WRITING ROBERT GREENE

Writing Robert Greene
Essays on England's First Notorious Professional Writer

Edited by

KIRK MELNIKOFF
University of North Carolina-Charlotte, USA

and

EDWARD GIESKES
University of South Carolina-Columbia, USA

ASHGATE

Published by
Ashgate Publishing Limited
Gower House
Croft Road
Aldershot
Hants GU11 3HR
England

Ashgate Publishing Company
Suite 420
101 Cherry Street
Burlington, VT 05401-4405
USA

Ashgate website: http://www.ashgate.com

British Library Cataloguing in Publication Data
Writing Robert Greene: new essays on England's first notorious professional writer
1. Greene, Robert, 1558?–1592 – Criticism and interpretation 2. Authors, English – Early modern, 1500–1700
I. Melnikoff, Kirk II. Gieskes, Edward, 1968–
828.3'09

Library of Congress Cataloging-in-Publication Data
Writing Robert Greene: essays on England's first notorious professional writer / edited by Kirk Melnikoff and Edward Gieskes.
p. cm.
Includes bibliographical references and index.
ISBN 978-0-7546-5701-9 (alk. paper)
1. Greene, Robert, 1558?–1592—Criticism and interpretation. 2. Authors, English—Early modern, 1500–1700. I. Melnikoff, Kirk, 1969– II. Gieskes, Edward, 1968–

PR2546.W75 2008
828'.309—dc22
[B]

2007039644

ISBN: 978-0-7546-5701-9

Printed and bound in Great Britain by MPG Books Ltd, Bodmin, Cornwall.

Contents

Acknowledgements		*vii*
Contributors		*ix*
Introduction: Re-imagining Robert Greene *Kirk Melnikoff and Edward Gieskes*		1
1	Robert Greene and the Theatrical Vocabulary of the Early 1590s *Alan C. Dessen*	25
2	"That will I see, lead and ile follow thee": Robert Greene and the Authority of Performance *Kirk Melnikoff*	39
3	Staging Professionalism in Greene's *James IV* *Edward Gieskes*	53
4	From *Homo Academicus* to *Poeta Publicus*: Celebrity and Transversal Knowledge in Robert Greene's *Friar Bacon and Friar Bungay* (c. 1589) *Bryan Reynolds and Henry S. Turner*	73
5	Robert Greene, "Author of Playes" *Ronald A. Tumelson II*	95
6	Forming Greene: Theorizing the Early Modern Author in the *Groatsworth of Wit* *Steve Mentz*	115
7	A Looking Glass for Readers: Cheap Print and the Senses of Repentance *Lori Humphrey Newcomb*	133
8	Robert Greene and the Uses of Time *Robert W. Maslen*	157
9	Transplanting Lillies: Greene, Tyrants, and Tragical Comedies *Katharine Wilson*	189

10 Recent Studies in Robert Greene (1989–2006) 205
Kirk Melnikoff and Edward Gieskes

Appendix A: Apocrypha 225
Appendix B: Edition Information 227
Appendix C: Editions Published by Year 235
Index 239

Acknowledgements

> As *Achilles* tortured the deade bodie of *Hector*, and as *Antonius*, and his wife *Fuluia* tormented the liuelesse corps of *Cicero*; so *Gabriell Haruey* hath shewed the same inhumanitie to *Greene* that lies full low in the graue.
>
> From Francis Meres, *Palladis tamia Wits treasury* (London, 1598).

This collection has been in the works for many years, and from the start, has been conceived as an answer to Greene's mistreatment by the many heirs of Harvey. A decade ago, its impetus came directly from James R. Siemon, professor of early modern literature and the leader of many provocative graduate seminars on Elizabethan culture at Boston University. Both of us still remember a certain fateful day when "Jim" closed a particularly thought-provoking class on *A Looking Glass for London and England* with the hope that some of us might someday undertake a different, more theory-inflected project on Robert Greene. That class began what would become a long engagement with this prodigal "University Wit" and derider of "upstart crows." Notably, it has included a multimedia, sold-out production of *James IV* at Boston University's Playwrights' Theatre in 1997, a donated fifteen-volume set of Grosart's *Life and Complete Works in Prose and Verse of Robert Greene*, and a surprisingly well-subscribed and well-attended Shakespeare Association of America seminar on Greene in 2002.

Through all of this, we both have enjoyed the help and encouragement of a number of people. With Jim at Boston University, Michael Arner, Jason Beals, Roger Grabowski, Colin Harris, Andrew Hartley, Eric Johnson-Debaufre, Lauren Kehoe, Christian Knapp, Peter Lurie, Sarah Lyons, Christopher Martin, Tom McLellan, Jonathan Mulrooney, Marc Olivere, Elaine Perlov, Kaara Peterson, Christopher Ricks, Justin Shilton, Kate Snodgrass, Michael Walker, Andrew Watson, and especially William C. Carroll all participated in one way or another in the launching of this project. Since our BU days, Kent Cartwright, Alan Dessen, Lukas Erne, Helen Hull, Suzanne Keen, Arthur Kinney, Jennifer Munroe, Alan Rauch, Bill Richey, Esther Richey, Alan Stewart, Fran Teague, and Virginia Mason Vaughan have also supported us either as readers or as willing auditors in what at times has seemed like a dubious project. We are grateful as well to the Shakespeare Association of America for providing a forum for considerations of Greene's work, to the University of North Carolina at Charlotte for granting funds in support of this project, and to the Boston University Humanities Foundation for its generous underwriting of our 1997 *James IV* production.

We also owe many thanks to the staffs at the Folger Shakespeare Library, at Boston University's Mugar Library, and at the University of South Carolina's Thomas Cooper Library for their friendly assistance. And it needs to be said that our editor Erika Gaffney's enthusiasm and guidance has again and again proven invaluable as we moved closer and closer to print.

And finally we owe more than we can say to our parents and grandparents, to Lisa, to Lara, and to Fin for weathering our inevitable musings on conies, Norwich, Harvey, Nashe, romance, print culture, "the loathed stage," professionalism, and repentance; on the people, themes, and issues that only work on Robert Greene can so specifically inspire.

Contributors

Alan C. Dessen, Peter G. Phialas Professor of English (emeritus) at U. of North Carolina, Chapel Hill, is the author of eight books, four of them published by Cambridge U.P.: *Elizabethan Stage Conventions and Modern Interpreters* (1984); *Recovering Shakespeare's Theatrical Vocabulary* (1995); *Rescripting Shakespeare: The Text, the Director, and Modern Productions* (2002); and *A Dictionary of Stage Directions in English Drama, 1580–1642* (coauthored with Leslie Thomson, 1999). Between 1994 and 2001, he was the Director of ACTER, now AFTLS (Actors from the London Stage). For roughly twenty years, he has been writing about current productions of Shakespeare's plays in *Shakespeare Quarterly* and *Shakespeare Bulletin*.

Edward Gieskes is Associate Professor of English at the University of South Carolina. He is the author of *Representing the Professions* (Delaware, 2006). He has published on Jonson, Shakespeare, and Middleton (in the forthcoming *Thomas Middleton and Early Modern Textual Culture: A Companion to the Collected Works*). He is at work on a book about generic innovation in early modern drama.

Lori Humphrey Newcomb is Associate Professor of English at the University of Illinois at Urbana-Champaign, where she teaches early modern drama and popular print culture. Her *Reading Popular Romance in Early Modern England* (Columbia University Press, 2002) traces the reception of Greene's most enduring work of fiction. Her current research explores the hybrid literacies that the new public theatres demanded of their audiences.

Robert W. Maslen has written two books: *Elizabethan Fictions* (Oxford, 1997) and *Shakespeare and Comedy* (Arden, 2005). He has also completed editions of Sidney's *Apology for Poetry* (Manchester, 2002) and Middleton and Dekker's *News from Gravesend* (Oxford, forthcoming), as well as a number of essays on Renaissance and modern literature. He is Senior Lecturer at the University of Glasgow.

Kirk Melnikoff is Assistant Professor of English at the University of North Carolina at Charlotte. His essays have appeared in *Mosaic*, *Studies in Philology*, and *Literature/Film Quarterly*, and he is editor in charge of the *Shakespeare on Screen Newsletter*, which is published as part of *Shakespeare Bulletin*. He is currently writing a book on early modern publishers like Nicholas Ling, Thomas Hacket, and Richard Jones.

Steve Mentz is Associate Professor of English at St. John's University in New York City, where he teaches Shakespeare and early modern literature. He is the author *of Romance for Sale in Early Modern England: The Rise of Prose Fiction* (Ashgate, 2006), coeditor of *Rogues and Early Modern English Culture* (Michigan, 2004), and articles in *Studies in English Literature*, *Studies in Philology*, *Renaissance Drama*, *TEXT,* and several edited collections. His current project explores shipwreck narratives from Shakespeare to Defoe.

Bryan Reynolds is Professor, Chancellor's Fellow, and Head of Doctoral Studies in Drama and Theatre at the University of California, Irvine. He is the author of *Transversal Enterprises in the Drama of Shakespeare and His Contemporaries: Fugitive Explorations* (2006), *Performing Transversally: Reimagining Shakespeare and the Critical Future* (2003), and *Becoming Criminal: Transversal Performance and Cultural Dissidence in Early Modern England* (2002); co-editer, with William N. West, of *Rematerializing Shakespeare: Authority and Representation on the Early Modern English Stage* (2005), and co-editor, with Donald Hedrick, of *Shakespeare Without Class: Misappropriations of Cultural Capital* (2000). His next book, *Transversal Subjects: Influential Performances in Critical Theory from Psychoanalysis to Poststructuralism beyond Cognitive Neuroscience*, will be out in 2008. Reynolds is also a playwright and cofounder of the Transversal Theater Company. With Elaine Aston, Reynolds coedits *Performance Interventions*, a book series in performance studies from Palgrave Macmillan.

Ronald A. Tumelson II (PhD, University of Alabama) is a former fellow of the Hudson Strode Program in Renaissance Studies. His contribution to this collection derives from the first chapter of his dissertation, "Mobilities: Social Change and the Plays of Robert Greene" (Tuscaloosa, 2005). When he is not revising this study for publication or researching other aspects of Greene's life and career, he teaches early modern English literature at the University of Alabama.

Henry S. Turner is Associate Professor in the Department of English at Rutgers University-New Brunswick. He is the author of *The English Renaissance Stage: Geometry, Poetics, and the Practical Spatial Arts in England, 1580–1630* (Oxford, 2006), the editor of *The Culture of Capital: Property, Cities, and Knowledge in Early Modern England* (Routledge, 2002), and coeditor of the series "Literary and Scientific Cultures of Early Modernity" (Ashgate Press). His essays have appeared or are forthcoming in *Shakespeare Quarterly*, *ELH*, *Renaissance Drama*, *Twentieth Century Literature*, and the History of Cartography project. He is currently writing a book on the history of the concept of the corporation in the early modern period.

Katharine Wilson has taught at the universities of Newcastle upon Tyne and Oxford. She is the author of *Fictions of Authorship in Late Elizabethan Narratives: Euphues in Arcadia* (Oxford, 2006), and is writing on Robert Greene for the forthcoming *Oxford Handbook of Tudor Literature, 1485–1603*, edited by Mike Pincombe and Cathy Shrank.

Introduction

Re-imagining Robert Greene

Kirk Melnikoff and Edward Gieskes

> I but answere in print, what they haue offered on the Stage: but leauing these phantasticall schollers, as iudging him that is not able to make choice of his chaffer, but a pedling chapman, [I turn] at last to *Perymedes the Black Smith* ... .
>
> Robert Greene, "To the Reader," *Perimedes the blacke-smith* (1588)

> Gentlemen, I know you ar not vnacquainted with the death of *Robert Greene*, whose pen in his life time pleased you as well on the Stage, as in the Stationers shops.
>
> Cuthbert Burbie, "The Printer to the Gentlemen Readers," *The repentance of Robert Greene Maister of Artes* (1592)

Written midway into what would be a short but prolific career, *Perimedes the Blacksmith* bears many intriguing traces of Robert Greene's vocational assumptions and practices half a decade before his death in 1592.[1] Significantly, this text for the first time bears clear witness to Greene's tense familiarity with London's burgeoning professional stage.[2] Responding in his dedication to "two Gentlemen Poets" who "had it in derision, for that I could not make my verses iet vpon the stage in tragicall buskins," Greene shows an awareness of the current popular repertory by alluding both to *Tamburlaine* (1587) and to the now lost *The Mad Priest of the Sun* (1587) as well as of the then current rage for unrhymed iambic pentameter, questioning those who would see "the end of scollarisme in an English blanck verse."[3]

---

1 Greene's titles in this introduction and the annotated bibliography that follows have been modernized for spelling, capitalization, and punctuation except those indicating specific early modern or modern editions. First references in this introduction to titles, unless otherwise indicated, are first given in "full" and subsequently shortened.

2 This passage is usually taken to suggest that Greene had already begun writing plays for the professional stage. See Stanley Wells, ed., *Perymedes the Blacksmith and Pandosto by Robert Greene: A Critical Edition* (New York: Garland Publishing, Inc., 1988), pp. xix–xxi. The "derision" to which Greene refers has commonly been associated with the reception of his *The Comical History of Alphonsus, King of Aragon.*

3 See Wells, pp. xxiii–xxv for a discussion of the plays possibly referenced by Greene's "the mad preest of the sonne."

This prefatory defense of what Greene calls his "wonted method" as a pamphlet writer in the face of criticism born in the theatre supplements a number of elements within the fiction itself that reference Greene's own singular engagement with the print trade. Described as an account of the nightly "prattle" between an Egyptian blacksmith named Perimedes and his wife Delia, *Perimedes* initially offers an intriguing explanation of its own inception. "[T]he Egyptians," Greene writes, "as a great monument kept diuerse of their [Perimedes and Delia's] discourses, which some by chance had overheard, and put downe as a Iewell in their librarie, I meane as their recordes doe rehearse, to set downe in brief two of their nights prattle."[4] "[O]verheard" by "chance" and selectively "put downe" by "some," the "discourses" of Perimedes and Delia are represented by Greene to have neither a traceable beginning nor a clear process of transmission. In effect, *Perimedes* begins by mystifying its own commodity status. At the same time, the work ultimately "set[s] downe" three, not "two of [Perimedes and his wife Delia's] nights prattle." This discrepancy between what he promises at the beginning and delivers at the end likely indicates Greene's failure to revise *Perimedes* before selling it to its publisher Edward White. Such a failure to revise also seems to explain the text's inconsistent marginalia that inexplicably ends one third of the way through. The ending of *Perimedes* is similarly fraught. Added to the end of the text, yet not a part of Perimedes and Delia's "two" nights of "discourse," are four "sonets" claimed to be from the "Chest" of Delia. The appending of these poems to *Perimedes* is explained by a prefatory letter from William Bubb and a following note penned by Greene. In the letter "William Bubb Gentleman, to his freend the Author," Bubb tells Greene that after becoming inspired by a "vewe" of the unpublished manuscript of *Perimedes* and "the last sheete hanging in the Presse, comming into your studie, I found in your Deske certaine Sonets, ... [and] I charge thee by that familiar conuersing that hath past betweene vs, that thou annex them to the end of this Pamphlet" (G4v). Greene's note then offers his audience this explanation: "I dare not but rather hazard my credit on your courtesies then loose for so small a trifle his freendship whome I haue euer found a: faithfull as familiar" (G4v–H1).

We begin with this short description of some of the substantive and material peculiarities of *Perimedes* because these features do much to demonstrate the complicated contours of Greene's writerly identity at a moment when he would start writing plays for the professional adult theatre companies. Greene's prefatory attack upon the "two Gentlemen Poets" constructs a particular relationship between the professional stage and the print market, and offers a tantalizing glimpse of one professional pamphlet writer's sense of the cultural and social significance of Marlovian verse and tragedy. At the same time, Greene's mystifying account of the text's origin coupled with his concluding explanation of the text's additions indicates the range of Greene's professional practices: his circulation of manuscript copies of his work, his collaborations with both friends

4 *Perimedes the blacke-smith* (London, 1588), B1v.

and patrons, his apparent disregard—in his failure to revise—for the literary value of his publications, and his wary approach to a print market driven by commodity and "pedling chapmen." And last, his composition of a text with a series of framed tales—a structure that Greene had been utilizing in such works as *Morando* (1584) and *Planetomachia* (1585) and would continue to utilize in *The Scottish History of James the Fourth* ("*James IV*")—suggests both Greene's interest in and particular understanding of audiences and their reception of fictional narratives.[5]

Intriguing contours, however, have rarely been conceded when the shape of Greene's career has been outlined. Of the few book-length studies of Greene since his death in 1592, all are apologist in tenor, compelled to admit that Greene lacked literary ability; that he was a popular writer primarily driven to ensure that his audience was "pleased" (to borrow Cuthbert Burbie's term); that he was often a money-driven hack.[6] Thus, John Clark Jordan warned potential readers in his 1915 monograph *Robert Greene*, "Whenever he saw an opportunity, in season or out, he was ready in a moment with something for the market. Hasty in publication, and desiring nothing beyond the immediate sale, Greene took no thought to finishing his work to a degree of perfection, or for removing from it flaws that might easily have been removed ... . Much of it, consequently, is slip-shod" (201–2). Seven decades later, Charles Crupi—in what is still the last book published on Greene—took up the tattered gauntlet of the Greene apologist in his 1986 Twayne-series *Robert Greene*:

> Greene deserves a serious reading, unbiased by his biography, his reputation as a popular writer, or his capacity to be fit into developmental schemes that celebrate modern taste as the goal of history. To grant him that reading is to find works that vary greatly in quality, originality, and significance but that repay close attention and sometimes surprise us with their complexity. Claiming for Greene a place in the small circle of our greatest writers would be pointless, but equally pointless is denying him a place in that larger circle whose merits are sufficient to inspire us to set aside the instinct to judge in favor of the need to understand.[7]

Crupi's more measured, historicist-inflected approach offers an important contribution to the critical tradition of Greene studies. Yet even as he suggests that modern readers "understand" Greene's writings in the terms of their era, Crupi is compelled nevertheless throughout his book to point out that the "complexity" of

---

5 For a general discussion of the sixteenth-century prose subgenre of the framework tale, see Wells, pp. xxvi–xxix.

6 John Clark Jordan, in *Robert Greene*, 1915 (New York: Octagon Books, 1965), concludes, "Greene was not great,–but a man does not have to be great to be worthy of study" (8). Three decades earlier in 1878, Nicholas Storojenko, in *Robert Greene: His Life and Works*, reprinted in *The Life and Complete Works in Prose and Verse of Robert Greene, M.A.*, 15 Vols., ed. A.B. Grosart (New York: Russell & Russell, 1964), tried to challenge such a perception. See particularly pp. 157–66 and pp. 221–6.

7 *Robert Greene* (Boston: Twayne Publishers, 1986), p. 145.

certain of Greene's prose works like *Alcida*, *Planetomachia*, and *Philomela* has been underappreciated.

More recently, Greene has enjoyed unprecedented public attention as the focal point of a chapter in Stephen Greenblatt's 2004 popular biography of Shakespeare *Will in the World*, a finalist for the 2004 National Book Award in Non-Fiction.[8] This book ultimately offers a familiarly dismissive image of Greene. In Greenblatt's imagination, Greene was the "grotesque" ringleader of a university-educated gang of bohemian writers, a man who abandoned his wife and children, who pursued bodily excess with unrivaled energy, and who was right at home with the "cheats, swindlers, and pickpockets" that he wrote about in his cony-catching pamphlets. Partner in crime with Marlowe, Nashe, and Lodge, Greene was a man, according to Greenblatt, whose only "dream, realized with perfect success, was to transform himself into a cynical swaggering bully" (206). Ultimately, in what may prove to be his book's most striking claim, Greenblatt concludes that, in response to Greene's attack upon him in *Greene's Groatsworth of Wit*, Shakespeare—in yet another of his acts of "imaginative generosity"—transformed the thievish, bohemian Greene into Falstaff.

While approaches that sensationalize a writer's life and/or apologize for a writer's aesthetic shortcomings (Greenblatt says that in the group of university-educated bohemians, "Greene was by no means the most accomplished" [203]) are less and less obligatory in today's normative critical climate of poststructuralism and cultural materialism, they are, at least in one ironic sense, very appropriate when talking about Greene. As has recently been pointed out by Lori Humphrey Newcomb, Greene and his prose work played an important role in a late Elizabethan and Jacobean discourse that sought to distinguish elite from popular culture.[9] Less than a year after Greene's death, for example, Henry Chettle in his *Kind-Hart's Dream*, wrote of Greene that "He was of singuler pleasaunce the verye supporter, and to no mans disgrace bee this intended, the only Comedian of a vulgar writer in this country."[10] Two decades later, additions to the sixth edition of Thomas Overbury's *Wife ... and Diverse More Characters*, elaborated on Chettle's alignment of Greene's writing with the low. In its description of "A Chamber-

---

8 Greenblatt's book, *Will in the World: How Shakespeare Became Shakespeare* (New York: W.W. Norton & Company, 2004), received a huge amount of public attention. When invited by Renee Montagne, in a radio interview aired on *Morning Edition*, Natl. Public Radio, WBUR, Boston. 17 Nov. 2004, to reveal his "favorite example" of Shakespeare's penchant for concealing the personal in his poems and plays, Greenblatt talks extensively about what he argues in his book to be Greene and his powerful influence upon Shakespeare.

9 See in particular "'Social Things': The Production of Popular Culture in the Reception of Robert Greene's *Pandosto*," *English Literary History* 61.4 (1994): 753–81 and "The Triumph of Time: The Fortunate Readers of Robert Greene's *Pandosto*," *Texts and Cultural Change in Early Modern England*, eds Cedric Brown and Arthur Marotti (New York: St. Martin's, 1997), pp. 95–123. See also her *Reading Popular Romance in Early Modern England* (New York: Columbia University Press, 2002).

10 *Kind-harts dreame* (London, 1593), B3–B3v.

maide," the work connects an interest in Greene with not just lower-order women but also with ambitions to transcend normative class and gender roles. "She reads *Greenes* works ouer and ouer," it says, "but is so carried away with *the Mirrour of Knighthood*, she is many times resolu'd to run out of her selfe, and become a Lady Errant."[11] As Newcomb has written specifically with regard to *Pandosto*, "The anxieties Greene has excited among modern critics–about popular literacy, plagiarism, roguery, superstition, and mimetic imaginings–had all emerged in the first generation after *Pandosto*'s publication [in 1588]" ("Social Things" 755).[12] This early emergence suggests both the force of Greene's writing and the power of its questions about cultural production and reception.

In that it establishes his significance in a way that has little to do with gauging his work's quality, originality, or aesthetic influence, Newcomb's research exemplifies a relatively new critical attitude towards Greene, and her exploration of *Pandosto*'s reception-history illustrates just one of the many untapped lines of approach to one of sixteenth-century England's most prolific writers. Other relatively recent work by A.R. Braunmuller, W.W. Barker, Ian McAdam, and Daniel Vitkus that is respectively informed by New Historicist, narrative, gender, and postcolonial theory has similarly opened up new vistas onto Greene. One hopes that the recent publication of new editions of *Menaphon*, *Perimedes*, *Pandosto*, *Greene's Groatsworth of Wit*, *The First Part of the Tragical Reign of Selimus*, and *The Honorable History of Friar Bacon and Friar Bungay* will make Greene's writing more accessible to new lines of critical inquiry.[13]

This collection continues this ongoing reappraisal of Greene's work. The essays in this volume, many by scholars who are already distinguished in their respective fields, collectively consider Greene's writings in the context of his extensive engagement with the popular print market and his efforts as a professional dramatist for the London-based theatrical companies. Unlike much of the previous work on Greene, many of these essays do not unduly stress the distinction between Greene's pamphlet writing and his playwriting; rather, they trace the ways in which Greene's work negotiates with and/or between these two very different cultural and economic fields. In effect, like Cuthbert Burbie in his prefatory elegy to Greene in his "The Printer to the Gentlemen Readers," which introduces *The Repentance of Robert Greene Master of Arts* (1592), they often imagine Greene's writing for the pamphlet market and the theatrical market as a continuum.[14] The essays in this volume

11 *Sir Thomas Ouerbury his VVife. With additions of nevv nevves, and divers more characters* (London, 1618), G8.

12 For a list of the editions of Greene's work published after his death, see Appendix C.

13 See our "Recent Studies in Robert Greene (1989–2006)" at the end of this volume for citations of these and other recent work on Greene.

14 Greene's major critics—Storojenko, Jordan, and Crupi—have all organized his career according to genre. Such a split focus is endemic to Greene studies in general: not only do the book-length studies organize Greene's literary output according to genre rather than

accordingly explore Greene's relatively unique position and particular practices as a writer working for two different industries. They also collectively reconsider how Greene's plays and pamphlets contributed to what were emergent understandings of authorship, popular print, and theatrical culture.

***

Greene was likely born in Norwich in early July 1558.[15] His family and place-of-residence during his boyhood years have yet to be definitively established.[16] We do know, however, that Greene was university-educated. References on the title-pages of his work and in university records suggest that Greene received a B.A. from St. John's College in Cambridge in 1580 and an M.A. from Clare Hall in Cambridge in 1583. Greene received an M.A. from Oxford in 1588. In his short lifetime, Greene published more than three dozen prose works, composed at least five plays, and was one of the period's most recognized—if not notorious—literary figures.[17] Greene infamously died in London in 1592.[18]

Endowed neither with a "players hide" nor a strictly "bibliographic ego," Greene, nevertheless, offers a particularly compelling case of involvement with the early modern culture industry.[19] For much of his career, Greene's perspective was the unique sum of engagements with two very different burgeoning

---

according to chronology but most essay-length studies of Greene are either focused on Greene's prose or his drama.

15 Biographical details offered in *The Repentance of Robert Greene*, Greene's signing "Nordovicensis" and "Norfolciensis" in two separate works during his lifetime, and finally city records all suggest that Greene was born in Norwich sometime in 1558.

16 Two theories about Greene's family and boyhood home have been offered. The earlier theory was put forward by John Churton Collins, in his *The Plays & Poems of Robert Greene*, 2 Vols (Oxford: Clarendon Press, 1905). Collins argues that Greene was the son of the Norwich saddler "Robert Greene" and that Greene spent his formative years in Norwich. Arata Ide supports this conclusion with further compelling evidence in her "Robert Greene *Nordovicensis*, the Saddler's Son," *Notes & Queries* 53.4 (2006): 432–6. Brenda Richardson, in "Robert Greene's Yorkshire Connexions: A New Hypothesis," *Year's Work in English Studies* 10 (1980): 160–80, however, has argued that Greene was more likely born the son of a Norwich cordswainer-turned-innkeeper who spent significant time in Yorkshire. According to her, Greene's tendency to dedicate his works to Yorkshire elite families and his social conservatism make Yorkshire a more likely choice for his adolescent home. For a judicious weighing of the evidence of Greene's life, see Crupi.

17 Greene has been named as the playwright of what has become a long list of anonymously published plays. See Appendix A for a list of Greene's apocrypha.

18 For a more extended discussion of Greene's biography and career, see the recent entry in the Oxford *Dictionary of National Biography* (written by Lori Humphrey Newcomb).

19 For a discussion of "bibliographic ego," see Joseph Loewenstein's *Ben Jonson and Possessive Authorship* (Cambridge: Cambridge University Press, 2002), pp. 1–4 and his "The Script in the Marketplace," *Representations* 12 (1995): 101–14.

economies: the print trade and the professional theatre. Greene's dealings with the former likely began around 1580 with his selling of a manuscript of *Mamilia* to the bookseller Thomas Woodcocke.[20] While we do not know exactly when Greene began writing for the professional stage, a good case can be made for dating what has been taken to be his first play, *The Comical History of Alphonsus, King of Aragon*, around the time of *Tamburlaine* (1587–88).[21] Indeed, Greene's pamphlets increasingly betray a theatrical focus after 1586.[22] In his preface to *Penelope's Web* (1587), for example, Greene imagines that the reception of his previous work may be as inscrutable as the physical responses of Roman theatre audiences. "[I]t may be," Greene writes, "the forehead is not alwayes a true heralt of affections, neither the rules of Phisiognomie infallible principles: for they which smiled in the *Theatre* in Rome, might assoone scoffe at the rudenesse of the *Scane*, as giue a Plaudite at the perfection of the action, and they which passe ouer my toyes with silence, may perhappes shrowde a mislike in such patience."[23] As mentioned above, Greene also introduces his *Perimedes* with a particularly rich reference to the professional stage. And in one of his longest engagements with the professional theatre aside from his *Greene's Groatsworth of Wit*, Greene includes a 1000-word digression by his narrating Palmer about "Playes, Playmakers and Players" in the second part of *Greene's Never Too Late* ("*Francesco's Fortunes*"), which was published in 1590. In it, the Palmer concludes, "Menander deuised them for the suppressing of vanities, necessarie in a commonwealth, as long as they are vsed in their right kind: the playmakers

---

20 Woodcocke entered *Mamillia* in the Stationers' Register (*A Transcript of the Stationers' Registers, 1554–1640 A.D.*, 5 vols, ed. Edward Arber [New York: Peter Smith, 1950]) on 3 October 1580. The entry reads, "Lycenced vnto him *Manilia. A lookinge Glasse for ye ladies of England*" (vol. 2, p. 378). For a short description of Woodcocke's stationer career, see R.B. McKerrow, *A Dictionary of Printers and Booksellers in England, Scotland and Ireland, and of Foreign printers of English Books 1557–1640* (London: The Bibliographical Society 1968), p. 300.

21 See Crupi, pp. 101–2.

22 Greene makes a theatrical reference in *Mamillia*: "*Astorides* seeing *Roscius* gestures, durst neuer after come on the stage ... . Two thinges daunte the minde of a young man; eyther the skill or person of the hearer" ([London, 1583], F4). This, however, is an isolated instance.

23 *Penelopes vveb* (London, 1587), A3v. Crupi theorizes that *Greene's Farewell to Folly* was written about this time as well. Significantly, in this work's "To the Gentlemen Students of both Vniuersities health," Greene writes, "And he that can not write true Englishe without the helpe of Clearkes of parish Churches, will needes make him selfe the father of interludes ... . As for example two louers on the stage arguing one an other of vnkindnesse, his Mistris runnes ouer him with this canonicall sentence, A mans conscience is a thousande witnesses, and hir knight againe excuseth him selfe with that saying of the Apostle, Loue couereth the multitude of sinnes. I thinke this was but simple abusing of the Scripture" (*Greenes farewell to folly* [London, 1591] A4v).

worthy of honour for their Art: and players, men deseruing both prayse and profit, as long as they wax neither couetous nor insolent."[24] Significantly, as opposed to what has essentially become the orthodox critical opinion that Greene consistently had an anti-theatrical bias, this passage points to a relationship with the theatre that is less adversarial than is often allowed to Greene.[25] Indeed, many of the essays in this collection rethink Greene's relationship with the professional stage, questioning in a number of different ways the usefulness (even accuracy) of attributing to Greene such a bias.

Greene's introduction to the labor economies of the professional theatre would, nevertheless, likely have been a startling one. Working first as a pamphlet writer who very quickly made a name for himself in the print market, he would have been accustomed to a specific set of vocational practices. He first would have been used to negotiating directly with booksellers and other members of the Stationers guild. In his first six years as a pamphlet writer (1580–86), Greene sold his work to no less than seven different stationers, suggesting that his work was initially a risky venture or possibly that Greene was a writer who was unafraid to look for the best possible price for his copy.[26] Even at the height of popularity, however, Greene likely received no more than two to three pounds for a single manuscript.[27] This was commonly a one-time payment. Before the Statute of Anne in 1710, England had no formal system of copyright. In selling a manuscript to a bookseller or a printer, an author essentially conferred the right to copy that work upon that member of the Stationers guild. Greene suggests this lack of control in his preface "To the Gentlemen Readers Health" in his *Orpharion* (1599) when he writes, "at last it is leapt into the Stacioners Shoppe, ... marry whether his presse were out of tune, Paper deere, or some other secret delay driue it off, it hath line this twelue months in the suds."[28] A stationer's right to copy included subsequent editions, meaning that an author, unless he was enlisted to revise, would not share in the further profits if his work proved to be popular.[29] Thus, Greene had to continue

---

24 *Greenes neuer too late* (London, 1602), J4v–K1.

25 See Crupi, pp. 20–21. For recent contributions to this critical orthodoxy, see James P. Bednarz, "Marlowe and the English Literary Scene," in Patrick Cheney (ed.), *The Cambridge Companion to Christopher Marlowe* (Cambridge: Cambidge University Press, 2004), pp. 98–100 and Arul Kumaran, "'Hereafter Suppose Me the Said Roberto': Greene's *Groatsworth of Wit* as Allegorizing Pamphlet," *Yearly Review* 10 (2001): 39–42.

26 These stationers were Thomas Woodcocke, William Ponsonby, Hugh Jackson, Roger Ward, Edward White, George Robinson, and Thomas Cadman. See Appendix B.

27 See A.W. Pollard, *Shakespeare's Fight with the Pirates* (Cambridge: Cambridge University Press, 1924), and Edwin Haviland Miller, *The Professional Writer in England: A Study of Non-Dramatic Literature* (Cambridge: Harvard University Press, 1959).

28 *Greenes Orpharion* (London, 1599), A3.

29 The exception to this rule seems to have been if a stationer asked an author to make revisions to the first edition. For more detailed discussions of these practices, see Loewenstein, *Ben Jonson*, pp. 3–9; Pollard, "The Regulation of the Book Trade in the

turning out new products in order to make a living even as works like *Gwydonius* and *Pandosto* were twice reprinted in his lifetime.

Working for the Elizabethan print market, however, offered other incentives for ambitious writers besides paltry payments. A residual vestige of a precapitalistic manuscript culture, patronage also played a role in the early English print market. Works of all sizes and in a variety of genres often included dedications to powerful men and women.[30] Writers had a variety of motives for seeking patrons for their printed works. Besides (1) the possibility of financial support, they sought (2) a continuation of already-established associations, (3) support for their political and theological causes, and (4) shielding from potential criticism.[31] Greene wrote dedications for almost all of his prose pamphlets, and as we saw in *Perimedes*, he apparently made a habit of circulating his work among potential patrons. Greene's dedications are telling in that they show him pursuing each of these motives at different points in his career.[32] His earliest extant dedications in the first and second part of *Mamillia* fall generally into the second category.[33] His subsequent dedications before 1586 are more requests to patrons that he does not know personally for financial support. In his dedication to Edward de Vere, Earl of Oxford in *Gwydonius* (1584), for example, Greene compares Oxford to the great classical patron of the Arts Maecenas: "Wheresoeuer *Maecanas* lodgeth, thether no doubt will schollers flocke. And your honour being a worthie fauourer and fosterer of learning, hath forced many through your exquisite vertue, to offer the first fruits of their studie at the shrine of your Lordships curtesie."[34] After 1583, Greene's dedications to patrons not only seek economic support but also shielding against what apparently was a growing body of Greene's critics. In the first part of *Morando*, Greene asks Phillip, Earl of Arundel, to "shrowde my simple woorke

---

Sixteenth Century," *The Library*, series 3, 7 (1916): 18–43; and W.W. Greg, *Some Aspects and Problems of London Publishing Between 1550 and 1650* (Oxford: Clarendon Press, 1956).

30 See Franklin B. Williams, Jr., *Index of Dedications and Commendatory Verses in English Books before 1641* (London: The Bibliographical Society, 1962) for a sense of just how wide-spread such a practice was in the sixteenth century.

31 See H.S. Bennett, *English Books & Readers* (Cambridge: Cambridge University Press, 1965), pp. 30–55.

32 As suggested before, Richardson has traced many of Greene's early dedicatees to Yorkshire and has argued that these dedications suggest that Greene may have spent the years of his boyhood and young manhood there. Greene's early dedications thus could suggest an effort on his part to profit from some of his early associations.

33 His dedication to "Lord Darcie of the North" in *Mamillia* elusively represents Greene's choice of patrons as the repaying of a "debt" (A2v) to the York aristocrat. His dedication of the second part of *Mamillia* (London, 1583) similarly thanks Robert Lee and Roger Portington for "the innumerable benefites and infinite good turnes which I haue receiued at your worships handes" (A2–A2v).

34 *Gvvydonius. The carde of fancie* (London, 1584), A3v.

vnder your Honours winges, thinking one dramme of your Lordships favoure sufficient to fence me from the venemous teeth of those byting Vipers, who seeke to discredite all, hauing themselues no credite at all."[35]

The momentum of Greene's dedications is suggestive. Veering from an early attempt to secure the approval and support of the elite, Greene's dedications show him quickly concerned with the reception of his works. Greene's broadened petitions seem to be at least partially the result of his general failure to garner patronage, a failure indicated by the fact that most of his dedications are directed to different people (see Appendix C).[36] Indeed, Greene admits that only "some" of his potential patrons had been receptive in his *Farewell to Folly*. To Robert Carey, Greene writes, "Hauing waded (noble minded Courtier) through the censures of many both Honourable and worshipfull, in cōmitting the credite of my bookes to their honourable opinions, as I haue found *some* of them [our emphasis] not onely honourably to patronize my workes, but curteouslie to passe ouer my vnskilfull presumption with silence, so generally I am indebted to all Gentlemen that with fauors haue ouerslipt my follies."[37] Greene's changed motivation seems also to have had something to do with his being drawn more deeply into a culture of professional writers in the mid 1580s.

Greene's early involvement with the print market would have offered little preparation for the relatively extensive requirements of London professional theatre writing. Late sixteenth-century professional playwrights wrote mainly for the adult acting companies and were essentially their employees.[38] Although some finished plays were doubtlessly offered to the acting companies, the majority of plays would have been commissioned, mostly because they had to fulfill the aesthetic and pragmatic requirements of the specific company to whom they were offered. For a professional playwright, the first step in garnering a commission would have been an "audition reading" where he presented the general outline of

---

35 *Morando the tritameron of loue* (London, 1587), A3v.

36 There are two exceptions to this: Greene dedicates both *Pandosto* and *Greene's Mourning Garment* to George Clifford; he dedicates both parts of *Never Too Late* and *A Quip for an Upstart Courtier* to Thomas Burnaby. Greene seemingly chose Burnaby because of a previous association. In the first part of *Never Too Late*, Greene writes, "[I have been] desirous a long time to gratifie your Worship with something that might signifie, how in al bounden duetie I haue for sundry fauors bin affected to your Worship" (A2). In the second part, Greene talks of receiving "many friendly, nay fatherly fauours at your hands" (A2) and says that Burnaby "gratefully accepted" *Never Too Late* (A2v). Two years later, Greene similarly refers to Burnaby as a "frend" and signs his dedication to *A Quip* "your duetifull adopted sonne" ([London, 1592] A2). For Greene's late disillusionment with the patronage system, see Arul Kumaran, "Patronage, Print, and an Early Modern 'Pamphlet Moment,'" *Explorations in Renaissance Culture* 31.1 (2005): 59–88.

37 *Greenes farewell to folly* (London, 1591), A2.

38 See G.E. Bentley, *The Profession of Dramatist in the Time of Shakespeare, 1590–1642* (Princeton: Princeton University Press, 1971), pp. 62–87.

the play to one or more principal members of the company.[39] If interested, the company would then give the dramatist a commission to complete the play. After finishing the play, a dramatist would then have had to read his manuscript to the assembled acting company for its approval (he might also have had something to say about the play's casting). If approved, the dramatist would receive the sum of his prearranged fee.[40] For unattached professional playwrights, involvement with the production of their play usually ended at this point; for attached professional playwrights, part of their contracted duties may have involved "instructing" the actors in their parts and helping out with "practical aspects" of the production.[41]

Although Greene's particular arrangements with the players remain unclear, conventional practices would have required him to have had a relatively close relationship with his company employers. Greene's work bears such an assumption out. Both *Francesco's Fortunes* and *Greene's Groatsworth of Wit* suggest that Greene's relationship with the players was close.[42] In the former, Greene's main character Francesco "*fell in* [our emphasis] amongst a companie of Players, who perswaded him to trie his wit in writing of Comedies, Tragedies, or Pastorals, and if he could performe any thing worth the stage, then they would largelie reward him for his paines" (B3v). In the latter, Roberto is represented as being "lodgd ... at the Townes end in a house of retayle" by a player in order to write plays.[43] The letter "*To those Gentlemen his Quondam acquaintance, that spend their wits in making plaies*," towards the end of the pamphlet, also suggests a close albeit uncomfortable attachment: "Base minded men all three of you, if by my miserie you be not warnd: for vnto none of you (like mee) sought those burres to cleaue: those Puppets (I meane) that spake from our mouths, those Anticks garnisht in our colours" (F1v).[44] That players tried "to cleaue" to him like "burres" suggests that the actors tried to

---

39 For a fuller description of such readings, see Tiffany Stern, *Rehearsal from Shakespeare to Sheridan* (Oxford: Clarendon Press, 2000), pp. 59–61.

40 W.W. Greg, in his edition of *Henlowe's Diary* (London, 1904–1908), concludes that £6 would have been the standard rate for a play.

41 For a detailed differentiation between attached and unattached professional playwrights, see Bentley, pp. 25–37. For a discussion of an attached playwright's role in the rehearsal process, see Stern, pp. 84–92.

42 Critical consensus now appears to be that *Greene's Groatsworth of Wit* is at least partially a forgery by Henry Chettle. See John Jowett, "Johannes Factotum: Henry Chettle and *Greene's Groatsworth of Wit*," *Papers of the Bibliographic Society of America* 87.4 (1993): 453–86, and D. Allen Carroll, ed., *Greene's Groatsworth of Wit* (Binghamton, NY: Medieval and Renaissance Texts & Studies, 1994), pp. 1–31. Carroll believes that most of Roberto's story was originally by Greene. Even if wholly by Chettle, it makes sense to assume that Chettle was careful to make the pamphlet sound like Greene.

43 *Greenes, groats-vvorth of witte* (London, 1592), E1.

44 Critics have identified the first "acquaintance" ("thou famous gracer of Tragedians") to be Marlowe, the second ("young *Iuvenall*") to be either Nashe or Lodge, and the third to be either Peele or Lodge.

attach themselves permanently to Greene.[45] Indeed, Greene may have had a close working relationship with the most successful company of his day, the Queen's Men.[46] *Selimus*, *The History of Orlando Furioso* and *Friar Bacon and Friar Bungay* indicate that they were "plaid by her Majesties seruants" on all their title pages, and *The Defense of Cony Catching* tells us that Greene sold *Orlando Furioso* first to "the Queenes Plaiers."[47] *Alphonsus*, *James IV*, *Selimus*, and *A Looking Glass for London and England* were all published by Thomas Creede, a stationer who may have had an exclusive arrangement with Elizabeth's company.[48]

Like Dekker and Middleton, whose positions in and relation to a broader cultural market have been obscured by a sustained focus on other writers, Greene had complex relations with his fellow writers, with the adult players, and with the stationers. Greene's complicated social position, however, has been greatly overshadowed by his reputation as *the* Elizabethan "hack writer" who wrote prolifically, lived profligately, and died squalidly. Much in the vein of Greenblatt's recent book, E.H. Miller's important and still profoundly useful *The Professional Writer in Elizabethan England*, while acknowledging Greene's influence and popularity, depicts him as a colorful, alternately tragic and tawdry figure who serves as an icon of 1580s and 1590s "bohemia":

> Fervently desirous of acceptance among gentlemen and hostile to vulgar commoners, they [young writers] often affected the dress and manners of what since has become known as the artist-type or the bohemian. Greene stalked about with the handsome peak which the beardless Nashe admired, but Gabriel Harvey, who "was altogether unacquainted with the man," ridiculed Greene's "fond disguisinge of a Master or Arte with ruffianly haire, unseemely apparel, and more unseemelye Company."[49]

Noting Greene's death in his "squalid room with his squalid mistress" more than once, Miller contributes to the image of Greene as an oft-tawdry hack writer whose bohemia stands in for the social world of prose writing in the period. Ironically, even a book dedicated to the culture of what Miller calls "professional" writing

---

45 Stern has suggested that Greene's use of the word "puppet" to describe an actor may imply that Greene was, in fact, a part of the rehearsal process (69). This, in turn, would mean that Greene was likely an attached playwright and that he would have spent much time with the Queen's Men.

46 For an excellent study of the Queen's Men, see Scott McMillin and Sally-Beth MacLean, *The Queen's Men and their Plays* (Cambridge: Cambridge University Press, 1998).

47 *The defence of conny-catching* (London, 1582), D2.

48 See G.M. Pinciss, "Thomas Creede and the Repertory of the Queen's Men, 1583–1592," *Modern Philology* 67.4 (1969): 321–30.

49 E.H. Miller, *The Professional Writer in Elizabethan England* (Cambridge: Harvard University Press, 1959), pp. 14–15. The book focuses exclusively on nondramatic writing which excludes consideration of how the professional writers who are its subject engaged in the market for drama, an engagement that shaped both dramatic and nondramatic writing. See below.

ends up obscuring the specific contours of Greene's vocational practices with sensational biography.[50]

Greene's close arrangements with acting companies and stationers, though, suggest that he was less a bohemian—defined by the *OED* as "A gipsy of society; one who either cuts himself off, or is by his habits cut off, from society for which he is otherwise fitted; especially an artist, literary man, or actor, who leads a free, vagabond, or irregular life, not being particular as to the society he frequents, and despising conventionalities generally"—than a professional writer. By "professional," though, we do not only mean that Greene wrote for money rather than some hypothetical love of letters, but that his practice was structured by a distinctly "professional" space of cultural production. A profession is an occupation which depends on the deployment of a particular kind of knowledge—of cultural capital—and can, therefore be defined by its always unstable control over a specific area of intellectual labor.[51] This control depends on the existence of a market for the professional's products—in this case plays and printed books—and that professional's awareness of the norms of that market. The boundaries of a profession develop out of conflict—conflict between producers and consumers and, quite importantly for Greene, between groups of producers. Professions and their practitioners are thus social products, and to label a figure a "professional" is to assert that that figure occupies a particular position—a position characterized by a degree of self-awareness and control—in a more or less well-developed area of work. Gieskes's essay below offers a longer version of this argument, but for our purposes here it is sufficient to note that our use of the term "professional" in reference to Greene implies that he was neither a helpless client of predatory printers nor an alternately desperate and sloppy hack selling whatever he could write as fast as he could write it, but rather a shrewd and engaged participant in a rapidly developing cultural market. In his career, Greene shows an awareness of differing audiences for different kinds of work, an ability to recognize and exploit changes in the market, a profound if not always coherent grasp of the possibilities of distinct forms, and a sense of himself as a writer; all of these are elements of his practice that have yet to be adequately described.

Communal relations are a fundamental characteristic of what we are defining as a "profession," and our approach has much in common with recent critical work on the early modern pamphlet and on early modern collaboration. Sandra Clark's *The Elizabethan Pamphleteers: Popular Moralistic Pamphlets, 1580–1640*, for

---

50 Biographies of Nashe, Harvey, Dekker, and others have also proven to be similarly sensational.

51 For an extended discussion of this definition, see Andrew Abbott's *System of Professions* (Chicago: University of Chicago Press, 1988), and Magali Larson's *Rise of Professionalism* (Berkeley: University of California Press, 1977). Though these two sociologists differ in their understandings of the professions, their work is complementary in this respect.

example, similarly maps a space of what she also calls "professional writing," defined by university-educated writers on one hand and "hackwriters of the crudest kind" on the other with semiprofessionals in between. "The milieu in which the pamphleteers lived and wrote," she writes, "was a small and intimate one. Writers of all kinds congregated in London, then a city of perhaps 160–180,000 people, and their own world formed an integrated community within the larger one."[52] Jeffrey Masten's more recent *Textual Intercourse* discusses writing in the social context of early modern male friendship and argues that writers' professional practice needs to be seen as part of a broader social pattern.[53]

Elizabethan writing has, of course, been described as "professional" for quite some time, with influential books dating to the early decades of the twentieth century. Many of these accounts, however, take up isolated elements of the field—prose writers, dramatists, poets, pamphleteers—and imagine a writing profession composed of more or less distinct groups whose work and social world seem curiously disconnected. Even Miller's work on Elizabethan professional writers excludes dramatists and poets from its purview. What such work has offered instead of a complicated constellation of social relations is a basic opposition between an amateur and the professional. As an example, David Margolies sees the work of the professional writer as defined by the tension between the aristocratic "stigma of print" and the desire to use writing as a vehicle of social advancement. Margolies writes, "The professional is different from the amateur not so much in degree of skill as in the qualitative difference of exercising his talents for gain."[54] Ignoring the communal aspects of professionalism, Margolies argues that the primary distinction between professional and amateur was financial.

More recent scholarship, though, has turned to "professional" as a way of characterizing certain aspects of early modern English society. Wilfred Prest, a prominent legal historian, has edited a collection of essays on early modern professional communities and has also written an important essay on the lack of an adequate history of the professions.[55] Rosemary O'Day's 2000 book *The Professions in Early Modern England, 1450–1800* offers an account of early-

---

52 *The Elizabethan Pamphleteers: Popular Moralistic Pamphlets, 1580–1640* (Rutherford, NJ: Fairleigh Dickinson University Press, 1983), p. 31.

53 Jeffrey Masten, *Textual Intercourse: Collaboration, Authorship, and Sexualities in Renaissance Drama* (Cambridge: Cambridge University Press, 1997).

54 *Novel and Society in Elizabethan England* (Totowa, NJ: Barnes & Nobles Books, 1985), p. 13. This position also depends on the existence of a "stigma of print," a stigma whose force has been questioned at least since Steven May's 1980 article in *Renaissance Papers* ("Tudor Aristocrats and the 'Stigma of Print,'" *Renaissance Papers* 1980: 11–18).

55 See Wilfred Prest, ed., *The Professions in Early Modern England* (London: Croom Helm, 1987), and "Why the History of the Professions Is Not Written," in G.R. Rubin and David Sugarman (eds), *Law, Economy, and Society: Essays in the History of English Law* (Oxford: Professional Books, 1984).

modern society as being in the process of professionalization. Her account is more generous in scope than traditional accounts of the professions that generally locate the advent of modern professions in the nineteenth century. While her focus is the three traditional "learned professions" of divinity, law, and medicine, she also considers the way in which other vocations were beginning to claim professional status.[56] Most recently, Edward Gieskes's *Representing the Professions: Administration, Law, and Theatre in Early Modern England* argues that a wide range of fields of endeavor can most helpfully be characterized as professional and that early modern England saw the professionalizing of ever larger numbers of occupations.[57]

This volume collectively reconceptualizes Greene's work in these professional terms. It traces the various ways in which Greene as a professional producer engaged with a broad social space of fellow writers, audiences, patrons, and employers. These essays show how the manifold changes over time in Greene's writing and publication practices serve as traces of his imbrication with an emerging social space of professional literary production at the same time that those changes outline some of that space's contours. Various sites of production influenced the development of professional and literary writing in the period, and writers like Greene found themselves in a rapidly changing and unpredictable social and economic space. The social world can be seen as being constituted by an array of fields (the field of writing being just one of many), which interact with each other in complex ways as relatively autonomous spheres of activity—each governed by internal rules and dominated by internal competitions for success in terms defined by the field.[58] These "spaces of possibles" operate to define for agents the available positions and the steps necessary to achieve them.[59] Those who occupy various positions in the field do so as the result of

56 Rosemary O'Day, *The Professions in Early Modern England, 1450–1800* (Harlow, United Kingdom: Pearson Education, 2000).

57 Edward Gieskes, *Representing the Professions: Administration, Law, and Theatre in Early Modern England* (Newark, DE: University of Delaware Press, 2006).

58 "Relative autonomy" is a crucial notion in Pierre Bourdieu's sociology. To say that fields are relatively autonomous is to say that the field in question, the field or writing, for example, has a set of norms and practices that structure terms of success or failure that are specific to that field. But, at the same time, the logic of the field exhibits a homology with the logic of what Bourdieu calls the "field of power." The intellectual field is autonomous, but still responds to external determinations.

59 Bourdieu writes, "The field as a field of possible forces, presents itself to each agent as a *space of possibles* which is defined in the relationship between the structure of average chances of access to the different positions (measured by the 'difficulty' of attaining them and, more precisely, by the relationship between the number of positions and the number of competitors) and the dispositions of each agent, the subjective and objective basis of the perception and appreciation of the objective chances" (Pierre Bourdieu, *The Field of Cultural Production* [New York, NY: Columbia University Press, 1993], p. 64).

their perception of their chances of access to those positions based on their capacities (dispositions) to deploy their varying endowments of cultural capital in the ongoing struggle that defines the field. Thus, individual agents like Greene succeed or fail because of the objective availability of positions as well as on their individual capacity to judge the "objective chances" of attaining a given position in the field. Dessen, Melnikoff, and Newcomb all describe aspects of the particular aggregation of cultural capital that Greene brought to the field of writing and suggest ways that his deployments of that capital depend as much on its origins in his Norwich background and his theatrical education as they do on his perceptions of the kinds of uses to which it might be put in a dynamic field. The success or failure of any of Greene's various interventions in the larger field of writing can, therefore, be said to depend on a combination of his cultural capital and the availability of positions in this field.

As Gieskes's and Reynolds and Turner's contributions to this collection will demonstrate, fields such as writing do not exist in isolation. They often interact, however, in a mediated way, responding to outside influences through the logics of their own particular discourses. Professional writing in Elizabethan England, for example, existed in many different social spaces—the printing house, the theatre, the court—and these spaces often overlapped and, at times, conflicted with each other. All of these social spaces exerted specific influences on the professional writers, and these influences were sometimes, but not always, compatible. Professions in general and the literary profession in particular develop in response to interactions such as these.[60]

Such interactions have a homologous relationship with struggles over definitions internal to the field of writing—struggles undergirding Greene's "upstart crow" comments in *Greene's Groatsworth of Wit*. Fields develop not only from external pressures but also from internal conflicts over, in the case of the field of writing, generic distinctions (as Mentz, Wilson and Maslen show in their contributions to this collection) and (as Tumelson's contribution suggests) definitions of important terms like "author," "writer," "reader."[61] That an emerging and disputed range of categorical distinctions was a defining feature of the

60 Andrew Abbott, in his *System of Professions*, argues that professions and professionalization develop as part of an interlocking system of occupations that, as they develop towards public recognition as professions, engage in a constant struggle over what definitions and practices make one profession distinct from another as well as what separates a profession from a mere occupation. Abbott's example is medicine, specifically the battle between physicians and other practitioners in the nineteenth century.

61 Bourdieu writes, "The very notion of writer, but also the notion of lawyer, doctor, or sociologist … is at stake in the field of writers (or lawyers, etc.): the struggle over the legitimate definition, whose stake—the word definition says it—is the boundary, the frontiers, the *right of admission*, sometimes the *numerus clausus*, is a universal property of fields" (Pierre Bourdieu and Loic Wacquandt, *Invitation to Reflexive Sociology* [Chicago, IL: Chicago University Press, 1992], p. 245).

discourse of professional writers at the end of the sixteenth century is intimated by Reid Barbour in his *Deciphering Elizabethan Fictions*:

> [Writers such as Greene, Nashe, and Dekker] adopt and change ... strategic terms, in sympathy, in antipathy, or more often in something between the two. In their relations, these three authors and their key terms show us something larger than the strategies of prose narrative: that is, the closely knit, though not monolithic or static, community of values exchanged and negotiated among the prosers.[62]

Barbour's characterization of the shifting and competing terms that build a "community of values" points towards the way that professional writing helped to constitute the larger field of writing. Debate over and competing uses of terms of judgment structure fields, and many of this volume's essays suggest that the social and cultural space of a profession can be usefully understood as the product both of (1) jurisdictional or border conflicts and (2) internal definitional struggles within the field of writing.

***

The essays in this volume reconsider Greene's practices as a writer and his varying contributions to the the shape of imaginative writing in the 1580s and early 1590s. In their organization, they also collectively stand apart from a critical orthodoxy that has primarily understood Greene as *either* a pampheteer *or* a playwright. The first two essays collected here are specifically concerned with Greene's particular practices as a professional writer. Alan C. Dessen's contribution "Robert Greene and the Theatrical Vocabulary of the Early 1590s" reconsiders some of the overlooked origins of Greene's specific practices as writer, specifically as a professional playwright. He begins by asking: even if fourteeners, overt allegory, and heavy-handed didacticism did more or less disappear, was the break with the dramatic form and procedures of the 1570s and early 1580s as severe as assumed in the prevailing narrative? Especially in the canon of plays from the late 1580s and early 1590s, what kinds of carry-overs can be discerned? Dessen thus starts with the slippery question: why does X happen at a given moment in a given play? Setting aside such stock answers as (1) to advance the plot or narrative, (2) to develop "character," and (3) to provide "comic relief," he focuses on less common yardsticks wherein X (4) provides symbolic or imagistic value and 5) makes a contribution to "structure" or patterning. Initially using examples from an assortment of plays with overt allegory (e.g., *Apius and Virginia* [1564], *A Warning for Fair Women* [1599]), Dessen ultimately focuses upon two plays by Robert Greene. According to Dessen, *Alphonsus, King of Aragon*, a jumbled response to (or imitation of) *Tamburlaine*,

62 *Deciphering Elizabethan Fiction* (Newark, DE: University of Delaware Press, 1993), pp. 13–14.

displays an intermittent attempt to enhance the main narrative by means of the choric appearances of Venus. In contrast to this early and somewhat primitive play, in *Friar Bacon and Friar Bungay* Greene skillfully uses his fool Rafe Simnell to orchestrate the "folly" of Prince Edward (the fool-as-prince) and his clownish servant Miles to orchestrate the limitations of Friar Bacon (the clown-as-magician). Here and in other examples, Dessen reconsiders episodes that apparently serve no visible-verisimilar-"realistic" function but, nonetheless, may contribute something distinctive to the overall effect or available meanings—at least when interpreted in terms of an original theatrical vocabulary. He concludes by underscoring "Greene's growth as a playwright, in particular his ability to use his legacy from the plays of the previous generation to forge something new and distinctive in Elizabethan drama."

Kirk Melnikoff's "'That will I see, lead and ile follow thee': Robert Greene and the Authority of Performance" is also interested in Greene's literacy in the theatrical conventions of the late 1580s and early 1590's stage and the practices that resulted from it. The essay begins by considering Robert Weimann's recent suggestion that we consider relations of writing and playing in their early modern context and attempt to answer the question of how and to what extent performance in Shakespeare's theater actually *was* a formative element, a constituent force, and together with, or even without, the text as a source of material "imaginary puissance" (5). Thinking about what Weimann characterizes as the "bi-fold" relationship between actorly and writerly modes of authorization that particularly characterizes the late 1580s drama of Greene, this essay ultimately challenges the critical commonplace that Greene was necessarily a consistent adversary of the performative tradition represented by "upstart crows." It argues not only that Greene began his theatrical career with *Alphonsus, King of Aragon* as an unselfconscious producer of actorly entertainments, but it also argues that in *James IV* Greene's approach to performance is much less devaluative than that articulated by Marlowe in *Tamburlaine*. Instead, Greene's use of both actorly and writerly modes of authorization in *James IV* can more usefully be described as collaborative, albeit apprehensive.

Other essays in this collection turn to Greene's role in the construction of a literary field and a model of authorship. They suggest, in one way or another, that Greene's works are themselves frequently engaged in defining the stakes in the emerging English literary tradition. In "Staging Professionalism in Greene's *James IV*," Ed Gieskes argues that Greene's work points to the advent of a theatrical field in which playwrights work as part of a broad group of theatrical professionals. At the same time, Gieskes's essay traces the way in which the craft practices of the Revels Office and their various possible meanings are refracted into the drama at a relatively early stage of its professionalization. According to Gieskes, Greene's play *James IV* demonstrates a sophisticated and ambivalent awareness of theatrical convention in the many metatheatrical comments that appear throughout the play. The play's literary self-consciousness derives from Greene's academic training, which steeped him in a deeply allusive and imitative style of composition. Greene is not only aware of a literary tradition, but also of a theatrical tradition—of a craft tradition of staging—and Greene alludes to and exploits the resources of these theatre-based traditions as much he does traditionally literary ones. Ultimately, contends Gieskes, *James IV* represents one professional writer's accommodation between a moralist's desire to instruct and the playwright's need to entertain. This accommodation is specifically professional—emerging from Greene's experience with page and stage—and points to the beginning of a contest over the profession's self-definition that shapes its development in profound ways.

Bryan Reynolds and Henry Turner's essay also points to the ways that Greene engages in the struggle for authority within the profession. According to them, Greene constructs his authorial identity in the context of conflict. They argue that among the writers known as "the University Wits" reputation depended on claims of status that, at the same time, denied that same status to others. Greene's refashioning of his public image follows this logic—he claims recognition in the act of denying it to others—and what they term the "dialectic of celebrity" in Greene's career has durable, structural effects on the profession of writing in early modern England. In *Friar Bacon and Friar Bungay*, a play where the powers of scholars who specialize in necromancy are celebrated and employed by sociopolitical conductors of state machineries to facilitate everything from international to interpersonal relations, an unexpected source of what Bryan Reynolds calls "transversal power" emerges triumphant yet ominous. Transversal power, a fluid and discursive phenomenon that can be found in anything from witchcraft to heart-wrenching poetry to philosophical inquiry, induces people to permeate the organized space of subjectivity—of all subjective territory and the state machinery that works to delineate it—and venture into the inestimable space where learning and metamorphosis can be dynamic and limitless. In the play, transversal power operates in conjunction with and/or through the love relationship between Margaret and Edward Lacy. Specifically, it is the force of love that fuels them, and such love is defined through its manifestations and influences vis-à-vis the ideologies of the official culture that simultaneously herald necromancy and paradoxically support rhetorically a transcendental notion of God as prescribed by the Christian tradition. Whereas necromancy functions to endow or trigger objects with agency (Bacon's crystal ball and brazen head), love, as articulated within the play, imbues objects of desire with the power to stimulate deviations by sociopolitical conductors that would otherwise seek to manufacture, manipulate, and/or negotiate an idealized concept of love that mutually advances state power. In effect, the magic of love "out magics" the respective authority of both scholarly and Christian discourse, presenting the play's audience with a less cynical but also more threatening concept of love than represented in most drama of the period.

Ron Tumelson's essay "Robert Greene, 'Author of Playes'" is particularly concerned with Greene's negotiations with the idea of dramatic authorship. It asserts the importance of Greene's role in both the emergent discourse on and the legitimation of play-writing's cultural status within England. Whereas most discussions on the cultural estimation and elevation of English plays center on the writings of Ben Jonson—particularly on the 1616 folio *Works*—Tumelson's essay argues against this commonplace within contemporary "historical" scholarship. According to Tumelson, Greene's authorial identity evolved in little over a decade between the publications of *Mamillia* (which may have been printed as early as 1580) and *Greene's Groatsworth of Wit* (which was printed posthumously in 1592), by which time his name was prominently displayed on several of his works' title-pages. Yet whereas much of Greene's writing in the 1580s centered on a variety of prose forms, by the end of his life, he had become something of a *Roberto fac totum*, having added plays to his trade-in-writing. Unlike his numerous prose works, however, not one of Greene's plays was published during his lifetime. Despite the fact that his plays had not appeared "on page" prior to the publication of *Greene's Groatsworth of Wit*, in the final, quasi-autobiographical prose works Greene renegotiates his authorial identity: he attempts to elevate the cultural status of play-writing, and to insist on his identity as an author and more specifically as an "Author of Playes." Consequently, if there is a "divide between Greene's dramatic production and his fiction," it is a divide that he himself initiated in *Groatsworth*.

Tumelson's focus on *Greene's Groatsworth of Wit* as a pivotal text in Greene's negotiations with dramatic authorship is more than apt. Since its publication in September 1592, *Greene's Groatsworth of Wit* has been infamous, in large part because of its attack on a certain not-yet famous "upstart crow." The massive critical attention this near-naming of Shakespeare has attracted has kept Greene's name in the critical spotlight and continues to associate him, albeit negatively, with the professional stage. In "Forming Greene: Theorizing the Early Modern Author in the *Groatsworth of Wit*," Steve Mentz shows how *Greene's Groatsworth of Wit* offers more than a vehicle for score-settling among playwrights; *Greene's Groatsworth of Wit* also constructs a complex fictional *summa* that retraces the twelve-year career of Robert Greene, the "King of the Paper Stage." Mentz's essay shows how the text explores nearly all the phases of Greene's career through its copious presentation of formal alternatives, including an abruptly truncated prodigal son narrative, two inset tales, a list of ten moral precepts, a poem, a beast fable, the famous attack on playwrights, and a deathbed letter supposedly penned by Greene to his estranged wife. According to Mentz, this composite text can be better read not as autobiography or pure fiction but as a practical form of literary theory: a work that enacts a self-conscious appraisal and review of what popular print culture had become by Greene's death. Greene would become a public symbol for published prose fiction in the years following his death, and in this deathbed text he both creates and becomes a contested metaphor for how prose fiction interacts with the marketplace of print and how the new medium positions itself against its great rival, drama. *Greene's Groatsworth of Wit*, along with a series of texts written by Greene or written about Greene after his death, provides a theory of early modern fiction as it was being articulated by such writers as Greene himself, his editor Chettle, and friends and rivals like Thomas Nashe, Barnabe Riche, and others. Contrary to what we might expect, given the relative paucity of critical work on early modern fiction as opposed to drama, *Greene's Groatsworth of Wit* presents prose fiction as having voracious formal ambitions and a capacity to embrace disparate audiences and forms. This text and the print culture from which it emerges create a proleptic self-portrait of the emerging cultural viability of printed narrative, the literary form that would come to dominate English letters but that conventional wisdom insists did not emerge until the eighteenth century. Renewed attention to *Greene's Groatsworth of Wit* and Greene, says Mentz, will require us to revise this and other accepted pieties about English narrative history.

Greene's direct, sometimes self-conscious, contributions to the varied shapes of English print narrative provide the focus of our collection's next two essays as well. Lori Humphrey Newcomb's "A Looking Glass for Readers: Cheap Print and the Senses of Repentance" traces the way in which Greene inventively crosses cultural registers—dramatic and nondramatic, sacred and secular, visual and verbal—as his plays and autobiographical pamphlets respond to new rhetorical and graphic conventions in the emergent literature of Puritan repentance. Focusing on *The Repentance of Robert Greene* (published posthumously in 1592), Newcomb argues that the pamphlet is a precursor to later spiritual texts. Although she cannot open a direct lineage to later spiritual autobiography or commercial devotional tract, Newcomb suggests that the first-person pamphlet, the form with which Greene is most associated, offered great promise as a medium for popular devotion. *The Repentance* is thus a precocious document of a textualizing impulse that would become central to popular Protestant experience, all the rarer because its author was noted for his sinfulness rather than his godliness, and perhaps possible only because its author's very soul approached being a textual creation. Like the ineffectual prophets who populate Greene's coauthored biblical drama *A Looking Glass for London and England* (performed 1589?), the experiences in this pamphlet explore the gap between the media that communicate the Word and the senses of resistant readers and listeners.

Robert W. Maslen's "Robert Greene and the Uses of Time" is similarly interested in Greene's contribution to Elizabethan narrative, particularly with how he writes himself into "the gaps, so to speak, in the Elizabethan canon." According to Maslen, Greene's work anxiously questions status quo understandings of productive labor, of time well spent, even of value or worth itself. The brand of fiction he wrote—failing to fall into any of the received categories of poetry, infected by the reviled forms of romance and continental prose narratives—exacerbated his anxiety and enabled him to recast these questions in a bewildering range of forms. Texts like *Penelope's Web* and *Euphues his Censure to Philautus*, for instance, articulate the problem of their own function by situating themselves in moments outside the orderly narrative of history. At the same time, Greene's brilliant use of the Faustian countdown of minutes towards his own death in his last publications makes conventional Elizabethan wisdom on the function of time well or badly spent look fundamentally inadequate to the needs of a sophisticated urban culture. Focusing particularly on

Menaphon, *Friar Bacon and Friar Bungay*, and *Greene's Vision*, Maslen traces how Greene's later writing opens the way to a range of new literary and dramatic forms well equipped to cope with new social, technological, religious, and economic realities. Greene's oeuvre is involved, in fact, with the triumph of time over the crude moralism that dominated literature and drama when he began to write.

The last essay included in this collection, Katherine Wilson's "Transplanting Lilies: Greene, Tyrants, and Tragical Comedies," looks at the influence of John Lyly's play *Campaspe* upon *Pandosto* and *Friar Bacon and Friar Bungay*, providing along the way another strong example of the benefits of reading Greene's work for the print market and the professional theatre as a continuum. It suggests not only that Lyly's tragicomic tonalities and plot progressively influenced Greene's popular romance and comedy but also that Lyly and his recognized style were employed by Greene in both works as benchmarks of an idealized popular cultural literacy. *Pandosto* contains direct quotations from *Campaspe* in the form of dramatic dialogue, but the themes of tyranny, male sexual exploitation, and social rank also recur throughout his story collections, for example in the inset tales in *Penelope's Web* and *Farewell to Folly*. Wilson's essay considers why the themes of Lyly's play held such a lasting appeal for Greene, and what the implications are for our understanding of Greene's attitude to genre, allusion, and the literary knowledge of his readership. Wilson stresses the extent to which Greene saw prose romance as a site for generic experiments; the awkward endings of many of his texts signal an attempt to achieve a form of "tyrant tragicomedy" in prose.

As is suggested by *Greene in Conceit*'s 1598 title-page illustration of a dead Greene in his winding sheet "raised from his graue to write the Tragique Historie of faire *Valeria* of London" (Figure 1), Greene continued to haunt London's burgeoning culture of writing.[63]

---

63 For an overview of Greene's continued influence after his death and a consideration of this woodcut, see Newcomb, *Reading Popular Romance*. For evidence of such influence, see Appendix C. That the woodcut gracing the title page of *Greene in Conceit* was specifically commissioned as a representation of Greene is impossible to know. Dickenson does include a reference to Greene writing in a winding sheet in his "aduertisement to the Reader" ("I saw standing before me, the shape of a well-proportioned man suted in deaths liuery, who seemed to write as fast as I could read" [A3]), suggesting the specific image on the title page.

60 GREENE IN CONCEIPT.

New raiſed from his graue to write the Tragique Hiſtorie of faire *Valeria* of London.

WHEREIN IS TRVLY DISCOVERED the rare and lamentable iſſue of a Husbands dotage, a wiues leudneſſe, & childrens diſobedience.

Receiued and reported by I.D.

Veritas non quærit angulos, vmbra gaudet.

Printed at London by RICHARD BRADOCKE for *William Iones*, dwelling at the ſigne of the Gunne neare Holborne conduit. 1598.

Fig. 1 The earliest known image of Greene

This woodcut, in which the first known image of Greene is captured, conjures more, however, than ghostly influence; it also demarcates a variety of the unique features of Greene's career as a writer, features to which this collection has been dedicated. Seated in a lofty chair, quill in hand with ink, sharpening knife and scholarly resource at the ready, Greene appropriately looks in this image, in the words of Newcomb, like "the scholarly romance writer." Such a visual representation counters Harvey's vagabond images of Greene and, with other equally different, posthumous representations, contributes to our sense of Greene as a much-disputed figure of discourse both before and after his death. More than this, though, the woodcut in its figuration of Greene writing underneath a framing proscaenium also offers an image which connotes the two different professional worlds in which Greene labored. Representing Greene as a writer on stage, the woodcut constructs Greene-the-writer as a public figure, one who was self-consciously performing every time he picked up a pen.

That the pamphlet's author John Dickenson could confidently turn to Greene six years after his death as both a marketing stratagem and a ploy at literary distinction well shows that Greene and his work persisted in informing later writing and professional position-takings.[64] The essays in this collection similarly attempt to conjure up a vision of Robert Greene writing. Together, they reimagine Greene by collectively asserting that England's first writer-by-trade be recognized as an exemplary figure in early modern professional writing and by collectively contending that his multiple engagements with the literary field index authorial and literary sophistication rather than bohemian disinterest or pecuniary desperation.

64 Dickenson specifically associates Greene with the misanthrope Timon of Athens in his "aduertisement," writing that it was only after "reading with some pleasure *Lucians Timon*" (A3) that he fell asleep and encountered Greene in a dream. Such an association of Greene with the Timon constructed in Lucian's dialogue-version suggests a very different vision of Greene's final years, one intriguingly more akin to Greene's construction of Bohan in *James IV* than to the contemporary accepted vision of Greene as simply a repentant prodigal. Unlike some of the other pamphlets that sought to capitalize on Greene's name after his death, Dickenson's pamphlet also does not clearly associate Greene with popular, debased culture. Instead, he represents Greene in his dedication to his readers as a well-respected writer. Toward the end of this preface, Dickenson not only confesses that some will view his use of Greene as an attempt "to picke vp some crummes of credit from anothers table" (A4), but he also admits that Greene well knows many other writers of more "sufficiencie" (A4v) than himself.

Chapter 1

Robert Greene and the Theatrical Vocabulary of the Early 1590s

Alan C. Dessen

Here is a familiar tale found in literary handbooks for much of the twentieth century. Once upon a time in the 1560s and 1570s (the boyhoods of Marlowe, Shakespeare, and Jonson), English drama was in a deplorable state characterized by fourteener couplets, allegory, the heavy hand of didacticism, and touring troupes of players with limited numbers and resources. A first breakthrough came with the building of the first permanent playhouses in the London area in 1576–77 (The Theatre, The Curtain)—hence an opportunity for stable groups to form so as to develop a repertory of plays and an audience. A decade later, the University Wits came down to bring their learning and sophistication to the London desert, so that the heavyhandedness and primitive skills of early 1580s playwrights such as Robert Wilson and predecessors such as Thomas Lupton, George Wapull, and William Wager were superseded by the artistry of Marlowe, Kyd, and Greene. The introduction of blank verse and the suppression of allegory and onstage sermons yielded what Willard Thorp billed in 1928 as "the triumph of realism."[1]

---

1 According to Willard Thorp, in *The Triumph of Realism in Elizabethan Drama, 1558–1612* (Princeton: Princeton Studies in English 3, 1928), early Elizabethan drama "was often rambling in structure and its realism was still of the sort which the miracles supported, horse-play, tumbling, and the antics of rustics, tavern-brawlers and half-witted clowns." Such plays lacked "strongly individualized characters belonging to a higher order of society" and were characterized by a heavy-handed didacticism. In contrast, by the death of Queen Elizabeth, an "evolutionary process" had taken place wherein plays preserve "a complete panorama of English life." The most important feature of this evolution, he argues, "is the loss of didactic purpose," for him "the predominant characteristic of early Elizabethan drama": "Before plays could be written which would show men as they are, writers had to believe that this was a better thing to do than to show them as the church or any other regent of morals thought they should be." His goal therefore is to trace "the decline of didacticism in theme and plot and the consequent triumph of realism" (Thorp, pp. vii–ix). For a representative account of the University Wits, see chapter four of Thomas Marc Parrott and Robert Hamilton Ball's *A Short View of Elizabethan Drama* (New York: C. Scribner's Sons, 1943). According to this mid twentieth-century handbook, these figures (Lyly, Peele, Greene, Kyd, and Marlowe) "shared the tastes of their public, but their

Theatre and drama historians have picked away at some of these details (in particular, 1576 has lost some of its luster or uniqueness), but the narrative of the University Wits's resuscitation of a moribund English drama has retained its status as received truth. No one, myself included, would deny that something changed in the mid-to-late 1580s with the appearance of *1 Tamburlaine* and *The Spanish Tragedy*, two items that irrevocably shifted the paradigm. In this watershed period that lasted through the early 1590s (Marlowe's death in 1593 provides one possible terminus), fresh materials and experiments abound, as evidenced in such landmark items as *The Jew of Malta*, the three parts of *Henry VI*, *Titus Andronicus*, and *Arden of Feversham*. If not a triumph of *realism* (a term notoriously difficult to pin down), a notable change from the pre-Kyd and pre-Marlowe dramatic fare cannot be disputed.

My focus, however, is upon continuity rather than breakthroughs. Few plays have survived from the London theatre company repertories of the early-to-mid 1580s. Of those few no one chooses to weigh *The Three Ladies of London* and *The Rare Triumphs of Love and Fortune* in the same scale as *Doctor Faustus* and *Friar Bacon and Friar Bungay*. Marlowe, moreover, in his Prologue to *1 Tamburlaine* clearly thumbed his nose at "the jigging veins of rhyming mother wits" of the previous generation. Nonetheless, I wish to pose the question: Even if fourteeners, overt allegory, and onstage sermons did (more or less) disappear, was the break with the dramatic forms and procedures of the 1570s and early 1580s as severe as assumed in the prevailing narrative? Especially in the canon of plays from the late 1580s and early 1590s what kinds of carry-overs can be discerned?

As a point of departure, consider a fundamental yet very slippery question: Why does X happen at a given moment in a given play? Generations of readers, at least up through the early 1980s, would provide such stock answers as 1) to advance the plot or narrative and 2) to develop "character." The latter answer may be out of fashion among academics and postmodernists who talk in terms of "subject positions" but is still prevalent among theatrical professionals (and my undergraduates). Another stock response is 3) to provide "comic relief" wherein the main action of a play becomes comparable to heartburn or a headache. Less common would be the response that X might be present at a given point 4) for its symbolic or imagistic value and least common would be 5) for its contribution to "structure" or patterning. My goal in this essay is to explore, briefly and tentatively, categories 4 and 5, with particular reference to Robert Greene's *Alphonsus of Aragon* and *Friar Bacon and Friar Bungay*.

Let me start with a stock device found in the late moral plays: the choice to break down X (an individual, a key choice, a kingdom) into its component parts that in turn can be represented onstage. A particularly revealing example is to be found in R.B.'s *Apius and Virginia* (1564) where, after Apius agrees to the Vice's

---

education and their inborn talent enabled them to guide, purify, and elevate these tastes till at last they trained an audience ready to receive and applaud the work of Shakespeare" (64).

plan (that will wrest Virginia from her family), the stage direction reads: "*Here let him make as though he went out and let Conscience and Justice come out of him, and let Conscience hold in his hand a lamp burning and let Justice have a sword and hold it before Apius' breast.*"[2] Although Conscience and Justice have no lines while Apius is onstage, the judge himself supplies their half of the argument:

> But out I am wounded, how am I divided?
> Two states of my life, from me are now glided,
> For Conscience he pricketh me contemned,
> And Justice saith, judgment would have me condemned:
> Conscience saith cruelty sure will detest me:
> And Justice saith, death in the end will molest me,
> And both in one sudden me thinks they do cry,
> That fire eternal, my soul shall destroy. (501–8)

Haphazard the Vice, however, mocks Conscience and Justice ("these are but thoughts" [510]) and argues instead: "Then care not for Conscience the worth of a fable, / Justice is no man, nor nought to do able" (521–2). After Apius agrees to forgo his scruples ("let Conscience grope, and judgment crave"), Conscience and Justice are left alone onstage to lament his decision in psychological terms (e.g., Conscience complains: "I spotted am by willful will, / By lawless love and lust / By dreadful danger of the life. / By faith that is unjust" [538–41]).

To act out the central decision in his play, R.B. has not resorted to a soliloquy or even to straightforward temptation by the Vice but has chosen to break down Apius's choice into its component parts. Somehow, at the moment when the judge is leaving the stage under the influence of the Vice and his own lust, Conscience and Justice are to "*come out of*" Apius (or "glide" from him, according to the dialogue), whether from behind his cloak or through some stage device (as in the genealogy of Sin sequence in *All for Money* [1577]). The theatrically emphatic presence of these two figures (with their striking entrance, their emblems, and their gestures) is then linked verbally to Apius's own conscience and sense of justice. Apius's subsequent exit with the Vice acts out his choice and spells out how he has abandoned his conscience and sense of justice in favor of his lust. Both the stage direction that indicates that Conscience and Justice are to "come out of" Apius and the Vice's insistence that "these are but thoughts" underscore how the inner workings of the protagonist's mind have been made external in a fashion particularly suited to onstage presentation.

---

2 *Apius and Virginia*, ed. Ronald B. McKerrow and W.W. Greg (London: Malone Society, 1926), l. 500. Dates attached to plays are for the convenience of the reader and are taken (often with a substantial grain of salt) from *Annals of English Drama 975–1700*, ed. Alfred Harbage, rev. S. Schoenbaum (London, 1964). With *Apius and Virginia*, *A Warning for Fair Women*, *Alphonsus of Aragon*, Brooke's Marlowe, and Greg's *Doctor Faustus*, I have modernized the spelling.

The late moral dramatists regularly used such onstage psychomachias to display at length pivotal decisions, whether the choice of Faith over Despair (*The Tide Tarrieth No Man* [1576]), the effect of Knowledge of Sin upon Infidelity (*The Life and Repentance of Mary Magdalene* [1558]), or the choice of Covetous over Enough (*Enough is as Good as a Feast* [1560]). The technique survives in the 1590s, as witnessed by the Good and Evil Angels of *Doctor Faustus* and one or more angels who flank a despairing figure in Lodge and Greene's *A Looking Glass for London and England* (1590). Consider in particular *A Warning for Fair Women* (1599) where a pivotal event, the seduction of Mistress Sanders, is presented not through dialogue among the characters but by means of a dumb show:

> *next comes Lust before Brown, leading Mistress Sanders covered with a black veil: Chastity all in white, pulling her back softly by the arm: then Drury, thrusting away Chastity, Roger following: they march about, and then sit to the table: the Furies fill wine, Lust drinks to Brown, he to Mistress Sanders, she pledgeth him: Lust embraceth her, she thrusteth Chastity from her, Chastity wrings her hands, and departs: Drury and Roger embrace one another: the Furies leap and embrace one another.*[3]

To underscore the effect, Tragedy as presenter explicates this dumb show for the spectator (e.g., "Now blood and *Lust*, doth conquer and subdue, / And *Chastity* is quite abandoned"). Clearly, the anonymous dramatist has not opted for the temptation scene expected by a modern reader but instead has provided a breaking down of the event into components that include both verisimilar figures (wife, seducer, bawds) and allegorical forces (Chastity, Lust, the Furies). In place of a soliloquy or a speech of acquiescence for the protagonist, the dramatist provides as major signals the thrusting away of Chastity and the embracing of Lust. Like R.B., Wapull, and Wager (or Marlowe with his good and evil angels), this dramatist felt that such an orchestration of component parts was a workable method of putting the mind of his protagonist on theatrical display at an important moment.

I invoke R.B.'s use of Conscience and Justice along with the dumb show from *A Warning for Fair Women* to suggest some of the expertise in the late moral drama that regularly goes unrecognized and to call attention to comparable devices (part of what I term *theatrical vocabulary*) in the 1580s and thereafter. My larger goal is to isolate and develop further these and comparable techniques in the plays that precede Kyd and Marlowe and then to deal with a wide range of plays from the late 1580s and thereafter in which playwrights somehow incorporate or adapt such devices. In this essay my primary focus will be on some of Robert Greene's

---

3 *A Warning for Fair Women*, ed. John S. Farmer (Amersham: Tudor Facsimile Texts, 1912), D1.

distinctive choices in an early, even primitive play, *Alphonsus of Aragon*, and his subsequent comic masterpiece, *Friar Bacon and Friar Bungay*.

A passage from Greene's prose would support the familiar tale with which I started. In his *Groatsworth of Wit* (1592), the Player tells Roberto that he was once "a country Author, passing at a Morall, for 'twas I that penned the Morall of man's wit, the Dialogue of Dives, and for seven years' space was absolute Interpreter to the puppets. But now my Almanac is out of date: *The people make no estimation, / Of Moralls teaching education*."[4] Clearly Greene knew well the drama of the previous generation, here characterized by the term *morall* (a dramatic kind surprisingly difficult to pin down), which by the early 1590s is seen as "out of date" and lacking any "estimation" as entertainment or edification. Greene, moreover (like Kyd and Marlowe), is far more skillful as a theatrical poet and craftsman than Wilson and his predecessors. But what happens when one looks for continuity rather than breakthroughs, especially in Greene's most fully realized plays?

Of the plays scholars have linked to Greene, certainly the least impressive is *The Comical History of Alphonsus, King of Aragon* whose title page asserts "Made by R.G." and "*As it hath been sundry times Acted*." Though not printed until 1599, this play was clearly written a decade or so earlier (*Annals of English Drama* dates it in 1587) and in language and action is heavily indebted to, even derivative from, Marlowe's *Tamburlaine*. For example, Alphonsus's boast: "I clap up Fortune in a cage of gold, / To make her turn her wheel as I think best"[5] is a clear echo of Tamburlaine's vaunt to Theridimas: "I hold the Fates bound fast in iron chains, / And with my hand turn Fortune's wheel about."[6] Similarly, the slaughter of the kneeling, pleading virgins of Damascus by a black-clad Tamburlaine in act 5 of part I is echoed with a difference in *Edward III* and *Alphonsus*. In their final sequences both plays provide kneeling figures (the six burghers of Calais; Amurack, Fausta, and Iphigina) who at first confront a stern figure who imposes a death sentence (Edward III, Alphonsus) but are spared owing to the intervention of another figure (Queen Phillipa; Alphonsus's father, Carinus). The link between *1 Tamburlaine* and *Alphonsus* is clearest when Iphigina first rejects her conqueror's offer of marriage (hence the three figures are doomed to death) but later kneels and pleads that he revoke his sentence "for that love if any love you had" (1902).

---

4 *A Groatsworth of Wit*, ed. G.B. Harrison (London and New York: Bodley Head Quartos, 1923), p. 34. For an extended account of the *morall* as a dramatic kind along with my struggle to make sense of the evidence (e.g., many of the allusions refer to a post 1600 phenomenon), see "The Morall as an Elizabethan Dramatic Kind: An Exploratory Essay," *Comparative Drama*, 5 (1971): 138–59.

5 *The Comical History of Alphonsus, King of Aragon*, ed. W.W. Greg (London: Malone Society, 1926), ll. 1614–15.

6 *Tamburlaine*, in Tucker Brooke (ed.), *The Works of Christopher Marlowe* (Oxford, 1910), ll. 369–70.

Alphonsus answers in a clear echo of Tamburlaine's white-red-black policy (submit when you have the opportunity or face death thereafter): "If that you had when first I proffer made, / Yielded to me ... / I would have done, but since you did deny, / Look for denial at *Alphonsus*' hands" (1906–9).

Despite the 1599 publication date, various features of this play point to its early, even primitive status. In particular, the stage directions are couched in a vocabulary that would disappear by the early to mid 1590s. Typical are the three uses of *let*, as in "*Let there be a brazen Head set in the middle of the place behind the Stage*" (1246–7; see also 2–3, 2109–10), a locution common in the 1580s but hard to find thereafter. Also not typical of later usage are the two "*as soon as* ..." items: "*as soon as they are in, strike up alarum a while*"; "*As soon as he is gone, sound music within*" (373, 923) and the repeated uses of "*toward*" (e.g., "*Albinius and Fabius go toward Alphonsus*" [337]), "*in this sort*" ("*Enter Laelius, who seeing that his King is slain, upbraids Alphonsus in this sort*" [401–2]), *thy-thou*, and *say* ("*Fabius give Belinus thy sword drawn, Belinus say as followeth*" [603–4]).

Another feature of *Alphonsus* typical of the 1580s and early 1590s is the presence of a framework to the action consisting of allegorical or mythical figures—here Venus and the Muses. Venus opens the play (4–43) lamenting the absence of poets to sing the praises of Alphonsus ("And all his acts drowned in oblivion" [33]) and then "*Stands aside*" (57) at the entrance of the Muses "*playing all upon sundry Instruments, Calliope only excepted*" (44–5), with Calliope, as the champion of epic poetry, mocked by Melpomene, Clio, and Erato. Venus asks Calliope "To entertain Dame *Venus* in her school, / And further me with her instructions" (97–8) so that she can "describe *Alphonus*' warlike fame: / And in the manner of a Comedy, / Set down his noble valor presently" (109–11). This opening sequence thereby suggests a connection between comedy, the epic or heroic, and Venus-love as might be expected from the title page's characterization of this work as a "Comical History."

What then is of particular interest for my purposes is how little is done in what follows with the presence of Venus in relation to the play proper (as opposed to Thomas Kyd's suggestive integration of Revenge and Don Andrea into the various actions of *The Spanish Tragedy*). The goddess does appear before each of the subsequent acts (which consist largely of the rise of Alphonsus, a series of battles, and some supernatural events involving Mahomet, a brazen head, and Medea the conjurer) and with the Muses in a coda at the end of the action, but these appearances provide little more than a narrative preview of what is to happen in acts 2 through 5. Typical is Venus's prologue to act 5 (1656–74) where she tells of the battle to come between Alphonsus and Amurack, the former's victory, and Amurack's being taken prisoner "until his daughter came: / And by her marrying, did his pardon frame" (1673–4).

That Venus serves as little more than a choric program note for acts 2 through 4 should not surprise a reader or playgoer, for the onstage events have little to do with Love. What *is* surprising is how little is made of Venus's presence in act 5 where the power of Love does have a significant effect on key choices and where allusions to Venus, Mars, and Cupid do appear in the dialogue. Initially, the all-conquering Alphonsus flees from Iphigina on the battlefield saying that he is not afraid to fight a woman, "But love sweet mouse hath so benumbed my wit, / That though I would, I must refrain from it" (1744–5). She replies in mythological terms: "Your noble acts were fitter to be writ / Within the Tables of dame *Venus* sun, / Than in God *Mars* his warlike registers" (1547–9) and adds mockingly: "When as your Lords are hacking helms abroad, / ... Your mind is busied in fond Cupid's toys. / Come on I'faith, I'll teach you for to know / We came to fight, and not to love I trow" (1750–54) and refuses to be his wife or concubine, though eventually she too flies and re-enters with her father and mother "*all bound with their hands behind them*" (1783–4).

Though Iphigina does change her tune and offer her love, the triumphant Alphonsus (as noted above) is intransigent, so that the impasse is only resolved with the appearance of Carinus, Alphonsus's father, who is moved by "Her sighs and sobs" and "store of Crystal tears" (1966–8) and, after observing that Alphonsus has "Been trained up in bloody broils of *Mars*" (1976), notes: "I should account that maid / A wanton wench, unconstant lewd and light, / That yields the field, before she venture fight" (1980–82). Here again the gods enter into the equation, at least verbally, so that Carinus, seeing that Alphonsus is fitter "to enter Lists and combat with your foes, / Then court fair Ladies in God *Cupid's* tents" (1987–8), pleads to Iphigina in behalf of his son, and she responds: "But *Cupid* cannot enter in the breast, / Where *Mars* before had took possession: / That was no time to talk of *Venus* games, / When all our fellows were pressed in the wars" (2021–4). Eventually, Alphonsus can talk of "my joy, since that I now have got, / That which I long desired in my heart" (2035–6).

The coda that brings back the Muses tells of the marriage of Iphigina and Alphonsus and Venus's return to heaven but does little to develop the triumph of Venus over Mars (or resolve the presence of Mahomet in the midst of the classical pantheon). The power of Venus, even over an otherwise all-conquering hero dedicated to Mars, is evident in act 5 and is signaled in the passages cited, but, despite various key choices and actions in act 5, the actual appearances of this figure before acts 2, 3, and 4 and in the coda add little to the mix. Kyd's provocative use of *his* choric figures may or may not have been available as a model, but other comparable plays before and after *Alphonsus* (e.g., *The Rare Triumphs of Love and Fortune*, *Soliman and Perseda*, *Mucedorus*, *Two Lamentable Tragedies*) do integrate their allegorical personae into the main action in ways not visible in Greene's play.

My goal here is not to belittle this early work but rather to use its shortcomings, particularly the missed opportunities in Venus's presence, to highlight the skillful development of comparable devices and motifs in Greene's most successful play, *Friar Bacon and Friar Bungay*. This comedy has no equivalent to Venus and the Muses and makes no overt use of allegory as in *Apius* or *Warning for Fair Women*.

Nonetheless, a close look at the function of two figures, the fool and the clown, can demonstrate how Greene has successfully adapted such techniques to his own purposes.

Consider first Rafe Simnell, Prince Edward's fool, who, along with Friar Bacon's servant Miles, elicits much of the play's laughter and, like comparable later and better known figures (e.g., Feste, Lear's fool), highlights the folly of others. What is of particular interest is how both Rafe and Miles serve to spell out the folly or weakness of their masters in a manner akin to the supposedly primitive techniques of the previous generation. First, in the opening scene after the prince reveals he has been struck by Margaret's beauty, it is Rafe who suggests that they turn to Friar Bacon for help. The fool's original notion may be comically absurd (that Bacon "shall turn me into thee; and I'll to the court and I'll prince it out" whereas Edward will be changed into "either a silken purse, full of gold, or else a fine wrought smock"[7] to gain access to his lady, but Edward does seize on the fool's suggestion: "Lacy, the fool hath laid a perfect plot," for if Margaret is coy and demands marriage, "it must be nigromantic spells / And charms of art that must enchain her love" (118, 122–3). The fool's (foolish) notion—to use Bacon's magic to gain Margaret—has quickly become the prince's strategy.

After Lacy has been delegated to woo Margaret in the prince's behalf, Rafe, Edward, Warren, and Ermsby appear again with the fool "*in Edward's apparel*" (5.0.s.d.). Not only has Rafe assumed the prince's garb, but the fool gives (comical) orders to the lords, entitles himself their "master" (2), is verbally deferred to as "your honor" and "my lord" (3, 6, 13), and is told "see you keep your countenance like a prince" (17). Here and in scene 7 where Rafe, Warren, and Ermsby confront the Oxford dignitaries, the playgoer witnesses princely folly in action wherein the fool-as-prince visibly supersedes the true prince (and both scenes are linked to violence, actual or threatened). This ascendancy (or mastery) of fool over prince is spelled out at the close of scene 5 when Edward, about to head off to Bacon's study, tells his two lords: "take the fool; / Let him be master, and go revel it," and Rafe responds: "Faith, Ned, and I'll lord it out till thou comest. I'll be Prince of Wales over all the blackpots in Oxford" (111–12, 116–17). This masquerade does not deceive Bacon, who tells the prince "Thy fool disguis'd cannot conceal thyself" (5.70), or even the Oxford dons ("I cannot believe that this is the Prince of Wales"—7.55). Rather, this easily penetrable disguise is for the benefit of the playgoer and serves as Greene's version of R.B.'s "*let Conscience and Justice come out of him*" or *A Warning for Fair Women*'s "*Lust embraceth her, she thrusteth Chastity from her*"—here to spell out Edward's folly in his pursuit of Margaret and in his subsequent vengeful anger at Lacy. The onstage deference of lords and

7 *Friar Bacon and Friar Bungay*, ed. Daniel Seltzer (Lincoln: The University of Nebraska Press, 1963), 1.98–101. All further citations are from Seltzer's edition, though I have consulted *Friar Bacon and Friar Bungay*, ed. J.A. Lavin (London: New Mermaid, 1969) and *Friar Bacon and Friar Bungay*, ed. W.W. Greg (London: Malone Society, 1926).

dignitaries to the fool-as-prince may be mocking or grudging, but the situation, the language, and the likely stage business (both deferential and violent) add up to a telling comment on Edward's foolishness.

In addition to costume and onstage behavior, the placement of scenes in this sequence is also significant, for Edward's use of the prospective glass, which allows him to see Margaret, Lacy, and Friar Bungay but not hear what the playgoer hears, is bracketed by the two Rafe-as-prince scenes in what John Weld terms "clever cross-cutting."[8] Edward's use of Bacon to prevent the marriage ("stop the marriage now, / If devils or nigromancy may suffice") and his determination to "hie me to Fressingfield / And quite these wrongs on Lacy ere it be long" (6.146–147, 179–80) are framed by the antics of his foolish counterpart "*in Edward's apparel.*" In the second Rafe scene, moreover, we are told that the false prince and his lords "have made a great brawl, and almost kill'd the vintner," and Rafe himself claims "These are my lords, and I the Prince of Wales" and adds that when the dons "see how soundly I have broke his head, they'll say 'twas done by no less man than a prince" (7.38–39, 48–9, 52–4).

This defense of princely violence is then followed by the key moment in the first half of this comedy, Edward's confrontation with Lacy and Margaret, which starts with menace (the prince enters "*with his poniard in his hand*" [8.0.s.d.]), moves to each lover's selfless plea to spare the other, and climaxes with Edward's self-examination that starts with questions ("art thou that famous Prince of Wales / Who at Damasco beat the Saracens"; "Is it princely to dissever lovers' leagues, / To part such friends as glory in their loves?") and builds to a recognition of a different kind of conquest: "So in subduing fancy's passion, / Conquering thyself, thou get'st the richest spoil"; "Lacy, rise up. Fair Peggy, here's my hand. / The Prince of Wales hath conquered all his thoughts, / And all his loves he yields unto the earl" (8.112–113, 116–17, 120–4). For the playgoer, this conquest of love and self ("subduing fancy's passion, / Conquering thyself"), Edward's crowning achievement, is linked not only to famous battles but also to the fool-as-prince

---

8 See John Weld, *Meaning in Comedy: Studies in Elizabethan Romantic Comedy* (Albany: State University of New York Press, 1975). Here and elsewhere the innovative Greene comes up with a device that Shakespeare will later adapt for his own purposes. I.e., Edward's seeing but not hearing is an early version of Iago's "ocular proof" in *Othello*, IV.i wherein initially Othello sees but does not hear Cassio talk about Desdemona-Bianca. Similarly, the Bacon-Miles combination in which the magus has a servant whose nature cannot be nurtured anticipates Prospero-Caliban (*Meaning in Comedy*, p. 138). My reading of Rafe-as-prince is comparable to Weld's "dramatic metaphor" analysis in terms of "the overthrow of reason by passion" wherein "The inversion of order in the band [of courtiers], folly on top, reason below, thus duplicates the inversion in Edward's own psyche." For Weld, when "Edward views the lovers in the enchanted glass of his own passion and mistakes their murder for his good," that metaphor provides "an alternative statement of the moral-psychological inversion writ large in the riot scenes that precede and follow it" (pp. 138–9).

scenes that have preceded it.[9] As Margaret notes, the prince's "conquest is as great, / In conquering love, as Caesar's victories" (137–8).

In the second half of the play, the roles of prince and fool are much diminished, for the focus turns primarily to Friar Bacon's magic and Margaret's beauty (the combination noted in 1935 by William Empson in *Some Versions of Pastoral*). In several of these scenes, Miles serves a function roughly comparable to Rafe's—and the two have already been linked in a variety of ways, as when the fool-as-prince commands "I will lead the way; only I will have Miles go before me, because I have heard Henry say that wisdom must go before majesty" (7.119–121). Miles is as far from being a scholar or magician as Rafe is from being a prince (as is evident in the former's clownish quips and Bacon's labeling of him twice as a dunce—5.24, 36), so that both the clown and the fool can highlight the folly or limitations of their respective masters and supposed superiors.

As befits his titular status, Friar Bacon's strengths or skills are central to a series of scenes, starting with the putting down of Burden and building to the triumph over Vandermast and the two uses of the prospective glass, and serve as a major source of this play's appeal. Less obvious but equally important are Bacon's limitations. As early as the second scene, Burden, skeptical about the notion of a brazen head that can "tell of deep philosophy," objects: "But Bacon roves a bow beyond his reach, / And tells of more than magic can perform" (2.82, 76–7). Bacon can embarrass and thereby undercut this skeptic by magically bringing the hostess from Henley, so that his critic is abashed by "his guilty conscience" and "mated by this frolic friar" (149–50), but the ability to use a devil to move figures around geographically (here with the hostess and later with Bungay to stop the wedding) or to use a prospective glass to see far off events does not counter Burden's critique. That the users of the glass (first Edward, then young Lambert and Serlsby) are provoked to deadly violence or near-violence indicates the presence of seeing or knowledge without true understanding or control, just as the failure of the brazen head project points to limitations that correspond to Burden's "beyond his reach."

Here is where Miles, like Rafe, contributes to a playgoer's fuller understanding. As with many such clowns, the series of quips provide not only fun but also a parody of the learning of his master and regularly convey the ineducable status of the would-be student-magician. The key scene is the failure of the brazen head where, after seven years of preparation and threescore days of watching, Bacon must rest and, therefore, must trust in Miles to watch (i.e., to stay awake) and to wake him. As with the fool-as-prince, the clown-as-magician is programmed to fail (Greene's version of the sorcerer's apprentice story), so that, after having slept

9 Perhaps worth noting is that this conquest of love/conquest of self as part of the first movement of a play is also found in the Edward III-Countess of Salisbury pre-France action of *Edward III*, the section of that history play regularly attributed to Shakespeare.

through the critical moments, Bacon can conclude, "My life, my fame, my glory, all are past" (11.95).

Scholars and editors have puzzled over the staging of the brazen head sequence, but these discussions rarely take into account what Miles is doing during his "watch."[10] After Bacon "*falleth asleep*," Miles comments on the head (especially the nose), announces "Well, I am furnished with weapons," and adds: "Now, sir, I will set me down by a post, and make it as good as a watchman to wake me if I chance to slumber" (11.37.s.d., 46–8). The Quarto's marginal stage direction then reads: "*Sit down and knock your head*" (49.s.d.), to which Miles reacts: "Passion a'God, I have almost broke my pate! Up, Miles, to your task; take your brown bill in your hand; here's some of your master's hobgoblins abroad," at which point: "*With this a great noise. The Head speaks*" (50–52). As Daniel Seltzer spells out the action in his note (74), apparently Miles has injured his head "by falling asleep and letting it knock against the column." The clown then falls asleep a second time even though he has sought to forestall this lapse by setting "a prick against my breast" (60–61)—here Seltzer adds a bracketed stage direction: "*Places the point of the halberd against his breast*" (J.A. Lavin inserts a comparable signal in his New Mermaid edition). When the third noise is heard that leads to the destruction of the brazen head, Miles reacts: "What, a fresh noise? Take thy pistols in hand, Miles" (73–4). Apparently the weapons the clown is "furnished with" include both a "brown bill" or halberd and pistols, none of which proves to be of much help.

Perhaps the stage business here should be written off as no more than "comic relief" supplied by the play's clown. But, as with Rafe-as-prince, Miles here is a stand-in (or sleep-in) for his master, and both of them fall asleep at pivotal moments, with the result that great plans fail owing to simple human weakness, the inability to sustain a watch. Bacon's magical tools are far more potent than Miles's weapons, but the magician's grand project also fails and his prospective glass will soon be destroyed in an act of repentance. That a sleepy Miles bangs his head against a stage post can, therefore, serve as a comment on the failure of "the head" in Bacon's plans, a failure to take into account human weakness (whether his own or that of Miles). Similarly, the failed attempt to stay awake by means of a halberd placed against his breast displays the clown-as-magician using a tool that is potentially self-destructive and almost leads to the demise of the user, a comical version of the danger inherent in Bacon's projects. These two images (neither of which is to be found in *The Famous Victories of Friar Bacon*), along with the taking "in hand" of two useless pistols, are designed to tell the story and elicit laughter, but they also comment on Bacon's failures.

By means of secondary figures and framing actions, the folly and weakness of both the prince and the magician have thereby been made explicit or further

---

10 See, for example, ed. Daniel Seltzer's Appendix A, pp. 98–100 and ed. J.A. Lavin's introduction, pp. xvii–xxi.

explored, a form of theatrical vocabulary widespread in the drama to follow (including the plays of Shakespeare) but with its roots in the pre-University Wits plays. Our notions of "character" or psychological realism may blur such effects or reduce our ability to recognize them, but Greene's combination of lively entertainment and potentially meaningful images is here delivered in a manner that likely made excellent sense to his playgoers. Indeed, such onstage techniques call attention to a liminal area between outright allegory (as in *Apius and Virginia* and other plays of the previous generation) and the supposed verisimilar-literal 1590s triumph of realism.[11]

By way of conclusion, consider a change made by a Royal Shakespeare Company director in his playscript for Marlowe's *Doctor Faustus*. In his 1989 production in the Swan, Barry Kyle chose to build on the shorter A-text and, in addition, work with thirteen actors, all of them men. To no one's surprise, some elements in the A-text were gone or transposed, with several of the alterations of potential interest. For me the most revealing change came late in the action. Few readers of this tragedy will leap to the defense of its "middle" (acts 3 and 4 in modernized editions), the scenes that depict Faustus's activities during his twenty-four years of "profit and delight"[12] after signing his pact with Lucifer. The last such episode in both A- and B-texts is the protagonist's encounter with the Vanholts where he supplies out-of-season grapes for the pregnant Duchess, a scene that follows the practical joke Faustus plays on the horse-courser. Kyle transposed these two scenes so that the interaction with the Vanholts preceded that with the horse-courser; moreover, he omitted the speech that closes the horse-courser sequence (the punch line for the episode in both early texts) in which the

11 I am sliding over several other items of potential interest. e.g., another much discussed moment (one not prized highly by many readers) is the Griselda-like testing of Margaret (perhaps comparable to the duke's testing of Isabella by not telling her that Claudio is alive) who eventually does choose Lacy over God. Here our sense of psychological realism or plausibility (why put either Margaret or Isabella through such hoops?) is superseded by Greene's strategy of setting up various parallels between his heroine and Bacon. For Greene, X can take precedence over Y when Y is *our* sense of plausibility and X represents a pattern to be fulfilled or a thesis to be sustained. Also, having Miles ride off to Hell on a devil's back (see 16.48–64) demonstrates Greene's awareness of one of the two most often alluded to features of the late moral plays (the other being the Vice's dagger of lath)—but with a twist. i.e., usually the figure in question is the Vice (Nichol Newfangle in *Like Will to Like* [1568]) or a fallen earthly protagonist (Worldly Man in *Enough is as Good as a Feast*), so that, according to previous theatrical tradition, if Bacon had not repented, he should have been the one to exit in this manner. To have Miles go to Hell willingly in the hopes of future profit as a tapster (42–4) adapts the still familiar moral play device to something suitable to clowns and comedy while separating Miles' folly or false expectations from those of his former (and now repentant) master.

12 Christopher Marlowe, *Marlowe's Doctor Faustus 1604–1616*, ed. W.W. Greg (Oxford: Oxford University Press, 1950), A. 83.

protagonist gloats that "Faustus has his leg again, and the Horse-courser, I take it, a bottle of hay for his labor" (A.1217–19).

Behind this change lay a desire by director and actor to improve Marlowe's presentation of Faustus's growing torment or apprehension, a progression that started in this production with his evident discomfort in his scene with the Emperor and was followed by the show for the Vanholts and finally by a reconception of the horse-courser encounter, which was played as a nightmare vision (the horse-courser was portrayed as a diabolic figure with talons). What in both early printed texts is a successful practical joke at the expense of the horse-courser became something decidedly different at the Swan.

Two incompatible senses of theatre or structure collide here. Although such reflexes may be deplored in academic circles, many readers, actors, and directors are most comfortable with some form of psychological realism and, therefore, seek to establish a progression of states of mind that makes best sense in such terms. The RSC Faustus, who lost his leg while writhing on the floor in pain, was clearly not a practical joker duping a bargain hunter. Readers may disagree about the function of this episode (at least those readers who assume it *does* have a function), but for me the point lies in a fairly obvious analogy: both the horse-courser and Faustus have made a bargain (for a horse at a low price, for twenty-four years of indulgence) that seemed like a good idea at the time but has a catch (don't ride the horse into the water; you must sign away your immortal soul) that leads to an unfortunate conclusion. The tragic fate of Faustus (like the folly of Prince Edward or the dangerous practices of Friar Bacon) is here previewed in comic terms by the discomfiture of the bargain hunter whose horse turns into a bundle of hay. Such use of prolepsis or analogical reasoning, however, is unlikely to work for playgoers at the Swan, so the director's choice here is an excellent example of rescripting to make a 1590s play conform to 1990s play logic.

That rescripting in turn brings me back to the various moments I have singled out from Greene's two plays. In keeping with the prevailing narrative about the role of the University Wits in the mid 1580s, Greene clearly does bring new expertise and professionalism to the popular stage. That expertise and professionalism, however, include an awareness of the potential in the pre-1585 drama for putting ideas and images in action onstage. In particular, his exploration of the folly and limitations of Prince Edward and Friar Bacon by means of Rafe and Miles (as with the link between Faustus and the horse-courser) demonstrates how the overt allegory of *Apius and Virginia* or *A Warning for Fair Women* can be metamorphosed into a new theatrical vocabulary rich in potential meanings. The gap between the relatively primitive use of Venus in *Alphonsus* and the fully realized Rafe-Miles scenes in *Friar Bacon* point to Greene's growth as a playwright, in particular his ability to use his legacy from the plays of the previous generation to forge something new and distinctive in Elizabethan drama.

Chapter 2

"That will I see, lead and ile follow thee": Robert Greene and the Authority of Performance

Kirk Melnikoff

> "[L]atelye two Gentlemen Poets, made two mad men of Rome beate it out of their paper bucklers: & had it in derision, for that I could not make my verses iet vpon the stage in tragicall buskins, euerie worde filling the mouth like the faburden of Bo-Bell, daring God out of heauen with that Atheist *Tamburlan*, or blaspheming with the mad preest of the sonne ... such mad and scoffing poets, that haue propheticall spirits as bred of *Merlins* race, if there be anye in England that set the end of scollarisme in an English blanck verse, I thinke either it is the humor of a nouice that tickles them with selfe-loue, or to much frequenting the hot house ... . If I speake darkely Gentlemen, and offend with this digression, I craue pardon, in that I but answere in print, what they haue offered on the Stage." (A3–A3v)
>
> —from *Perimedes the blacke-smith* (1588)

In his book *Author's Pen and Actor's Voice: Playing and Writing in Shakespeare's Theatre*, Robert Weimann has suggested that we "reconsider relations of writing and playing in their early modern context and ... attempt to answer the question of how and to what extent performance in Shakespeare's theatre actually *was* a formative element, a constituent force, and together with, or even without, the text as a source of material 'imaginary puissance.'"[1] The late Elizabethan professional theatre should not, he contends, "be subsumed under any one purpose of playing; it must be viewed as plural, as serving a number of diverse functions, as—far from being unified or unifying—a contested field in which early modern literary meanings can be constructed but also interpreted" (8). Focusing specifically on *Richard III*, *A Midsummer Night's Dream*, *Hamlet*, *Troilus and Cressida*, *Macbeth*, and *Cymbeline*, Weimann argues that "dramatic writing and theatrical performing in the English Renaissance ... [were] in a socially and culturally precarious state of both cooperation and confrontation, interaction and 'interface'"(6).

As one articulation of what he describes as the "bi-fold" relationship between actorly and writerly modes of authorization that particularly characterize

---

1 Robert Weimann, *Author's Pen and Actor's Voice: Playing and Writing in Shakespeare's Theatre* (Cambridge: Cambridge University Press, 2000), p. 5.

Shakespeare's drama, Weimann identifies the essentially confrontational mode of authorization inscribed in the late 1580s drama of university-educated playwrights, particularly that of Christopher Marlowe. According to Weimann, Marlowe's early conception of the purposes of playing is well encapsulated in his prologue to the first part of *Tamburlaine the Great* (1590), which "aggressively fashion[s] ... a new writerly authority" (57). Marlowe's inscription of textual authority, suggests Weimann, is echoed by the late writing of Robert Greene. "The inscribed sense of superiority in the shoemaker's son's condescension to the players," writes Weimann, "is perhaps best spelled out in the words of Robert Greene, one of his 'shifting companions,' when the latter, in his polemic against a certain player-playwright, presumes to view the players as 'those Antics,' 'such rude groomes,' and 'such peasants'" (57). Weimann's invocation of Greene and his infamous attack upon the players is perhaps only meant as an enlivening analogy, but, as the above prefatory material from Greene's 1588 pamphlet *Perimedes the Blacke-Smith* suggests, it is an analogy that needs qualification.

Greene's preface to *Perimedes* represents the first reference in his pamphlets to the London professional stage.[2] In it, Greene puts his own writing in opposition to both the form—"blanck verse"—and content—"Athiest"—of Marlowe's own. Moreover, Greene's ire in this passage is directed not at the players but presumably at other playwrights, the "two Gentlemen Poets" who "had it in derision, for that [he] could not make [his] verses jet vpon the stage." At the beginning of his dramatic career, then, Greene clearly did not consider himself simply to be a "companion" of Marlowe, and unlike Weimann's Marlowe, his identity as a professional playwright did not singularly depend upon "a biased and sharply contestatory devaluation of performance practices" (Weimann 57). Examining the different approaches to performance articulated by the texts of both *Alphonsus, King of Aragon* and *The Scottish History of James the Fourth*, this essay will attempt to reassess Greene's relationship with the players. Not only will it argue that Greene's working understanding of performance practice should not be seen as simply devaluative, but it will also contend that Greene ended his dramatic career by producing a "bi-fold" engagement with Elizabethan performance practice that is reminiscent of Shakespeare in a play like *A Midsummer Night's Dream*.

Greene's career as a professional playwright most probably began with *Alphonsus*.[3] Likely written a short time after the first part of Marlowe's

---

2 Greene's preface to this work, "To the Gentlemen readers, *Health*," in which he defends his "verses" from the derision of "two Gentlemen Poets," has proven to be provocative for a variety of reasons. Its citation of Marlowe's overreaching protagonist has reinforced our sense of the profound impact of Marlowe's first professional production. At the same time, its elusive reference both to "two Gentlemen Poets" and to the now lost play *The Mad Priest of the Sun* has inspired a variety of critical detective work. See David Farley-Hills, "Tamburlaine and the Mad Priest of the Sun," *Journal of Anglo-Italian Studies* 2 (1992): 36–49.

3 As Charles Crupi in *Robert Greene* (Boston: Twayne Publishers, 1986) has rightly stressed, "the dates of the plays are uncertain, and, indeed, the canon itself remains a matter

Tamburlaine, *Alphonsus* is significant both because it appears to be Greene's first play and because it shows many signs of being printed directly from an authorial draft.[4] Many of these signs are of the sort identified by Greg and others as indicative of authorial copy-texts. They include a host of permissive stage directions and "fictional signals" along with the absence of stage directions that warn of actions to come.[5]

For my purposes, *Alphonsus* is significant because it contains stage directions that suggest Greene's particular position with respect to the professional theatrical culture of the late 1580s and early 1590s. As one might expect from what likely was Greene's first professional play, some of these directions reveal a lack of familiarity with the developing conventions of the professional theatre manuscript.[6] Most obviously, the text of the play is awkwardly marked by Greene's combined use of narrative speech cues and speech prefixes.[7] After Albinius (one of Alphonsus's loyal followers) is directed to enter, for example, the stage direction and the first subsequent line read:

---

of debate" (100). Nevertheless, *Alphonsus*'s "general awkwardness" (100) and its parodic relationship with the first part of *Tamburlaine* suggest that the play is Greene's earliest surviving dramatic piece. For further arguments supporting a 1587 date for *Alphonsus*, see John Clark Jordan, *Robert Greene* (New York: Octagon Books, 1965), pp. 175–7. Stylistic and thematic similarities with Greene's other writing along with the authorial attribution of "R.G." on the 1599 title page provide compelling reasons to believe that *Alphonsus* is a Greene play.

4 This is not a new observation. W.W. Greg in his "Introduction," *Alphonsus King of Aragon* (The Malone Society Reprints, 1926), p. viii; G.B. Harrison in *Elizabethan Plays and Players* (Ann Arbor: University of Michigan Press, 1956); Alan C. Dessen in *Elizabethan Stage Conventions and Modern Interpreters* (Cambridge: Cambridge University Press, 1984), p. 26; and others have all suggested a strong authorial presence in the first quarto. According to Harrison, "The text is interesting because of its stage directions, which suggest that it was printed direct from an author's manuscript, and that he was a literary man, visualizing his play, than anyone actually writing in the theatre itself" (83).

5 Dessen, p. 28. William B. Long, in 'A bed / for woodstock': A Warning for the Unwary," *Medieval and Renaissance Drama in England* 2 (1985): 91–118, has argued that stage directions are almost always the work of a playwright, whether the copy-text consists of "foul papers" or a theatrical fair copy. "There is no evidence," he writes, "in the surviving playbooks that theatre personnel removed, simplified, or regularized such playwrights' directions in preparing a playwright's manuscript to be a 'promptbook'" (94). *Alphonsus* also has many examples in the text of what appear to be compositor errors.

6 As Dessen, Linda McJannet in *The Voice of Elizabethan Stage Directions* (Newark: University of Delaware Press, 1999); David Bradley in *From Text to Performance in the Elizabethan Theatre: Preparing the Play for the Stage* (Cambridge: Cambridge University Press, 1992); and others have observed, a "common code" or group of shared conventions did exist in the stage directions written for the Elizabethan professional theatre.

7 For a history of these speech attributions, see McJannet, pp. 58–65.

> Alphonsus *make as though thou goest out,*
> Albinius *say.*
> *Albi.* What loytring fellow haue we spied here?[8]

The direction "Albinius *say*" not only renders the following speech tag "*Albi.*" redundant, but it also had the potential of misleading an actor into delivering the tag. To cite another of the many examples, at the beginning of Act two, before Alphonsus's tagged speech "*Alphon.* Go packe thou hence ...," Greene's stage direction reads, "*Strike vp alarum. Enter* Flaminius *at one doore*, Alphonsus *at an other, they fight*, Alphonsus *kill* Flaminius, *and say*" (B4v). As Linda McJannet has pointed out, narrative speech tags were common in medieval dramatic texts but were quickly superceded by speech prefixes in plays written for the London professional theatres. Greene's combination of narrative cues and speech prefixes in *Alphonsus*, then, seemingly constitutes his failure to produce a conventional working manuscript for his London employers.

Such a textual oddity may have been the product of Greene's familiarity with an older dramatic tradition; it may also have been the product of his early work as a professional pamphlet writer. While undoubtedly evocative of medieval theatrical manuscripts, Greene's use of narrative cues is also reminiscent of writing strategies in his earlier prose work *Planetomachia* (1585). Towards the end of this framework tale, Greene's combination of narration and dialogue is as awkward as his combination of narrative cues and prefixes in *Alphonsus*. Introducing a cued exchange between Saturn and Venus, Greene writes,

> Venus had no sooner ended her tale, but Saturne rising out of his seate, as one in a chase, fell into these Chollericke tearmes.
> Saturne.
> Venus, you play ... .[9]

Just as his narrative cue "say" renders his speech tags redundant in *Alphonsus*, Greene's signal that Saturn will next "[fall] into ... Chollericke tearmes" makes his speech tag "Saturne" unnecessary. That Greene's early pamphlet-writing practices did inflect his early playwrighting is perhaps best corroborated by Greene's awkward inclusion of the section heading "*Of the Historie of* Alphonsus" (B4v) at the beginning of the second Act of *Alphonsus*. Patently untheatrical, section headings were a conspicuous part of Greene's prose work in the late 1580s. Works such as *Euphues his Censure to Philautus* (1587), *Perimedes* (1588), and *Ciceronis Amor* (1589) all include headings before letters, stories, histories and orations, even when such shifts in content were clearly implied.

---

8 Robert Greene, *Alphonsus King of Aragon*, 1599 (The Malone Society Reprints, 1926), Blv.

9 Robert Greene, *Planetomachia* (London, 1585), F3.

Greene's unconventional stage directions in *Alphonsus*, however, should not be taken to suggest his complete unfamiliarity with the contemporary conventions of professional playwrighting.[10] On the contrary, *Alphonsus* also contains elements that reveal Greene's literacy in a 1580s shared theatrical vocabulary.[11] To begin with, Greene's stage directions for Alphonsus at the beginning of the play to "*make as though thou goest out*" (B1v) and for Amuracke midway through Act three to "*Lay hold of* Fabius, *and make as though you carrie him out*" (G1v) are strongly evocative of the pre-1590s London theatre in their use of the construction "make as though."[12] Also a part of the shared theatrical vocabulary of the 1580s and 1590s is Greene's frequent use of the word "toward" in stage-directions like "*Point toward* Alphonsus" (B3v), "Albinius *go towards* Alphonsus" (B4), and "*Go toward Alphonsus and speake to one of his soldiers*" (H4).[13] And lastly, three of Greene's stage directions in the play include "let" in the imperative form.[14] As Dessen and Thomson point out in their *Dictionary of Stage Directions in English Drama, 1580–1642*, "[t]he imperative *let* is found regularly in the 1580s and early 1590s but not thereafter" (131).

Greene's tenuous familiarity with professional theatrical culture can also be seen in *Alphonsus*'s mixture of literary and theatrical directions. At times, Greene constructs stage directions in fictive terms. At the beginning of the play, he offers a stage direction that in its clarification of familial relations addresses a readerly audience: "*Enter* Clarinus *the Father, and* Alphonsus *his sonne*" (A4v). Later, Greene provides a direction for the character Laelius that speaks from the fictional context of a recent regicide: "*Enter* Laelius, *who seeing that his King is slaine, upbraides alphonsus in this sort*" (C1). More often, however, Greene provides stage directions that speak directly to actors concerned with the complexities of staging. At the beginning of Act four, Greene identifies the theatrical space in which the important prop of the brazen head should be located: "*Let there be a brazen Head set in the middle of the place behind the Stage, out of which, cast flames of fire, drums rumble within*" (F1v). Similarly, at the end of the play, Greene provides a direction for a dramatic spectacle that in its use of "chaire" and "top of the stage" is couched in the material reality of the theatre: "*Exit* Venus. *Or if you can conueniently, let a chaire come downe from the top of the stage, and draw her vp*" (I3).

10 I am indebted to Dessen for this important caveat and many of the observations in this paragraph.

11 Dessen, in his contribution to this collection, makes something of the same assertion: "Clearly," writes Dessen, "Greene knew well the drama of the previous generation ... . Greene, moreover (like Kyd and Marlowe), is far more skillful as a theatrical poet and craftsman than Wilson and his predecessors."

12 See Alan C. Dessen and Leslie Thompson, *A Dictionary of Stage Directions in English Drama 1580–1642* (Cambridge: Cambridge University Press, 1999), pp. 138–9.

13 See Dessen and Thomson, p. 234.

14 See stage directions on A3, F1v, and I3.

The printed 1599 quarto of *Alphonsus*, then, provides evidence not simply of Greene's inexperience with the professional Elizabethan stage; it suggests his relative familiarity with both its material reality and its playwrighting conventions as well. Greene may never have made his "verses iet vpon the stage in tragicall buskins," but *Alphonsus* suggests that this was not because he was completely out-of-touch with the 1580s professional stage. Greene had a sense—limited though it may have been—of the professional theatre's shared vocabulary, and he shows himself willing to work from the material perspective of his employers.

Greene, however, also had a sense of the capacities of the players for which he wrote his scripts. In *Alphonsus*, he consistently assumes that professional actors need much guidance, that they would be unable to figure out even the most obvious actions implied by his text. There are many examples of these kinds of unnecessary directions.[15] After Belinus tells Albinius and Fabius to "prithie goe, and aske him [the disguised Alphonsus] presently, / What countrey man he is, and why he comes / Into this place," the stage direction reads: "Albinius *and* Fabius *go toward* Alphonsus" (B3v–B4). This is an action necessarily implied by the fact that after the stage direction Albinius directly addresses Alphonsus with "My friend, what art thou?" Similarly, at the conclusion of a *Tamburlaine*-inspired early scene showing Alphonsus crowning three of his loyal followers, the stage direction tells the actor playing Alphonsus to "*set the Crowne on his* [Albinius's] *head*," even though Alphonsus's following line "Arise *Albinius* King of *Aragon*, / Crowned by me" (D3v) makes this action obvious. Greene's sense that he must continually guide the actors is not limited to just action; he also provides direction on emotional response. After Fausta accosts Amuracke for approving in his dream a vision of their daughter's marriage to Alphonsus, the stage direction reads "Amuracke *rise in a rage from thy chaire*" even though Amuracke's following lines—"What threatning words thus thunder in mine eares? / Or who are they amongst mortall troupes, / That dares presume to vse such threats to me?" (E3)—make such a reaction very clear.

Greene's lack of confidence in the deductive abilities of actors is perhaps not surprising. It correlates well with his figurative attack upon "those Puppets" and "vpstart Crow[s]" in his *Groatsworth of Witte* that Weimann and a host others have used to suggest Greene's antipathy towards the players. It also similarly anticipates an attack upon the players in his pamphlet *Francesco's Fortunes* (1590) where, through the voice of a "Palmer," Greene defines acting as nothing more than a "mechanical labour." Recounting a conversation between Cicero and the famed Roman actor Roscius, the Palmer approvingly quotes Cicero as saying, "why *Roscius*, / art thou proud with *Esops* Crow, being pranct with the glorie of others feathers? ... I graunt your action, though it be a kind of mechanical labour; yet wel done tis worthie of praise: but you worthlesse, if for so small a toy you waxe proud."[16] Greene's lack of confidence in *Alphonsus*, however, should not be

15 See stage directions on B2, B3v, B4, C1, C1v, C4, D2v, D3, E3v and others.

16 Robert Greene, *Francescos Fortunes* (London, 1590), B4v–C1.

confused with the overt antipathy toward and frustration with the actors of these later pamphlets. Instead, Greene's unnecessary promptings should be correlated with the play's ample encouragement of unscripted performance.

This encouragement takes many forms. It is most obvious in Greene's permissive directing of the play's musical elements.[17] At the beginning of the play, for example, Greene neither prescribes the music nor the specific instruments that the nine muses should be playing when the first enter the stage. The stage direction only says: "*Enter* Melpomine, Clio, Errato, *with their sisters, playing all vpon sundrie Instruments*" (A3v). Greene closes the play with a similar open direction. After the muses have bid farewell to Venus, they are directed to "*Exeunt omnes, playing on their Instruments*" (I3). A similar open invocation for music occurs in the third Act when Medea enchants Amuracke into sleep. Before her entrance, the stage direction reads: "*sound musicke within*" (E1). Greene is also permissive about the specific course of much of the play's spectacular action. Not only are many of its scenes of battle described in the stage directions using open language like "*they fight*" (B4v), "*flie*" (G4), and "*take him prisoner*" (G4), but many of its supernatural elements are unrestricted as well. The most obvious example of Greene's permissive approach to the performance of magic occurs during Medea's enchantment of Amuracke. After he has been soothed to sleep by the aforementioned "*musicke*," Medea enters and is directed to "*do ceremonies belonging to coniuring*" (E1). The omnipresence of unnecessary staging cues along with the play's broad allowance for unscripted performance suggests that although Greene initially presumed that his actor-employers had limited abilities, he at the same time was not actively hostile towards actorly purposes of playing on the professional stage.

Sometime around 1590, Greene wrote *James IV*.[18] In this play, Greene's perspective upon performance seems to change significantly. Like *Alphonsus*, the first extant edition of *James IV* (1598) offers a copy of what would seem to be an authorial manuscript. As such, it provocatively offers perhaps Greene's last attempt to construct a theatrical script for the professional stage.[19] This endeavor is less suspicious than *Alphonsus* of the deductive abilities of the actors, and this is certainly the natural result of Greene having become more experienced with the

---

17 Besides what I describe below, the play is full of alarums, and soundings of drums and trumpets.

18 All quotations are from Robert Greene, *The Scottish History of James the Fourth*, 1598, ed. W.W. Greg (The Malone Society Reprints, 1921). Working from a combination of historical and literary evidence, Norman Sanders, in his edition of the play (*The Scottish History of James the Fourth* [London: Methuen & Co. 1970]) forwards a 1590 date for *James IV* (pp. xxv–xxix). Sanders's gathering of evidence for this date is admirably complete and compelling.

19 In coming to the conclusion that *James IV* was printed from an authorial draft, Sanders points to literary stage directions, permissive stage directions, and inconsistent speech prefixes (pp. lvii–lix).

everyday working of the professional stage.[20] Even though *James IV* is in many ways a much more dramatic work than *Alphonsus*, almost entirely gone are Greene's redundant stage directions.[21] Greene's new trust in the "mechanical labour"'s of the players is perhaps best illustrated in the play's opening induction. When the angry Bohan finds that Oberon has enchanted his sword so that he cannot draw it from its sheath, no stage directions accompany either Bohan's initial discovery that "Gos sayds what wilt not out? whay thou wich, thou deele, gads fute may whiniard" (A3v) or his subsequent find (after Oberon has freed it from its sheath) that he cannot move his sword to strike the Fairy King.

What does not accompany Greene's more experienced understanding of the player's practices, however, is a lessening of Greene's permissive stage directions. If anything, these directions dramatically increase in variety. *James IV* contains little of *Alphonsus*'s martial elements, but even in its rare scenes of violence, the play is open about their staging. When Dorothea is forced to fight Jaques towards the end of the fourth Act, the stage direction only states, "*They fight, and shee is sore wounded*" (H1). Like *Alphonsus, James IV* is consistently permissive about the play's musical entertainments. The play's first direction is the vague "Musicke playing within" (A3). Similarly, when Ida and her mother, the Countess, begin the second Act "*in theyr porch, sitting at worke*," Greene vaguely directs that "*A song*" (D1v) be given before the two characters begin their dialogue.[22] Music accompanied by dance, however, far outweighs sung or unaccompanied music as a performative spectacle in the play. Not only is there at least one dance number in every Act of *James IV*, but without exception, all of these numbers are conceived by Greene to be open to the interpretive and performative skills of the players. The play opens with one of these unscripted dance numbers. Before Oberon and Bohan exchange any words, the stage direction dictates, "*Enter* After Obero, *King of Fayries, and Antique, who dance about a Tombe, plac'st conuentiently on the Stage, out of which, suddainly starts vp as they daunce*, Bohan, *a Scot*" (A3). Afterwards, during the course of his play, Greene requires "*a gig deuised for the nonst*" (A4v), "*a rownd of Fairies, or some prettie dance*" (C4), "*a hornpipe*" (E4), "*three Antiques, who dance round*" (G4), "*a rownd, or some daunce at Pleasure*"

---

20 Like *Alphonsus*, *James IV* has stage directions that are both fictive ("*in a marbell tombe*" [D1], "*in theyr porch*" [D1v], "*widdowes house*" [H4v], "*the gates*" [I1v]) and theatrical ("*on the Stage*" [A3], "*a noyse of hornes and showtings*" [Gv1]). Gone, however, are *Alphonsus*'s awkward directions.

21 *James IV* does contain redundant directions, but they are not nearly as frequent as in *Alphonsus*. See D2 ("*He carries the letter*"), D2v ("*Offer to exeunt*") and D4v ("*They all are in a muse*").

22 See G1v as well. Dessen and Thomson's work on stage directions has clearly shown that such a direction was highly conventional during the period (207–8). My only point is that this particular stage direction relies upon the players to choose the lyrics and tune of this particular "song."

(H3), and finally "*a solemne service*" followed immediately by "*a service, musical songs of marriages, or a maske, or what prettie triumph you list*" (H4v).

Yet even as Greene in *James IV*, as he does in *Alphonsus*, routinely makes use of modes of performance authority in his construction of theatrical entertainment, he at the same time shows himself to be newly aware of and interested in modes of textual or representational authority. In other words, it is only toward the end of Greene's dramatic career that we can usefully describe his vision of theatre as "bi-fold." Like *Richard III*, *A Midsummer Night's Dream* and *Hamlet*, *James IV* offers a self-conscious rumination upon relations between playwriting and performance. Akin to Hamlet, Greene's surly Scotsman Bohan prefers self-contained writerly drama, and his willful production of his dramatic illusion is an important element of both the play's action and thematic concerns.

When we first meet Bohan at the beginning of the play, he has removed himself from society and is living in a tomb because he "hate[s] the world." Drawn out of his grave by Oberon, King of the Fairies, in order to explain why he has chosen such a life, Bohan supplements the short account of his life's downward course in the play's induction (A3v–A4v) with a history play of his own devising about James IV's fall into corruption. Bohan addresses Oberon with little doubt that his play will amply demonstrate why he has chosen to forsake the world:

> Now King, if thou be a King, I will shew thee whay I hate the world by demonstration, in the year 1520. was in *Scotland*, a king ouerruled with parasites, misled by lust, & many circumstances, too long to trattle on now, much like our court of *Scotland* this day, that story haue I set down, gang with me to the gallery, & Ile shew thee the same in Action, by guid fellowes of our country men, and then when thou seest that, iudge if any wise man would not leaue the world if he could. (A4v)

Bohan's didactic play becomes the two-hour centerpiece of *James IV*'s action, and it is only disturbed by short but relatively frequent choric interruptions by Bohan and Oberon that many times contain dramatic interludes. As the play progresses, it becomes more and more clear that Bohan is a playwright who is overtly concerned that his message be clearly communicated. As such, Bohan constantly focuses on the course of his own play. At the end of the first interlude, Bohan quickly draws Oberon's attention back to his play: "Then marke my stay, and the strange doubts, / That follow flatterers, lust, and lawlesse will, / And then say I haue reason to forsake the world, / And all that are within the same" (C4v). His focus is the same after the second interlude. "Now marke my talke," Bohan strongly advises Oberon, "and prosecute my gyg" (C4v). This is matched by his demand that Oberon "marke mee more" (D1) at the end of the third interlude. Ultimately, Bohan loses control over his play, and it is both the course and the cause of this division between playwright and play that Greene sets out to explore in *James IV*.

Oberon, too, is a producer of dramatic entertainment in the play, and he performs an important role in Greene's thematization of the relationship between actor and dramatist. Oberon represents actorly driven performance, one based upon song, dance, clowning, spectacle, and extemporal and melodramatic acting. Ultimately, his drama originates in the festive, holiday tradition, where dramatic art both mended and fashioned communal relations as it offered a sanctioned release from the concerns of everyday existence. Oberon's love of a festive, performative art that is opposed to a world of static meanings at first connects him to Bohan. Thus, when Bohan asks him "what art thou," Oberon replies, "*Oberon* King of Fayries, that loues thee because thou hatest the world, and to gratulate thee, I brought those Antiques to shew thee some sport in daunsing, which thou haste loued well" (A4). Throughout the play, Oberon continually offers Bohan his own brand of theatre. Not only does he enter dancing with an "Antique," but after the first Act, upon seeing the beginning of Bohan's play, it is Oberon who presents to Bohan the play's dramatic interludes.[23] These, as Oberon tells Bohan, are essentially his own competing shows:

> Here see I good fond actions in thy gyg,
> And meanes to paint the worldes in constant waies:
> But turne thine ene, see which for I can commaund.
>
> *Enter two battailes strongly fighting, the*
> *one* Simi Ranus, *the other,* Staurobates, *she flies, and her*
> *Crowne is taken, and she hurt.* (C4v)

In the place of Bohan's writerly desire of rendering a didactic message using the history play's more realistic characters and action, Oberon shows "what [he] can commaund": a dumb show on the fleeting nature of worldly pomp. Oberon continues to offer these dances and dumbshows in the face of Bohan's scripted play, setting up what is essentially a dramatic competition between the two.

Greene's use of this framing device also allows him to dramatize the Elizabethan clown's disruptive relationship with the playwright and the playwright's texts. Greene initially offers a patriarchal understanding of the former relationship in making Bohan Slipper's father. In this formulation the playwright engenders the role of the clown, creating not just the temper of his performances but the world he inhabits. Bohan makes this patrimony clear when, after ordering

---

23 The first quarto of *James IV* is notoriously corrupt in its placement of these dramatic interludes. They all appear, one after another, at the end of the first Act. Sanders has suggested that the first misplaced interlude follow the first scene, the second follow the second scene, and the third follow the second scene of the third Act (128–32). Experience in the theatre has shown that Sanders is right about the first and third interludes but that it makes more sense to place the second interlude after the first scene of the second Act. This is because Oberon's question, "How shuld these crafts withdraw thee from the world?" (C4v), is more logically a response to the clumsiness of Ateukin's attempt in this scene to get the Countess to agree to let her daughter Ida become James's courtesan.

Slipper and his brother Nano to dance a jig, he gives Slipper his inheritance of knavery and dismisses him into "the wide world": "Now get you to the wide world with more thẽ my father gaue me, thats learning enough, both kindes, knauerie & honestie: and that I gaue you, spend at pleasure" (A4v). Slipper, however, like most clowns on the Elizabethan stage, is far from obedient to his playwright father. When he and his brother Nano first enter at Bohan's call, his energy will not be bridled. To Bohan's command, "Haud your clacks lads, trattle not for thy life, but gather vppe your legges and daunce me forthwith a gigge worth the sight," Slipper replies, "Why I must talk on Idy fort, wherefore was my tongue made?" (A4).

Slipper owes a debt of existence to his playwright father, but to Oberon he owes a debt of influence. At the beginning of the play, before Bohan's show commences, Oberon blesses Slipper, highlighting what will be his connection to him and the Fairy King's preferred mode of dramatic activity: "to loggerhead your sonne, I giue a wandering life, and promise he shall neuer lacke: and auow that if in all distresses he call vpon me to helpe him" (A4v). Oberon's gift of "a wandering life" does not simply invoke the professional actor's perceived vagabondage; it also confers upon Slipper the unpredictability of his theatre's extemporal and extradramatic stars, the Vice and the clown. Just as these characters unpredictably "wandered" between the world of the play and the world of the audience, Slipper will wander as well. At times, Slipper disrupts the course of the play's action by directly communicating with the audience. When Sir Bartram gives him ten pounds to steal a lease from Ateukin, for example, Slipper quickly turns to the audience and says, "Now roome for a Gentleman, my maisters, who giues mee mony for a faire new Angell, a trimme new Angell?" (F1). At other times, Slipper disrupts with his clownish performances. When Ateukin tries to convince the Countess to let her daughter become a mistress to the King, Slipper interrupts and asks, "Now I pray you sir what a kin are you to a pickrell?" (D3).

Not suprisingly, it is Slipper who begins the transformation of Bohan's play from tragedy to what is essentially tragicomedy. Up until the third Act, Bohan's play proceeds along the course of tragedy, and when Bohan and Oberon enter, Bohan makes it clear that he sees the play as still proceeding according to his dark intentions, that his "jig will prove no jest":

> So *Oberon*, now it beginnes to worke in kinde,
> The auncient Lords by leauing him aliue,
> Disliking of his humors and respight,
> Lets him run headlong till his flatterers,
> Sweeting his thoughts of lucklesse lust,
> With vile perswations and alluring words,
> Makes him make way by murther to his will. (E4)

It is in the next few scenes, however, the tide begins to turn. Bribed to steal a lease from his master Ateukin, Slipper also accidently steals Dorothea's death warrant from James and gives it to Sir Bartram. Slipper's fortunate thievery thwarts

James's plot. It allows Sir Bartram to warn Dorothea and ultimately puts her in the company of her saviors, Nano and Sir Cuthbert.

From this point on, the play moves in a direction away from Bohan's tragic intentions—Dorothea's wounds inflicted by Jaques do not prove mortal, James repents his actions against his Queen and turns on Ateukin, and in the finale, Dorothea forgives James his transgressions against her. The play ends on a happy note—virtue is shown to be triumphant, and all is well in the world. Yet in the face of this, Bohan not only remains convinced about the wickedness of the world, but he also refuses to recognize the transformation of his play, as is apparent in his final words to Oberon:

> An he weele meete ends: the mirk and sable night
> Doth leaue the pering morne to prie abroade,
> Thou nill me stay: haile then thou pride of kings,
> I ken the world, and wot well worldly things.
> Marke thou my gyg, in mirkest terms that telles
> The loathe of sinnes, and where corruption dwells. (D1v)

To Bohan, rather than showing the ultimate reformability of man and the power of virtue in the face of vice, his play speaks "in mirkest terms" and "telles / The loathe of sinnes, and where corruption dwells." In effect, he has completely misread the transformed production.

Bohan's failure to recognize the transformation of the play is shown by Greene to be the direct product of Bohan's inability to overcome his own self-focus and obsession with intellectual property. Bohan's self-centeredness goes beyond a need to be in complete control of his play; it also manifests itself in his responses to Oberon's interludes. The narcissism behind Bohan's rejection of Oberon's opening dance is only eclipsed by his responses to Oberon's dumbshows. In the first jig showing the fleetingness of pomp, Bohan characteristically assumes that Oberon's show is an exercise in self-representation. "I see," Bohan replies, "thou art thine ene. / Thou bonny King, if Princes fall from high, / My fall is past, vntill I fall to die" (C4v). Bohan's response to Oberon's second jig that is about the unavoidability of death is similarly self-focused: "What recke I then of life," he says, "Who makes the graue my tomb, the earth my wife?" (D1). And to Oberon's last dumbshow about the fickleness of fortune, Bohan responds, "How blest are peur men then that know their graue" (D1). Bohan's self-indulgence ultimately achieves its zenith in his esoteric response to the ending of the production. What was at first a search for reflections of his own concerns in Oberon's entertainments in the end becomes an unselfconscious projection of these concerns onto what was once his own play. *James IV*, thus, ends as a tragedy of writerly alienation: Bohan is not completely reconciled with Oberon, and the angry Scot's final action is to walk off towards the only object that he can with certainty call his own, a "graue of [his] owne prouiding" (A4).

This essay has attempted to revise the critical commonplace that Greene was necessarily a consistent antagonist to "upstart crows." Not only has it demonstrated how Greene began his playwriting career as a vocationally literate—albeit novice—producer of actorly entertainments, but it has also suggested that in *James IV* Greene significantly revises his earlier "bi-fold" practice. His later approach, however, is still very different from the devaluative one that Weimann contends is articulated by Marlowe in *Tamburlaine*; instead, Greene's use of both actorly and writerly modes of authorization in *James IV* is patently more cooperative.[24] It can also be described as deeply apprehensive about the limitations of textual authority. Bohan's ambition that both his text and its production will smoothly reflect his intentions is shown to be not simply deluded but narcissistic and self-destructive. That Bohan fails in his bid for control and ends up alienated, bitter, and alone can be read as a strong critique of what Weimann has described as a devaluative writerly mode. Ultimately, his description of Greene as the "shifting companion" of Marlowe—given what Greene articulates about the purposes of playing in both *Alphonsus* and *James IV*, and given what he would come to articulate in his *Groatsworth of Wit*—is truer than perhaps even Weimann realized.

24 That Marlowe's *Tamburlaine* does in fact support writerly authority in its prologue could also be called into question. See my "'[I]ygging vaines' and 'riming mother wits': Marlowe, Clowns and the Early Frameworks of Dramatic Authorship," *Early Modern Literary Studies* 13.2 (October, 2007) / Special Issue 16.

Chapter 3

Staging Professionalism in Greene's *James IV*

Edward Gieskes

> Changes as decisive as an upheaval in the internal hierarchy of different genres, or a transformation of the hierarchy within genres themselves, affecting the structure of the field as a whole are made possible by the *correspondence between internal changes* (themselves directly determined by the transformation in the chances of access to the literary field) *and external changes* which offer to new categories of producers (successively, the Romantics, Naturalists, Symbolists, etc.) and to their products consumers who occupy positions in social space which are homologous to their own position in the field, and hence consumers endowed with dispositions and tastes in harmony with the products these producers offer them.
>
> —Pierre Bourdieu, *The Rules of Art*[1]

This essay makes a double argument about Robert Greene's *James IV* and its place in both literary and dramatic history. First, it demonstrates that *James IV*, a play that juxtaposes different kinds of dramaturgy, illustrates the way that craft practices and their various possible meanings are refracted into the drama at a relatively early stage of its professionalization. Greene makes use of these refractions to make an argument, "by demonstration" (to use the play's language), about what plays can and should do. Greene's play stages a debate over the *ends* of drama by representing a conflict between *kinds* of drama and the kinds are signaled by reference to particular kinds of stagings. Neither side in the staged contest emerges victorious—Bohan's asceticism is contaminated by Oberon's aestheticism and vice versa—but what does emerge is a sense of the representational capabilities of the professional theatre. Second, I will argue that this awareness of the capacities of the theatre is in turn a sign of Greene's professionalism, a professionalism that is defined by his embeddedness in a multiplicity of cultural fields.

It has been a commonplace observation that early modern drama is "professional." Our understanding of profession, however, has a long and

1 Bourdieu's focus in this book is on the French field in the nineteenth century (which explains his focus on the novel), but the idea that generic upheavals depend on this kind of conjunction of changes makes sense of the transformation of the early modern literary field in the period following about 1570.

complicated history, a history that can partially be traced through the various permutations of the word's definition from the early modern period to the present.[2] Moreover, there has been an extensive and contentious debate in the sociology of the professions over such matters as when professions begin, what constitutes a profession, how different professions relate, and so forth. The model that seems both most adequate and most relevant to the case at hand—that of Robert Greene and the emergence of professional theatre—is Andrew Abbott's whose *System of Professions* offers an alternative to other sociologists' models of historical development by analyzing the professions according to a system model. Abbott does not focus exclusively on any particular profession, nor does he offer any kind of reductive unitary definition of what constitutes a profession. Abbott's book instead focuses on *relations* between professions in an effort to make sense of the way they develop by acting on each other as well as by refining and theorizing their own particular areas of expertise.[3]

Relational at the core, Abbott's theory actively situates particular professions in a dynamic social context and suggests that such a context has a profound influence over the shape of each profession's work, training, and organization. The context of that work has as much of a constitutive role in defining a profession as the profession's expertise does. Abbott argues that:

> the professions make up an interacting system, an ecology. Professions compete within this system, and a profession's success reflects as much the situation of its competitors and the system structure as it does the profession's own efforts. From time to time, tasks are created, abolished, or reshaped by external forces, with consequent jostling and readjustment within the system of professions. Thus, larger social forces have their impact on individual professions through the structure of within which the professions exists, rather than directly ... Professions are never seen alone, but they are also not replaced by a single encompassing category of "the professions." They exist in a system.[4]

Changes in one profession necessarily affect the other professions, to a greater or lesser degree, as they are nearer or further apart in social space. Abbott describes a vacancy model of the "ecology of the professions" in which professions compete for position within a semiclosed set of jurisdictions.[5] In such a system, change in one profession's claimed area of expertise necessarily demands a response from

2 For more complete discussion of this issue, see my *Representing the Professions: Administration, Law, and Theater* (Newark, DE: The University of Delaware Press, 2006).

3 Theatre and playwriting thus develop in a complex interaction with each other, other professions, and the economy in which they operate.

4 Andrew Abbott, *The System of Professions: An Essay on the Division of Expert Labor* (Chicago: The University of Chicago, 1988), p. 33.

5 Vacancy models describe systems in which change only occurs when a position becomes vacant for whatever reason. Abbott's example is the episcopate where bishoprics only change when an occupant vacates his position, either taking up a new one, itself opened by a vacancy or by leaving the system altogether.

other professions upon whose jurisdictions that claim impinges. Those responses themselves demand responses until the system settles into a new equilibrium.[6] In this model, professions close to each other in social space necessarily, if not directly, influence each other's patterns of success, training, expectations, mechanisms of distinction, and definitions of professionalism and professional conduct. To cite one illustrative case, as sixteenth-century lawyers developed a sense of themselves as serving the "freedom of Englishmen," writers also began to stress their educative role in the culture. Thus Sir Philip Sidney describes poetry as his "unelected calling" and makes an argument for the usefulness and worth of writing in his 1583 *Apology*.[7] Defining the poet, he writes:

> that it is not rhyming and versing that maketh a poet—no more than a long gown maketh an advocate who though he pleaded in armor should be an advocate and no soldier. But it is that feigning notable images of virtues, vices, or what else, with that delightful teaching, which must be the right describing note to know a poet by.[8]

The poet's work, says Sidney, is as immutable a principle of identity as that of the lawyer who even in armor would still be a lawyer. Understood through Abbott, Sidney's comparison of poet and advocate is not mere coincidence but serves as an example of the way that the discourse and status of one occupation affects those around it in social space.[9] Abbott's definition is thus more dynamic and situational

---

6 Abbott, p. 90. Vacancies occur when a profession vanishes or is suppressed and "bumps" are the product of one profession seizing the jurisdiction of another. Often, both occur at the same time. The history of public administration in early modern England can be seen in these terms. As the clerical role in government declined (and was actively suppressed in some cases), a new professional grouping formed to take over that part of the clergy's former jurisdiction.

7 Profession language such as this recurs at several points in the *Apology*. Sidney is, of course, responding to Stephen Gosson's *Schoole of Abuse* (London, 1579), which reviled plays and poetry as incitements to vice rather than spurs to virtue. This exchange was followed by a whole series of controversial writings that increasingly recognized writers and actors as being engaged in a profession (see Heywood's *An Apology for Actors* [London, 1612], Field's *The Remonstrance of Nathan Field, One of Shakespeare's Company of Actors* [London, 1616], and Field's *Actors' Remonstrance or Complaint* [London, 1643] for examples). According to Abbott, public debate such as this is an integral part of the development of professions and is a primary source of the contacts with adjacent professions that define the system as a whole. The *Apology* also makes a claim for the dignity of the poet's calling by asserting that it is a vocation given by God—exploiting the resources of the religious dimensions of the term.

8 Sir Philip Sidney, *An Apology for Poetry*, 1583, in Hazard Adams (ed.), *Critical Theory Since Plato* (San Diego: Harcourt, 1971), p. 159.

9 Ben Jonson is, perhaps, the best example of a poet taking a moralist's role. His close ties to the Inns of Court put him in contact with lawyers' developing self-definitions, and he began formulating an ideal of the poet's role, an ideal expressed in *Pöetaster*.

than that of earlier scholars; he defines profession simply as an aspect of the division of "expert labor," not in terms of some abstract list of essential qualities necessary for an occupation to qualify as a profession. Professionalization is less an overarching developmental pattern common to all professions than, as Abbott argues, the product of ongoing interactions such as those between law and writing.

I

Greene's relation to the professional theatre has often been seen as combative—based largely on his confessional pamphlets and accounts that emphasize the profligate waste of his talents on the "puppets" of the stage—but this depiction simplifies a far more complicated and interesting situation. In his brief career, Greene engaged with most of the major modes of cultural production in the period—the press, the stage, manuscript circulation (apparently), and while it does not seem that he produced court or civic entertainments, his plays contain elements not unlike both—and the range of these engagements argue against any straightforward ranking of his preferences. Unlike the later Ben Jonson, we do not have an "ode to himself" bidding farewell to either the loathed stage or the presses. And, of course, Jonson's own farewell has to be balanced with his various returns to the stage. What we do have from Greene, however, is a number of discussions of and responses to the theatre in Greene's prose that can illustrate his deep awareness of theatrical practice and his complicated attitude towards it.

In 1590, *Greenes Neuer Too Late* appeared in two parts, and the second part (*Francescos Fortunes*) contains several pages discussing the theatre. The Palmer is telling a story about Francesco's response to a bout of poverty. Having not been trained up in any "mechanicall courfe of life," he finally decides that some profit ought to derive from his being a scholar:

> [A]lthough in these daies Arte wanted honor, and learning lackt his due, yet good letters were not brought to so lowe an ebbe, but that there might some profite arise by them to procure his maintenance. In this humour he fell in amongft a companie of Players, who perswaded him to trie his wit in writing of Comedies, Tragedies, or Pastorals, and if he could performe any thing worth the stage, then they would largelie reward him for his paines.[10]

Finding that he can write something worth the stage, Francesco becomes a highly successful playwright and fills his previously empty purse.The account closes with the Palmer averring that since they suppress vanities, plays are

10 *Francescos Fortunes, or The second part of Greenes Neuer too late* (London, 1590), B3v. It is interesting that Greene uses the verb "performe" here to describe the audition process Francesco's work undergoes. It is as if there is some slippage between the actorly and the authorly here as Francesco begins to make his way as a writer of plays.

> neceffarie in a common wealth, as long as they are vfed in their right kind; the play makers worthy of honour for their Arte: & players, men deferuing both prayse and profite, as long as they wax neither couetous nor insolent. (C1)

This statement resembles those of many other period defenders of the stage and of poesy more generally and, like those other defenses, focuses on the good use of drama as a legitimation of the quality of playwriting and playing. This is a fairly clear statement in favor of the usefulness of theatre, as long as the players grow neither covetous nor insolent, and is not far from Bohan's justificatory explanation of his own play in *James the IV*. Greene's famous complaint in *Groatsworth* is, in fact, precisely about the players being both greedy and insolent, not about playing per se. Greene appears to have seen the stage as one of several venues for his work, one that was as good as any other so long as the players bargained fairly and performed decorously.

As both Kirk Melnikoff and Alan Dessen note in their contributions to this volume, Greene demonstrates a sophisticated and developing awareness of stage convention that in itself argues against any easy account of his relations with the players. For my purposes here, it is sufficient to note that Greene clearly sees a place of honor for the drama in the commonwealth and that place is based on its ability to be useful—to teach. Following the Horatian precept that the best teaching is the most delightful, Greene's drama strives to yoke theatrical pleasure and profit together. *James the IV*, the subject of the rest of this essay, represents Greene's most elaborated representation of the tensions implicit in this yoking—Greene seems to be uneasy, or at least unconvinced, that pleasure and profit can be easily united in a stage play—and the play develops out of a meditation on the capacities of the theatre to provide both.

II

Greene's generic experimentation (demonstrated by his prose romances as much as his plays as discussed by other contributors to this volume) bears witness to the kind of generic upheaval Bourdieu describes in this essay's epigraph. Generic upheavals, in Bourdieu's view, depend on the coincidence of changes in education and reading practices—changes that depend on differing "chances of access" to the means of cultural production—with changes in audience—the appearance or disappearance of consumers whose tastes are aligned with the products offered because of a homology of social position between the producer and consumer. Greene occupies an exemplary position in the changing field as an example of the new kind of producer to which Bourdieu refers. He was educated in the humanist moral tradition but found himself working for audiences whose tastes lagged behind at least some of the kinds of products he had been trained to produce. The success of Marlowe's plays influenced Greene's dramaturgy (his early works imitate the Marlovian "mighty line" and the spectacular sweep of *Tamburlaine*). Marlowe blended classical learning and popular dramaturgy in a way that transformed Elizabethan playwriting. Greene's early plays reflect his searching for models in a radically changed (and radically unstable) professional theatre. His work seems to have been intended to appeal to both learned and unlearned audiences in much the way that Marlowe's seems to have.[11] This effort, an effort to produce and respond to "external changes" depends as much on Greene's sense of the dispositions of the audiences for which he wrote as it does on his awareness of other changes, changes in the technical side of the theatre in which he worked.[12] The kinds of changes Bourdieu describes depend both on educational shifts and a shifting and developing sense of what is possible in the theatre—an awareness of the practical aspects of production helps audiences respond to new work at the same time that those changes help make that new work possible. Greene's plays represent a provisional accommodation between the theoretical knowledge of drama derived from his Cambridge education (see the learned historical defense of theatre cited above) and a practical sense of what the actually existent theatre was capable.

James IV opens with the interruption of the rest of a stoical Scot named "Bohan" by a visit by the King of the Fairies, Oberon, who appears to be curious about why Bohan hates the world and has decided to live in a tomb. Bohan proposes to explain by presenting a play that demonstrates his position by exposing all the vices from which he has fled. The play proper then begins and presents the youthful James marrying the virtuous daughter of the King of England while at the same time finding himself consumed with lust for a Scottish lady named "Ida." With the aid of a bad counselor, he pursues the virtuous Ida unsuccessfully and plots to have his queen killed. James thinks he has had Dorothea, his queen, murdered so he can pursue the "Scottish Ida" who, being virtuous, wants nothing to do with him. Dorothea's father, the King of England, vows revenge and attacks Scotland, winning battles and killing thousands as he makes his way to meet James. When they meet, James makes lame offers of ransom or reparation and matters seem headed for disaster when the disguised Dorothea reveals herself and almost instantaneously resolves the situation. She forgives James for his adulterous plot and attempt to murder her ("Tush, but a little fault") and causes her father to vow continued friendship with James. Then all parties go in to dinner. If this synopsis sounds contradictory, it is because the narrative *is* contradictory, largely due to the way Greene orchestrates Oberon's intervention in Bohan's play. It would seem that James is heading toward disaster, toward the end of a *de casibus* tragedy, but does not get there because of Oberon's active presence.

---

11 His "imitations" of Marlowe are evidence of his search for ways to unite his learning to more popular elements by imitating Marlowe's successful combinations.

12 See Dessen, Tumelson, and Melnikoff in this collection for discussions of Greene's theatrical sophistication.

In fact, the various and seemingly disparate elements of the play make sense *as a play* only in the context of the frame. In other words, the play makes no narrative sense without the constant presence of Bohan and Oberon.[13] The best example of this is the all-but incredible resolution of what is set up as a tragic plot in a comic scene of reconciliation. In the chorus after act 3, Bohan claims that the rest of the play will be "ruthful," but his claim is not borne out by the action:

> ... it would make a marble melt and weep
> To see these treasons gainst the innocent;
> But since she 'scapes by flight to save her life,
> The king may chance repent she was his wife.
> The rest is ruthful, yet to beguile the time,
> 'Tis laced with merriment and rhyme.[14]

---

13 Greene's reputation as a dramatist has suffered due to readings of the play that fail to situate it in the context of theatrical production in the 1590s. To take a characteristic example, in an essay tellingly entitled "Robert Greene as Dramatist" (in R. Hosley [ed.], *Essays in Elizabethan Drama* [Columbia, MI: The University of Missouri, 1962]), Kenneth Muir writes: "Although rash critics have compared Bohan to Shakespeare's Oberon and Prospero, the induction and choric interludes between the acts are tedious and unnecessary. It is absurd for Bohan's sons to appear as characters in the play he is presenting before Oberon, especially as the events are supposed to have taken place in an earlier age; it is artistically confusing when Slipper is rescued from the gallows by the intervention of Oberon; and Greene does not explain how Nano, who takes service with Ateukin in the first act, should be in Dorothea's service in the second. It may be added that the scenes in which Lady Anderson falls in love with the disguised Dorothea are bungled, and nothing is made of Sir Cuthbert's jealousy. The debate between a Lawyer, a Merchant, and a Divine (5.4), which was presumably intended to illustrate the evil results of James IV's misgovernment, is never once brought into focus" (50). Muir's reaction is typical of critics of this play and Greene's drama in general. He likes the story of James' temptation, fall, and redemption, but sees the frame and other "interludes" as tedious or unnecessary. Ironically, without the frame, the internal narrative makes almost no sense: the abrupt fairy-tale resolution is a direct result of Oberon's intervention in the didactic story Bohan attempts to tell. Muir also misrepresents the "problem" of Nano's service: Ateukin takes him into service intending to present him to Dorothea as his gift. Even the otherwise strange conversation between the Lawyer, Divine, and Merchant makes sense in the context of the frame's debate. All of the elements for which Muir castigates the play are precisely those that make it interesting as theatre, and, more important for my argument here, offer insight into the field of production of which it is a product. The play combines multiple genres (romance, comedy, dance, etc)—making use of the multiple possibilities available to a dramatist at this early stage in the development of the professional theatre—as part of Greene's attempt to instruct while entertaining. The combination is far from seamless, as Muir recognizes, and this indicates not only Greene's uncomfortable relationship with theatre, but also the field's inchoate state.

14 Chorus III.3–9. All quotations from Greene's play are from Norman Sanders's edition in the Revels series (London: Methuen, 1970).

Instead, the play ends in reconciliation and feasting, not the "ruthful" tragedy Bohan promises. Merriment and rhyme take over completely by the end of the play, driving the action rather than being merely a palliative to the "ruthful" play Bohan promises here. In fact, the primary focus of the play turns from the narrative of James' corruption to the relationship between Bohan and Oberon whose details emerge through the contested staging of the play.[15] Bohan clings to his aesthetic even at the end of the play despite losing control of his narrative to Oberon. After the final scene, he tells Oberon:

> Mark thou my jig, in mirkest terms that tells
> The loath of sins and where corruption dwells.
> Hail me ne mere with shows of guidly sights;
> My grave is mine, that rids from despites.
> Accept my jig, guid king, and let me rest;
> The grave with guid men is a gay-built nest. (Chorus V.5–10)

Bohan's "jig" does not, however, "in mirkest terms" tell a story of corruption and punishment.[16] The moral tale Bohan that he claimed would show why he hates the world becomes a pastoral, comic play that culminates in a mass reconciliation between couples, nations, and kings in which only the servants are punished. Oberon, not Bohan, has the final word and his antics sing and dance Bohan to rest.[17]

---

15 In one of the most affecting moments in the play, Bohan begs Oberon to save Slipper from execution for colluding with Ateukin—forgetting for the moment that what he's watching is only a "demonstration"—Oberon obliges out of "love."

16 See the discussion of the generic significance of the term "jig" below. Bohan always refers to his "demonstration" with this term, which locates the play, or, better, Bohan's part of it, in a particular theatrical tradition distinct, I will argue, from Oberon's interventions in the play. Bohan's words also call attention to the built nature of his tomb-retreat.

17 My own "demonstration" depends, in part, on the production of the play (produced by Willing Suspension Productions) at Boston University in 1997. Kirk Melnikoff directed, and Mike Walker and I served as assistant directors. Our direct engagement with Greene's dramatic practice clarified many of the oddities of the play and pointed toward some of my conclusions here. The conflict the play dramatizes is a long-lasting one that provides one of the structuring oppositions of the literary field. In our staging, Bohan and Oberon were seated just off the stage proper (in front of the curtain) throughout the play, visibly reacting to and, at times, intervening in the action. Oberon's antics danced before, after, and during the play, and served as the actors in the dumbshows. Modern editions of the play print the several dumbshows as appendices ("additional choruses"). In the several readings we gave the play, it became clear that the choruses reflect moments where Oberon's aesthetic gains ground on Bohan's and that there were logical places in the text to insert them. On stage, as the play progressed and Oberon's influence became more and more important, the action of the choruses spill over more and more into the starker play world of Bohan's narrative. The

The play is thus less about the (totally unhistorical) fall and dubious redemption of James IV, than about the current state of the field of cultural production, and more specifically of the subfield of writing for the theatre. Greene worked in a theatre that was fundamentally collaborative, and his play reveals the signs of this collaborative field. Bohan's refusal to see how his play has changed in production—in the process of collaboration—is only one of these signs. The jigs, dumbshows, and other apparently extradramatic interludes are, as Kirk Melnikoff points out in his Director's Notes to the 1997 Willing Suspension Productions staging of the play, the product of a theatre that was "still in the early stages of professionalization [and] popular elements like jigs and hornpipes would have been seen as no more extraneous to a play than a good story."[18] Greene's innovation as playwright is to attempt to unify these popular elements with the plot of his play and, more interestingly, to do so in such a way as to make a point about the purpose of writing plays. The play thematizes a *dramatic* contest, constantly reminding the audience that Bohan and Oberon are staging a struggle between two kinds of drama not least by keeping them onstage, or, as in our production of the play, just offstage, throughout the performance. The resolution of Bohan and Oberon's contest is a kind of rapprochement between didacticism and, for lack of a better term, aestheticism. It is not, though, a resolution that synthesizes or simply combines these modes. Instead, what Greene does is exploit the representational resources of disparate literary and stage traditions in the service of his argument about the purpose of playing and, more importantly, to make a good play.[19]

James IV begins this argument by depicting Oberon's fairies dancing about the tomb where Bohan lives with his sons Slipper and Nano in stoical retreat from the corrupt world. After some dancing and stage business, Oberon questions Bohan about why he "dwellest in a tomb and leavest the world" (Ind.38–9). This question is the opening gambit in a play-long conversation about Bohan's retirement. Bohan begins by offering a biographical explanation—he lived in the court, in the country, and in the city, but found all these ways of life wanting and thus has retreated to his tomb—and then offers to show Oberon why he hates the world "by demonstration" (Ind.106):

---

spillover suggests the contest between the principles represented by Oberon and Bohan—which we came to see in terms of a professional conflict.

18 Kirk Melnikoff, Directors' Notes, Program for Willing Suspension Productions *James IV*, 1997.

19 It is not my intention to posit some kind of teleological movement here—out of the meeting of these two traditions comes the theatre of the later 1590s—but to describe tensions in the field, problems writers and companies appear to have faced, and to suggest that the failure to resolve these problems and tensions helps define the field by defining the terms of discussion. It is not, in other words, solutions that describe the theatrical field, but the enacted discussion of failures in a wide range of plays.

> *Boh.* In the year 1520 was in Scotland a king, overruled by parasites, misled by lust, and many circumstances too long to trattle on now, much like our court of Scotland this day. *That story I have set down.* Gang with me to the gallery, and *I'll show thee the same in action* by guid fellows of our countrymen; and then *when thou seest that*, judge not if any wise man would not leave the world if he could.
>
> *Ober.* That will I *see*; lead and I'll follow thee. (Ind.109–14 [my emphasis])

Bohan imagines his play as a visual demonstration—the enactment of a treatise on world-loathing—and envisions his audience judging what they are shown after the demonstration ends. He introduces the play by talking about writing—setting down the story—and then stages it "in action" with good fellows who mysteriously appear to act the story. The opening scene of the frame stresses Bohan's authorial position, one of stoical remove and moralistic intention, while Oberon is represented as being a member of the audience—passively watching the demonstration of why one ought to forsake the world. Both Bohan and Oberon speak of seeing the play, placing emphasis on the visual impact of the action, but, as the play proceeds, the kinds of vision they imagine become increasingly distinct.[20] Bohan's "demonstration" is meant to show the reasons for his retreat "in action"—it is a thesis-driven show—where Oberon seems more interested in the visuals of the play as visuals, bracketing the thesis of the production as Bohan imagines it. The framing device calls attention to the artificiality of the play—its composedness—and, more importantly, initiates a debate over the form and intentions of its artifice.

Bohan's stark, world-forsaking aesthetic comes into conflict with Oberon's more luxuriant and visual one throughout the choruses, and those conflicts go some distance towards explaining the otherwise totally inexplicable happy ending of the play by demonstrating Oberon's increasing influence over the action. The Oberon-Bohan conflict also refracts what seem to be Greene's ideas about different kinds of staging. In one of the first of the choric interludes, Oberon recognizes Bohan's skill in depicting the way of the world: "Here see I good fond action in thy jig, / And means to paint the world's inconstant ways; /But turn thine eyen, see which I can command" (Chorus VI.1–3).[21] What Oberon commands is a dumbshow, a pageant of sorts, depicting "*two battles strongly fighting the one [led by]*

---

20 Greene appears to be calling attention to the visual aspect of the play even at the level of the terms used to describe how it is to be received. The stress on vision, on looking at the show, remains constant throughout the play and both Oberon and Bohan call attention to the particular things they are looking at ("jig" vs. "pomp," for example). This is despite the fact that James's story could be told with almost no set and little in the way of props. The technically demanding part of Greene's play lies in the dumbshows.

21 Placement of the choruses is a major difficulty in the play—the Quarto of 1598 prints several of them following the first act, but it seems clear that they belong elsewhere in the play. It is not obvious, however, where they do belong. Sanders' edition prints them as "Additional Choruses" in an appendix to the play.

SEMIRAMIS, the other [by] STABROBATES. She flies, and her crown is taken, and she [is] hurt" (Chorus VI.3.1–3). The dumbshow is introduced here as a demonstration of Oberon's skills—skills put into competition with Bohan's "jig."[22]

Jig has a very specific theatrical meaning and both Bohan and Oberon consistently refer to Bohan's play by this term. Jigs are common features of the public stage—one of the things *Tamburlaine*'s induction claims to be distancing itself from—and Greene, influenced as he is by Marlowe, knew this as well as his audience. Oberon's dumbshow—the performance *he* can command—is a very different kind of display. Bohan tells us that "two battles" enter and fight, leaving "everywean … betaint with bloud," and Oberon has to gloss the show's allegorical significance because Bohan cannot tell what it means: "What gars this din of mirk and baleful harm, / Where everywean is all betaint with bloud?" (Chorus VI.4–5). Oberon explains that this shows "what is worldly pomp" by describing the fall of Semiramis "in her pride."

The "din of mirk and bloud" to which Bohan responds is a spectacle that depends on visual effects for its force—how else is an audience to recognize Semiramis and Stabrobates but by some kind of visual cue—and Oberon's shows all depend on this kind of display. Bohan's appreciation of Oberon's skill is tempered by his desire to have Oberon "mark [his] talk and prosecute [his] jig" (Chorus VI.14–15). The chorus calls attention to several distinct aspects of performance. By labelling Bohan's play a "jig" and linking its presentation to "talk," the chorus locates it firmly on the public stages and connects it to a particular kind of staging—one that relies on the spoken word and what Bohan calls action more than iconic staging or costume. Oberon's show, however, is pure spectacle—mystifyingly so—and requires explication from its creator. Significantly, this type of display is characteristic of Revels Office productions.[23]

III

Most accounts of the emergence of writing for the theatre in the sixteenth century have focused on matters that can more or less comfortably be labeled literary—matters of education (with the appearance and subsequent decline of the University Wits), of competition between non-affiliated playwrights, of stage language, or of

22 Using the OED, Sanders glosses "jig" as "a performance normally of a lively or comical nature usually applied to a piece given in the intervals or at the end of a play" and suggests that here it refers to the play as a whole. The more usual sense of the word has to do with a dance at the end of a play. Why Bohan would call his "ruthful" play a jig is difficult to say, but the term allies the work with a particular kind of theatre.

23 Interestingly, the pamphlets recording Lord Mayor's Shows include detailed explications of the meaning of the various figures and props in the shows.

influence of writer upon writer.[24] Theatrical history has also offered provocative accounts of what William Ingram calls the "business of playing" that point to the influence economic considerations have on the emerging professional theatre and on playwriting.[25] The institutional context of what could be called the theatre trades, however, is less often discussed. Books like Streitberger's *Court Revels* have described the changing structure of the Revels Office, and Bergeron's *English Civic Pageantry* has described the City dramatic tradition, but the focus remains on the plays or masques and their writers with less attention being given to the relationship between those masques and plays and the craftsmen called upon to realize the designs.[26] Dramatic possibilities, however, have much to do with technical ones—without the ability to build certain things (a flying chair, say) certain kinds of dramatic action are impossible if not strictly unimaginable—and developments in the one influence and structure developments in the other. As Abbott argues, professions interact in a complex ecology and to understand developments in one profession (here playwriting), one must understand its relations to professions close to it in social space. In other words, the practices of a group of craftsmen who worked in the Revels Office and for civic entertainments, such as the Lord Mayor's Show, must have had an influence upon the development of professional playwriting in early modern England. These craftsmen provided an important part of the dramatic vocabulary employed by professional playwrights and the acting companies.[27]

The Revels Office's functions were many throughout the period: it was the site of theatrical censorship since all playtexts had to pass under the scrutiny of the master, it was responsible for a wide range of entertainments for the monarch, and it contributed to the construction and maintenance of festive facilities such as the Banqueting Hall and other examples of what John Orrell calls "festive

---

24 See G.E. Bentley, *The Profession of Dramatist in Shakespeare's Time* (Princeton: Princeton University Press, 1971); James S. Shapiro, *Rival Playwrights* (New York: Columbia University Press, 1991); and Lynne Magnusson, *Shakespeare and Social Dialogue* (Cambridge: Cambridge University Press, 1999).

25 William Ingram, *The Business of Playing* (Ithaca: Cornell University Press, 1992).

26 See W.R. Streitberger, *Court Revels* (Toronto: University of Toronto Press, 1994), and David M. Bergeron, *English Civic Pageantry* (Columbia: University of South Carolina Press, 1971). There are notable exceptions to this, Orgel and Strong's work on the masque and Inigo Jones being chief among them, but in general scholars have not focused much attention on craftspeople since the major transcription projects of the first third of the 20th century (Stephen Orgel, *The Jonsonian Masque* [Cambridge: Harvard University Press, 1965], and Stephen Orgel and Roy Strong, *The Theatre of the Stuart Court* [Berkeley: University of California Press, 1973]). The ongoing Malone Society *Collections* series offers vitally important access to records as well.

27 This is analogous to the way that John Bulwer's *Chirologia* (London, 1644) describes how gesture conveys meaning in great detail. Regrettably, we do not have a similar work on props, but the plays provide evidence of a kind of language of the prop.

architecture."[28] It also conducted annual inventories and maintenance of the "stuffe" associated with its responsibilities. Records of these operations—called "airings"—provide some of the most useful information about the range of the Office's activities and the size of its staff. The airings were large events employing significant numbers of people on a regular basis to evaluate, catalog, and repair items ranging from costumes to furniture to lighting apparatuses. Period discussions of the Revels—broadly understood to encompass theatrical performance, dance, music, and other forms of entertainment—point to an awareness of the importance of craft traditions to the production of entertainments and, indeed, sometimes downplay the role of the writer in favor of the designer or artificer.[29] In his description of London's educational institutions, Sir George Buc writes that he

> might hereunto adde for a Corollary of this discourse, the Art of Reuels, which requireth knowledge in Grammar, Rhetorike, Logicke, Philosophie, Historie, Musick, Mathematickes, & in other Arts (& all more then I understand I confesse) & hath a setled place within this Cittie. But because I haue described in, and discoursed thereof at large in a particuler commentarie, according to my talent, I will surcease to speake any more therof: blazing onely the armes belonging to it, which are Gules a crosse Argent, and in the first corner of the scutcheon, a Mercuries Petasus Argent, and a Lyon Gules in cheefe.[30]

Unfortunately, the "particuler commentarie" did not survive.[31] Often attached to Stowe's Survey, Buc's *Third University* deals with London's educational institutions—making a claim that London is the third university—and the inclusion of the Revels in this work underscores the recognized institutional status of the Revels establishment. Not only is the Revels Office important to the Crown, London chorography recognizes it as well. The traditional trivium of grammar, rhetoric, and logic is joined in this theatrical curriculum by a slightly revised quadrivium which substitutes history and philosophy for geometry and astronomy. In Buc's vision, the art of the Revels requires knowledge of these arts and these

28 See John Orrell's work on theatre architecture. The Works Office was in charge of the actual construction, but the Revels establishment seems to have been involved in design and, most importantly, in stagecraft.

29 Most famously, Inigo Jones's fights with Jonson turn on the relative importance of stage and script. Less well known are the repeated references to the artificers of civic pageantry who are often recognized above the writers of the various shows.

30 Sir George Buc, *The Third Universitie of England* (London, 1615), Oooo3v. Copy in the British Library.

31 Nor does the treatise described in the section on poets and musicians. Buc's *Third University* is appended to Stowe's *A Survey of London* in the editions of 1615 and 1632. Buc discusses every conceivable educational institution in London—from the churches to the Inns of Court and chancery to schools of music, dancing, and fencing; and he includes the Revels in his list of things taught in London.

same arts have a recognized place in London.[32] His assertion derives from and reflects the regular and central part played by staged entertainment in his London. Whether in the Revels Office proper or in the public theatres or on the streets, playing had a place in London and so, too, did the artificers supporting those entertainments. Stage production, then as now, demanded large numbers of technical professionals to provide the stages, props, lighting, and costumes essential to mounting a performance and their influence on the early modern population of such theatrical artificers and their "art" on the development of early modern drama was considerable.[33]

The records of the Revels Office suggest that the Office's needs for stage carpenters, painters, tailors, designers must have had much in common with the needs of professional acting companies and theatre managers. So, too, the Lord Mayor's Shows employed a wide range of craftsmen, designers, and writers. In response to the demand for skilled theatre workers, a regular population of theatre craftspeople emerges in the course of the sixteenth and seventeenth centuries, which points to the existence of a body of skills and techniques that actors, producers, and playwrights would have both known of and been able to depend on in their work. Moreover, as Buc attests, these skills and techniques were at least somewhat rationalized and thus teachable—having such a body of skills is one of the defining features of a profession.

Several important conclusions can be drawn from an examination of the Revels, Works, and City records related to dramatic production. First, regular patterns of staffing can be discerned in the records of the Revels Office, the Works, and the Lord Mayor's Shows all through the period. The Revels Office tended to employ the same group of craftsmen year after year and each livery company tended to hire the same writers and designers from show to show. The Works' responsibilities at times overlapped with those of the Revels Office and at least some of the craftsmen worked for both and, at least once, the Works made use of Peter Street's skills.[34] It also appears that certain families tended to provide the same kinds of services for each office.[35] Second, the Revels and Lord Mayor's

---

32 This institutionalization—the imagination of a curriculum—marks the regularization and rationalization of specifically Revels-related skills. This kind of rationalization in an educational context is a mark of a profession. Buc may be imagining this—motivated by his own position as master—but the fact that such a thing is imaginable is important to the development of a profession (or group of them).

33 See my *Representing the Professions* for a more detailed discussion of these points.

34 See John Orrell's *The Human Stage: English Theatre Design 1567 to 1640* (Cambridge: Cambridge University Press, 1988), pp.162–3. Street's specialized tools and skills were used by the Works office in making some stage pillars.

35 One example is Richard Munday—Anthony Munday's son—who was employed as a painter on a series of Lord Mayor's Shows in the early seventeenth century only some of which were written by his father. Richard's employment extends past his father's death. James Peele and his son George offer devices and scripts for several Lord Mayor's Shows

Shows employed a wide range of craftsmen doing specifically theatrical tasks. "Property-makers," painters, tailors, "other artificers," wiredrawers, and carpenters all provided various essential services to what amount to more or less permanent production companies.[36] Third, in the case of the Lord Mayor's Shows, production responsibilities shifted over time from being primarily in the hands of the livery company, who had elected that year's Mayor, to being contracted out to individuals or groups who promised to provide the pageants in exchange for a lump payment that would cover the expenses of the production.[37] This may be an analogous phenomenon to the increasing reliance on professional players in the Revels Office after the 1580s.

The contracting out of these tasks by the livery companies and by the Revels Office to increasingly well-organized groups demonstrates the professionalization of these practices. Where amateur members of the livery companies once wrote, designed, built, and performed the Shows, by the end of the period, all aspects of production save funding were the province of professionals—actors, stage architects, musicians, and others. Many definitions of professionalization hold that professions are defined by the specialization of skills and the contracting out of tasks by the livery companies suggest that this was occurring in early modern London's theatrical trades. The example of "property-making," a term first used in the Revels records, underscores the specialization of skills that developed on the production end of the theatre. This process occurs in tandem with the professionalization of writing.

IV

Greene's play, an example of a professional dramatist's appropriation of available theatrical discourses, also stages the complex and sometimes conflicted effects that those discourses can (or cannot) achieve. Bohan's demonstration and Oberon's complementary interventions are at times incompatible, or at least mutually incomprehensible. Oberon's dumbshow may be illegible to Greene's onstage audience, but Bohan's "demonstration" is also unclear. Like the audience in the

over the period as well. In the Revels records, one John Ogle and his son (John Ogle "iunior") are paid as "propertymakers" in many of Cawarden and Blagrave's accounts. This is also true of several other father/son teams among the artisans working for the Revels Office. See Malone Society, *Collections III* (Oxford: The Malone Society, 1954) for Munday and Albert Feuillerat, *Documents Relating to the Office of the Revels in the Time of Elizabeth* (Louvaine, 1908) for details.

36 See the discussion of property-making in my *Writing the Professions*.

37 Malone Society *Collections III* contains a variety of citations to people like Munday, Dekker, John Grinkin, Middleton, and others being paid large sums (£190 and upwards) for the pageants. The scale of these payments suggests that they were coordinating the whole of the production for the year. See discussion below.

theatre, neither Oberon nor Bohan appears capable of easily interpreting the performance before them. In chorus VII, for example, Oberon expresses confusion about the importance of what he has just witnessed: "How should these crafts withdraw thee from the world?" (chorus VII.1).[38] Why, in other words, should the relatively innocuous events depicted have led Bohan to renounce the world and flee to the wilderness to live in a tomb? Prompted by the apparent inadequacy of Ateukin's "crafts" to explain Bohan's loathing of the world, Oberon presents a vision of "pomp" which presumably does give a reason to "withdraw … from the world" (chorus VI.1):

> *Enter* CYRUS, Kings *humbling themselves; himself crowned by olive, that at last dying* [is] *laid in a marble tomb with this inscription*:
>
> *Whoso thou be that passest, for I know one shall pass, know that I am Cyrus of Persia, and I prithee envy me not this little clod of clay wherewith my body is covered.*
>
> *All exeunt.*
>
> *Enter the* King in *great pomp who reads it, and issueth,* [and] *crieth, 'Ver meum.'* (chorus VII.2.1–8)

Craft in this chorus most immediately refers to Ateukin's trickery, but by opposing it to Oberon's pomp, Greene draws an analogy between that craft and the play itself. In other words, the play's craft, its art, is at this point inadequate to explain Bohan's motivations, which calls forth Oberon's "pomp" in an effort to do what the play produced by Bohan cannot. Oberon supplements the Ateukin-as-Machiavel plot with this visual show that, by being seen, is meant to convey a meaning Bohan's play does not. Oberon's productions appeal to an audience trained in reading visual allegory, the kind of stage design Orrell describes as being one of the foundations of English theatre architecture, a dramaturgy distinct from, or maybe supplemental to, the word-oriented drama Bohan strives to produce.[39]

Bohan's insistence on calling his play a jig—no matter how unlike a jig it is—locates his work in a popular tradition that, it could be argued, Bohan is trying to revise into a useful form. While *Tamburlaine*'s induction scorns the "jigging vein of rhyming mother-wits," Bohan embraces at least the label, appropriating the social and institutional capital associated with it, in order to revise it and attempt to

38 Sanders conjectures that the chorus may have appeared after 1.2 where Ateukin employs his craft, but to no harmful ends—thus not justifying Bohan's loathing of the world.

39 See Orrell, *Stage Design.* Note, too, that unlike the Semiramis show, this one comes with signs that are read by the performers. Oberon seems to be responding to Bohan's earlier inability to understand what the dumbshows mean without commentary. Bohan's orientation is consistently toward words and away from spectacle and Oberon revises the dumbshows in light of this.

produce a satire of courtly corruption. Likewise, Oberon's "pomp" and the series of dances, dumbshows, and tableaux that constitute it owe a great deal to the kind of visual spectacle characteristic of both the Revels and the Lord Mayor's Shows and put that immediately recognizable symbolic capital in service of an analogous agenda of demonstration, of entertainment, and finally, like Bohan after all, of instruction. Both presenters depend implicitly on the audience's awareness of and response to different traditions of staging, traditions which here, as elsewhere, are represented by quite specific technical elements—elements that derive from an established craft tradition that helped produce the theatres on whose stages Greene's play was produced.

Both stage traditions, curiously, fail here. Neither Bohan nor Oberon understands the other's show. The kinds of representations offered are insufficient to the task at hand, whatever it may be. Greene, unlike Bohan or Oberon, does not restrict himself to one or another kind of representational strategy—both Bohan's "jig" and Oberon's "pomp" are available to him for strategic use. Greene's juxtapositions of failed shows in *James IV* point to his own difficult relationship with the stage and to a larger and longstanding crisis in the field, a crisis that cannot be explained solely in literary terms. Nor can it be explained in craft terms. This crisis is a representational one—archly looked back on by *Henry V*'s chorus—that Greene resolves by foregrounding it. In *James IV*, Bohan's thesis-driven demonstration founders at the time that Oberon's spectacle does and out of that conjoined failure emerges the play. Greene's play makes itself out of a set of references to theatrical practices and thus comments on the state of the field at the same time it offers itself up as a different kind of representation—that also represents the professional theatre. Greene's experiment may not be as successful as those of other writers, but his experimentation, like that of Marlowe or Shakespeare, relies on an encounter between a well-understood set of staging traditions and the body of skills the playwrights brought to the theatres.

V

Greene's play *James IV* thus demonstrates a sophisticated and ambivalent awareness of theatrical convention in the many metatheatrical comments that appear throughout the play (one character, Slipper, functions as an incarnate comment on the conjunction of the play world and that of the audience).[40] The play's generic hodgepodge (its mixture of romance, pastoral, and tragedy [finally undermined by the other elements] under the rubric of a history play), points to

40 The position of slipper and his brother Nano, both inside the play and outside of it, resembles that occupied by Rafe in Beaumont's later *Knight of the Burning Pestle* and that liminal position enables the characters to comment (if not explicitly) on the ways the plays they occupy operate.

Greene's painfully self-conscious dramaturgy. The play's literary self-consciousness—its pointing to the tradition of the Machiavel, its allusions to pastoral, and its announcement of itself as artifice—derive, at least in part, from Greene's academic training which steeped him in a deeply allusive and imitative style of composition. This feature overall is well-established but Greene's self-awareness in the play also points to the advent of a theatrical field in which playwrights work as part of a broad group of theatrical professionals. Greene is not only aware of a literary tradition, but also of a crafts tradition—of traditions of staging. Greene alludes to and exploits the resources of these craft traditions as much he does traditionally literary ones.[41]

Several recent critics have pointed to Greene's conscious artistry in the play—calling attention to the way he plays with generic conventions, to the frame, and to Greene's staging of a kind of dramatic theory. A.R. Braunmuller writes that Greene:

> Probes ... the relation between dramatic illusion and the dual realities represented by the theater audience and the stage audience ... Greene has encircled the conventions of the internal play with another illusion having conventions of its own and dramatic aims necessarily different from those implicit in the internal play.[42]

Braunmuller's attention is mostly given to "literary" aspects of the play—seeing it as a strong precursor to Shakespearean romantic comedy—and he stresses Greene's authorial experimentation. Likewise, Alexander Leggatt describes an internal debate in the play between the "satiric, moralizing, finally despairing" Bohan and the "festive, comic, life-affirming" Oberon. Leggatt argues that "the conflict between them is one familiar elsewhere in Greene's work… the conflict between a celebration of the pleasures of life and the impulse to repent and renounce those pleasures."[43] These concerns are literary and more or less biographical, focused on what Greene is doing with specifically writerly conventions. Finally, Clinton Crumley's discussion of the play as "historical romance" pays careful attention to the way the frame narrative works with history and romance to gesture "towards a domain somehow untouched by chronicle history."[44] All of these welcome reappraisals of the play, and of Greene's

---

41 See Timothy Reiss, *Meaning of Literature* (Ithaca: Cornell University Press, 1992).

42 A.R. Braunmuller, "The Serious Comedy of Greene's *James IV*," *English Literary Renaissance*, 3 (1973): 338. Braunmuller also notes the resemblance of the framing situation to the inductions of later plays by Jonson (e.g., *Bartholomew Fair* and *Every Man Out of His Humour*).

43 Alexander Leggatt, "Bohan and Oberon: The Internal Debate of Greene's *James IV*," in Lynne Magnusson and C.E. McGee (eds), *The Elizabethan Theatre XI* (Ontario: P.D. Meany, 1985), pp. 98–9.

44 J. Clinton Crumley, "Anachronism and Historical Romance in Renaissance Drama: *James IV*," *Explorations in Renaissance Culture* 24 (1998): 88.

dramaturgy more generally, focus on what amount to philosophical questions about aesthetics, about history, and about genre.[45] These approaches to the play need to be supplemented by more attention to the material underpinnings of the questions the play asks—the aesthetics of Greene's play, in other words, are grounded in a theatre where craft traditions, kinds of staging, were as subject to contestation as written traditions.

James IV thematizes a dramatic contest, constantly reminding audiences that Bohan and Oberon are staging a struggle between what the play imagines as two kinds of drama not least by keeping them onstage throughout the performance.[46] The resolution of Bohan and Oberon's contest is a kind of provisional synthesis of didacticism and aestheticism (for lack of a better and less anachronistic term). This stage-debate between kinds of theatre depends as much on these "literary" categories as it does on the existence of recognized patterns of staging that derive from the practices of theatre craftsmen. In other words, these patterns signal distinctions between kinds of playing practice. Where the Revels Office produced the kinds of shows Oberon's fairies perform, the itinerant professional acting companies of the earlier sixteenth century produced sparer shows more akin to that which Bohan strives to present. The aesthetic questions of the play depend on an awareness of the material conditions of different styles of playing. Greene strove to straddle what emerge in the play as the extremes of professional practice, and this straddling produces *James IV*'s often confusing blend of stoic *contemptus mundi* and luxuriant visual pleasure. Rather than synthesize what McCluskie terms a "theatre of spectacle" with a theatre of ideas or choose one above the other, Greene appears to have juxtaposed them, playing with already established visual and material languages, in an effort to call attention to various conventions of playing. This kind of attention to convention, a key feature of later drama like Beaumont's *Knight of the Burning Pestle*, is specifically professional and here depends on the existence of conventions of staging that derive from a combination of court and city traditions. To use Abbott's terminology, Greene's play represents a moment when the new professional theatre and a craft performance tradition are coming into "equilibrium." The play's dramatic debate presents that process from Greene's position as a university-educated professional writer—and thus also represents a

---

45 The same applies to the critical discussion of Jonson's *Poetaster*, a play often discussed more in terms of its philosophical or biographical interest than in terms of its place in a changing theatrical field.

46 The two poles imagined here come to be associated with the comic realism of Heywood, for example, on the one hand, and what Kathleeen McCluskie terms "the elite style of satiric iconoclasm" on the other (in *Dekker and Heywood: Elizabethan Dramatists* [New York: St. Martins, 1994], p. 15). McCluskie argues that Heywood linked himself with a "theatre of exciting physical action, a theatre which was a spectacle and an entertainment, a magical vision of unexperienced riches before it was a theatre of ideas" (15). What is interesting here is the way that Greene juxtaposes these poles rather than necessarily choosing one over the other in any kind of clear fashion.

position-taking in the ongoing struggle to define the dramatic field. The uneasiness and problems inherent in staging the play bear witness to the difficulty of the project Greene and his contemporaries undertook.

The choruses engage in the kinds of debates that Braunmuller, Leggatt, and Crumley describe, but also, in their emphasis on distinct kinds of theatre craft, represent an uneasy linking-together of very different stage traditions in the service of Greene's dramaturgical intent. Moreover, the questions Greene appears to be asking have as much to do with fundamentally theatrical questions about communicating across the stage-audience divide as they do with philosophical questions about pleasure and renunciation, satire and comedy, and so forth. The more abstract questions that Braunmuller, Leggatt, Crumley, and others rightly discuss find their root in Greene's wrestling with the varied technical tools at hand in order to convey his meaning in the play. The conflict between the two aesthetics in this play refracts a struggle with what Greene found to be refractory materials. The illegibility of both Oberon and Bohan's productions at various times in the play and their ongoing mutual revisions of the performance raise questions about the didactic usefulness of drama by struggling with the material components of that drama—the struggle with the material precedes the questions and drives the kinds of resolutions Greene comes to, however provisional they may be.[47]

Finally, Greene's play enacts a contest between kinds of drama by testing the representational capacities of two kinds of theatre. In this contest between spectacle and action, the contest attempts to work out so-called literary questions by using all the means available at the time Greene wrote. Those resources are literary, deriving from Greene's education, and artisanal, deriving from the craft of the theatre in which he was working. In *James IV*, both sets of practices, of resources, are mutually dependent, and the play as a whole emerges out of Greene's use of both. The craftsman's artifice is no more a means to Greene's artistic ends (a notion that in terms of the period makes little sense) than the script is a means to the ends of the craftsman. Theatrical artifice, in all senses of the term is both the form of Greene's play and, in a sense, the content.

---

47 Greene remains dubious about the play's capacity to convey a message to the end—Bohan's final speech tells the audience that they have witnessed a kind of morality play, but his remarks bear almost no resemblance to the action actually presented.

Chapter 4

From *Homo Academicus* to *Poeta Publicus*: Celebrity and Transversal Knowledge in Robert Greene's *Friar Bacon and Friar Bungay* (c. 1589)

Bryan Reynolds and Henry S. Turner

The Dialectic of Celebrity

By the time Robert Greene received his second Master of Arts degree from Oxford in 1588—having already been awarded both a BA (1580) and an MA (1583) from Cambridge—he had long since established his position outside the university in the precarious and often contentious world of professional writing.[1] Soon it would be impossible for readers to overlook Greene's most recent distinction, which became a regular fixture of his title pages and prefaces; to one reader in particular, the humanist Gabriel Harvey, the phrase "Robert Greene, Master of Arts in both Universities" became a particularly irritating display of humane learning in the interest of naked ambition. Ironically, Harvey himself was hardly coy about self-promotion, and the famous quarrel among Harvey, Greene, and Thomas Nashe remains one of the most colorful surviving examples of how early modern *homo academicus* sought to define a new position for himself in the public market for printed books, once he had left the familiar, if not always comforting, walls of collegiate life and began to feel his way toward a new system of employment and reward, faculty and task, reputation and identity.[2]

---

1 See René Pruvost, *Robert Greene et Ses Romans* (Paris: Les Belles Lettres, 1938), the first biographer to point out the correct date of Greene's degrees; also Johnstone Parr, "Robert Greene and his Classmates at Cambridge," *PMLA* 77 (1962): 536–43. For additional biographical information on Greene, see John Clark Jordan, *Robert Greene* (New York, NY: Columbia University Press, 1915/New York, NY: Octagon Books, 1965); Edwin Haviland Miller, *The Professional Writer in Elizabethan England* (Cambridge, MA: Harvard University Press, 1959).

2 We have taken the term *homo academicus* from Pierre Bourdieu's *Homo Academicus*, trans. Peter Collier (Stanford, CA: Stanford University Press, 1988); as we discuss below, the work of Bourdieu has been central to our analysis in the essay that follows.

And what was this world that *homo academicus* sought to enter, the world of the "professional writer"? No doubt it could be many things: prolific, and thus exhausting; self-indulgent, and thus at times highly gratifying; outspoken, and as a consequence genuinely dangerous to personal freedom and bodily integrity. But above all it was "poor," in all the senses of the term: a world where the symbolic currencies of credit, favor, and reputation barely compensated for the paucity of hard cash, the fickle ignorance of buyers, and the iron-fisted acumen of publishers; a world viewed with a mixture of distaste and distant curiosity by those in a position to lead opinion and determine matters of degree. That the stakes of the period's most famous literary quarrel could be at once so petty and so enormous is easy to see: the oblique jabs, glancing comments, invidious comparisons, and posthumous insults were the only resources available to Greene, Harvey, and Nashe as they sought to leverage what little symbolic power they had in the face of the Stationer's monopoly, the Bishop's license, or the patron's favor. Nor is it any wonder that their writings sometimes strike us as narrow and self-regarding: bruised egos and narcissistic consolation are perhaps all that remains when resources are scarce, temporary alliances pass for friendship, and personal ambition becomes the only stay against the threat of a penniless and lonely death.

In many ways Greene was luckier, or cannier, than either Harvey or Nashe, since he seems to have realized early on that a carefully managed persona would become his only reliable resource and that the more ubiquitous and variable that persona became—even to the point of self-contradiction—the more likely it was to find a market. His greatest misfortune was to die before them, unwittingly bequeathing control of that persona to at least one avowed enemy and a friend of dubious commitment. In a moment of astonishing vindictiveness and determination, a grudging Harvey could track down the charitable shoemaker's wife who had lodged Greene as he lay dying and then publish the miserable details of his final moments, ladling on self-righteous derision; Nashe, meanwhile, only weakly contested the portrait and offered a tepid defense of his one-time ally and fellow alumnus.[3] "There is no telling," Lori Humphrey Newcomb has recently written, "when his usual title-page billing 'Robert Greene, Master of Arts in both Universities' ceased to claim courtly status and began to flaunt his dramatic fall": the market had welcomed *homo academicus*, used what it could, and moved on.[4]

Scholars writing on the rise of the professional author have long looked to Greene, Harvey, and Nashe as exemplary of the "university wits" who abandoned a career within the walls of the university or the Church in favor of a more public and less secure vocation in London's literary marketplace. But these accounts have largely overlooked the fact that the primary point of contention among writers such

---

3 See Edwin Haviland Miller, "The Relationship of Robert Greene and Thomas Nashe (1588–92)," *Philological Quarterly* 33 (1954): 353–67.

4 Lori Humphrey Newcomb, *Reading Popular Romance in Early Modern England* (New York, NY: Columbia University Press, 2002), 28.

as Harvey, Greene, and Nashe was an emerging notion of *celebrity*: the symbolic power celebrity conferred, of course, but, even more crucially, the way celebrity was defined through legitimate acts of recognition. As Pierre Bourdieu has argued:

> Symbolic power—as a power of constituting the given through utterances, of making people see and believe, of confirming or transforming the vision of the world and, thereby, action on the world and thus the world itself, an almost magical power which enables one to obtain the equivalent of what is obtained through force (whether physical or economic), by virtue of the specific effect of mobilization—is a power that can be exercised only if it is *recognized*, that is, misrecognized as arbitrary. This means that symbolic power does not reside in "symbolic systems" in the form of an "illocutionary force" but that it is defined in and through a given relation between those who exercise power and those who submit to it, i.e. in the very structure of the field in which *belief* is produced and reproduced.[5]

At stake in the quarrels among the so-called university wits was precisely the terms of recognition through which the authority of the professional writer and his product might be evaluated. Each man sought to construe his contemporaries as unworthy of recognition, in a double sense: unworthy to be recognized by others, and even more importantly, unworthy of *bestowing recognition on others*. For the act of recognition implies an act of investment, as Bourdieu has observed: recognition becomes a form of capital when it takes the form of "degree specific consecration ... i.e., the degree of recognition accorded by those who recognize no other criterion of legitimacy than recognition by those whom they recognize."[6]

The "dialectic of celebrity," as we term it, emerges out of this process whereby competing public personae are composed through acts of public recognition that are bestowed by others already recognized as worthy of performing these acts. When these acts of recognition all derive from within the same field and the agents involved are competing over the same tokens of value and modes of power, this dialectic approaches a self-sustaining process that marks the relatively autonomous nature of the field. Because the early modern literary field was still in the process of establishing the terms of definition and value that could be specific to it, the struggle between Harvey, Greene, and Nashe over "literary" authority and the celebrity it might bring was particularly sharp. Writing for commercial publication, after all, was one of only several career paths that the former university man might pursue, typically in alternation or combination with a residency at one of the Inns of Courts; serving as a private tutor or public lecturer, acting as secretary, translator, "reader,"

5 Pierre Bourdieu, *Language and Symbolic Power*, ed. John B. Thompson (Cambridge, MA: Harvard University Press, 1991), 170.

6 Pierre Bourdieu, "The Field of Cultural Production, or: The Economic World Reversed," trans. Richard Nice in *The Field of Cultural Production: Essays on Art and Literature*, ed. and introduction by Randal Johnson (New York, NY: Columbia University Press, 1993), 29–73, p. 38.

or intelligencer for powerful patrons or, on occasion, for the government.[7] Indeed, a writer such as Harvey only partially sought to become a "literary" figure in the modern sense: his goal was less to write poems, plays, romances, or other forms that might appeal to a commercial audience of readers than it was to enter political service, and he used his writings to position himself in this sphere. Greene and Nashe, we might say, were *reduced* to seeking recognition as celebrities in a literary market because they found themselves unable to secure reliable sources of patronage, employment, and power outside of the field of commercial publication—their celebrated "authorial" personas were the virtue that resulted from their necessity.

For *homo academicus*, finding success in the market for printed books rather than in more traditional patronage or employment required unusual ingenuity, flexibility, and stamina, as Greene's own work attests: romances, short moral tales, repentance narratives, cony-catching "exposés" (largely borrowed from other writers),[8] satire, one work of astrology, and at least five plays—dramatic writing being an area in which Greene, it seems, never enjoyed the success of some of his contemporaries. The rest of this essay examines one of the most successful of Greene's plays, *Friar Bacon and Friar Bungay* (c. 1589), and proposes that Greene uses it to undertake an intricate account of the conflicted places that *homo academicus* occupied in late-sixteenth century English culture and of how he might come to occupy a newly emergent position: what we call "*poeta publicus*," the celebrity author. We will provisionally describe the relationship between *homo academicus* and *poeta publicus* as one of "homology," as Bourdieu has articulated the term, in order to demonstrate a series of structural analogies between two sociocultural fields that would seem, despite all Greene's efforts, to remain quite distinct from one another. We will use the principle of homology, first, to describe

---

7 See for instance the work of Anthony Grafton and Lisa Jardine on Gabriel Harvey, especially "'Studied for Action': How Gabriel Harvey Read his Livy," *Past and Present* 129 (1990): 30–78, and *From Humanism to the Humanities: Education and the Liberal Arts in Fifteenth- and Sixteenth-Century Europe* (Cambridge, MA: Harvard University Press, 1986); also that of Jardine and William Sherman on Henry Wotton, "Pragmatic Readers: Knowledge Transactions and Scholarly Services in Late Elizabethan England," in Anthony Fletcher and Peter Roberts (eds), *Religion, Culture and Society in Early Modern Britain: Essays in Honour of Patrick Collinson* (Cambridge: Cambridge UniversityPress, 1994), pp. 102–24; Sherman, *John Dee: The Politics of Reading and Writing in the English Renaissance* (Amherst, MA: University of Massachusetts Press, 1995); Warren Boutcher, "Pilgrimage to Parnassus: Local Intellectual Traditions, Humanist Education and the Cultural Geography of Sixteenth-Century England," in Yun Lee Too and Niall Livingstone (eds), *Pedagogy and Power: Rhetorics of Classical Learning* (Cambridge: Cambridge University Press, 1998), pp. 110–147; Paul E. J. Hammer, "The Earl of Essex, Fulke Greville, and the Employment of Scholars," *Studies in Philology* 91 (1994): 167–80.

8 For discussion of Greene's borrowings from other writers, see Bryan Reynolds, *Becoming Criminal: Transversal Performance and Cultural Dissidence in Early Modern England* (Baltimore, MD: Johns Hopkins University Press, 2002), pp. 64–94.

aspects of the constitution of these fields in general where analogies in their respective structures are particularly visible; second, we will examine homologies of position that individual agents might occupy in, between, and/or linking these two fields, circumstances for which terms like "lamination," "stratification," "amalgamation," or "collapse" will prove themselves to be more appropriate than "homology." Since Greene himself was so self-conscious about his position in both fields and actively sought to forge connections between the persona of *homo academicus* and that of *poeta publicus*, he stands as a strong example of how both fields were changing during the period and of how the professional writer—and notably the writer of plays—understood his new liabilities and potential for success.

The "Friar Bacon Formation": Affective Presence and Articulatory Space

As a first step in our analysis of how the figure of Friar Bacon in Greene's play should be understood as an avatar for Greene's own transitional position among several overlapping social fields, it will be necessary to examine the constitution of the "academic" and "literary" fields in general at the end of the sixteenth century and to point out salient points of homology between them. Specifically, we will argue that the definition of *magic and mathematics* (and the interface between them) in the intellectual field of the university provides a model for Greene to assess the place of *poetics*, and especially of *dramatic poesy*, in the literary marketplace. The structural position of these two fields of knowledge within their own institutional spheres, we will go on to argue, were homologous to one another for the simple reason that both fields of knowledge were viewed as fundamentally heterodox or transversal by early modern contemporaries.

The definition and place of magic in the university field occupy much of Greene's play and account for its most engaging elements. Ever since the pioneering work of historians such as D.P. Walker and Francis Yates, critics have recognized the enduring influence that hermetic, cabalistic, and other occult philosophies exercised on figures such as Marsilio Ficino, Giovanni Francesco Pico della Mirandola, Henry Cornelius Agrippa, Giordano Bruno, John Dee, and Tommaso Campanella, although in light of more recent scholarship, it is no longer quite true to say, with Yates, that "If there was any interest in [occult hermeticism] in England, it was not in officially established circles in Church or University, but in private circles, such as Sir Philip Sidney's group of courtiers studying number in the three worlds with John Dee, or survivals of the More-Colet tradition."[9] Keith Thomas has demonstrated how widely

9 Francis Yates, *Giordano Bruno and the Hermetic Tradition* (Chicago, IL: University of Chicago Press, 1964), p. 187. For the discussion of occult knowledge that follows, we have drawn on (in addition to the work of Yates) D.P. Walker, *Spiritual and Demonic Magic from Ficino to Campanella* (London: The Warburg Institute and the University of London, 1958/Nendeln: Kraus Reprint, 1969); Wayne Shumaker, *The Occult Sciences in the*

various occult practices extended in early modern English social life and called attention to the extraordinary persistence of both astrology and alchemy well into the seventeenth century. Charles Schmitt has shown that interest in astrology, alchemy, and magic *did*, in fact, penetrate quite far into the sixteenth-century university curriculum, providing topics of disputation for the MA degree and capturing the attention of well-regarded Oxford doctors such as John Case, Everard Digby, Matthew Gwinne, and John Williams, the last eventually to rise to the position of Lady Margaret Professor of Divinity.[10] To be sure, this interest was a cautious one and always with an eye to the crucial distinction between so-called "white," "spiritual," or "natural" magic and the more dangerous "black," "necromantic," or "demonic" magic. In the former, the special operations of the practitioner animated latent natural forces in order to achieve natural effects or effects that, however artificial they might seem, nevertheless depended on natural processes; in the latter, demons were invoked as intermediary causes in order to produce effects that directly contravened natural processes and that were often undertaken to procure some immediate material advantage for the practitioner.

As is clear from Greene's play, however, the boundary between natural and demonic forms of magic was, in fact, a much fuzzier one than many writers cared to admit, their different means and ends often difficult to distinguish from one another. An important reason for this convergence may be attributed to the fact that both forms of magic were still intimately associated with the "mathematical sciences" more broadly, as the character Mason, Friar Bacon's colleague in *Friar Bacon and Friar Bungay*, avows:

> No doubt but magic may do much in this;
> For he that reads but mathematic rules
> Shall find conclusions that avail to work
> Wonders that pass the common sense of men.[11]

Renaissance (Berkeley: University of California Press, 1972); Eugenio Garin, *Astrology in the Renaissance*, trans. Carolyn Jackson and June Allen, revised by Clare Robertson (London: Routledge & Kegan Paul, Ltd., 1983/London: Arkana and Penguin, 1990); Anthony Grafton, *Cardano's Cosmos* (Cambridge, MA and London: Harvard University Press, 1999); Don Cameron Allen, *The Star-Crossed Renaissance* (Durham: Duke University Press, 1941/New York: Octagon Books, 1973); John S. Mebane, *Renaissance Magic and the Return of the Golden Age* (Lincoln, NE and London: University of Nebraska Press, 1989).

10 See Charles Schmitt, *John Case and Aristotelianism in Renaissance England* (Kingston and Montreal: McGill-Queen's University Press, 1983), pp. 53–4, 118–21 and 191–216; Keith Thomas, *Religion and the Decline of Magic* (New York, NY: Charles Scribner's Sons, 1971); Mordechai Feingold, "The Occult Tradition in the English Universities of the Renaissance: a Reassessment," in Brian Vickers (ed.) *Occult and Scientific Mentalities in the Renaissance* (Cambridge: Cambridge University Press, 1984), pp. 73–94.

11 All citations are to *Friar Bacon and Friar Bungay*, ed. Daniel Seltzer (Lincoln: University of Nebraska Press, 1963), by scene and line number, the passage cited above appearing at 2.72–75; cf. also 4.53.

As a consequence of this association, the line between what early modern authorities called "magia" and what we today would describe as "applied mathematics" or "technology" was indistinct, since many of the preoccupations of writers on magic concerned not its theoretical consistency but its practical application, in fields as diverse as optics, mechanics, medicine, horticulture, and pharmacology.[12] Furthermore, interest in occult theories and methods was by no means limited to figures on the margins of institutionalized intellectual life but extended to scholars at the center of the university field, like Case, Gwinne, or Williams, as well as to more public statesmen, and even as far as Elizabeth herself. On March 10, 1576, Elizabeth visited Dee's house at Mortlake in order to be entertained in his garden by his magic glass, and the efforts of Dee and Kelley to secure the secret of the philosopher's stone were followed with equal interest by Case at Oxford and by Elizabeth and Lord Burghley, although no doubt for somewhat different reasons. Even a sober scholar such as Case failed to recognize that Kelley was a self-serving charlatan, and although Rudolf II had expelled Dee and Kelley from Prague for suspicion of fraud, Burghley continued to court Kelley in the hopes that he would return to England with his alleged alchemical solutions.[13]

Among English writers, no figure was more representative of the mysteries and promise of magic and mathematics than the historical person of Roger Bacon, who had long been an outstanding figure in the various occult traditions that had grown out of medieval Arabic manuscripts, such as the *Picatrix*, or that had been disseminated through Ficino's translation of the *Corpus Hermeticum*, where Bacon appears, along with Albertus Magnus and Robert Grosseteste, as a magus renowned for his production of mechanical animals, talking statues, and the

---

12 See, in addition to the works cited in n. 9 above, J. Peter Zetterberg, "The Mistaking of 'the Mathematicks' for Magic in Tudor and Stuart England," *Sixteenth Century Journal* 11 (1980): 83–97; Nicholas Clulee, *John Dee's Natural Philosophy: Between Science and Religion* (New York and London: Routledge, 1988); William Eamon, *Science and the Secrets of Nature* (Princeton: Princeton University Press, 1994).

13 For Elizabeth's visit to Dee and dealings with Dee and Kelley, see Samuel Clyde McColloch, "John Dee: Elizabethan Doctor of Science and Magic," *South Atlantic Quarterly* 50 (1951): 75–7 and 84 and Charles Nicoll, *The Chemical Theater* (London; Routledge & Kegan Paul, 1980), pp. 20–21; on Case's interest in Dee and Kelley, see Schmitt, *John Case*, p. 121 and p. 210 ("We now believe that Sir Richard [sic] Kelly is producing gold itself by the use of the philosopher's stone and without deceit or fraud," Case, *Lapis philosophicus* [Oxford, 1599], cited by Schmitt, p. 183). The interests of the government are clear, too, from John Dee's enthusiastic letter to Lord Cecil (15 February 1562) announcing that while in Paris he had discovered a manuscript copy of Johannes Trithemius's *Steganographiae*, a treatise on cryptography that offered, in addition to its methods for secret codes, elaborate formulas for communicating over great distances through the aid of angels. See Clulee, "John Dee's Early Natural Philosophy," p. 644 n. 41; Gatti, p. 74 and n. 32. Trithemius's work was printed in 1606 but in MS much earlier; see Walker, *Spiritual and Demonic Magic*, pp. 86–90.

infamous brazen head.[14] Despite the fact that Bacon himself took pains to distinguish the practice of magic from the study of properly natural forces, by the early seventeenth century, his name had become an important symbolic token for writers seeking to legitimate their inquiries into the relationship between art and nature or their curiosity about a wide range of occult practices: Ficino, Pico, Agrippa, Dee, Bruno, Case, Raleigh, and Sir Thomas Browne, among others, all looked to him as a model for the legitimacy of natural magic as both a theoretical and a practical pursuit.[15] At Oxford, Bacon's reputation as a mathematician, mechanician, alchemist, and natural occultist may have helped to establish a continuous *institutional* tradition of occult inquiry, and this perhaps explains why Case's friend John Williams prepared an edition of Bacon's *Libellus* or *Epistola Rogerii Bacon ... de retardandis senectutis accidentibus et de senisbus conservandis* (1590), published at Oxford by Joseph Barnes, Case's own publisher. Many of Bacon's writings also circulated in manuscript during the period, especially among men interested in mathematical, mechanical, and occult problems: Thomas Harriot, for instance, read with interest Bacon's treatises on alchemy, his rejection of Democritian atomism, his experiments with burning mirrors, his defense of mathematics, and his comments on various aspects of legitimate experimental method (*arte experimentali*).[16] Mathematical practitioners such as Robert Recorde or Leonard and Thomas Digges wrote admiringly about Bacon's technical experiments with optical glasses and his theories of perspective;

14 On Bacon's reputation in general, see A.G. Molland, "Roger Bacon as Magician" *Traditio* 30 (1974): 445–60, esp. p. 450, with additional bibliography. Stories of speaking statues had long been associated with the ancient Egyptian priests who were believed to have authored the hermetic writings and had passed from Augustine to Aquinas, Ficino, Agrippa, Dee, Recorde, and many others; see Yates, *Giordano Bruno*, *passim*.

15 See Molland, "Roger Bacon as Magician"; Mebane, *Renaissance Magic*, p. 76, pp. 80–83; P.M. Rattansi, "Alchemy and natural magic in Raleigh's *History of the World*," *Ambix* 13 (1966): 122–38.

16 See Stephen Clucas, "Thomas Harriot and the Field of Knowledge in the English Renaissance," in Robert Fox (ed.) *Thomas Harriot: An Elizabethan Man of Science* (Aldershot: Ashgate Press, 200), p. 100 and n. 33; p. 109 and n. 68, citing the mathematician Thomas Allen and Robert Payne as reading Bacon in manuscript; p. 117 and n. 103; p. 128 n. 141, on William Warner's interest in Bacon; also Hilary Gatti, "The natural philosophy of Thomas Harriot" also in Fox (ed.), *Thomas Harriot*, pp. 75–7. As Stephen Clulee has shown, Dee passed through a two-year period (1556–58) of fascination with Bacon's work during which he acquired manuscript copies of nearly all of Bacon's writings, wrote a defense of Bacon against the charge of necromancy (which he never published), and annotated Bacon's *Epistola de secretis operibus artis & naturae, & de nullitate magiae* (not printed until 1618). See Clulee, "Astrology, Magic, and Optics: Facets of John Dee's Early Natural Philosophy" *Renaissance Quarterly* 30 (1977), esp.pp. 642–3 and n. 35, p. 663, pp. 669–72, pp. 672–5 and ns. 128–9 and Clulee, "At the Crossroads of Magic and Science: John Dee's Archemastrie," in Vickers (ed.), *Occult and Scientific Mentalities in the Renaissance*, pp. 57–71.

at the same time, editions of Bacon's own work (and spurious works attributed to him) gradually began to make their way into print.[17]

Like Cicero, Erasmus, and other key figures in Renaissance thought, although to a more circumscribed degree than these more famous writers, Roger Bacon was starting to emerge in early modern culture with what we call an "affective presence," a distinct discursive cultural force or vitalizing authority whom men such as Dee, Case, or Williams could imitate as they sought to define their own intellectual identities around novel, and often unorthodox, problems of inquiry. According to the transversal theory that guides our investigation, affective presence can be understood as the combined material, symbolic, and imaginary existence of a concept, object, subject, and/or event whose multiplicities radiate through and around environments.[18] As a result, affective presence often brings otherwise disparate constituents and forces into play with each other to produce at least one prominent formation, an "articulatory space" comprised of avenues for knowledge transfer, communication, and interfacing experiences and phenomena.[19] When encountering or embodying any media conceptually and/or materially imbued with the affective presence of icon, an event, or series of related events (a "movement"), we become a participant in a variety of articulatory spaces, in much the same way that subsets and their elements work in mathematical set theory.

---

17 In addition to the *Libellus* or *Epistola Rogerii Bacon ... de retardandis senectutis accidentibus et de senisbus conservandis* prepared by Williams, these include the *Epistola fratris Rogerii Baconis de secretis operibus naturae et de nullitate magieae* or *De mirabilis potestate artis et naturae*, published in Latin and two English translations. On Williams's interest in Bacon, see Schmitt, *John Case*, p. 112, p. 119, p. 195; the work was eventually printed in an English translation as *The Cure of Old Age, and Preservation of Youth* (London 1683), prefaced by a life of Bacon and a list of his writings. The *Epistola ...* first appeared in Paris (1542) and then at Oxford in an edition (1594) that no longer survives (see Little, in *Bacon Essays*, no. 18, and Schmitt, *John Case*, p. 195 n. 14); the work was translated into English and printed twice, first as part of the *Mirror of Alchemy* (London, 1597) and then again as *Frier Bacon his Discovery of the Miracles of Art, Nature, and Magick* (London, 1659). The title page of the 1659 edition announces that it is "Faithfully translated out of Dr. Dees own Copy" and prefaces the text with an account of Bacon's life and a list of authorities who approved his piety and learning. On the *Mirror* and its relation to Bacon see Nicoll, *The Chemical Theater*, pp. 23–32.

18 For more on "affective presence" and "transversal theory," see Bryan Reynolds, *Becoming Criminal*, pp. 1–22; *Performing Transversally: Reimagining Shakespeare and the Critical Future* (New York, NY: Palgrave Macmillan, 2003), pp. 1–28; and *Transversal Enterprises in the Drama of Shakespeare and his Contemporaries: Fugitive Explorations* (London: Palgrave Macmillan, 2006), pp. 1–26; also Bryan Reynolds, "The Devil's House, 'or worse': Transversal Power and Antitheatrical Discourse in Early Modern England," *Theatre Journal* 49.2 (1997): 143–67.

19 For more on "articulatory spaces," see Bryan Reynolds, *Performing Transversally*, pp. 1–28 and *Transversal Enterprises*, pp. 1–26.

Like all celebrities with affective presence, the symbolic power of Friar Bacon—the icon and concepts associated with him—grew precisely *through* acts of reference, imitation, and efforts to become like him, thereby both endowing him with an authority that tended to reflect back on the historical figure and helping to legitimize those problems to which he had contributed solutions. The "Friar Bacon formation," as we call it, allowed Greene to bring into focus the two primary social positions that were fundamental to the emerging identity as *poeta publicus* that he sought to fashion for himself. As a poet, pamphleteer, and conspicuous university "master," Greene was himself becoming a sociopolitical conductor with new symbolic power, a power that grew to the degree that his celebrity, as a distinctive form of affective presence, also increased.[20] Because of its historical novelty and because the terms of its definition were changing by the year, the identity of the professional writer was difficult for Greene to imagine and to project with critical distance in his writing. With his play, Greene was able to capitalize on the distinct articulatory space that was beginning to form around the cultural figure of "Friar Bacon" and his affective presence, partly through the accident of existing source materials and partly through the growing awareness of Roger Bacon's legacy in university circles with which Greene himself was familiar. The position of *homo academicus*, particularly when imagined retrospectively and over a long historical trajectory, offered a familiar homological model that Greene could use to examine his own position as a professional writer, as well as that of contemporaries such as Harvey or Nashe, as they sought to establish themselves in the literary—and especially in the *dramatic*—marketplace.

Rivalry, Transversality, and Dramatic Form

The significance of "Friar Bacon" as an affective presence for Greene, we propose, lay chiefly in his marginal, embattled position within the university field and his longstanding affiliation with heterodox epistemologies. For this reason, Bacon provided Greene with a model for ways in which *homo academicus* might oppose official culture, journeying beyond the traditional parameters of his sanctioned subjective territory as academic or scholar and moving into alternatively subjective territories. In this way, the "Friar Bacon formation" demonstrates another aspect of *homo academicus*-becomings-*poeta publicus* that has been overlooked by scholarship on the so-called university wits: his *transversality*, his capacity to influence radical changes within himself and in society, which both generated and

---

20 In our analysis, "sociopolitical conductors" are the familial, educational, juridical, and religious structures that promote or oppose, often contradictorily, the prevailing ideology of the society in which they function. For detailed discussion on sociopolitical conductors, see Bryan Reynolds, "The Devil's House, 'or worse,'" pp. 143–67; *Becoming Criminal*, pp. 1–22; and *Performing Transversally*, pp. 1–28.

was generated by the new challenges he presented to the regulating endeavors of early modern English society's sociopolitical conductors and official culture.[21] The very field in which Greene sought to make his reputation and the very forms he employed to do so, after all, carried many of the same transversal associations and objections that were leveled against the occult sciences, with their mysterious symbols and incantations, their proximity to mathematics and assorted practical arts, and their seeming affiliation with the demonic.[22] The persistent objections to the public theatre by many of the city's aldermen are well-known, and the writings of antitheatricalists, such as by John Greene, John Northbrooke, Stephen Gosson, John Rainolds, and Phillip Stubbes, would have been very familiar to Greene, especially since many of these men were his teachers and peers at Oxford and Cambridge. Consider John Greene's *A Refutation of the Apology for Actors* (1615), which rebuts playwright Thomas Heywood's *An Apology for Actors* (1612) with a striking account of "a Christian woman [who] went into the Theater to behold the plaies":

> She entered in well and sound, but she returned and came forth possessed of the Diuell. Wherevpon certaine Godly brethren demanded Sathan how he durst be so bould, as to enter into her a Christian. Whereto he answered, that *hee found her in his owne house*, and therefore took possession of her as his own.[23]

If the church is the house of God, the public theater is the Devil's "*owne house*": its "Sathans Synagogue."[24] But the many pamphlets, too, that began to flower in

21 According to transversal theory, "Becoming is a desiring process by which all things (energies, ideas, people, societies) change into something different from what they are. If the things had been identified and normalized by some dominant force, such as state law, religious credo, or official language, then any change in them is, in fact, becomings-other" (Reynolds, *Becoming Criminal*, pp. 20–21). On the other hand, as Reynolds explains in *Transversal Enterprises*, "comings-to-be occur when people lose control during the process of becomings-other and become more of/or something else than anticipated and/or desired. In other words, becomings are active processes, often self-inaugurated and pursued intentionally, whereas comings-to-be, however induced by becomings, are generated by the energies, ideas, people, societies, and so on to which the subject aspires, is drawn, or encounters by happenstance" (2–3).

22 On relations between poetics, drama, and practical mathematics more broadly during the period, see Henry S. Turner, "Plotting Early Modernity" in *The Culture of Capital: Property, Cities, and Knowledge in Early Modern England* (New York, NY: Routledge, 2002), and Turner, *The English Renaissance Stage*: *Geometry, Poetics, and the Practical Spatial Arts* (Oxford: Oxford University Press, 2006).

23 John Greene, *A Refutation*, p. 44.

24 Ibid., p. 43. In *The Anatomie of Abuses*, Phillip Stubbes also refers to the theatre as "Sathan's Synagogue" (143) and in *A Second and Third Blast of Retrait from Plaies and Theatres* (London: 1580), Anthony Munday calls "the Theater" "the chappel of Satan" (quoted in Stubbes, p. 302). For a detailed account of antitheatricality in early modern England, see Bryan Reynolds, *Becoming Criminal*, pp. 95–125.

the 1580s, as Joad Raymond has recently demonstrated, and by which Greene made his enduring reputation, soon drew the anger of those who viewed the entire form as so much seditious waste paper and gutter trash from the suburbs. "A *Pen*!," Thomas Dekker would later write of pamphlets and pamphleteers, as he turned, for a moment, on his own company, with one of the many legends associated with Roger Bacon in mind: "the invention of that, and of *Inke* hath brought as many curses into the world as that damnable Witch-craft of the *Fryer*, who tore open the bowels of Hell, to find those murdering engines of mankind, *Guns* and *Powder*."[25]

One of the most significant mythical figures associated with both poetry and music in the period, furthermore—Orpheus—was also one of the most important figures in the hermetic genealogy of ancient magi, second, in some accounts, only to Hermes himself; the Orphic hymns sung by Ficino and Pico offered some of the most powerful modes of magical incantation: "in natural magic nothing is more efficacious than the Hymns of Orpheus," Pico affirmed,

> the names of the gods of which Orpheus sings are not those of deceiving demons, from whom comes evil and not good, but are names of natural and divine virtues distributed throughout the world by the true God for the advantage of man, if he knows how to use them.[26]

Thus when Sidney refers to Orpheus as "Father in learning" to all historians in the *Defense* or when he compares Orpheus's power to move trees to Stella's ability to "charm" men's ears in his lyric "If Orpheus voice had force to breath such music's love," his invocations draw the "art of poesy," through its associations with number, harmony, and song, more closely toward ancient occult knowledge than we might recognize if we hear only a more conventional mythic genealogy.[27] For Agrippa, who condemned the occult arts along with all other forms of human learning in his *De vanitate scientiarum* (1530)—and who promptly published his own compendia of magic, *De occulta philosophia libri tres*, only three years

25 Thomas Dekker, *The Dead Terme* (1608), in *Non-Dramatic Works*, ed. Grosart, 4 vols (privately printed, 1884–86), vol. 4, p. 65; cited by Joad Raymond, *Pamphlets and Pamphleteering in Early Modern Britain* (Cambridge: Cambridge University Press, 2003), p. 53.

26 Cited by Yates, *Giordano Bruno*, p. 89; see pp. 78–80, pp. 89–91, pp. 136–7; also Walker, *Spiritual and Demonic Magic*, pp. 12–24.

27 Cf. also Harvey's *Pierces supererogation, or A new prayse of the old asse* (1593), linking "Hermes ascending spirit" with "Orpheus enchanting harpe," "Homers diuine furie," "Tyrtaeus enraging trumpet," "Pericles bounsinge thunderclaps," and "Platos enthusiasticall rauishment" (24); also the Christianized treatment of Orpheus as ancient poet and mystical philosopher throughout the English translation (partially by Sidney) of Phillipe Du Plessis Mornay's *A woorke concerning the trewnesse of the Christian religion* (1587), as observed by Yates (1964), p. 178, p. 188.

later—poets are first natural philosophers because they inquire into the secrets of nature.[28] For this reason, poetry was very similar to astrology: if poetry was the "Authore of lies, and the maintainer of peruerse opinions" (30), Agrippa maintained, and even the "mother of lies" (32)—here using a phrase that Sidney would also use in his *Defense*, where he alludes directly to Agrippa's work—then "... the Astrologers" were "themselues no lesse Fabulouse then Poetes," since they "haue written rules in their bookes of Elections, with whiche one seruice of bawdrie, al Astrologers, and diuinours make no small gaine: next vnto which magicke doth present her selue as healper" (214).[29] Like poetry, which "Augustine willeth ... shoulde be banished out of the Citte of God: Plato the Pagane diueth ... out of his Common Weale. Cicero forbiddeth ... to be admitted" (32), so also arithmetic or geometry should also banished from the commonwealth; rhetoric, too, is a lying discourse (43) and should have no place in the commonwealth (44); as an art of persuasion, it resembles nothing so much as magical incantations (128).

Not only did Greene's contemporaries perceive a fundamental homology between magic and poetry, therefore, but Greene himself had a demonstrable interest in the occult sciences even before writing his play and certainly was aware of the link between magic and poetry that Orpheus represented. In 1585 Greene had published his *Planetomachia*, a series of dialogues and tragic stories exchanged between the seven planets that illustrated the predominant astrological influences of Venus and Saturn;[30] Greene's "Apology" for astrology in that work maintains that

> The *Gretians* neither receiued the knowledge of Astrologie of the *Ethiopians* nor *Egiptians:* But *Orpheus* the sonne of *Aeagar* and *Calliope*, was there first Schoolemaister, who taught them no plaine way but in darke problemes and misteries: For he instituted certaine Feastes called *Orgia:* wherein vpon his Harpe he deliuered them in Sonnets the principles of Astrologie. Furthermore, by his Harpe which had seuen strings, he did represent the consent of the moueable Starres: which when he did strike he did ouercome all things, and mooued both Stones, Birds and Beastes. (2)

---

28 All following citations are from Henry Cornelius Agrippa, *Of the Vanitie and Vncertaintie of Artes and Sciences*, English trans. by James Sanford (1569, 1575) ed. Catherine M. Dunn (Northridge, CA: California State University, 1974), p. 143.

29 For Sidney's attitudes to occult knowledge, see Turner, *The English Renaissance Stage*, Ch. 3, with additional bibliography.

30 Greene dedicated the book to the Earl of Leicester who took an interest in astrology and included two defenses of the science, one in English and one in the form of a Latin dialogue. See Don Cameron Allen, "Science and Invention in Greene's Prose," *PMLA* 53 (1938): 1007–18, who provides a detailed inventory of Greene's many "scientific" allusions and discusses the *Planetomachia* on pp. 1014–18, identifying his primary sources as Johannes Pontanus's "Aegidius Dialogus" (from which Greene has lifted *verbatim* his Latin defense, changing only the names of the interlocutors) and Melancthon's edition of Ptolemy's *De Praedictionibus Astronimicis* (Basel, 1543).

In the case of the *Planetomachia*, too, Greene's engagement with the occult sciences must be understood as an act of position-taking, as Bourdieu has described it, within the larger contest over defining the identity, expertise, and affective presence of *homo academicus*: Greene's biographer René Pruvost speculates that the *Planetomachia* may have been inspired by the fact that both Richard and John Harvey—Greene's exact contemporaries at Cambridge—had recently published books of astronomical predictions in 1583, and that Greene's book may also have provoked Gabriel Harvey's annoyance.[31]

Like many of his contemporaries, Greene was particularly attracted to the figure of Roger Bacon: many of the legendary stories associated with the "Friar"—his construction of automata, including the brazen head, his attempts to build a wall of brass around England, his collaborations with Bungay, and his debate with the foreign scholar Vandermast—were circulating in the anonymous mid-sixteenth century romance, the *Famous History of Fryer Bacon*, that served as an immediate source for Greene's own play; since the *Famous Historie* incorporated several passages from Bacon's *The Mirror of Alchemy*—itself circulating in manuscript well before its publication in 1597—we can assume that Greene had at least an indirect acquaintance with Bacon's work. As a model for contemporary *homo academicus*, the "Friar Bacon formation" is defined by the intersection and friction among positions that are partly intellectual and partly sociological. Having developed into a distinct affective presence, he represents a constellation of points distributed within a spectrum of ideas, methods, and vocabulary that were

31 See Pruvost, *Robert Greene*, pp. 207–18, discussing Richard Harvey's *Astrological Discourse* (1583) and John Harvey's *An Astrological Addition ...* (1583), with John's translation of the *Iatromathematica* attributed to Hermes Trismegistus and *An Almanacke, or annual Calender, with a compendious Prognostication ...* (1589). Their elder brother Gabriel's position on astrology seems to have varied throughout his life; he owned copies of several astrological works and made extensive astrological annotations during the period when he was studying civil law. Cf. Virginia F. Stern, *Gabriel Harvey: A Study of His Life, Marginalia, and Library* (Oxford: Clarendon Press, 1979), p. 71, p. 93 and her discussion of Gabriel's changing attitudes to astrology, pp. 168–71 and n. 58. On July 26, 1578, Harvey participated in a three-hour disputation at Cambridge before Burghley and Elizabeth, in which he argued the opposing position to the question of whether "astra non imponunt necessitatem"; see Stern, *Gabriel Harvey*, p. 40, p. 204, p. 216, and p. 68 n. 61; Harvey's astrological books include Luca Gaurico's *Tractatus Astrologicus* (1552), which he was reading in 1580, and Bonetus de Lates's *Hebrei medici Provenzalis Annuli per eum compositi super astrologiam utilitates incipiunt* (Paris, 1527); cf. Harvey's *marginalia* to his edition of Dionysius Periegetes, *The Surveye of the World ... englished by T. Twine* (1572), in *Gabriel Harvey's Marginalia*, ed. G.C. Moore Smith (Stratford-Upon-Avon: Shakespeare Head Press, 1913), esp. pp. 159–62. Harvey also owned four manuscript treatises on magic that he annotated in approximately 1577 (now collected as BL Add. MS 36674). One had been passed to him via different Cambridge men, and Harvey associates it with "Agrippas Occulta philosophia"; another had been written by the astrologer Simon Foreman, and Harvey's copy was probably in Foreman's own hand; Stern, *Gabriel Harvey*, p. 242; Feingold, "Occult Tradition," p. 81–2.

competing for epistemological authority at the close of the sixteenth century: we may provisionally distinguish neoscholastic natural philosophy, occult philosophies and mathematics, and the humanist "arts of discourse," including rhetoric, dialectic, and poetics. At the same time, he operated as a sociopolitical conductor within the institutional structures and official territories of the college and the university at large, as these were defined internally among rivals and externally in relation to the state machinery of both domestic and foreign powers.[32]

Viewed in this light, the epic disputation between Friar Bacon and Vandermast in Greene's play is best understood as a hyperbolic representation of actual university practice, in which a contemporary interest in all aspects of mathematics and magic, natural and otherwise, have been accentuated and submitted to scrutiny. What is at stake in the debate between the two scholars is partially their own expertise (and thus their symbolic power) over a vocabulary, a set of concepts, and a series of well-defined problems, but also at stake is the very status of magic and mathematics in general as new fields of knowledge that might be of potential service to the emerging nation-state.[33] The stakes of the debate, as in the quarrel among Harvey, Greene, and Nashe, are precisely the affective presence of celebrity and the power that the recognition by others, whether colleagues or kings, endows. As Clement somewhat disingenuously claims:

> Bacon, we come not grieving at thy skill,
> But joying that our academy yields
> A man suppos'd the wonder of the world;
> For if thy cunning work these miracles,
> England and Europe shall admire thy fame,
> And Oxford shall in characters of brass,
> And statues, such as were built up in Rome,
> Eternize Friar Bacon for his art. (2.36–43)

---

32 On the institutional nature of Bacon's position, see Reynolds and Turner, "Performative Transversations: Collaborations Through and Beyond Greene's *Friar Bacon and Friar Bungay*," in Reynolds, *Transversal Enterprises*, pp. 240–50.

33 On this point see Reynolds and Turner, "Performative Transversations"; Turner, *The English Renaissance Stage*. Certainly there were several immediate models for Greene to draw upon, most famously Giordano Bruno's visit to Oxford in 1583, where he disputed (to his great disdain) with Dr. John Underhill before the Polish Count Laski and "others of the English nobility." Although Bruno later recounted a stunning victory over his opponent—"the wretched doctor who was put forward as the leader of the Academy on that grave occasion came to a halt fifteen times over fifteen syllogisms, like a chicken amongst stubble"—other evidence indicates that contemporaries viewed it as the public humiliation of a famous foreign scholar by the Oxford faculty, when one of them realized that much of Bruno's discourse consisted of unacknowledged quotation from Ficino's *De vita coelitus comparanda*. See Robert McNulty, "Bruno at Oxford," *Renaissance News* 13 (1960): 300–305; Yates, *Giordano Bruno*, pp. 206–10, citing Bruno's account; Feingold, "The occult tradition," pp. 76–7.

The structure of Clement's disavowal as it unfolds across the first three lines of the passage converts the professional jealousy that flourished among Greene, Harvey, and Nashe into an affirmation of the institution that presided over *homo academicus*: paradoxically, rivalry no longer threatens to dissolve the academic field by pitting colleagues against one another but becomes instead a field-defining gesture. At the same time, however, Clement's comment reveals how insecure *homo academicus* remained within the walls of his institution, since the legitimacy of his research program, and thus of his entire field of expertise, depended on outside recognition and reward. Whatever the outcome of the disputation with Vandermast, Friar Bacon needs the imprimatur of an international community of scholars and of King Henry, who, as we have argued elsewhere,[34] stands ready to annex the epistemological authority of either Bacon or Vandermast for his own purposes:

> We'll progress to Oxford with our trains,
> And see what men our academy brings.—
> And, wonder Vandermast, welcome to me.
> In Oxford shalt thou find a jolly friar,
> Called Friar Bacon, England's only flower;
> Set him but nonplus in his magic spells,
> And make him yield in mathematic rules,
> And for thy glory I will bind thy brows,
> Not with a poet's garland made of bays,
> But with a coronet of choicest gold. (4.56–65)

The desirability of the "coronet" that Henry will bestow lies less in its precious substance than in the royal recognition of authority that it signifies, an authority that the King opposes to the "poet's garland" but which is, at root, of the same nature, bays and gold forming only two different material forms for the symbolic power that public recognition brings when it is bestowed by a recognized authority. The real difference between the two rewards is to be found in the two fields in which the consecrating authority is situated: the King's gesture asserts the field of politics over that of poetics, the authority of the monarch over scholars or poets. And he knows that while both scholars and poets are hungry for the recognition of colleagues, the real prize it to be found in the power, influence, and wealth that public legitimacy and celebrity made possible—and Greene knew it, too.

Indeed, the King's comparison between the "coronet of choicest gold" and the "poet's garland made of bays" reveals the full stakes of Green's play: for if we regard the entire struggle between Friar Bacon, Friar Bungay, and Vandermast as a homology for the kinds of struggles over reputation, recognition, and reward that also engaged Greene and his contemporaries, we may grasp that one of the significant prizes at stake is precisely the power that *homo academicus* might

34 See Reynolds and Turner, "Performative Transversations," pp. 240–50.

achieve by forging an alignment between university accreditation and expertise, on the one hand, and public celebrity in the literary marketplace, on the other. After all, Greene wrote *Friar Bacon* in the first place in order to strengthen his bid for the public favor that other dramatists of the 1580s were beginning to enjoy. Greene's most famous words are words of rivalry against an emerging professional competitor, a warning to university men such as Marlowe and Nashe to beware the "upstart crow" who had begun to stalk the boards among them. This commercial rivalry and the fragile, occasional collaborations that it sponsored among university men were a foundational condition of the emergence of the theatre as a public institution; in Greene's play, we find its homological image in the tenuous collaboration between Friar Bacon and Friar Bungay against Vandermast.

But we also find the traces of the market in professional theatre embedded within the very form—in the structure and stylistic features—of a play whose double action pits contemporary satire of academic life against the pastoral *topos* and romance phrasings that a playwright such as Lily had made popular. The result is a peculiar generic hybrid assembled out of literary conventions that were competing for the attention of audiences and playwrights alike in the 1580s, a play in which the classicism of university drama meets estates satire, revenge tragedy, romantic comedy, and the sonnet, as in the following description of Margaret:

> I tell thee, Lacy, that her sparkling eyes
> Do lighten forth sweet love's alluring fire;
> And in her tresses she doth fold the looks
> Of such as gaze upon her golden hair;
> Her bashful white mix'd with the morning's red,
> Luna doth boast upon her lovely cheeks;
> Her front is beauty's table, where she paints
> The glories of her gorgeous excellence;
> Her teeth are shelves of precious marguerites
> Richly enclosed with ruddy coral cleeves.
> Tush, Lacy, she is beauty's over-match,
> If thou survey'st her curious imagery. (1.50–61)

One of the most remarkable aspects of *Friar Bacon and Friar Bungay* is the way in which Greene attempts to demonstrate his currency as a playwright by containing stylistic variety within a single generic framework: that of the history play, a comparatively novel and specifically English dramatic genre that would eventually become the vehicle for Shakespeare's own emergence as a celebrity playwright. Having renounced his magic and embraced both "Mercy and Justice" and "pure devotion" (13.100, 107) at the end of the play, Bacon steps forward to declare "Old Plantagenet" the ruler of "Albion diadem" (16.6–7) and then offers a "prophecy ... mystical" (16.63):

> That here where Brute did build his Troynovant,
> From forth the royal garden of a king
> Shall flourish out so rich and fair a bud
> Whose brightness shall deface proud Pheobus's flower,
> And over-shadow Albion with her leaves." (16.44–48)

By this point at the end of his play, Greene has begun to move beyond the competing genres of the history play or court romance and toward a new form—a fusion of native English historical traditions, popular prophecy, and mythological romance—that anticipates Shakespeare's much later *Cymbeline*.

But Greene's play finally has loftier ambitions than a garland of bays strung from assorted scenes, images, and turns of phrase: as we have been arguing, it stages a confrontation between two epistemological traditions out of which dramatic poesy itself, as a coherent intellectual system for generating knowledge about the world, might draw its power and legitimacy. These are the occult and quasi-occult sciences of magic, astrology, alchemy, and mathematics, on the one hand, and the classical, mythological tradition of the university humanist and his arts of discourse, on the other. Both epistemological traditions were aggressively textual, and both lend Greene a vocabulary, range of imagery, and set of proper names with which he could construct dramatic blank verse that might rival Marlowe's "mighty line." Compare the technical language of Vandermast in the first disputation with Friar Bungay (9.28–40),[35] or the self-importance of Bacon's account of his own scholarly labors, in the third person (10.11–20),[36] with Margaret's lines as she reads Lacy's letter (10.117–121)[37]: the passages, and others like them, demonstrate how Greene turns on the one hand to the classical mythological tradition and on the other to the occult sciences in order to generate a suitably "dramatic" line of blank verse. Indeed, the competing authority of these

---

35 "The cabalists that write of magic spells, / As Hermes, Melchie, and Pythagoras, / Affirm that, 'mongst the quadruplicity / Of elemental essence, *terra* is but thought / To be a *punctum* squared to the rest; / And that the compass of ascending elements / Exceed in bigness as they do in height; / Judging the concave circle of the sun / To hold the rest in his circumference. / If, then, as Hermes says, the fire be greatest, / Purest, and only giveth shape to spirits, / Then must these daemones that haunt that place / Be every way superior to the rest'" (9.28–40).

36 "The rafters of the earth rent from the poles, / And three-formed Luna hid her silver looks, / Trembling upon her concave continent, / When Bacon read upon his magic book. / With seven years' tossing necromantic charms, / Poring upon dark Hecat's principles, / I have framed out a monstrous head of brass, / That, by the enchanting forces of the devil, / Shall tell out strange and uncouth aphorisms / And girt fair England with a wall of brass" (10.11–20).

37 "The scrolls that Jove sent Danaë, / Wrapt in rich closures of fine burnished gold, / Were not more welcome than these lines to me. / Tell me, whilst that I do unrip the seals, / Lives Lacy well? How fares my lovely lord?" (10.117–121).

two traditions assumes a particularly spectacular *scenic* form at the center of the play, when Friar Bungay first conjures:

> …the tree leav'd with refined gold,
> Whereon the fearful dragon held his seat,
> That watch'd the garden call'd Hesperides,
> Subdued and won by conquering Hercules. (9.79–82)

and Vandermast responds by summoning Hercules himself to "pull off the sprigs from off the Hesperian tree" (9.95). But when Bacon finally enters the scene, Hercules stands powerless before the demons he commands:

> Bacon, that bridles headstrong Belcephon,
> And rules Asmenoth, guider of the north,
> Binds me from yielding unto Vandermast. (9.141–43)

Here magic and mathematics have explicitly and literally triumphed over a separate humanist literary tradition, just as the English history play and vernacular romance rises to eclipse learned translations of the Senecan tragedies of Hercules, such as Thomas Newton's *Seneca His Tenne Tragedies* (London, 1581). The struggle—simultaneously formal, ideological, intellectual, and professional—may be summed up in the competing lists of proper names invoked throughout the play by characters distributed across its two actions: Jove, Danae, Daphne, Phoebus, Apollo, versus Pythagoras, Belcephon, Asmenoth, Hecat, Demogorgon, Lucifer, "Sother, Eloim, and Adonai/ Alpha, Manoth, and Tetragrammaton" (13.93–94).

Greene has written a play in which he uses Bacon's growing affective presence and the unique articulatory space his persona made available to comment on the nature of theatre as a distinct mode of representing and understanding the social world and to launch a vehicle in which his own power over this form is displayed as clearly as possible. The homologies are particularly visible in those moments when Bacon uses his famous "glass prospective" to structure viewing positions and reveal forces—the psychological forces of desire and ambition, as well as their moral implications—that lie hidden to characters and audience alike:

> I will, my lord, strain out my magic spells;…
> But come with me; we'll to my study straight,
> And in a glass prospective I will show
> What's done this day in merry Fressingfield. (5.100–106)
> …
> Now, frolic Edward, welcome to my cell;…
> Within this glass prospective thou shalt see
> This day what's done in merry Fressingfield
> 'Twixt lovely Peggy and the Lincoln Earl.
> …

> Stand there and look directly in the glass. (6.1–10)
>
> ...
>
> Sit still, my lord, and mark the comedy. (6.48)

By juxtaposing the lines with one another, we can see the basic homology between magic and the theatre leap into focus, as the stage splits into two simultaneous scenes, ostensibly separated by hundreds of miles ("'Twere a long poniard, my lord, to reach between / Oxford and Fressingfield" [6.131–32]). Greene has literalized the definition of comedy traditionally ascribed to Cicero—*imitatio vitae, speculum consuetudinis, imago veritatis*—and recast it so that the audience is invited to understand the conventions of theatrical performance not in terms of a humanist literary tradition but as a distinct mode of occult mathematics and technology. The scenes are a theatrical demonstration of Sidney's famous mathematical metaphor in his *Defense*:

> as in geometry the oblique must be known as well as the right, and in arithmetic the odd as well as the even, so in the actions of our life who seeth not the filthiness of evil wanteth a great foil to perceive the beauty of virtue.[38]

Like a "great foil," these split scenes, too, imitate, mirror, and show, since Margaret appears in the glass, like Edward, in the company with a friar whose initials are also FB (Friar Bungay) and who uses his "art and cunning" (6.21) to reveal the real Earl of Lincoln beneath his disguise, just as Bacon has just done to Edward in an earlier scene and as he does now in real time. Bacon's power, in short, is nothing less than the power of Greene's theatre: the power to penetrate beneath superficial appearances to reveal occult processes that would be impossible to view directly. But for Greene these occult processes are finally social, political, and professional, and the image he makes of them is a projection of his own not-so-secret desires: a fantasy of social mobility and sudden transformation in status, as Margaret rises from the position of a pastoral buttery maid to become the rival of a Spanish princess; a fantasy of professional rivals vanquished and of international celebrity; a fantasy of grateful royalty, crossing the threshold of a humble lodging to sit at the sparsely furnished table of the scholar.

To a greater degree than his contemporaries, perhaps, Greene sought to forge a permanent identity that was somehow *between homo academicus* and *poeta publicus*, as a third position distinct from them: a university man-about-town who was as famous for his degrees as he was infamous for his dissolute habits. For Greene, the credibility, longevity, and profitability of this new identity depended on his ability to use the tokens of his past learning as capital for his current life. He attempted to legitimate his writing and his emerging position in the literary field by

---

38 Sir Philip Sidney, *The Defense of Poesy*, in *Miscellaneous Prose of Sir Philip Sidney*, ed. Katherine Duncan-Jones and Jan van Dorsten (Oxford: Clarendon Press, 1973), 96.2–6.

invoking ethical imperatives that derived from the academic-theological field of the humanist university—an institution still strongly oriented toward the Church but increasingly organized around a distinct neoclassical textual tradition—and transporting them to the print marketplace, where they could form the dominant system of valuation by which "professional" writing might be evaluated and designated as "literary." His title pages register a convergence between two distinct cultural and economic systems of valuation—the currency of the college and the coin of the printing house—and attempt to convert the former into the latter: they parade the conspicuous *signs* of Greene's academic history in a bid to transform sensational topics into edifying material. For this reason, the recurring trope of repentance finally was significant to Greene's authorial self-definition, since it enacts rhetorically as autobiography the very process of ideological and institutional legitimation that his title pages announce for his written works. And it is no accident that the most conspicuous, homological similarity between Greene and the figure of Friar Bacon is the latter's sudden repentance at the end of Greene's play: his abjuration of magic in favor of a holy life, much the way Greene abjured romantic fictions—the *inventions* of a *poietic* mode—for a narrative of (putatively) authentic confession and spiritual awakening. This, finally, was Greene's most enduring hope: a fantasy of rehabilitated reputation as the favorite son of Oxford whose accomplishments might outlast the centuries.

Chapter 5

Robert Greene, "Author of Playes"

Ronald A. Tumelson II

In a commendatory poem that served to introduce the publication of Ben Jonson's *Catiline his Conspiracy* (1611), John Fletcher complains about what he regards as print culture's wrong-headed consumers. The jeering rhetoric of his poem implies that these people have no business reading literary works like Jonson's play. Because a market-place does not discriminate between consumers of its wares, however, Fletcher is forced to admit that such readers are inevitable. These consumers, he tells Jonson,

> must see your Booke, and reade; and then,
> Out of their learned ignorance, crie ill,
> And lay you by, calling for mad *Pasquill*,
> Or *Greene's* deare *Groatsworth*, or *Tom Coryate*,
> The new *Lexicon*, with the errant Pate.[1]

The texts Fletcher mentions circulated, like Jonson's play, as "pamphlets," an often denigrated bibliographic format. Discussing the commonplace attitude toward such textual artifacts, Alexandra Halasz argues that "the categorization of pamphlets by their commodity status, rather than by their authors, titles, or discursive kind draws attention to them as *only* pamphlets and thus distinguishes them from other discourses produced in small formats and sold in the marketplace."[2] Yet, in his allusions, Fletcher names authors (Thomas Coryate) and titles (*Pasquill*); in the case of "*Greene's* deare *Groats-worth*" (chronologically the most distant author and text to which he alludes), he names both.[3] Contrary to the dominant mode of

---

1 Ben Jonson, *Catiline his Conspiracy* (London, 1611), A3v.

2 *The Marketplace of Print: Pamphlets and the Public Sphere in Early Modern England* (Cambridge: Cambridge University Press, 1997), p. 3.

3 Fletcher seems to have in mind Nicholas Breton's *Pasquils Mad-Cap*, the earliest surviving editions of which, prior to Fletcher's allusion, date from 1600; but their popularity suggests numerous editions. Either *Coryats Crambe* or *Coryats Crudities*, or indeed both, could be referred to, as these were published in 1611, and entered on the Stationers' Register on 26 November 1610 and 7 June 1611, respectively. See Edward Arber, ed., *A Transcript of the Registers of the Company of Stationers of London, 1554–1640*, 5 vols (1875; rpt. New York: Peter Smith, 1950), 3.449, 459. The reference to "The new *Lexicon*" appears to

categorization that Halasz describes, Fletcher attempts to distinguish the pamphlet containing Jonson's play from similar mass-market publications. Thus, Fletcher calls attention to the role of the market in the production of early modern literature, a role that he regards with trepidation. While acknowledging that heterogeneous interests or tastes comprise the market, Fletcher wants to control the consumption of Jonson's play. He suggests that if the city of London can "purge her iudgement presently" (A3v), then its reformed consumers will possess the wit to purchase and read Jonson's play alone. The complaint clearly betrays an anxiety concerning the marketplace of print, for Fletcher prefers a homogeneously composed market, one whose readers possess the wit to distinguish Jonson's play from other pamphlets with merely pseudo-literary pretensions.

Stemming from an anxiety about market forces, then, Fletcher's complaint heightens the tension between memory and forgetfulness (or neglect). *Catiline* had failed in its original marketplace, the public stage; it could also fail in the marketplace of print, for potential consumers may "lay you by." Serving as both signifier of the text on the bookstalls (*Catiline*) and of its absent author (Jonson), *you* indicates the extent to which printed books and authors were identified with, and could be substituted for, each other. The possibility of neglecting the text of *Catiline* would also mean neglecting Jonson. This is surely not Fletcher's aim; rather, he proposes that "things" like Robert Greene's *Groats-Worth of Witte* will eventually leave "no more behind / But a thin memory (like a passing wind) / That blowes, and is forgotten, ere they are cold" (A4r). Hence, Fletcher anticipates a time when Greene's work will die just as Greene has already died. Despite this expectation for textual and authorial demise, however, the allusion to Greene may be seen as an articulation of a crisis: nearly twenty years after its initial publication, Greene and his "deare *Groatsworth*" refuse to go away, refuse to be forgotten.

The last (surviving) edition of the pamphlet prior to the appearance of Fletcher's poem dates from 1596. Why, in 1611, call attention to *Groats-Worth* at all? A likely possibility is that there was at least one edition of *Groats-Worth* published about this time in order to meet the apparent consumer demand implied in Fletcher's lines. Jonson implied a similar demand two years earlier in his comedy *Epicoene*, in which he lampooned *Groats-Worth* as an inexpensive inducement to sleep.[4] If Fletcher was aware of Jonson's opinion of Greene or of *Groats-Worth*, then he may have intended to compliment Jonson by recalling this particular allusion in Jonson's play. Nevertheless, these details do not explain entirely Fletcher's singling out this particular text from among Greene's works. For, even if we were to posit a recent reprint of *Groats-Worth* that has subsequently been lost, there were several, equally

modify "*Tom Coryate*," but could refer to any number of dictionaries printed about this time. Jonson's *Catiline* does not appear to have been entered on the register before its publication in quarto; thus, its date in relation to these other texts is difficult to ascertain.

4 *The Complete Plays of Ben Jonson*, ed. G.A. Wilkes, 4 vols (Oxford: Clarendon Press, 1982), 3: 189–90.

popular works by Greene on the bookstalls in 1611.[5] To any one of those texts Fletcher could have alluded; he chose "*Greene's* deare *Groatsworth*," ensuring if only nominally the survival of author and text in the cultural memory.

In singling out this text and in defaming a writer who had been dead for nearly twenty years, Fletcher accords text and author an importance meriting closer scrutiny. I submit that the claims within *Groats-Worth* regarding Greene's status as a playwright were at the heart of Fletcher's allusion. *Groats-Worth* was both a culmination of Greene's thoughts about play-authorship and a signal reference point for many of his playwriting contemporaries. Well before Jonson and Fletcher began writing for the stage, *Groats-Worth* proffered a renegotiation of the cultural status of the early modern English playwright. One of my arguments in this essay is that Fletcher's critique of "*Greene's* deare *Groatsworth*" was both a textual and discursive strategy to elevate Jonson's own authorial identity at the expense of Greene's. Part of that strategy consisted in forgetting all about Greene, replacing his memory with a more suitable author of plays. There is good reason to believe that Fletcher's strategy was partly successful, for we have mostly forgotten about Greene's role in the discourse on play-authorship's cultural status. Indeed, most scholarly accounts of the cultural status and legitimation of English plays center on Jonson—particularly on the 1616 folio *Workes*, which both in its title and bibliographic format profoundly shaped the rhetorical and material discourses on play-authorship, and helped to renegotiate the perceived status of play-texts.

Arguing against this commonplace within accounts of the emergence of the playwright-as-author, I assert the importance of Greene's role in the emergent discourse on play-authorship's cultural status in early modern England. *Groats-Worth* was demonstrably important in this process of renegotiation, and evidence both from contemporary allusions and from the period's literary anthologies further serves to emphasize the significance of his contribution to the cultural legitimation of plays. Greene's place at the forefront of this discourse merits serious consideration; doing so will enable us to view more accurately the historical emergence of the playwright-as-author, and confer on Greene the cultural status "Author of Playes."

Ben Jonson has long been recognized for championing both the cultural status of his own plays and his status as a playwright. Over thirty years ago, Gerald Eades

---

5 In the year prior to Fletcher's complaint, the fourth edition of *Menaphon* was rechristened "*Greenes Arcadia*." Also available were the fifth edition of *Greenes Neuer Too Late* (*Francescos Fortunes* inclusive), and a seventh edition of *Pandosto* in 1609. See Gordon Coggins, "Greene's *Pandosto*: A 'Ghost' of 1584," *The Library* series 6.2 (1980): 448–56. More recent grist for Fletcher's mill might have been *Ciceronis Amor*, which was reprinted a fifth and sixth time in 1609 and 1611, respectively. Its popularity may have been revitalized by *Every Woman in Her Humour* (1609), a dramatic adaptation of Greene's work. See Archie Mervin Tyson, ed., *Every Woman in Her Humor: A Critical Edition* (1952; rpt. New York and London: Garland, 1980), pp. 36–48. Given its then current popularity, *Ciceronis Amor* would have been a more relevant text for Fletcher's aims. For a list of Greene's many posthumous editions, see Appendix C at the end of this volume.

Bentley asserted that Jonson's 1616 *Workes* "constituted a direct claim to status and permanence [for plays] unprecedented in the English theatre world."[6] What ultimately set Jonson apart from other playwrights, Bentley avers, was his "deep involvement with the preservation of his plays and his ideas for posterity" (291). A sense of literary self-preservation enabled this undertaking in which Jonson constructed a heretofore unheard of authorial identity. Revising select plays for inclusion in this monumental collection, the first of its kind to publish in folio the publicly performed plays of an Englishman, Jonson exerted considerable control over the volume's printed matter. Jonson's thinking about play-authorship has been characterized by Joseph Loewenstein as the operations of a "bibliographic ego." As a consequence of his "nascent awareness of the new value that was beginning to accrue to dramaturgy," Loewenstein argues, Jonson turned to the printing press with the view of regaining artistic control over his works, a form of control unavailable to him within the playhouses' "disorderly market" (270).[7] The marketplace of print met Jonson's alleged needs for order and permanence.

Jonson's "bibliographic ego" now occupies a prominent role in studies of early modern notions of play-authorship; in fact, the printed book continues to remain at the center of discussion on authorship in general.[8] Yet scholarly emphasis on print culture's relation to authorship entails what we might call a bibliographic *ergo*, whose logic goes something like this: Jonson oversaw the publication of his plays in print; *therefore*, he anticipated modern definitions of authorship. Predicating the authorship of plays on printing assumes a necessary connection between the two. Hence, in a recent collection of essays by leading scholars of early modern English drama, Jeffrey Masten epitomizes the bibliographic *ergo* when he rephrases Michel

6 *The Profession of Dramatist in Shakespeare's Time, 1590–1642* (Princeton: Princeton University Press, 1971), p. 290.

7 "The Script in the Marketplace," *Representations* 12 (1985): 101–14; rpt. in *Representing the English Renaissance*, ed. Stephen Greenblatt (Berkeley: University of California Press, 1988), pp. 265–78.

8 For the 1616 folio, see Jennifer Brady and W.H. Herendeen, eds., *Ben Jonson's 1616 Folio* (Newark, DE: University of Delaware Press; London and Toronto: Associated University Presses, 1991). Working backward from the Jonson folio, recent scholarship on the publication of his plays in quarto has seen an ongoing construction of Jonson's text-based authorial identity. See especially discussions of Jonson's *Sejanus* by John Jowett, "Jonson's Authorization of Type in *Sejanus* and Other Early Quartos," *Studies in Bibliography* 44 (1991): 254–65; and Evelyn B. Tribble, *Margins and Marginality: The Printed Page in Early Modern England* (Charlottesville: University Press of Virginia, 1993), pp. 146–57. For a critique of the bibliographical imperative, see Bruce Boehrer's "The Case of Will Kemp's Shoes: *Every Man Out of His Humour* and the 'Bibliographic Ego,'" *Ben Jonson Journal* 7 (2000): 271–95, where he argues that Jonson's "emergent sense of the 'bibliographic ego' tends to be more egotistical than bibliographic" (288).

Foucault's famous question, then offers its unequivocal answer: "*Where* is an Author? In the bookshop."[9]

None of Greene's plays could be obtained from stationers or booksellers in 1592, the year of his death; in fact, editions of his plays began to appear in print only posthumously. If we follow the so-called logic of the bibliographic *ergo*, Greene could not have been an "Author of Playes." How, in the absence of a printed play to his credit, do we account for this seemingly brash claim? To begin with, the turn to print may have been somewhat facile for Jonson; it was not so for precursors like Greene, whose relationship to early modern print culture differed markedly from Jonson's. Various inhibiting factors in the last two decades of the sixteenth century printing industry may have discouraged Greene from attempting to print his own plays. Unlike textual conditions in the first two decades of the seventeenth century, when Jonson oversaw the printing of his plays, printed commercial plays in the early 1590s neither guaranteed authorial attribution nor assured artistic control and permanence. By 1592, few plays written for the commercial playhouses had been published in print, and those that were—*Tamburlaine the Great* (1590), *The Troublesome Raigne of Iohn King of England* (1591), *Arden of Feversham* (1592), *The Spanish Tragedie* (1592)—did not give any indication as to their authorship.[10] So, even if Greene's plays had been printed, he could not reasonably expect his name to appear on their title pages. (Indeed, when John Danter and Cuthbert Burbie, the same printer-publisher duo that produced Greene's *Repentance*, issued *Orlando Furioso* in 1594, they did so without authorial attribution.)[11]

---

9 "Playwrighting: Authorship and Collaboration," in *A New History of the Early English Drama*, eds John D. Cox and David Scott Kastan (New York: Columbia University Press, 1997), p. 371. Contributors to this important volume make only passing references to Greene; indeed, he does not merit a place in the collection's extensive index. However, the editors do allow space for a lost play that was in repertory with the King's Men: "Cloth Breeches and Velvet Hose" (387, 562), which, judging from its title, was a play based on Greene's *A Quip for an Upstart Courtier* (1592).

10 W.W. Greg, *A Bibliography of the English Printed Drama to the Restoration* 4 vols (London: Bibliographic Society; Oxford University Press, 1939-59), 1: 171–2, 178, 183, 187.

11 Compilation of title-page data suggests that mention of play-authorship lagged behind mention of the company that performed the play. See James P. Saeger and Christopher J. Fassler, "The London Professional Theater, 1576–1642: A Catalogue and Analysis of the Extant Printed Plays," *Research Opportunities in Renaissance Drama* 34 (1995): 63–109. Among the first commercial plays to specify authorship, *A Looking Glasse for London and England* (London, 1594) and *Frier Bacon, and Frier Bungay* (London, 1594) declared on their title pages that the plays were made by "*Thomas Lodge* Gentleman, and *Robert Greene. In Artibus Magister*" (A2) and "*Robert Greene* Maister of Arts" (A2), respectively. These ascriptions were, I submit, a consequence of Greene's posthumously acknowledged status as a playwright.

Even if a title-page attribution of a play were a certainty, a playwright could not reasonably expect that his "work" would appear on the book's pages. Richard Jones illustrates this point in his well-known address to the first edition of the two-part *Tamburlaine* when he informs readers that he has "*(purposely) omitted and left out some fond and frivolous Jestures, digressing (and in my poore opinion) far unmeet for the matter, which I thought, might seeme more tedious unto the wise, than any way els to be regarded.*"[12] Whatever the source of that material—Marlowe? The Lord Admiral's Men for whom the play was originally written?—Jones betrays his proprietary ownership of the work and his control over its printed form. To those who had authorial pretensions and were keen observers of the marketplace of print, *Tamburlaine* exemplified the control stationers had over play-texts. The same observers may have been aware of the stationers' lack of control, too. The title page of the earliest surviving edition of *The Spanish Tragedy* declares that it had been "Newly corrected and amended of such grosse faults as passed in the first impression."[13] When printed, play-texts of the early 1590s often passed to the stationers from the players, who occasionally altered the texts they purchased from playwrights in order to meet with the censor's approval or to satisfy the demands of performance. The first edition of Greene's *Orlando Furioso* (1594) states on its title page that its text is "as it was plaid before the Queenes Maiestie." This printed text differs from the manuscript that contains the part for Orlando, but whether changes to the play were made for the specific performance mentioned on the title page, or for a reduced touring troupe, is now impossible to determine.[14] The textual conditions in which plays were printed in the early 1590s might have given Greene, or any playwright who wished to assert his authorial identity via the medium of print, pause.

Greene might also have hesitated given his experiences as a writer of prose pamphlets. After an author sold a work to a stationer, ownership was fully in the

---

12 *The Complete Works of Christopher Marlowe*, ed. Fredson Bowers, 2 vols, 2nd edn (Cambridge: Cambridge University Press, 1981), 1: 77.

13 *The Spanish Tragedy*, ed. J.R. Mulryne, 2nd edn (London: Black; New York: Norton, 1989), p. 1.

14 *Orlando Furioso* (London, 1594), A2. The manuscript belonged to Edward Alleyn, who likely performed in the titular role. J. Churton Collins transcribed the manuscript in *The Plays and Poems of Robert Greene*, 2 vols (Oxford: Clarendon Press, 1905), 1: 266–78. Many of the issues raised by the relationship between the manuscript and the printed text are discussed in W.W. Greg, *Two Elizabethan Stage Abridgements:* The Battle of Alcazar *and* Orlando Furioso, *an Essay in Critical Bibliography* (Oxford: Clarendon Press, 1923), pp. 132–3, 135–41). Greg also provides a more accurate transcription of Orlando's part (142–200). For a wholesale critique of Greg's theories regarding so-called bad quartos, see Laurie E. Maguire's *Shakespearean Suspect Texts: The 'Bad' Quartos and Their Contexts* (Cambridge: Cambridge University Press, 1996); and for *Orlando Furioso* in particular see Michael Warren's "Greene's *Orlando*: W.W. Greg Furioso," in *Textual Formations and Reformations*, eds Laurie E. Maguire and Thomas L. Berger (Newark, DE: University of Delaware Press; London: Associated University Presses, 1998), pp. 67–91.

latter's hands; and any future monetary expenses and gains belonged solely to the stationer. By noting the recirculation of his earlier prose works, several of which were reprinted during his lifetime, Greene learned first-hand about the lack of authorial control. Originally printed in 1584, *Gwydonius. The Carde of Fancie* and *Morando the Tritameron of Loue* were reprinted in 1587, and *Arbasto, the Anatomie of Fortune* in 1589. While title-page imprints were brought up to date, the pamphlets were largely unaltered; in fact, with the exception of *Morando*, these were page-for-page, preliminary-for-preliminary reprints.[15] Hence, however much Greene may have wished to control his authorial identity, the printing industry militated against any such self-construction. Consider the following dilemma created by the simultaneous publication of earlier books alongside new ones: the "Robert Greene" presented to the reading public in 1584 was re-*present*ed in 1587 and 1589. If one "Robert Greene" sought to repent in later pamphlets for his misdeeds in writing earlier pamphlets—as Greene does in *Farewell to Folly* (1590)—the "Robert Greene" of the earlier pamphlets always came back to problematize the repentant one, or at least to compromise the sincerity of that repentance. Because they were mostly in the hands of producers and consumers in the market of printed goods, books had the potential to create a dispersal of authorial identity and control. Even if Jonson, who was not a popular author, ultimately managed to exert some control over his published work, in the final decades of the sixteenth century the printed book was not a reliable guarantor of a stable authorial identity.

Greene's conceptions about what the marketplace of print meant for his authorial identity were shaped by his relationship to early modern print culture. The difference between his and Jonson's attitudes toward a text-based authorial identity becomes sharper if we consider that, in predicating our constructions of the early modern period's "author" on printed matter, we may have inadequately represented the conditions in which authorship existed. Put more polemically, a conception of authorship that is inextricably linked to the publication in print of a "work" is misleading if not untenable. Kevin Pask provides a welcome alternative to authorship studies when he structures the concept of authorship around Pierre Bourdieu's notion of "cultural capital." Turning from, or at least downplaying, the concept of authorship derived from Foucault, Pask argues that "an examination of the sedimentary record of social struggles thus somewhat displaces the recent

15 Due to substantial additions, the second edition of *Morando* is considerably longer than the first. An extended list of first editions and reprints during Greene's lifetime includes: *A Notable Discouery of Coosenage*; *The Second Part of Conny-Catching*; and *A Quip*, which went to six editions in 1592 alone. See Edwin Haviland Miller, "The Editions of Robert Greene's *A Quip for An Upstart Courtier (1592)*," *Studies in Bibliography* 6 (1953–54): 107–16. In the last year of his life, Greene may have seen another edition of *Pandosto*, whose fascinating cultural peregrinations are treated admirably in Lori Humphrey Newcomb's *Reading Popular Romance in Early Modern England* (New York: Columbia University Press, 2002).

literary-historical practice of subordinating literary production to sociopolitical concerns." For Pask, "poetic authority [is] itself a site of social contestation."[16] Fletcher's allusion to "*Greene's* deare *Groatsworth*" illustrates perfectly the kind of "sedimentary record of social struggles" that Pask describes, for authorial identity is embedded in these cultural contests. Fletcher, we recall, attempts to shape and control what Bourdieu calls "the field of cultural production," by at once memorializing the work of Jonson and wishing oblivion on the works of authors like Greene.[17] Pask, who expresses little interest in allusions of this sort, focuses his research and analysis on a relatively ignored, albeit provocative, aspect of early modern authorial construction: the memorializing "life of the poet." These narratives, according to Pask, "constitute one of the earliest forms of literary-historical writing in the European vernaculars" (3); as such, they offer valuable testimony in the emerging discourse on early modern authorship. One of the signal weaknesses of Pask's study is his failure to mention Greene, an author represented by not one but two texts that delineate the "life of the poet": *The Repentance of Robert Greene Maister of Artes* (1592) and "*Greene's* deare *Groatsworth*."[18]

A little over two weeks after his death in the early days of September 1592, "Greenes Groatsworth of wyt" was entered on the Register of the Company of Stationers. When the pamphlet was published shortly thereafter, late sixteenth-century readers were offered a sensational, quasi-autobiographical account of what was arguably for the period one of England's most popular writers. Indeed, not

16 *The Emergence of the English Author: Scripting the Life of the Poet in Early Modern England* (Cambridge: Cambridge University Press, 1996), p. 3.

17 On his theory of fields in relation to cultural artifacts, see Pierre Bourdieu, *Distinction: A Social Critique of the Judgement of Taste* (Cambridge: Harvard University Press, 1984), pp. 226–30; and *The Field of Cultural Production: Essays on Art and Literature* (New York: Columbia University Press, 1993).

18 On 20 September, just seventeen days after the accepted date of Greene's death, *Groats-Worth* was entered on the Stationers' Register (Arber 2.620); *Repentance* was entered a little over two weeks later, on 6 October (2.621). More has been written concerning "*Greene's* dear *Groatsworth*" than any of his other works, due largely to the "upstart crow" allusion in the letter to Greene's fellow playwrights, an illusion that most scholars accept as a reference to Shakespeare. Consequently, legions of biographers and critics have mined the allusion for what it may tell us about Shakespeare. The narrow focus on Shakespeare's status as an author of plays obfuscates the pamphlet's other concerns and contributes very little to our understanding of Greene's authorial renegotiation elsewhere in the pamphlet. To counterbalance the focus on Shakespeare, I purposely resist the other "authorship question" that currently occupies scholarly discussion on *Groatsworth*: Is it Greene's? Nashe's? Chettle's? A collaboration between some or all them? For the most sophisticated hypotheses regarding the problems of attribution, see D. Allen Carroll, ed., *Greene's Groatsworth of Wit: Bought with A Million of Repentance (1592)* (Binghampton, NY: Medieval and Renaissance Texts and Studies, 1994), pp. 1–22; and John Jowett, "Johannes Factotum: Henry Chettle and *Greene's Groatsworth of Wit*," *Publications of the Bibliographical Society of America* 87 (1993): 453–86.

only did "*Greenes* ..." grace the title pages of several prose works printed during his lifetime, but in the years following his death several publishers and writers capitalized on his name by attributing, often dubiously, their wares to Greene.[19] Despite a prolific and highly visible career as a writer of prose narratives, however, *Groats-Worth* presented to its readers a putatively more reputable "author." While there is scant mention of his prose pamphlets in this narrative, Roberto (Greene's thinly veiled pseudonym) becomes in the course of his life "famozed for an Arch-plaimaking-poet."[20] This claim challenges the reputation already achieved by Greene's prose works, one that evolved in the decade between the publications of *Mamillia* (1583) and *Groats-Worth*. Whereas much of Greene's writing in the 1580s centered on a variety of lyric and prose forms, by the decade's end he had begun to write for the public playhouses. The emphasis in *Groats-Worth* on playwriting belies what we know, and presumably what late sixteenth-century English readers might have known, about Greene's career as a writer. Because none of his plays appeared in print prior to 1594, Greene's reading public may have been puzzled by this emphasis.

Nevertheless, Greene's emphasis on playwriting in *Groats-Worth* ought to be taken as a signal moment in the renegotiation of his authorial status. As the quotation above suggests, *Groats-Worth* privileges "plaimaking" over Greene's other literary output. The pamphlet's narrator engages in a similar kind of privileging by structuring the relationship between the university-educated Roberto and his brother, Lucanio, in terms of playwright and player, respectively. Lucanio is compared to "a plaier that being out of his part at his first entrance, is faine to haue the booke to speak what he should performe" (C3r). To assist his brother in wooing a courtesan, Roberto-as-playwright supplies the diction his brother lacks. This structuring of the brothers' relationship foreshadows the pamphlet's most well known section: Greene's infamous diatribe against the players in the epistle to his fellow, university-trained playwrights. Greene contrasts Marlowe, Nashe, and Peele with the players, "those Puppets (I meane) that spake from our mouths" (F1v). Lamenting the strained relationship between playwrights and players, Greene remarks, "it is pittie men of such rare wits, should be subject to the pleasure of such rude groomes" (F2). Greene's complaint stems from the fact that he and his fellow university graduates must "subject" themselves to social inferiors. In the epistle, Greene claims that the players have "driuen [him] to extreme shifts" by reducing him to poverty (F1v). His

19 Based on extant editions, the earliest examples come from 1590: *Greenes Neuer Too Late* and *Greenes Mourning Garment*; *Greenes Farewell to Folly* was printed in 1591. Posthumously titled pamphlets include: *Greenes Vision* (1592), *Greenes Orpharion* (1599), *Greenes Carde of Fancie* (1608), and *Greenes Arcadia* (1610). Titles by other writers include *Greenes News from Both Heaven and Hell* (1593), *Greenes Funeralls* (1594), *Greene in Conceipt* (1598), and *Greenes Ghost Haunting Conie-Catchers* (1602).

20 *Greenes, Groats-Worth of Witte Bought with a Million of Repentance* (London, 1592), E1.

present condition contrasts with the expectation that lured Roberto to write plays in the first place. According to *Groats-Worth*'s narrator, Roberto embarked on his career as a playwright after his dismissal from the home of his younger brother. In his destitution, Roberto shares his woes with a seemingly well-to-do stranger whom he meets. The stranger, mistaken by Roberto for "a Gentleman of great liuing," reveals that he is in fact "a player" (D1v). The encounter marks a pivotal moment in Roberto's nascent career as a professional playwright, for the player subsequently proffers employment "greatly to his [i.e., Roberto's] benefite." Hence, an important incentive for Roberto's turn to playwriting is financial. The financial rewards of the Elizabethan playhouses may have lured Greene to write plays, too. According to Phoebe Sheavyn, "rewards [for playwrights] were considerably higher than those available in the printed-book market."[21] Consequently, if "professional playwrights ... took in more cash from their professional activities than was usual for writers" (Bentley 89), then we might understand more clearly Greene's turn toward the theater. However much it may have been maligned, playwriting may have appealed to Greene as a more lucrative mode of literary production. A playwriting career appears to hold out for Greene the potential to earn a "living" that is consonant with his status as a "Master of Arts," and as a gentleman. The player's promises of monetary rewards are never realized, however.

A similar account of Greene's turn to playwriting can be found in the other posthumously published "life of the poet": *The Repentance of Robert Greene*. In this work, too, Greene clearly distinguishes between his narrative prose and his dramatic poetry. He writes, "I left University and away to London, where [...] I became an Author of Playes, and a penner of Love Pamphlets."[22] The hierarchy implied by the paired dichotomies—"Author"/"penner" and "Playes"/"Pamphlets"—privileges his plays over his prose narratives. It is impossible to know whether in doing so Greene was being sarcastic, as Lori Humphrey Newcomb opines (26). Her assessment rests on the unsupported assumption that Greene despised writing for the stage, an assumption promulgated by Greene's biographers. In 1909, Thomas H. Dickinson asserted that "Greene had no pride in his work as a playwright."[23] More recently, Charles W. Crupi avers, "every indication is that Greene, like most other writers of his day, saw play scripts as paid labor, not literature."[24] Surely, writing plays for the public stage in order to earn his living may have been demeaning for someone who, because of his social position and title, considered the players beneath him. But contempt for socially inferior players does not indict the authorship of plays. On the

---

21 *The Literary Profession in the Elizabethan Age*, rev. J.W. Saunders, 2nd edn (Manchester: Manchester University Press; New York: Barnes, 1967), p. 95.

22 *The Repentance of Robert Greene Maister of Artes* (London, 1592), C1v.

23 Thomas H. Dickinson, ed., *Robert Greene*, The Mermaid Series (London: Unwin; New York: Scribner's, 1909), p. xxvii. Dickinson affirmed further that this was a general trait of Elizabethan dramatists, who "looked with shame on their writing for the stage" (xiv).

24 Charles W. Crupi, *Robert Greene* (Boston: Twayne, 1986), p. 20.

contrary, two factors militate against the reductive assessment of Greene's attitude to plays. First, although Greene treats players with contempt, he makes few sustained comments regarding the writing of plays; second, favorable contemporary allusions to Greene's status as an "Author of Playes" reinforce the claim's sincerity.

Whereas *Groats-Worth* reveals a great deal of information concerning Greene's perceptions of players, it gives only fleeting glimpses of his attitude toward the authorial production of plays. His earliest commentary on plays appears four years earlier in the prefatory letter to the gentlemen readers of *Perimedes the Blacke-Smith* (1588). In this work, Greene attempts to answer the accusation that, as he puts it, "I could not make my verses iet vpon the stage in tragicall buskins."[25] The so-called attack is actually a defense of his own foray, generally believed to be with *Alphonsus, King of Aragon*, into this rapidly evolving mode of literary production. The defense was directed not at the players but at his fellow playwrights. At issue for Greene is the public fact of his artistic failure vis-à-vis the public fact of the artistic success of fellow university graduates, notably Marlowe. Writing against "these phantasticall schollers," Greene "but answere[s] in print, what they haue offered on the Stage" (A3v). A famously self-advertised scholar himself (although, atypically, *Perimedes* does not advertise his authorship or his academic credentials on its title-page), Greene resorts to a prose pamphlet in order to answer critics of his play. Prose, he seems to imply, surpasses verse: "if there be anye in England that set the end of scollarisme in an English blanck verse, I thinke either it is the humor of a nouice that tickles them with selfe-loue, or to much frequenting the hot house [...] hath swet out all the greatest part of their wits" (A3r-v). *Perimedes* thus sounds a retreat from stage to page.

Late the following year, several of Greene's friends flocked to his side in the prefatory material to *Menaphon* (1589). In the (often oblique) allusions contained in a well-known letter to the gentlemen of both universities, Thomas Nashe belittled contemporary writers of tragedy: "English *Seneca* read by candle light yeeldes manie good sentences [...] I should say handfuls of tragical speeches."[26] Nashe appears more concerned with contemporary playwrights' choice of models than with the authorship of plays per se. The injunction to playwrights in the opening stanza of Thomas Brabine's commendatory poem is more succinct:

> Come foorth you witts that vaunt the pompe of speach,
> And striue to thunder from a Stage-mans throate:
> View *Menaphon* a note beyond your reach;
> Whose sight will make your drumming descant doate:
> Players auant, you know not to delight;
> Welcome sweete Shepheard, worth a Schollers sight. ([*3v])

---

25 *Perimedes the Blacke-Smith* (London, 1588), A3.
26 *Menaphon* (London, 1589), **3.

Brabine ends the stanza with a curt, dismissive line that seems to conflate players and playwrights. He then introduces Greene, the "sweete Shepheard," before moving on to his praise of *Menaphon*. Unlike the spoken, ephemeral performance of plays, the printed text of prose romance is "worth a Schollers sight." As in *Perimedes*, the discussion concerning the legitimacy of plays is couched in terms of a struggle between university graduates vying for cultural cachet. Greene and his friends assert his cultural presence by turning to what appears to be the more durable medium: print. With several artistic successes in this medium behind him, Greene seems to have known, like Jonson after him, when the printing press could further assertions pertaining to cultural legitimacy. It appears to have done so when he, like Jonson, was driven to defend his artistic failures; indeed, it has been suggested that Nashe's letter and Brabine's poem were "written to comfort [Greene] for failure" (Collins 1.41–42). Yet whereas Jonson printed plays like *Catiline*, Greene printed prose.

Whatever the precise reasons for the debate, Greene himself may have had good cause to engage in these critiques and to encourage them from his friends. While his circle of supporters attacked only certain kinds of dramatic writing, Greene continued to write for the public playhouses until his death. It has been argued, in fact, that Greene's work on what has become his most familiar play, *Frier Bacon, and Frier Bungay*, began as early as 1588.[27] His attitude toward playwriting comes to center on a pressing issue: patronage. In 1589, some time prior to the publication of *Menaphon*, Greene dedicated *Ciceronis Amor* to Ferdinando Stanley. Though the date is uncertain, his bid for Stanley's patronage may have been early in the year—perhaps shortly after 28 January, the date of Stanley's summons to Parliament as Lord Strange.[28] In seeking support from a well-to-do and potentially influential patron, Greene disguises neither his academic credentials nor his financial want: "Meane schollers haue hie thoughtes; though low fortunes," he writes in the pamphlet's "Epistle Dedicatorie."[29] Whatever his own motives for refusing patronage to Greene, Stanley's interests clearly lay elsewhere. In the same year as Greene's dedicatory epistle, Stanley chose to patronize one of the leading professional playing companies, christening them Lord Strange's Men. In his own lifetime, Greene could have seen several of his plays performed under Stanley's auspices. Between February and June 1592, performances of *Frier Bacon*, *Orlando Furioso*, and *A Looking Glasse for London and England* were recorded by Philip

---

27 Greene may have written parts of the play prior to Richard Tarlton's death in September, 1588. See Richard Levin's "Tarlton in *The Famous History of Friar Bacon* and *Friar Bacon and Friar Bungay*," *Medieval and Renaissance Drama in England* 12 (1999): 84–98.

28 E.K. Chambers, *The Elizabethan Stage*, 4 vols (1923; rpt. Oxford: Clarendon Press, 1961), 2.118.

29 *Ciceronis Amor: Tullies Love* (London, 1589), A2v.

Henslowe as having been acted by "my lord stranges mene."[30] Stanley's support of mere players must have been a considerable blow to Greene's sensibilities if not to his esteem. The failure to secure Stanley's patronage for himself may serve to account for the attacks printed in *Menaphon* later that year.

Stanley's patronage of a company of players and Greene's subsequent disappointment may have furthered the discourse on play authorship. For his part, Greene took up at greater length the issue of playwright-patronage the following year in *Francescos Fortunes*, which constituted the second part of *Greenes Neuer Too Late* (both published in 1590). The narrative in this two-part work contains thematic links to *Groats-Worth* and *The Repentance*. After expending his income on a courtesan, the university-educated Francesco turns to playwriting to earn his living: "he fell in amongst a companie of Players, who perswaded him to trie his wit in writing of Comedies, Tragedies, or Pastorals, and if he could performe any thing worth the stage, then they would largelie reward him for his paines."[31] Lured thus by the monetary incentive to write plays, Francesco "thought it no dishonor to make gaine of his wit, or to get profite by his pen: and therefore getting him home to his chamber writ a Comedie, which so generally pleased all the audience, that happie were those Actors in short time that could get any of his workes, he grewe so exquisite in that facultie" (B3v). This episode in Francesco's adventures provides his narrator with an opportunity to offer his opinion regarding the status of plays, and the current conditions structuring the relationship between players and playwrights. In doing so, he provides a brief overview of the social relations existing in the Roman theater, which he argues should be emulated and re-implemented: "so highlie were Comedies esteemed in those daies, that men of great honor and graue account were the Actors, the Senate and the Consuls continuallie present, as auditors of all such sports, rewarding the Author with rich rewards, according to the excellencie of the Comedie" (B4v). Kirk Melnikoff has argued that this arrangement would eschew "the economic gains of the market," the operating principle within the Elizabethan professional theater, in favor of "an amateur system of theatrical production."[32] Equally important were the anticipated authorial gains: if implemented, the new system would reward the "Author" for his "workes." Greene must have been fully aware of English protocols governing sixteenth-century playhouses and patronage. In accordance with the 1572 "Acte for the punishment of Vacabondes," only play companies—like Lord Strange's Men—were

30 *Henslowe's Diary*, eds R.A. Foakes and R.T. Rickert (Cambridge: Cambridge University Press, 1961), p. 16.

31 *Francescos Fortunes: Or the Second Part of Greenes Neuer Too Late* (London, 1590), B3v.

32 "'[P]aines to prie into my imagination': Robert Greene and Authorial Identity," (paper presented at the annual meeting of the Shakespeare Association of America, Minneapolis, MN, March 23, 2002), p. 3.

patronized by the nobility.[33] While this kind of patronage was merely nominal for the players, the kind Greene appears to espouse would entail "rich rewards" for the author of plays.

A system of patronage modeled on the practices of antiquity would also confer cultural legitimacy on playwriting and the playwright. In sum, the digression in *Francescos Fortunes* reads as though Greene wanted to intervene in and restructure the terms of patronage within the marketplace of plays. Had he been able to influence the existing social conditions of play-patronage, he may have inaugurated a substantial change in the status of English plays, conferring on them a cultural legitimacy hitherto unknown.

After reviewing some of the same details I have discussed above, Crupi sees little to suggest that "Greene took drama seriously" (20). To speak of Greene's *attitude* toward the status of plays is to homogenize a multifaceted record of *attitudes*—some of which belonged to Greene, some to his friends. If we accept Crupi's assessment of Greene's attitude toward plays, then we are left with a puzzling fact: "Before 1592 his contemporaries and friends are [...] silent about his work as a playwright."[34] From this point forward, allusions to Greene as a playwright or to his plays are commonplace. Why should the year 1592 mark a decided shift in the perception of Greene's authorial identity? I submit that Greene's renegotiation of his authorial status, with its beginnings in *Perimedes* and its culmination in *Groats-Worth* and *Repentance*, met with pronounced success.

Between the publication of these later pamphlets and the year's end, several contemporaries acknowledged this change in their allusions to Greene. By October 1592, Cuthbert Burbie, the publisher of *The Repentance*, addressed the pamphlet's gentlemen readers by reminding them that Greene's "pen in his life time pleased you as well on the Stage, as in the Stationers shops" (A2r). The sequence of elements in Burbie's phrasing subordinates his own profession as stationer to the stage. The order here replicates the locution within the pages of *The Repentance*: Greene was an "Author of Playes and a penner of Loue Pamphlets." Burbie's mention of Greene's authorship of plays instantiates an early awareness of the status that was beginning to accrue to this field of literary production. Indeed, allusions to his playwriting increased in the years after Greene's death. Seven years after the publication of *Menaphon*, Nashe called attention to and emphasized the cultural significance of the change in Greene's authorial status while remarking on his erstwhile collaborator's skill in plotting plays. Nashe, in fact, extols Greene as

---

33 See Andrew Gurr, *The Shakespearean Stage, 1574–1642*, 3rd edn (Cambridge: Cambridge University Press, 1992), p. 27.

34 Collins did not substantiate his assertion that Greene "never once in his voluminous prose writings refers, except in the two pieces just mentioned [i.e., *Repentance* and *Groats-Worth*], to the fact of his having written plays" (1.38). Because of the status of Collins's edition as the standard edition of Greene's plays, his views have likely had much to do with Greene's absence from discussions on play-authorship.

"his crafts master."[35] After his own death, Nashe appears as a character in playwright Thomas Dekker's *A Knights Conjuring* (1607), where Greene's ghost accompanies those of other deceased playwrights—Kyd, Marlowe, and Peele—in a discussion on the current conditions existing between players and playwrights. The pamphlet tantalizingly ends just after Nashe arrives, "inuey[ing] bitterly [...] against dry-fisted Patrons, accusing them of his vntimely death."[36] Nashe was apparently influenced by Greene's attempted reconfiguration of the patronage system, and still lamenting its operating conditions.

Even if the conventions governing the early modern system of player-patronage remained unchanged and playwright patronage remained out of reach for Greene and his immediate contemporaries and successors, the allusions above attest nonetheless to the import of Greene's authorial renegotiation. His status as an "Author of Playes" gained in cultural significance in other ways, too. Equally if not more important were the allusions that recalled the classical model for patronage Greene articulated in *Francescos Fortunes*. For Henry Chettle, in the readers' epistle to *Kind-Harts Dreame* (1592), written some three months after Greene's death, Greene was "the only Comedian of a vulgar writer in this country."[37] The term *comedian* implies in its classical derivation a degree of cultural prestige for those who previously had been perceived as mere playwrights. Thus, according to Chettle, Greene was a "vulgar"—that is, vernacular—Aristophanes or Menander, Plautus or Terence.

These and other comedic writers from antiquity form a further link between Greene and classical literature in the "Comparative Discourse" of Francis Meres's *Palladis Tamia* (1598). Meres, who does not so much compare as juxtapose classical and vulgar authors, includes Greene's name in a list of English poets who are "the best for Comedy amongst vs."[38] As Lukas Erne independently argues, Meres's text "poses a problem if we believe that playbooks had to await the publication of Jonson's *Workes* until anyone started taking them seriously as dramatic *literature*."[39] Explicitly linking Greene to a classical heritage was serious business. The implications of this culturally significant gesture were not lost on Gabriel Harvey, who regarded the comparison a few years earlier as something of a cultural crisis. In his extended, postmortem attack on Greene in *Foure Letters* (1592), Harvey believed, with good reason, that Greene was not only the most culturally mobile author of the period but also a serious threat to what was for Harvey legitimate literature. Anticipating by nearly two decades Fletcher's anxieties concerning "errant Pate[d]" consumers in the marketplace of print,

---

35 *Haue with You to Saffron-Walden* (London, 1596; rpt. Menston: Scolar Press, 1971), V3.

36 *A Knights Conjuring: Done in Earnest, Discouered in Jest* (London, 1607), L1.

37 *Kind-Harts Dreame* (London, [1592]), B3v.

38 *Palladis Tamia* (London, 1598; rpt. New York: Garland, 1973), 2O3v.

39 *Shakespeare as Literary Dramatist* (Cambridge: Cambridge University Press, 2003), p. 69.

Harvey argues that although Greene's works were replacing those of Greek and Roman authors, they were not equal to them:

> Howe vnlike *Tullies* sweete Offices: or *Isocrates* pithy instructions: or *Plutarches* holesome Morrals: or the dilicate Dialogues of *Xenophon*, and *Plato*: or the sage Tragedies of *Sophocles*, and *Euripides* or the fine Comedies of the daintiest Atticke wittes: or other excellent monumentes of anitiquity, neuer sufficientlie perused? yet the one as stale, as oldest fashions: and what more freshly current for a while, then the other? Euen *Guicciardines* siluer Historie, and *Ariostos* golden Cantoes, grow out of request & the Countesse of Pembrookes Arcadia is not greene inough for queasie stomackes, but they must haue *Greenes* Arcadia: and I beleeue, most eagerlie longed for *Greenes* Faerie Queene. O straunge fancies: o monstrous newfanglenesse.[40]

Harvey, whom Nashe labeled "a forestaller of the market of fame," brazenly voices his anxiety over the market success of "*Greenes* Arcadia," which can be clearly identified as *Menaphon*.[41] Although he is fairly explicit about this text, Harvey's rhetoric betrays a concern for the cultural mobility of Greene's other works as well.

Specifically, embedded in Harvey's attack is an oblique acknowledgement of crisis centering on Greene's playwriting. On the pamphlet's preceding page, Harvey perceptively notes the discursive shift that had taken place regarding Greene's authorial identity. As a consequence, he criticizes what he refers to as Greene's "phantasticall interluding" (B2v). Used here in a pejorative sense, the term *interlude* was likely chosen to diminish the significance of Greene's comedies. Harvey jeeringly suggests later that, with Greene's death, "Phantasticality [will have to seek] for a new Autor" (D2).[42] Harvey sustains this

---

40 *Foure Letters, and Certaine Sonnets* (London, 1592; rpt. Menston: Scolar Press, 1969), D2v.

41 Nashe, *Strange Newes* (London, 1592; rpt. Menston: Scolar Press, 1969), B2. In her brief discussion on the Harvey passage, Newcomb treats the allusion to "*Greenes* Arcadia" as a reference to *Pandosto* (31). Based on the evidence of surviving editions to 1592, there is some reason to believe *Pandosto* was the more popular narrative, but apart from counting the number of editions, there is considerable evidence that Harvey alludes to *Menaphon*. Not only does Nashe, in his prefatory epistle to *Menaphon*, refer to the work as Greene's "*Arcadian Menaphon*" (**1v), the text begins with the following heading: "*Arcadia*. The reports of the Shepheards" (B1). Moreover, *Menaphon* was anthologized far more frequently than *Pandosto*. Several of *Menaphon*'s poems were printed in both *Englands Helicon* (1600) and *Englands Parnassus* (1600). Charles Crawford, in "*Belvedere, Or the Garden of the Muses,*" *Englische Studien* 43 (1910–11): 198–228, located forty-one passages from Greene's works in *Belvedere* (1600): "Thirteen from *Menaphon*; ten from *Never too Late*; nine from *Alcida*; seven from *Penelope's Web*; and two from *Alphonsus*. Of the *Menaphon* passages, ten are prose, made to resemble verse" (204–5). Harvey more likely refers to the more popular *Menaphon*.

42 If we are to trust Harvey's dating in *Foure Letters*, his underhanded affirmation of Greene's authorial identity preceded the claims to authorial status in both *Groats-Worth* and

attention to playwriting through to the passage cited above, where he names classical tragedians—Sophocles and Euripides—and refers to "the fine Comedies of the daintiest Atticke wittes." The omission of the comic authors' names might simply reflect commonplace notions about the hierarchy structuring literary genres, a hierarchy that placed tragedy above comedy. At the same time, though, Harvey's omission neglects Greene's classical predecessors. In *Francescos Fortunes*, Greene reverses this hierarchy by elevating comedy over tragedy. We recall that Francesco is given the option to write "Comedies, Tragedies, or Pastorals." When he returns to his chamber, Francesco chooses to write a *comedy*.

Greene's inversion of generic hierarchy becomes more pronounced in the subsequent digression on plays and playwrights, the exclusive focus of which is the "inuention of Comedies" and the genre's principle authorities: Menander, Plautus and Terence (B4–B4v). In their differing rhetorical strategies to control the field of cultural production, Greene and Harvey offer clear evidence of "social struggles" that center on play-authorship and the cultural legitimation a classical heritage entails. Harvey may have had good reason to refrain from calling too much attention to comedy. According to Nashe, in his rejoinder to Harvey's attack on Greene, "about twelue yeeres ago [Harvey] bepist his credite with *Three proper and wittie familiar letters*" (*Newes*, B1v). In one of those letters, Harvey encouraged "the new poet" of *The Shepheardes Calender* to write comedies. Richard Helgerson explains the context for Harvey's advice: "it was with the express purpose of getting Spenser to shift his efforts from *The Faerie Queene* to his nine comedies that Harvey addressed his friend." Harvey appears to have taken stock of the prestige within humanist circles that was accruing to comedic works. As Helgerson suggests, "comedy, with its laudable aim of reforming manners and morals, might in humanist eyes seem the appropriate labor of a great poet."[43] Despite Harvey's advice, Spenser may not have been up to this task, but Greene was.

Neither Spenser's comedies nor "*Greenes* Faerie Queene" survives. Yet as this strained chiasmus suggests, lurking between the above-quoted lines of Harvey's attack is an anguished acknowledgement of Greene's cultural mobility. If he had not died, Harvey implies, the market's "queasie stomackes" would have elicited from Greene an epic poem or a work of comparable cultural significance. Indeed, signs that Greene was already encroaching on this cultural domain are embedded in Harvey's attack. Harvey acknowledges both a decline in the demand for "*Ariostos* golden Cantoes"—that is, Lodovico Ariosto's *Orlando Furioso*, Spenser's principle model for *The Faerie Queene*—and the ascent of Greene's *Orlando Furioso*. In writing a play based on an Italian epic, Greene appears to have heeded Harvey's earlier advice to Spenser. The reference to "*Greenes* Faerie

Repentance. However, Harvey's pamphlet was not entered on the Stationers' Register until 4 December 1592 (Arber 2.623), nearly two months after *Repentance*.

43 *Self-Crowned Laureates: Spenser, Jonson, Milton and the Literary System* (Berkeley: University of California Press, 1983), p. 149.

Queene" echoes Harvey's lament for "*Ariostos* golden Cantoes": had Greene lived he may have done to Spenser what he did to Ariosto.

Greene takes considerable poetic license in adapting Ariosto's romance-epic for the stage. Nevertheless, he adheres in some places more closely to Ariosto's Italian than does Sir John Harington in his 1591 translation of the poem into English (Collins 1.217).[44] Greene inserts portions of two stanzas directly from Ariosto's poem into Orlando's diatribe against women. The spliced together Italian stanzas do not concern me here, but Greene's bonus translation of them into English does. In his jealous frenzy, Orlando rants in a familiar, misogynist strain:

> Discurteous women natures fairest ill,
> The woe of man, that first createst curse,
> Base female sexe, sprung from blacke *Ates* loynes,
> Proude, disdainefull, cruell, and vnuist,
> Whose words are shaded with inchaunting wiles,
> Worse then *Medusa*, mateth all our mindes,
> And in their hearts sits shamelesse trecherie,
> Turning a truthlesse vile circumference,
> O could my fury paint their furies forth,
> For hell, no hell compared to their hearts,
> Too simple diuelles, to conceiue their arts :
> Borne to be plagues vnto the thoughts of men,
> Brought for eternall pestilence to the worlde. *R Greene.*[45]

I quote these lines, not from an edition of Greene's play, but from *Englands Parnassus* (1600), one of the earliest printed collections to include "the choysest Flowers of our Moderne Poets." By doing so I want to divert attention both from the lines themselves and from their context in the play in order to focus on the cultural significance of their inclusion in the anthology.

Robert Allot, the anthology's compiler, adds a considerable layer to "the sedimentary record of social struggles" over Greene's authorial identity. By quoting

---

44 Harington appears to have rankled at Greene's presumption in adapting Ariosto's poem for the stage. In a list of play-texts in his possession, Harington pejoratively termed Greene's play "Orlando foolioso" (Greg, *Bibliography* 3.1311). A version of Greene's play was performed at the Rose in February 1592, but Henslowe does not mention the play again (16). It is mentioned later that year in *The Defence of Conny Catching* (London, 1592), a half-hearted critique of Greene's cony-catching pamphlets. The pseudonymous "penner" of the pamphlet (possibly Greene himself) enjoins Greene to "aske the Queens Players, if you sold them not *Orlando Furioso* for twenty Nobles, and when they were in the country, sold the same Play to the Lord Admirals men for as much more" (C3–C3v). Greene was clearly identified as this play's author well in advance of its publication in print.

45 Robert Allot, comp., *Englands Parnassus: Or the Choysest Flowers of Our Moderne Poets* (London, 1600; rpt. Amsterdam: Theatrum Orbis Terrarum; New York: Da Capo Press, 1970), X6.

this passage from *Orlando Furioso*, Allot makes several bold moves. In ascribing *these* lines to "*R Greene*," Allot performs an essential function in "precise" authorial attribution—what Masten refers to as "the urgency of knowing the lineage of plays and parts of plays." Tracing "the emerging regime of the author" to developments in the latter half of the seventeenth century, Masten argues that it was then that the modern concept of the author "was brought into being" (369). That "urgency," Masten implies, was something entirely new. Yet evidence from *Englands Parnassus* indicates that fragments from literary works, including plays, were attributed to individual authors much earlier than Masten would have us believe. Prior to the publication of Allot's anthology, neither of the two printed editions of *Orlando Furioso* (in 1594 and 1599) had indicated the play's authorship. Allot provides that information, as he does for other passages he culls from this play and other works attributed to "*R Greene*." Appropriating the lines from their original context in Greene's play (Orlando has clearly gone mad before speaking them), Allot asserts his control over the way in which "*R Greene*" is packaged and consumed. In quoting these lines, Allot accords Greene the status of an authority on a specific topic: the lines above appear beneath the rubric "Women" (X3v), a category that includes passages from the darlings, in Harvey's estimation, of Elizabethan literature: Sir Philip Sidney, Harington, and Spenser. By including "*R Greene*" in an anthology where he is cited alongside these and other English writers, Allot asserts another level of control. As a consequence of this inclusion, Allot ensures Greene's authorial identity: the quotation simultaneously canonizes Greene as an authority on women and a "Moderne Poet," an author of English literature. More importantly, because the passage comes from *Orlando Furioso*, Allot attests to the fact that plays had been elevated to such a degree as to form an integral part of at least one contemporary's conception of English literature. Working independently from the evidence of literary anthologies such as Allot's *Englands Parnassus*, Erne also recognizes "that dramatic texts were on the way to becoming part of the English literary canon well before Jonson and Shakespeare's plays were published in prestigious folio editions" (75). Indeed, of the thirty passages ascribed to "*R Greene*" in *Englands Parnassus*, roughly two-thirds are taken from his plays.[46] Allot's anthology not only confirms the cultural elevation of plays by 1600, it recognizes and rewards Greene's considerable contribution to the discourse on play-authorship.

The foregoing allusions to Greene and quotations of his works suggest that if no edition of his plays survived, there would remain several testimonials

---

46 Allot ascribes thirty-three passages to Greene, but it has long been known that Allot's attributions are occasionally wrong; indeed, Collins noted that he was "a most misleading guide" (1.59). See Charles Crawford, ed., *Englands Parnassus: Compiled by Robert Allot, 1600* (Oxford: Clarendon Press, 1913). Crawford located three of the thirty-three passages attributed to Greene in Spenser; he also located three passages in Greene that Allot attributed to other writers (542–44). One of the *Orlando Furioso* quotations, a single line, is attributed to George Peele (170).

acknowledging his status as an "Author of Playes": allusions by friends and enemies, as well as quotations by compilers of anthologies. Such a record may have been familiar to a university-educated writer like Greene. If there was anything classical literature had to teach scholar-poets like Greene it was that authorial identity was not predicated on the survival of a given author's texts. On the contrary, while many names of authors from antiquity survive, most of their works do not. The juxtaposition in Meres's "Comparative Discourse" of contemporary English playwrights, like Robert Greene, and classical dramatists includes some of those names: "Eupolis Atheniensis, Alexis Terius, Nicostratus, Amipsias Atheniensis, Anaxandrides Rhodius, Aristonymus, Archippus Atheniensis and Callias Atheniensis; and among the Latines, [...] Naeuius, Sext. Turpilius, Licinius Imbrex, and Virgilius Romanus" (203–203v).[47] If the survival of works from antiquity was not a prerequisite for achieving authorial identity, then the survival of his plays may not have concerned Greene.

In the liminal space between their ephemeral production on stage and their enduring production on the page, Greene articulated the cultural legitimacy of plays by invoking a classical model of author-patronage. Seeing the possibility of renegotiating his own authorial identity, Greene turned to the prose pamphlet in order to exploit further his cultural mobility. This generic medium allowed him to assert his cultural status as "an arch-plaimaking poet," an "Author of Playes." Yet his authorial identity was also negotiated within an emergent literary marketplace that was determined not only by the producers and consumers of the early modern stage and page but also by the differing cultural tastes of men like Harvey and Fletcher, Nashe and Chettle. The effects of that renegotiation are clearly discernable in Jonson, a Janus-like figure who looked backward to a time of patronage and forward to a print culture that ultimately bestowed on authors proprietary ownership of their works. In his dedicatory epistle to William, Earl of Pembroke, Jonson writes, "[*Catiline*] is the first (of this race) that euer I dedicated to any Person" (*Catiline* A2v; Jonson, *Plays* 3.359). In his "quick look through the published plays of Jonson's most prominent contemporaries" (including, at the head of the list, Greene), Helgerson notes, "the dedication of *Cataline* [sic] was a new departure not only for Jonson, but also for the playwrights generally" (167–8). Helgerson's cursory glance at "published plays" suggests both the bias in the bibliographic *ergo* and the extent to which Greene's contribution to the discourse on the cultural elevation of plays and playwrights has been forgotten. While the fact of the dedication itself may have been new, it is still rather difficult to imagine Jonson's bid for play-patronage without Greene or his "deare *Groatsworth*."

---

47 These classical authors were listed as well in Edward Phillips's comparison of ancients to moderns in *Theatrum Poetarum, or a Compleat Collection of the Poets* (London, 1675; rpt. Hildesheim, NY: Olms, 1970). Phillips, who constructs comparable lists for modern—principally English—poets, lists Greene (2G9–2G9v) alongside contemporaries like Jonson (2A10–2A10v).

Chapter 6

Forming Greene: Theorizing the Early Modern Author in the *Groatsworth of Wit*

Steve Mentz

> What matter who's speaking, someone said what matter who's speaking ... I'll be there, I won't miss it, it won't be me, I'll be here, I'll say I'm far from here, it won't be me, I won't say anything, there's going to be a story, someone's going to try to tell a story.
>
> Samuel Beckett, *Texts for Nothing*[1]

The publication of *Greenes, Groats-worth of witte, bought with a million of Repentance* (London: William Wright, 1592) was a literary scandal that produced one of the most oft-quoted passages in Elizabethan literature. Scholars of Shakespearean drama, whose interests have largely driven discussions of this text, repeatedly quote the book's ambiguous but suggestive attack on a certain "upstart Crow." Beyond questions of Shakespeare's biography, however, *Groatsworth* occupies an important place in the history of early modern print culture. It was one of many books published in or after late 1592 that document Elizabethan literary culture's fascination with the dissolute death of Robert Greene, the most popular and prolific writer of Elizabethan printed fiction. Three separate titles—*Groatsworth*, *The Repentance of Robert Greene*, and *Greenes Vision*—were published in the final months of 1592, each one claiming to represent Greene's final words.[2] The notorious *Groatsworth*, a loose collection that includes a prodigal tale, several novelle, and the famous letter to Greene's fellow dramatists, has long been deemed incoherent and fragmentary, possibly a forgery, or at best an unacknowledged collaboration. This dismissal of the book misreads its structural coherence and range, and also inappropriately judges it as sincere autobiography when it is better read as metaliterary commentary. When the text is considered a summatory response to Greene's twelve-year career in print—what the publisher

1 Samuel Beckett, *Stories & Texts for Nothing* (New York: Grove Press, 1967), p. 85.

2 Each of these books presents different authenticity problems. I discuss *Groatsworth*'s below. I omit discussion of the *Repentance* and note that *Greenes Vision* was almost certainly written around 1590 and expeditiously issued immediately after Greene's death. See Charles W. Crupi, *Robert Greene* (Boston: Twayne, 1986), p. 34–5.

William Wright in a prefatory letter calls "a period to his pen"—its supposed incoherence becomes less a matter of authorial incompetence than a drastic attempt to unify a multifaceted career.[3] The book is better read neither as autobiographical fiction nor as canny forgery, but as a practical form of literary criticism, a pioneering investigation into what we now call the "author function."

The author this text constructs is both collaborative and name-driven, and the "Greene" constructed is both a public persona and a recognizable individual. In 1592 Greene was a public symbol for published prose fiction; he, along with his sometime protégé Thomas Nashe, had already begun in a public polemic against early modern theater companies (which the letter to the dramatists extends); and this deathbed text elaborates a contested metaphor for how prose fiction authorship positioned itself in rivalry with drama and in relationship to existing conventions of the writing life.[4] The book's "Greene" represents many things—a dying author, an impostor, a marketable commodity in the late Elizabethan book market—but above all he is the early modern prose author as English literary culture imagined him in 1592. This author, pace Foucault, may be conceived of as the principle of profit in the proliferation of print, with "profit" taken in its full range of possible meanings, from humanist moral improvement to the exchange of goods and money in bookstalls at St. Paul's.[5] The portrait of print authorship under construction gives historical specificity to our evolving understanding of literary authorship in early modern England.

---

3 Robert Greene, *Greenes Groatsworth of Wit, Bought with a Million of Repentance (1592)*, D. Allen Carroll, ed. (Binghampton, NY: Medieval and Renaissance Texts & Studies, 1994), p. 41. All further citations to *Groatsworth* and Carroll's introduction taken from this edition. While I depart somewhat from Carroll's conclusions about authorship, I cite his careful and thorough edition as the best and most widely available edition of *Groatsworth*. He bases his edition on the 1592 quarto now in the Folger library. See Carroll, ed., pp. 33–6, for a survey of early modern and modern editions.

4 For the running polemic against drama, see Greene's *Perimedes the Blacke-Smith* (1588), Nashe's *Anatomy of Absurdity* (1590), and Nashe's preface to Greene's *Menaphon* (1589). In a prefatory letter to *Perimedes*, Greene attacks as his rivals "two Gentlemen Poets . . . [who] had it in derision, for that I could not make my verses iet vpon the stage in tragicall buskins, euerie worde filling the mouth like the farburden of Bo-Bell, daring God out of heauen with that Atheist *Tamburlan*" (A3). Nashe similarly attacks the stage, and probably Marlowe, in his preface to *Menaphon*: "I am not ignorant how eloquent our gowned age is grown of late, so that every mechanical mate abhors the English he was born to, and plucks, with a solemn periphrasis, his *ut vales* from the inkhorn, which I impute not so much to the perfection of arts as to the servile imitation of vanglorious tragedians … ." (Robert Greene, *Menaphon*, Brenda Cantar, ed. [Ottawa: Dovehouse Editions, 1996], p. 81).

5 The quotation from Foucault to which I allude reads, "The author is the principle of thrift in the proliferation of meaning ... . The author is therefore the ideological figure by which one marks the manner in which we fear the proliferation of meaning" ("What is an Author?", *The Foucault Reader*, Paul Rabinow, trans. [New York: Pantheon, 1984] pp. 101–20, 118–19).

Scholars of early modern prose fiction have for some time recognized that while the case of the young Shakespeare draws attention to *Groatsworth*, the letter to the dramatists is but one of many perplexing components that make up this text. The text's references to player-patrons, University Wits, prodigal sons, and its possibly topical beast fable make it an enticing target for students of late Elizabethan literary culture.[6] It announces a watershed event in Elizabethan letters: the death of Robert Greene touched off, in Thomas Nashe's phrase, "a coil ... with pamphleting on him after his death," including the long-running Nashe-Harvey controversy.[7] After a twelve-year career as playwright, university wit, and the most prolific and popular writer of prose fiction in early modern England, Greene died impoverished but flamboyant, after what his enemy Gabriel Harvey described as a "fatall banquett ... [of a] surfett of pickle herring and rennish wine."[8] This book purported to be, as Greene says in a letter prefacing *Groatsworth*, "the last I have writ, and I feare me the last I shall write" (42).

One conundrum about the book can be stated succinctly: we don't know who wrote it. When modern critics or bibliographers list Greene as the author, they assume what we cannot prove: that this text has a single author, and that this author is the one named in the title. I do believe that Greene wrote at least some of the text, but as I discuss below, we cannot determine exactly what. (My reading of *Groatsworth* attempts to turn this lack of precise knowledge into an analytical opportunity.) In strict bibliographical terms, the identity of the text's author, named "Greene" in the title, cannot be certain: Nashe was proposed with enough credibility that he denied it in the second edition of *Pierce Penniless* (1594), and Henry Chettle, the purported editor of Greene's deathbed papers, has been proposed as at least coauthor by the text's modern editor, D. Allen Carroll, and, in a series of influential articles, by John Jowett.[9] With attribution studies undergoing a revolution in methodology and new work on collaboration and anonymity revising accepted notions of authorship, the case of *Groatsworth* now seems particularly fraught.[10] The extant evidence suggests that the *Groatsworth* is better

6 Carroll argues that the beast fable is a veiled attack on Lord Burleigh, following Spenser's "Mother Hubbard's Tale" (107–13).

7 Thomas Nashe, *Pierce Penniless his Supplication to the Devil*, prefatory letter to the 2nd edn, *The Unfortunate Traveler and Other Works*, J.B. Steane, ed. (Harmondsworth: Penguin, 1971), p. 49.

8 Gabriel Harvey, *Foure Letters*, G.B. Harrison, ed. (London: Bodley Head, 1922) p. 13.

9 I cite Carroll's edition throughout this article, and I shall also cite Jowett's major study of *Groatsworth:* "Johannes Factotum: Henry Chettle and *Greene's Groatsworth of Wit*," *Publications of the Bibliographical Society of America* 87.4 (1993): 453–86.

10 For a recent summary of the state of attribution studies, see Harold Love, *Attributing Authorship: An Introduction* (Cambridge: Cambridge University Press, 2002). For recent work on collaboration, see, for example, Jeffrey Masten, *Textual Intercourse* (Cambridge: Cambridge University Press, 1997), and Brian Vickers, *Shakespeare,*

read as an unusual form of collaboration than a single-author book or a forgery. While work on collaborative authorship has recently renovated our understanding of early modern dramatic authorship, studies of prose fiction authorship have lagged in this area. The case of *Groatsworth* does not fit existing models of collaboration any more than our standard models of single authorship. The text is not clearly the product of an idealized comradeship like that of Beaumont and Fletcher, nor is it the result of a master (say Shakespeare) reworking an inferior text (say Twine's *Patterne of Painefull Adventures*, or a lost Ur-Hamlet), nor is it the result of the piecemeal labor we see in the various hands in *The Booke of Sir Thomas More*. Rather, this collaboration operates between a living author who claims to be merely an editor (Chettle) and a dead author whose role cannot be firmly fixed. At stake is not just the historical accuracy of saying that the text is or is not "Greene's"; we also need to determine what the consequences of reading the text as a destabilized collaboration are for early modern studies.[11] It facilitates an historicized response to Foucault's influential debunking of authorship; in the case of early modern print culture, it matters very much who's speaking, or at least who's supposed to be speaking.[12] The obsessive efforts of readers and critics to determine who's speaking in the *Groatsworth* reveal the controlling logic of modern and early modern understandings of authorship that it is naïve to think we can ignore.

To summarize the possible authors of this hybrid text, we can begin with the simplest possibility: that the Greene of the title is, in fact, the author, and that the text really was, as Chettle claims, part of the "many papers in sundry Booke sellers

---

Co-Author: A Historical Study of Five Collaborative Plays (Oxford: Oxford University Press, 2004). For an excellent study of anonymity in early modern literary culture, see Marcy North, *The Anonymous Renaissance: Cultures of Discretion in Tudor-Stuart England* (Chicago: University of Chicago Press, 2004).

11 Jowett claims that taking Chettle as the primary author may have a liberating affect: "[T]he fact remains that reassigning the authorship of the *Groatsworth* cannot avoid opening up new ways of reading it" ("Johannes Factotum," 485).

12 The "death of the author," announced by Barthes and Foucault in the 1970s, has met with increasing resistance since the mid-1990s. See, for example, Seán Burke, *The Death and Return of the Author: Criticism and Subjectivity in Barthes, Foucault, and Derrida*, 2nd edn (Edinburgh: Edinburgh University Press, 1998), 1st edn, 1992; Jorge Gracia, *A Theory of Textuality: The Logic and Epistemology* (Albany: State University of New York Press, 1995) and *Texts: Ontological Status, Identity, Author, Audience* (Albany: State University of New York Press, 1996); Adrian Wilson, "Foucault on the 'Question of the Author': A Critical Exegesis," *Modern Language Review* 99.2 (April 2004): 339–63. Lucas Erne's *Shakespeare as Literary Dramatist* (Cambridge: Cambridge University Press, 2004) has more recently sparked the reconsideration of early modern authorial practices.

hands" after Greene's death.[13] Even in this simplest case, however, we have to reckon with Chettle's admitted editorial hand: He admits to having made a fair copy, "as sometime *Greenes* hand was none of the best," and he also claims that he "stroke out what then in conscience I thought he in some displeasure writ: or had it been true, yet to publish it, was intollerable" (6). (The omitted details are usually taken to include a reference to Marlowe's homosexuality; his atheism remains in the letter.) Thus the Greene-as-author hypothesis shades into a second possibility, that the text is at least partly Chettle's, perhaps working from Greene's notes or, failing that, from his idea of what Greene sounded like.[14] A third possibility is deliberate forgery. Chettle admits elsewhere that he misattributed to Nashe another preface that he wrote in the summer of 1592 (for Anthony Munday's *Gerileon*); Carroll sees a pattern here.[15] Beyond these three possibilities—which are best thought of as comprising a continuum, with authenticity and forgery as extreme cases, and various forms of collaboration filling out the middle—there remain at least two other conceptual options. One is that the "Greene" of this text be read as a literary character, the product of Greene's own bibliography plus his notorious life, assembled to be as convincing as Chettle could make it.[16] Finally, my suggestion that the *Groatsworth*'s Greene should be read as the then-current idea of the marketplace author, a "principle of proliferation in the circulation of print," asserts that, while its exact attribution may be unrecoverable, the value of this text for early modern studies is its picture of early modern authorship. We have a "Greene" named in the title, and that figure dramatically intrudes on the story when the main narrative itself ruptures: "Heere (Gentlemen) breake I off *Robertos* speech; whose life in most parts agreeing with mine, found one selfe punishment as I have doone. Heereafter suppose me the saide *Roberto*, and I will goe on with that hee promised: *Greene* will send you now his groats-worth of wit" (75). The

13 Henry Chettle, *Kind-Hearts's Dream*, G.B. Harrison, ed. (London: Bodley Head, 1923), p. 5. This text, which contains Chettle's defense of Greene's authorship, was entered on 8 December 1592; the *Groatsworth* had been entered on 20 September. See Carroll, pp. 1–2.

14 Jowett thinks Chettle is the author, but he admits that much of the *Groatsworth* sounds like Greene "in his Nashean manner" ("Johannes Factotum," 476).

15 Chettle admits that he wrote the epistle, which appears over the initials "T.N.," but he claims these initials were set "by the workemans error" (*Kind-Heart's Dream*, 7). See Carrol 3.

16 This position, rather than the simple claim of forgery, seems to be Jowett's final stance on the text: "The work will demand a complex response that will take Greene not simply as another writer's representation of Greene, but as a figure offered to the reader as Greene's representation of himself" ("Johannes Factotum," 485). This line of reading resonates with a powerful strain in Greene criticism that sees him treating himself as a literary character, especially in the repentance tracts but also throughout his career in his front matter. For an influential statement of this thesis, see W.W. Barker, "Rhetorical Romance: The 'Frivolous Toyes' of Robert Greene," *Unfolded Tales: Essays on Renaissance Romance*, George M. Logan and Gordon Tesky, eds (Ithaca: Cornell University Press, 1989): 74–97.

text seems intensely aware of its authorial instability, and it claims that the disjunction between Roberto and Greene matters less than the value, monetary and moral, of the offered repentance. According to the book, it matters little whether Roberto is Greene or Greene's creation; the reader is invited to "suppose" (not absolutely believe) them equivalent. I take this to be a literary critical move of some sophistication; for a text that, as Alexandra Halasz has demonstrated, "locates its value in the marketplace and identifies it with the practice of usury," to claim further that its authorial identity matters less than its economic value forces the reader's focus away from Greene toward the groat, and away from the conundra of attribution toward a richer sense of what authors were becoming in Elizabethan print culture.[17] As I shall show, this text also includes a detailed structural summary of Greene's career in print, and an intellectual portrait of a struggling, ambitious author which reveals leading changes in Elizabethan literary culture.

Beautified Feathers

While part of my intent is to demonstrate that *Groatsworth* reveals at least as much about early modern print authorship as about dramatic culture, I shall begin with the book's most famous lines, those attacking Shakespeare. My point is not to reinforce the primacy of the Bard, but rather to expose how this familiar passage contains veiled reference to the print-drama rivalry that has largely gone unmarked. The passage, quoted in virtually every general introduction to Shakespeare, reads:

> [T]here is an upstart Crow, beautified with our feathers, that with his *Tygers hart wrapt in a Players hyde*, supposes he is as well able to bombast out a blanke verse as the best of you: and beeing an absolute *Johannes fact totum*, is in his owne conceit the onely Shake-scene in a countrey. (84–5)

While the play on Shakespeare's name (to which he would reply much later, *sotto voce*)[18] demonstrates that the letter addresses the not-yet-famous dramatist, the precise nature of the attack has long been in doubt. At issue is the identity of the upstart crow and the meaning of the "beautified feathers" that he appropriates: is this Aesop's crow, a mimic and thus implicitly an actor, or Horace's (from the third Epistle), a plagiarist and literary thief?[19] The history of this controversy, from

---

17 See Alexandra Halasz, *The Marketplace of Print: Pamphlets and the Public Sphere in Early Modern England* (Cambridge: Cambridge University Press, 1997), p. 35.

18 I discuss how Shakespeare uses the word "green" as part of a running commentary on Greene's career in "Wearing Greene: Autolycus, Robert Greene, and the Structure of Romance in *The Winter's Tale*," *Renaissance Drama* 30 (1999–2001): 73–92.

19 On the classical references, see Peter Berek, "The 'Upstart Crow,' Aesops Crow, and Shakespeare as a Reviser," *Shakespeare Quarterly* 35.2 (Summer 1984): 205–7; and

Edmund Malone's eighteenth-century assertion that Shakespeare began his career revising Greene's plays to the mid-twentieth century quarrel in which Peter Alexander crossed swords with John Dover Wilson, has been amply documented by the Shakespeare industry.[20] What seldom gets noticed about the debate between actors and plagiarists is how closely this distinction parallels the disjunction between the two modes of literary production that Greene and Shakespeare practiced: theater and print. If we can reasonably assume that both Aesop and Horace were known to Greene and Chettle—Carroll follows Wilson in claiming that Aesop's crow and Horace's were considered one composite image by early modern readers[21]—we can find in this familiar quotation a reiteration of the attack on "those Gentlemen his Quondom acquaintance, that spend their wits in making plaies" (80). The letter thus becomes part of Greene's long-running attack on his own playwriting career, and Shakespeare (not yet a "man in print" in 1592) becomes a foil for Greene and his peers who split their time between print and the theater.[22]

If the upstart crow is Aesop's, then the accusation is of mimicry and also of social opportunism: "Now the jackdaw [crow], realizing his own ugliness, went around gathering up the feathers which fell from the other birds, which he then arranged and attached to his own body. Thus he became the most handsome of all."[23] This image gave rise to Malone's thesis that Shakespeare began his career as a reviser of other playwrights' work, including Greene's.[24] Read from the point of

---

David Chandler, "'Upstart Crow': Provenance and Meaning" *Notes & Queries* 42.3 (September 1995): 291–4. Chandler cites the history of the controversy from Malone and John Dover Wilson forward. Thomas Merriam, in "Groatsworth's Added Value," *Notes & Queries* 43.2 (1996): 145–9, further notes that the image of the crow is made up of "virtually stock phrases from a pool of Greene-Nashe associations" (148), but that the misquotation of *3 Henry 6* identifies Shakespeare as the target.

20 A thorough exploration of responses to this passage appears in Carroll, Appendix G, 131–45.

21 Carroll cites Wilson and J.A.K. Thomson on this point, and notes that Wilson found evidence that a word of Horace's ("*cornicula*") sometimes replaced Aesop's "*cornix*" in early modern editions of Aesop (135).

22 Carroll reads the letter in slightly different terms: "The charge against Shakespeare ought to be seen as part of an ongoing conflict: first, between the University Wits (Greene, Nashe, Peele, and others) and actors, and second, between the Wits and the new, uneducated professional playwrights (Shakespeare, Munday, Kyd, and others)" (141). I concur that the letter participates in several ongoing struggles, and certainly do not deny either of the rivalries Carroll here identifies, but I also see a clear contrast being drawn between drama and print. That Greene himself (like Nashe) wrote drama as well as printed fiction makes his position somewhat self-critical, but that was not an uncommon position for Greene.

23 Aesop, *The Complete Fables*, Olivia and Robert Temple, trans., Robert Temple (London: Penguin, 1998), p. 119.

24 See S. Schoenbaum, *Shakespeare's Lives*, 2nd edn (Oxford: Oxford University Press, 1991), pp. 121–2. Schoenbaum's confident assertion that "the *Contention* and the

view of an author who was attempting to define himself outside of the theater, however, this accusation conveniently places Shakespeare as aspiring to the position that Greene (and/or Chettle and Nashe) intends to vacate. The crow's "feathers" are theatrical bombast—precisely what Greene rejects in the preface to *Perimedes*—not the purportedly more solid stuff of print.

Treating the text as an allusion to Horace, by contrast, emphasizes the role of the literary text as authorial property and artistic creation. In this view, rhetorical "feathers" are the tools of the literary trade. In his third Epistle, Horace provides two cautionary images of writers as thieves:

> What about Titius? He'll soon be the talk of the town
> Because he didn't turn pale at the notion of drawing
> From Pindar's well instead of the common cisterns.
> Does he ever think of me? How is he doing?
> Does he continue to study, watched by the Muses,
> Adapting the measures of Thebes to the Latin lyre?
> Or does he rant and rage in the tragic mode?
> And Celsus, too? He's been advised, and surely
> It's good advice for him, that he should write
> Out of himself and out of what he knows
> And stay away from those old writers he reads
> In Apollo's library on the Palatine.
> Someday the flock of birds might come back asking
> To have their brilliant feathers given back
> And the crow, stripped naked, is certain to be laughed at.[25]

The two poetic errors which Horace points out in this passage—Titius rants and rages, and Celsus plagiarizes from Apollo's library—parallel the flaws of writing for the stage that Greene and his sometime ally Nashe had been pointing out since *Perimedes* and *Menaphon*.[26] Horace's image of the crow seems substantially the same as Aesop's, but the social cost of failure has changed: in Aesop, the crow simply becomes a crow again (i.e., he loses his borrowed beauty), but Horace's bird is "certain to be laughed at." In the Horatian, humanist conception of authorship, a poet is answerable in social terms for the impact of his literary products on the public. The reason for a writer like Greene to attack a purely

---

True Tragedy are not independent plays but corrupt versions—memorial reconstructions—and *2* and *3 Henry VI*" (122)—has itself come under scrutiny more recently, as a new reviser hypothesis has gained sway.

25 Horace, "To Julius Florus," *The Epistles of Horace*, David Ferry, trans. (New York: Farrar, Straus and Giroux, 2001), p. 19.

26 As Carroll notes, "both the pilferage of Celsus and the bombast of Titius occur together in Shakespeare" (135).

dramatic career like the one he associates with Shakespeare seems to be public humiliation, the loss of status associated with borrowed feathers.[27]

One Groat

If the attack on Shakespeare and the other dramatists seems part of a larger distinction *Groatsworth* draws between page and stage, it remains to determine how the bulk of the text extends this meta-literary argument. I propose that not only is the Greene of the title a literary construct, but that the text as a whole recapitulates Greene's long and diverse career in print. Even when the half-dozen or so plays that he wrote are set aside, Greene's career as a prose writer has long baffled criticism because of its size and range. He published over three dozen books in his twelve-year career, and imposing order on this prolixity has long proved difficult. The most detailed study of Greene's career is still that of René Pruvost, who in 1938 proposed that Greene's twelve years as a writer saw him pass through no less than fourteen different phases, with each one usually marked by an overt departure from its predecessor.[28] Pruvost's scheme has proved unwieldy, and it also tends to minimize the continuities among Greene's various genres. More recent scholarship has pared down his categories to as few as two (W.W. Barker's "monologic" and "dialogic" phases) or, more commonly, three or four.[29]

Two things seem clear despite the critical confusion about Greene's career as prose author: first, he consciously selected and later eschewed several different genres of fiction, and second, his dramatic rejections of his own previous works often concealed a fundamental continuity. A progressive chronological model is

---

27 Shakespeare, of course, did turn to the publication of narrative poems in 1593–94. While it has often been assumed that these publications were products of the closing of the theaters for plague, he may have been following something like Greene's career advice to seek advancement through print and patronage rather than the stage. For a sensitive reading of the reception of Shakespeare's poems in print, see Sasha Roberts, *Reading Shakespeare's Poems in Early Modern England* (Houndmills and New York: Palgrave, 2003).

28 See René Pruvost, *Robert Greene et ses romans: Contributions á l'histoire de la Renaissance en Angleterre* (Paris: Société d'Editions 'Les Belles Lettres,' 1938).

29 For a reading that emphasizes continuity in Greene's career, see Barker. More conventional parsings of the career include John Clark Jordan's division of it into three phases, each marked by a different Latin tag: romances under *Omne tulit punctum*, moral fictions under *Sero sed serio*, and urban exposés under *Nascimur pro patria*. See *Robert Greene* (New York: Oxford University Press, 1915). Charles Crupi, in a more recent study, sees four notable divisions: early work (1580–86), romances and frame tales (1587–89), Farewells to Folly (1590), and finally cony-catching and repentance (1591–92). Arthur Kinney, in an influential study, sees Greene's career as a relatively unified application of humanist models to popular fiction (*Humanist Poetics: Thought, Rhetoric, and Fiction in Sixteenth-Century England* [Amherst: University of Massachusetts Press, 1986]).

thus both required—Greene self-consciously announces his successive transformations—and suspect. As Crupi notes, “Greene tended to work one vein through several pamphlets before going on to a new one” (70), although this linear progression does not always reflect the books as they appeared in print. With this in mind, I offer the following seven-part schematic of Greene’s career in prose (Table 1). While the first six categories move through the twelve years of Greene’s career more or less in order, in several cases (notably *Greenes Vision* [1592] and *Philomela* [1592]), individual pamphlets may have been published considerably after they were written. The seventh category, satire/invective, appears as a kind of sideline in Greene’s career, an ancillary mode to which he periodically turned. (I omit *A Maiden’s Dreame* [1591] from my list, since this dream vision, published on the death of Christopher Hatton, appears to have no clear relationship to Greene’s other works.)

Table 1 The Phases of Greene’s Career in Prose[30]

1. Lylian romance: Seven books (1580–86)	*Mamillia Parts 1 & 2* (1580,1583) *Arbasto* (1584) *Morando Parts 1 & 2* (1584, 1586) *Myrror of Modestie* (1584) *Planetomachia* (1585)
2. Novella collections: Five books (1585–90)	*Penelope’s Web* (1587) *Euphues his Censure* (1587) *Alcida* (1588?) *Perimedes the Blacke-Smith* (1588?) *Opharion* (1590)
3. Greek romances: Five books (1584–90)	*Gwyndonius* (1584) *Pandosto* (1588) *Menaphon* (1589) *Ciceronis Amor* (1589) *Philomela* (1592)
4. Farewells to Folly: Four books (1590–91)	*Greenes Mourning Garment* (1590) *Greenes Never Too Late* (1590) *Franciscos Fortunes* (1590) *Greenes Farewell to Folly* (1591, ent. 1587)
5. Cony-Catching: Six books (1591–92)	*A Notable Discovery of Cosenage* (1591) *The Second Part of Cony-Catching* (1591)

30 I use the simplest short versions of Greene’s sometimes lengthy titles. For the most comprehensive treatment of Greene’s bibliography, see A.F. Allison, *Robert Greene 1558–1593: A Bibliographical Catalogue of the Early Editions in English (to 1640)* (Kent: Wm. Dawson & Sons Ltd., 1975).

	The Third Part of Cony-Catching (1592) *The Defence of Cony-Catching* (1592) *A Disputation ...* (1592) *The Black Bookes Messenger* (1592)
6. Repentance tracts: Three books (1592)	*Groatsworth* (1592) *The Repentance of Robert Greene* (1592) *Greenes Vision* (1592, prob. written 1590)
7. Satire/Invective: Four books (1585–92)	*An Oration ... at Rome* (1585) *The Spanish Masquerado* (1589) *The Royall Exchange* (1590) *A Quip for an Upstart Courtier* (1592)

Several things must be noted about this table: First, the distinctions between genres are meant to be practical rather than exclusive; these categories provide a sense of how Greene appears to have wanted his evolving career to appear to readers who followed him from *Mamillia* to his deathbed.[31] Some flexibility in identification is especially evident in the first two categories: *Mamillia*, all readers concur, is a two-part romance explicitly modeled after Lyly's two *Euphues* volumes (1578 and 1580), but the distinction between the subsequent romance-collections that I label "Lylian" and those that I label "novelle collections" is less distinct than some of the other breaks in Greene's career.[32] I date *Greenes Farewell to Folly* in 1591, despite a Stationers' Register entry in 1587, on the assumption that it was published as part of Greene's rejection of his earlier romances after 1590. (If it was written in late 1587, than the *Farewell* is the first, not the last, book in this phase.) I also include *The Defence of Cony-Catching* among Greene's six cony-catching pamphlets, despite its being claimed by "Cuthbert Cony-Catcher" on its title page and being comprised of a series of attacks on Greene himself.[33] Finally, the last category, satire or invective, links four books that were not published in chronological proximity. This category seems to represent a local, topical urge that Greene sometimes gave vent to: Greene in his Nashean mode, in Jowett's phrase.

31 On generic flexibility in early modern literature, see Alistair Fowler, "The Formation of Genres in the Renaissance and After," *New Literary History* 34:2 (Spring 2003): 185–200.

32 I do see an increasing independence from Lyly over time, and I place my break between these phases at 1587 to signal that Greene's two Homeric-framed collections—*Penelope's Web* and *Euphues his Censure*, both published in 1587—mark a new ambition in Greene's fiction. Space prohibits elaborating this argument here.

33 On this text as a repositioning of romance tropes in an urban environment and thus an important part of Greene's larger literary project, see my "Magic Books: Cony-Catching and the Romance of Early Modern London," *Rogues and Early Modern English Culture*, Craig Dionne and Steve Mentz, eds (Ann Arbor: University of Michigan Press, 2004), pp. 240–58.

This categorization of Greene's career in prose is particularly valuable for my purposes because of how closely it mirrors the apparently slapdash construction of the *Groatsworth*. Chettle, we recall, explains the *Groatsworth*'s lack of organization by noting that he pieced it together from Greene's messy study after his death. For most readers of the text, this posthumous birth has explained the radical shifts of tone and subject matter, in which a fairly conventional, prodigal romance suddenly breaks off and gives place to an Aesopian fable, a list of moral precepts, a didactic poem, an attack on popular drama, and a melodramatic letter to Greene's estranged wife. If the individual sections of *Groatsworth* are parsed out, however, they clearly parallel, in range and content if not always in order, the many phases of Greene's career in prose. Thus I provide a second table that combines an outline of the organization of the *Groatsworth* with a suggested parallel for each section of the text from Greene's own career:

Table 2 The Structure of *Groatsworth* and Parallels to Greene's Career[34]

1.	"The Printer to the Gentle Reader" (41)	
2.	"To the Gentleman Readers" (42)	Farewell to Folly
3.	"Greenes Groates-Worth of Wit" (43–75)	Greek romance
	London section (69–75)	Cony Catching
4.	"Lamilias Song" (52–3)	Lylian romance
5.	"Lamilias Fable" (58–9)	Lylian romance[35]
6.	"Robertoes Tale" (60–63)	Novella
7.	Roberto's Poem (66–7)	Satire/Invective
8.	Break in text (75)	Farewell to Folly
9.	Repentant Poem (75–6)	Satire/Invective
10.	Moral Precepts (77–9)	Repentance tract
11.	"To those Gentlemen…" (80–87)	Satire/Invective
12.	Aesopian Fable (87–9)	Novella
13.	"A Letter written to his wife ..." (90–91)	Repentance tract

The twelve parts of the text that purport to be Greene's (excluding the letter from the publisher William Wright) lay out in full the seven genres that span Greene's prose career. The *Groatsworth* is not an arbitrary collection of scraps and leftovers but a complete and strategic *summa* of Greene's multifaceted career as prose author.

34 Page numbers in parentheses are to Carroll's edition. Titles in quotations marks appear in the text.

35 If Carroll's reading of this fable as a covert attack on Burghley (see 107–13) is correct, it may be more accurately considered as topical satire or invective.

The relationship that I assert between the structure of *Groatsworth* and that of Greene's career is not simply comprised of arbitrary similarities or broad parallels in plot or theme. Rather, each of the twelve sections contains explicit textual evidence linking it to a particular phase in Greene's life in print. The letter "To the Gentlemen Readers" establishes itself as one of the Farewells to Folly by laying open Greene's "sickenesse, riot [and] Incontinence" in order to "commend this [book] to your favourable censures" (42). This letter (which probably has as good a claim to be Chettle imitating Greene as any section of the text, except possibly the break in the main tale) asserts the radical dependence on its readers that has distinguished Greene's appeals to his audience since *Mamillia* (1580). Greene (or "Greene") notes that his book, "like an Embrion without shape, I feare me will be thrust into the world" (42), but he hopes that when readers connect the book to his penitence they will accept it despite its unfinished status: "Beseeching therefore so to be deemed hereof as I deserve, I leave the worke to your likinges, and leave you to your delightes" (42). As usual, Greene appeals to the pleasure-seeking reader, whose "delightes" may seem all the sweeter when counterbalanced against Greene's miseries.[36]

That the main story parallels the major trajectory of Greene's adaptations of Greek romance narrative appears obvious from the tale's opening lines: "In an Iland bounded with the Ocean there was sometime a Cittie situated, made riche by Marchendize, and populous by long peace" (43) and the nearly allegorical portrait of the usurious father Gorinius (Latin for "Greene"). The prodigal son storyline, in which Roberto and Luciano compete for their father's legacy, which Luciano then squanders, follows the "Elizabethan prodigal" storyline quite closely.[37] Carroll has helpfully pointed out verbal echoes of Lodge (48n and *passim*), Nashe (46n and *passim*), and other Elizabethan fiction writers, and many of the situations—from Lamilia's seduction of Luciano to Luciano's subsequent description as a "prodigall child" (55)—were conventional in this sort of fiction by 1592. What seems noteworthy is the varied texture of the material inside the main plot of *Groatsworth*: when Roberto reaches London and becomes "an Arche-plaimaking poet," for example, his story follows Greene's cony-catching pamphlets as much as his prodigal romances:

> His companie were lightly the lewdest persons in the land, apt for pilferie, perjurie, forgerie, or any villainy. Of these hee knew the casts to cog at cards, coossen at Dice; by these he learnd the legerdemaines of nips, foystes, connycatchers, crosbyters, lifts, high Lawyers, and all the rabble of that unclean generation of Vipers: and pithily he could paint out all there whole courses of craft. So cunning he was in all craftes, as nothing rested in him almost but craftines. (72–3)

36 W.W. Barker emphasizes the "devastating unseriousness" of Greene's playing up his deathbed misery in his final texts ("Repentant Romance" p. 97).

37 See Richard Helgerson, *The Elizabethan Prodigals* (Berkeley: University of California Press, 1976). For a recent response to Helgerson, see Derek B. Alwes, *Sons and Authors in Elizabethan England* (Newark: University of Delaware Press, 2004).

This detailed recitation of the technical terms of cony-catching is not simply a reference to Greene's previous works (and an advertisement for them, presumably); it also suggests the close relationship between the prodigal romance and cony-catching genres. As "Greene" constructs the *Groatsworth*, the criminal exposés that Greene wrote in 1591–92 appear less a rejection that a logical outgrowth of his earlier Greek romances.

Even in its references to other Elizabethan authors, the *Groatsworth* elaborates a detailed portrait of Greene's career. Lamilia's part in the main plot is to seduce Luciano and extract his fortune from him. In this, she plays the role of Lyly's *femme fatale* Lucilla (the echoes of their names cannot be coincidental), and her alliance with and later abandoning of Roberto inverts Greene's early imitation and later rejection of the Lylian model. Lamilia's fable, even if it has the topical meaning that Carroll attaches to it, relates a story of treachery that parallels the hothouse world of Lylian fiction with its betrayals and counter-betrayals.[38] The tale with which Roberto replies to Lamilia extends Lylian fiction to the somewhat broader scale characteristic of Greene's novella collections, although no precise source for this bed trick tale has been found.[39] Roberto's poem, however, makes a clear reference to one of Greene's sideline genres, invective: "What meant the Poets in invective verse / ... / Onley for this their vices they rehearse, / That curious wits which in this world converse, / May shun the dangers and enticing shoes, / Of such false Syrens" (66). Here hero (and text) suggest that the structuring prodigal tale gives rise to satiric attack, as it will later lead Roberto first to cony-catching and later to repentance. The Aesopian fable of the Ant and the Grasshopper (87–9) rounds out a similar moral, and by introducing these two figures "walking together on a Greene" (87), the fable misses no chance to recall the intimate relationship between the dying author and his disjunctive book.

The emphasis on repentance also connects *Groatsworth* to Greene's life story. Roberto's second poem, with which the book introduces his repentance, contains a satiric attack on the "Deceiving world, that with alluring toyes, / Hast made my life the subject of thy scorne" (75). What seems noteworthy here is not just the straightforward attack on Roberto/Greene's (the correspondence has become explicit) old songs "of Love" (76), but also the continuing emphasis on being read, even from beyond the grave: "Ah Gentlemen, that live to read my broken and confused lines, looke not I should (as I was wont) delight you with vaine fantasies, but gather my follies altogether, and as yee would deale with so many parricides,

38 On the development of Elizabethan prose romance through the rejection of this model, see my "Escaping Italy: From Novella to Romance in Gascoigne and Lyly," *Studies in Philology* 101.2 (Spring 2004): 153–71. On the "dominant reality of betrayal" in Lyly, see Madelon Gohlke, "Reading *Euphues*," *Criticism* 19 (1977): 103–17.

39 Carroll notes that Samuel L. Wolff has posited Achilles Tatius's *Cliophon and Leucippe*, a Greek romance that Greene drew on extensively in *Gwyndonius* and elsewhere. See Carroll p. 60n.

caste them into the fire" (76–7). Perhaps here we see Chettle's (and William Wright's) interest peering out from behind these words, in which what seems essential is that gentlemen read this book even as they cast "follies" into the fire.

The ten moral precepts (77–9) that follow the break in the text (75) make use of invective in a more straightforward and didactic way, as Roberto notes when he introduces them: "Learne wit by my repentance (Gentlemen) and let these few rules following be regarded in your lives" (77). Like the closing letter to his wife, these precepts emphasize their finality, and the "Greene" who writes them seems already beyond the pale. He still cannot resist making puns on his name; he describes his son in the letter as being "yet Greene, and may grow straight, if he be carefully tended" (90).[40] Between the moral precepts and the deathbed letter comes the anti-playwriting satire, and once again we see the transitional sentences of the *Groatsworth* as attempts to bridge apparent disparities, both within the text and over the course of Greene's career. "Greene" claims that his advice to his peers is valuable precisely because of his deathbed repentance; it is the "Swanne like" (42) nature of his song that makes it worth hearing. He thus introduces the famous letter by emphasizing its practical value for its intended recipients: "But now, though to my self I give *Consilium post facta*; yet to others they may serve for timely precepts. And therefore (while life gives leave) I will send warning to my olde consorts" (79). The claim is not just that repentance makes Greene more knowledgeable about the errancy of the dramatist's life, but (more particularly) that repentance makes his invective more readable. Everything that happens to Greene in the combined romance-autobiography-literary criticism that makes up the true genre of the *Groatsworth* conspires to make his work essential reading.

Who's Speaking?

Accepting that the *Groatsworth* may be better understood as a calculated attempt to summarize and unify the far-flung print career of Robert Greene leads to some preliminary conclusions about the nature of print authorship and the author-function in Elizabethan England. For one thing, the sense that the "author-function" is always under construction, always in the act of defining itself—which has become accepted wisdom since Foucault and Barthes—here receives historical evidentiary backing. While the *Groatsworth* seems as least as uncertain as Foucault about what an author is, it is less willing to debunk that figure's mystique. The motivating force behind the rearticulation of "Greene" as an author in this text seems to be proliferation rather than thrift: the connection with the "gentle reader" at which William Wright aims in his prefatory letter creates profit in several

40 If this son is the "Fortunatus Greene" buried in Shoreditch in August 1593 and mocked by Gabriel Harvey as "Infortunatus Greene," it seems that Greene's mixing of fiction with reality extended to his child's name. See Crupi, p. 9.

senses: financial for the publisher; moral, perhaps, for the reader; and the profit of increased visibility in the marketplace for the author or authors. Emerging ideas of print authorship appear to have more to do with the economics of the book market than ideological conflicts over status or authority. We may further conclude that a print author like Greene speaks at least as directly to the realities of the book market as figures like Shakespeare and Jonson, who dominate our drama-centered scholarship.[41] The *Groatsworth* finally suggests that collaboration, which is fast becoming a normative idea in discussions of early modern dramatic authorship, may not be limited to fraught or friendly relations between playwrights: dead writers, deceptive stationers, forgers, and other figures of murky motives and unknown tendencies may contribute materially to collaborations as well.

More specifically, reading *Groatsworth* as a very early work of literary theory allows it to engage directly with influential statements of theoretical principles like Foucault's "What is an Author?" This intentionally anachronistic engagement encourages several caveats to Foucault's conclusions. First, the fundamentally metaphorical connection that Foucault draws from the "kinship between writing and death" becomes literal in Greene's book.[42] In this case, the impending (and, by the time of reading, accomplished) loss of physical selfhood enables "Greene" to assume a quasi-theoretical position; he becomes a symbol of print authorship in the act of laying down his pen. Foucault seems to have anticipated part of this symbolic transaction when he writes, "[w]riting is now linked to sacrifice and to the sacrifice of life itself; it is a voluntary obliteration of the self," but when he extends the metaphor to assert that "[it] does not require representation in books because it takes place in the everyday existence of the writer" (102), he overlooks the way the literal truth of death underwrites the creation of a posthumous reputation for Greene, and, in different terms, for writers like Sidney and Marlowe as well. Second, the proliferation of meaning as this text initiates it may be less ideological than strategic; Greene's dying scene gets textualized in part to enable the circulation of the products of his authorial career through the dissemination of the *Groatsworth*. If contemporary criticism still wishes to follow the giant-killing strategy that New Historicism has taken from Foucault—"In short, the subject (and its substitutes) must be stripped of its creative role and analysed as a complex and variable function of discourse" (118)—we should take care not to exclude the individualist strategies of once-overlooked subjects like Greene, Chettle, and Wright, who clearly have local interests in particular strategies of creation and dissemination.

---

41 Among the best studies of early modern print authorship have been Joseph Loewenstein's books on the "bibliographic ego" of Ben Jonson: see both *The Author's Due: Printing and the Prehistory of Copyright* (Chicago: University of Chicago Press, 2002) and *Ben Jonson and Possessive Authorship* (Cambridge: Cambridge University Press, 2002).

42 Foucault, "What Is an Author?", p. 102. Further citations in the text.

Beyond this historicist and individualist criticism of Foucauldian theory, which has been articulated in broader terms by Brian Vickers and others, the construction of Greene as the author of the *Groatsworth* enables another way of thinking about the formation of the author in early modern England.[43] By quoting Samuel Beckett's *Texts for Nothing* in my epigram at greater length than Foucault does in his famous essay, I intend to draw out the fundamentally narrative basis of Beckett's dismissal of attribution.[44] What counts in literary culture, this passages suggests, is story itself. The basic literary and linguistic act for Beckett is the assertion of an at least minimally coherent narrative: "there's going to be a story, someone's going to try to tell a story." What distinguishes Greene's prose fiction is its melodramatic, sensationalist, and heavily plotted nature, its facility with a core narrativity that may be more accessible to comparative narratologists than to early modern historicist criticism. It is with a still-noticeable sense of embarrassment that literary critics describe Greene as the "apostle of entertainment in literature" or call his work "little more than popular trash."[45] Without disagreeing about the primacy of the marketplace in Greene's career, I believe that scholarly reluctance to take seriously an author so connected to the Elizabethan Grub Street has distorted our sense of what print was doing to authorship in this period. Greene's career, as miniaturized in the *Groatsworth*, demonstrates how print facilitated the proliferation of narrative modes in Elizabethan literary culture. In this reading, "Greene"—the symbolic author—is the basic achievement of both the *Groatsworth* and Greene's entire career; his authorial name asserts (or "supposes") a fundamental unity underlying the diversity of his output. Beckett's acknowledgement of the primacy of story, even if straightforward narrative is one of the things that his work explodes, reminds postmodern critics that we still read through the basic conventions of narrative. Whatever the precise circumstances of the *Groatsworth's* original composition and repackaging for the press, the two stories it tells—of the prodigal career of the fictional Roberto, and the multifaceted literary career of Robert Greene—commend themselves to the reader's attention as stories first, allegories second. In this sense, it may matter who is speaking simply because what is spoken is a story of disparity and achieved unity that still underwrites our basic notions of what authors do.

---

43 For an influential if sometimes shrill critique of postmodern theoretical approaches to early modern literature, see Brian Vickers, *Appropriating Shakespeare: Contemporary Critical Quarrels* (New Haven: Yale University Press, 1994). For an oblique response to this and other critiques of New Historicism, see Stephen Greenblatt and Catherine Gallagher, *Practicing New Historicism* (Chicago: University of Chicago Press, 2001).

44 Foucault quotes Beckett twice, at the beginning (p. 101) and end (p. 120) of his essay.

45 Crupi quotes David Bevington on Greene the entertainer (p. 38). The second quotation comes from Katherine Duncan-Jones, *Ungentle Shakespeare: Scenes from His Life* (London: Arden, 2001), p. 48.

Chapter 7

A Looking Glass for Readers: Cheap Print and the Senses of Repentance

Lori Humphrey Newcomb

The various repentance pamphlets published around Robert Greene's early death are notorious as biographical and literary documents, but seldom have been considered as devotional writing. Critical myth has it that Greene turned to writing these pamphlets to exploit the authorial potential of the deathbed, as though dying at thirty-four were a strong career option. Critics also have charged Greene with insincerity for claiming multiple acts of repentance in several pamphlets published over three years, even though period theology counseled that any believer's struggle to repent would be lifelong.[1] Thus, it has been assumed that a lay writer so marked by commercialism could not produce significant records of devotional experience. The work of historians of religion increasingly disproves that assumption, showing that commerce and devotion were inextricably bound together in the print culture of England's long reformation. Whatever Greene's pamphlets may have done (or not) for his soul or his purse, they were innovations in the field of cheap devotional writing in the 1590s. More specifically, the pamphlets associated with this sinful layman both reflected and advanced Reformation debate about the best media for addressing and converting sinners—a debate that also reflects on theatre as a complex medium for addressing new audiences. Greene's pamphlets question the reliability of the senses as means to repentance, much as later debates over theatre will question the senses as means to understanding.[2]

This essay focuses on *The Repentance of Robert Greene* (published posthumously in 1592) as it tests its era's devotional resources and their potential sensory effects. In two separate sections of this pamphlet, respectively narrating Greene's deathbed repentance and sinful life, the first-person persona testifies that sermon-going had failed to save him, that he had instead been saved by a printed

1 Peter Lake, *Moderate Puritans and the Elizabethan Church* (Cambridge: Cambridge University Press, 1982), p. 164.

2 See William N. West, "Understanding in the Elizabethan Theaters," *Renaissance Drama* 35 (2006): 113–43.

treatise, a lengthy devotional "steady seller." As the pamphlet rejects the performative immediacy of sermons in favor of recursive, solitary devotional reading, it contradicts the pastoral wisdom of its day and anticipates the next century's turn to personal and textualized forms of devotion. *The Repentance* is an idiosyncratic precursor to later brief, cheap, and highly affective spiritual texts that would roll off the presses, although it does not open a direct lineage to later spiritual autobiography or commercial devotional tracts. Instead, as *The Repentance* shapes appropriated biographical and theological material under the dubious aegis of a notorious author's name and habitus, it suggests that the immediacy and affordability of Greene's signature form, the first-person pamphlet, gave it enormous promise as a vehicle of popular devotion.

The originality of Greene's repentance pamphlets does not turn on Greene's sincerity; indeed, it is best appreciated by bracketing off the question of biographical sincerity or even of authorship. Greene's pamphlets suggest his fear of seeming insincere—in God's eyes as well as readers'—when he recorded a deathbed repentance in a culture that had foresworn that rite, and when he worried about exclusion from God's book of life given the sins on record in his past publications. *The Repentance* inscribes these fears in pervasive images of textuality, anticipating that signature of seventeenth-century English devotional practice, its constant reading and writing of the self. *The Repentance* is thus a precocious document of a textualizing impulse that would become central to popular Protestant experience, all the rarer because its author was noted for his sinfulness rather than his godliness, and perhaps possible only because its author's very soul approached being a textual creation. Like the ineffectual prophets who populate Greene's coauthored biblical drama *A Looking Glass for London and England* (performed 1589?), the experiences in this pamphlet explore the gap between the media that communicate the Word and the senses of resistant readers and listeners. If the pamphlet leaves modern readers in doubt about Greene's redemption (as if we could know), it is clearly important testimony to the early modern understanding of the senses, their roles in affect, and their ties to the experiences of reading and theatregoing. It testifies to early readers' growing faith in the efficacy of the written word, as instrument of salvation as well as entertainment, and to one playwright-turned-writer's sense that the printed word could outstrip even the most sincere pulpit performance.[3]

In 1592, no other English author, lay or clerical, would have preferred treatises to sermons as bearers of the Word to the populace. That aural experience was thought to trump reading experience is difficult to imagine now, since we tend to naturalize the alliance of print and Protestantism. But especially in England, it was by no means inevitable that Protestantism, the religion of the Word, would become

3 Bruce R. Smith, "Hearing Green," in Gail Kern Paster, Katherine Rowe, and Mary Floyd-Wilson (eds), *Reading the Early Modern Passions: Essays in the Cultural History of Emotion* (Philadelphia, PA: University of Pennsylvania Press, 2004), pp. 147–68.

a religion of the book, much less a popular culture of the book. Bryan Crockett notes "There was still considerable resistance in sixteenth-century England to a merely textual understanding of the faith."[4] Church reformers, in their eagerness to wean the populace from bodily ceremony to the ineffable Word, remained ambivalent about the dispersing of that Word in vernacular or affordable texts. No Tudor monarch championed universal literacy or a Bible in every household as a goal for the reformed English church. The Elizabethan solution was that God's chosen means for embodying his Word was the ear. The eye, looking or reading, was supposedly more prone to temptation and subjectivity, especially in the uneducated.[5] Alexandra Walsham confirms that well into the seventeenth century, divines "continued to regard the pen and press as inferior to the organ of the mouth as a mechanism for conveying divine truth, to privilege sound over sight, the ear over the eye, as a route to spiritual revelation and enlightenment."[6] Throughout Elizabeth's reign, Protestant leaders of all stripes recommended as the primary means of popular conversion and instruction replacing the suspect confession and the controversial mass, not the reading of scripture, but the hearing of sermons. Theologians praised the ear as the "ordinary" means for salvation, that is, the recommended salvific delivery system for all but those specially favored by education and divine calling. The felt primacy of hearing, based on physiognomic theories of the passions, would hold sway into the next century in secular contexts, as Bruce Smith has argued in "Hearing Green."

Greene, however, was less interested in hearing. Heterodox in many ways, he apparently also held unusual views about the sensory effects of devotional practices. The action of *A Looking Glasse for London and England*, the Bible play he coauthored with Thomas Lodge, relentlessly repeats sermon-like prophecies only to show their falling on unhearing ears in both Nineveh and London. *The Repentance* demonstrates that sermons fail even off-stage. The critique is most explicit in the pamphlet's accounts of Greene's life: these are passages of dubious authorship potentially enhanced by Greene himself, his "editor" Henry Chettle, or both, that we, nonetheless, should take as significant representations of the authorial self. The pamphlet suggests that the sermon's appeals to the ear are the rhetorical equivalent of spectacle: impressive but not durable enough to support a lively faith. Instead, the pamphlet locates truly affective experience in Greene's

---

4 Bryan Crockett, *The Play of Paradox: Stage and Sermon in Renaissance England* (Philadelphia: University of Pennsylvania Press, 1995), p. 55.

5 Crockett, *Play*, p. 53; Eric Josef Carlson, "The Boring of the Ear: Shaping the Pastoral Vision of Preaching in England, 1540–1640," in Larissa Taylor (ed.), *Preachers and People in the Reformations and Early Modern Period* (Boston: Brill, 2003), pp. 280–81.

6 "Preaching Without Speaking: Script, Print, and Religious Dissent," in Julia C. Crick and Alexandra Walsham (eds), *The Uses of Script and Print, 1300–1700* (Cambridge: Cambridge University Press, 2004), p. 229.

reading a treatise, which moves his body to shake, his teeth to chatter, and his soul to own up to its ineradicable records. The pamphlet's highly original approach to devotion is theatrically cued yet even more deeply textualized. It can best be appreciated by situating it alongside four key intertexts: the sermons of John More of Norwich (1594), the *Looking Glasse for London and England* (1594), Edmund Bunny's *Book of Christian Exercise* (1589), and Philip Stubbes's *A Christal Glasse for Christian Women* (1591). All four of these intertexts, like *The Repentance*, aim to bring the Word to ordinary persons, reflecting explicitly on their communicative means and the difficulty of moving inward motions to lively faith. As it happened, each publication ran into multiple reprints that echo the commercial-devotional liminality of *The Repentance*. Through its ties to these four intertexts, *The Repentance* records or imagines the quest for faith of a famous sinner. At the same time it assesses four potentially salvific practices—sermon-going, play-going, treatise-reading, and life-writing—as they textualize the Word to produce lay affect. Its views of these practices flag the changing social expectations for popular access to the divine Word: from the sixteenth century's eagerness for hearing and ambivalence about looking, to the seventeenth century's hunger for constant individualized reading and writing.

How English Protestants of these centuries sought to embody devotion for ordinary persons has been a crucial subject of historical inquiry since the 1970s, when revisionist, theological historians, above all Patrick Collinson and Eamon Duffy, began proposing that the English Reformation, far from being inevitable, was imposed by a godly elite on a confused and even unwilling populace. Collinson asked in his 1979 chapter "Popular and Unpopular Religion" whether Protestantism should be considered popular culture; only gradually has his own scholarship and his students' concluded it could. The question has lent itself well to the history of the book, and magisterial studies by Ian Green, Walsham, Tessa Watt, and others have recovered the slow production of England's Protestant popular print culture. Greene's pamphlet, which records a somewhat unwilling individual's attempt to impose Reformation on himself, presents a fascinating test case for this historiographical debate. Greene himself is not an ordinary believer; writers are "extraordinary readers," as Heidi Brayman Hackel points out, because they leave such ample traces of their reading experiences.[7] But this particular extraordinary reader speaks publicly for ordinary readers. In *The Repentance* Greene represents himself as made "ordinary," meaning something like today's "popular," or accessible and predictable, by his writing of plays and romances: he was so "famous in that qualitie, that who for that trade growne so ordinary about London as *Robin Greene*."[8] That "ordinary" persona is effectively the author of

7 Heidi Brayman Hackel, *Reading Material in Early Modern England: Print, Gender, and Literacy* (Cambridge: Cambridge University Press, 2005), pp. 7–8.

8 Robert Greene, *The Repentance of Robert Greene* (1592; reprint edn, New York: Burt Franklin, 1970), A2v. Further references will be noted parenthetically.

this posthumous pamphlet; Chettle, a stationer and writer, reports that he assembled it from fragments left by the historical personage Robert Greene after his death, but Chettle could easily have invented material in Greene's name. From the title onward, the pamphlet plays with Greene's ordinariness, for *The Repentance of Robert Greene Maister of Artes* signifies both education and ignorance: the M.A. is from St. John's, Cambridge, a hotbed of Puritan learning, but the stance is that of a lowly sinner turning in desperation to vernacular devotional resources. The sins its speaker most regrets are those forms of disorderly speech—"monstrous swearing and horrible forswearinge"—that historians of social control have attributed to the poor, and sixteenth-century ministers laid to the rich.[9] Yet for these oral sins, the pamphlet imagines deeply textual salves: reading, writing, erasing.

Beyond this pamphlet, Greene's career mixed the media of performance and textuality, script and print. His plays were highly rhetorical, spectacular—and among the earliest public-theatre scripts printed; his pamphlets, anti-Martinist to cony-catching to deathbed, create theatrical voices—and revel in print's new ubiquity. Finally, and crucially, Greene's last-ditch repentance suspended him between election and reprobation. Although the doctrine of double predestination would become an obsession of early seventeenth-century theologians and believers (what Ian Green calls "high Calvinism"), sixteenth-century Protestant divines tried to shield the laity from the terrors of the double decree.[10] Greene's fascination with the rigidity of predestination, although muddled in its doctrinal details, thus occupies a liminal place in the history of popular Protestantism, an idiosyncratic spurt of the hellfire about to be launched by the great popularizer of predestination, William Perkins. *The Repentance of Robert Greene* creates a *Robin Greene* who, in his notorious ordinariness, his educated popularity, his repentant reprobation, voices a need that other Elizabethan sinners must have felt but not yet dared to speak: not just to hear the promises of sermons or see the figures of ministers, but to read and write the marks of election that new theologies taught them to seek. Collinson suggests that English Protestantism became popular culture when individual laypersons began to voice desires to wrest control over their spiritual lives, shifting their centers from the performative examples of preaching ministers to believers' individualized experiences of reading and self-examination. In 1592, it took a well-educated, notorious reprobate on his deathbed to recognize, much less publish, that desire to read the self.

---

9 Gabriel Harvey, *Works*, 3 vols, ed. Alexander B. Grosart (1884–85; reprint edn, New York: AMS Press, 1966), 1: 169.

10 Ian M. Green, *Print and Protestantism in Early Modern England* (Oxford: Oxford University Press, 2000), pp. 74–5, 312–14. Patrick Collinson quotes one preacher: "what should such matters be spoken of among the people? They make men worse" (*The Elizabethan Puritan Movement* (Berkeley, CA: University of California Press, 1967), p. 37.

I. Hearing

The biographical sections of *The Repentance* detail two life-changing spiritual experiences: the narrating "Greene" recalls hearing a sermon in Norwich (his birthplace) at an unspecified earlier date, and he tells of reading, on his sickbed, a devotional work that compelled him to write this, his dying work. The reading experience is in the pamphlet's main section; the sermon-going experience, earlier in the sequence of his life, is appended in the next section, "The life and death of Robert Greene." This reversal, even in such a cobbled-together text, effectively signals the sermon's failure to save as inevitable. That impression is doubled by a passing reference, earlier in the "life and death" section, to Greene's general resistance to preaching:

> I seemed as one of no religion, but rather as a meere Atheist, contemning the holy precepts vttered by any learned preacher: I would smile at such as would frequent the Church, or such place of godly exercise, ... so that herein I seemed a meere reprobate, ... one wipt out of the booke of life. (B–Bv)

After reporting more about his youthful misdeeds, Greene admits that "yet but once, I felt a feare and horrour in my conscience & then the terrour of Gods judgementes did manifestly teach me that my life was bad, that by sinne I deserued damnation, and that such was the greatnes of my sinne, that I deserved no redemption" (C2v). The preacher who produced this "feare and horrour" was "a godly learned man, whose doctrine, and the maner of whose teaching, I liked wonderfull well: yea (in my conscience) such was his singlenes of hart, and zeale in his doctrine, that hee might haue conuerted the most monster of the world" (C2v).

Greene, who narrates himself as a near-monster, conspicuously omits to say that he himself was converted by this experience he "liked" so "wonderful well." As he goes on to detail his reactions, it is clear that he is moved only to "sighing" and longing for God's grace, responses which fall short of repentance. Furthermore, he concedes within two paragraphs that "this good motion lasted not long in mee ... . [A]lthough God sent his holy spirit to call mee, and though I heard him, yet I regarded it no longer than the present time, when sodainly forsaking it, I went forward obstinately in my misse" (C3). What he heard at this sermon made an impression, but was not internalized, if he could so easily "forsake" it. Greene does not explain why this experience failed to effect conversion, or even insist that the fault lay in the sermon not in his resistance. But he has selected the preacher reputed most capable of converting a sinner, and reported that even that preacher cannot reach him. The details of his response, when compared to period instructions about hearing sermons, imply the limited efficacy of sermons in reaching habitual sinners.

In questioning sermons as effective instruments of conversion, Greene rebutted a point on which mid-Elizabethan divines, from moderates to reformers, fundamentally agreed: that sermons were the primary and sufficient means for an English Protestant church to save its populace. One pastoral thinker after another echoed the questions of Romans 10:14: "Howe then shall they call on hym, on whom they have not beleved? Howe shall they beleve on hym of whom they have not hearde? Howe shal they heare, without a preacher? And howe shall they preache, except they be sent?"[11] The agreement of church leaders on this principle and their divergences over its execution reveal enormous confidence in the power of the Word delivered aurally and surprising ambivalence about the power of the Word distributed in print.

It was crucial for any Protestant church to displace popular belief in the saving efficacy of the mass and to emphasize logocentric rather than spectacular means of instruction. But Elizabeth's churchmen expected popular logocentrism to be auditory: although these divines had come to the new faith through reading scripture, they did not trust the uneducated to do so. The governors of church and state aimed to share the Gospel, but to limit lay opportunities for scriptural interpretation: for instance, there was no campaign to put a Bible on every lap, despite the famous frontispiece to Foxe that depicts every man and woman in the congregation following the lesson in his or her own text.[12] Of course, the Elizabethan injunctions of 1559 renewed the Edwardian order for "the whole Bible, of the largest volume" to be placed in each parish church so that "parishioners may most commodiously resort unto the same and read the same"; still, the 1559 renewal carefully specifies such reading as "out of the time of common service," as though to bar parishioners from questioning scriptural citations during service.[13] The Elizabethan settlement, such as it was, could make the priest the provider of scriptural interpretation because priests' stances were under the control of Crown and bishops. Priests were to administer the generally tight-lipped liturgy, to deliver homilies weekly and sermons at least quarterly. All priests were required to take the oath of supremacy, and preaching required a separate license. In a system that made sermons crucial to the communication of doctrine, the saving of the populace, and state control of the priesthood, the adequacy of their provision was bound to become a partisan issue.

Ministers were divided on whether sermons were *uniquely* salvific and whether the popular appetite for them might be excessive. Preaching was newly ranked as more important than the performance of sacraments, "first among ministerial duties in every official statement from the commencement of the English Reformation."[14] The shift did not please all: a 1560 order stipulated that no communion be offered

---

11 As given in the 1568 Bishops' Bible.

12 Patrick Collinson, *The Elizabethan Puritan Movement*, pp. 23–4.

13 Bray, p. 337.

14 Carlson, "Boring," p. 261.

without a sermon first, so that ministers and congregations, "by deferring of this sacrament to be ministered until doctrine be preached and received, may be thereby caused and occasioned more to desire and frequent preaching of the word."[15] But increasingly, the Elizabethan ministry divided over the warmth of their commitment to preaching. Reformists insisted that only preaching held scriptural authority to save: it was not just the ordinary means of salvation, but the "most" ordinary or "most principal" means.[16] But the episcopal conservative, reluctant to increase the emphasis on preaching, asserted God's right to save in mysterious ways, including through the sacraments. Thus, in a 1587 trial, the bishops told a nonconformist minister that to call preaching the "*only* ordinary means" of salvation was an "execrable heresy."[17] A commitment to preaching was widely understood as marking precisian believers, too: in a popular treatise of 1603, the godly protagonist is asked, "Are you one of those puritans who would have only preaching?"[18]

Especially in the early part of the reign, the shortage of licensed preachers was dire, yet Elizabeth was quick to punish those ministers who complained of the lack. The result was that committed preachers acquired the standing of protest leaders, and sermon-going a certain cachet of political resistance. In 1570, when Edmund Dering told the Queen she had been "carelesse" of her people in failing to provide more preachers, he delivered an insult that she never forgave—and the sermon that was the most reprinted single sermon of the era. Again, in 1576, Elizabeth asked Edmund Grindal, archbishop of Canterbury, to suppress "prophesyings," learned exercises in which clergy debated scripture before large lay audiences. In a long and agonized letter, Grindal refused to block what he argued was a form of preaching. The letter reminds the queen yet again that "Public and continual preaching is the ordinary mean and instrument of the salvation of mankind," and more cannily, that it promotes the security of the monarch: "[W]here preaching wanteth, obedience faileth."[19] Grindal intuited that the Queen's underlying worry was that prophesyings would become lay conventicles: these events, he assured her, train clergy to preach, not laity to interpret, and "no layman [is] suffered to

---

15 Alan Fager Herr, *The Elizabethan Sermon: a Survey and a Bibliography* (1940; reprint edn, New York: Octagon Books, 1969), p. 17.

16 Carlson, "Boring," p. 256.

17 Christopher Hill, *Society and Puritanism in Pre-Revolutionary England* (New York: St. Martin's Press, 1997), p. 17 (my emphasis).

18 Patrick Collinson, *Godly People: Essays on English Protestantism and Puritanism* (London: Hambledon Press, 1983), p. 1.

19 The letter is reprinted in David Cressy and Lori Anne Ferrell (eds), *Religion and Society in Early Modern England: A Sourcebook* (London and New York: Routledge, 1996), pp. 94–9. Lori Anne Ferrell and Peter McCullough (eds), *The English Sermon Revised: Religion, Literature, and History, 1600–1750* (Manchester: Manchester University Press, 2000), p. 67.

speak at any time."[20] Questioning interpretation was for the clergy, not the laity, but the laity could listen. For this letter Grindal was suspended, an action that confirms the Elizabethan reluctance to stir the laity to literacy.

However, there was no quelling the appetite for sermons, and the 1580s and 1590s saw the continued rise of lay "exercises" building on sermons: preachers leading post-sermon review, or "repetition," sessions; lay gatherings in homes to read scripture, and sermon "gadding"—parishioners traveling to other parishes to attend sermons. The claimed objective of gadders was to hear sermons weekly (each parish was asked to offer a sermon each month, with homilies read on intervening Sundays), but clearly many gadders sought preachers more sensational or famous or precise than those at home. If, as was suspected, they were eager to gather with others of the same appetite, their godliness risked sliding into separatism. Even if charismatic preachers did not attract sectarians, they certainly caused disorder by attracting crowds: hence the "political elite's suspicions of the preaching clergy."[21] It was widely acknowledged that for all the rivalry between sermons and plays, both were forms of urban entertainment. The St. Paul's sermons in particular attracted huge audiences and offered the bonus spectacle of parading penitents. Not every preacher could be a crowd-pleaser, but preachers were urged to adopt performative styles that would move listeners to livelier faith. To further engagement with congregants, preachers were admonished not to read from prepared scripts, but to speak *extempore* for maximum immediacy.[22] While celebrants of sacraments were forbidden to embellish the liturgy, and clowns were discouraged from ad libbing, preachers of sermons were urged toward a lively delivery that would encourage a lively inward faith.

Greene's *Repentance* attests that he saw the most charismatic of Elizabethan preachers and received an "inward motion" that was lively, but not lively enough to last. It says Greene received this motion "in Saint Andrews Church in the Cittie of Norwich, at a Lecture or Sermon then preached by a godly learned man, whose doctrine, and the maner of whose teaching, I liked wonderfull well: yea (in my conscience) such was his singlenes of hart, and zeale in his doctrine, that hee might haue converted the most monster of the world" (C2v). This "godly learned man" has long been identified as John More, the so-called apostle of Norwich (d. 1592), famous for preaching thousands of sermons over his career, including three or four most Sundays. The huge church of St. Andrews, Norwich was by then "virtually a gathered Puritan congregation," backed by the city's godly merchants, and attracting flocks of godly women, "Saint *Andrewes* birds," who would take their pews hours before the service.[23] Greene primarily evaluates More rhetorically,

20 Ferrell and McCullough, *English Sermon*, p. 97.

21 Crockett, *Play*, p. 15.

22 Carlson, "Boring," p. 256; Crockett, *Play*, p. 15.

23 Patrick Collinson, *The Religion of Protestants* (Oxford: Oxford University Press, 1979), p. 142.

repeatedly mentioning his disinterested, even technical, admiration for More's "pithie and perswasiue manner." If Greene "liked wonderfull well" both More's "doctrine" and the "maner of [his] teaching," "liking" is surely more apt for the delivery than the doctrine.

Greene is on better doctrinal grounds in attributing his "inward motion" not to More but to God: as Greene's contemporary William Perkins would urge: "[T]he hearers ought not to ascribe their faith to the gifts of men, but to the power of God's word."[24] Greene's *Repentance* reports that through More, "the "terrour of Gods judgementes did manifestly teach me, that my exercises were damnable, and that I should bee wipte out of the booke of life, if I did not speedily repent my loosenes of life, and reforme my misdemeanors" (C2v). Yet this sentence is also problematic, since Greene is vague about which exercises are damnable, and unsure about whether "reforme" can save him. A nearby sentence offers a worrying variant: "[T]he terrour of Gods iudgementes did manifestly teach me that my life was bad, that by sinne I deserved damnation, and that such was the greatnes of my sinne, that I deserved no redemption" (C2v). The inconsistency between the nearly-consecutive sentences points to Greene's real doubt: Is he redeemable, or are his sins unforgivable? Surely a saving sermon ought not to leave such questions unanswered. Was the confusion a failure of the sermon form, or a failure of Greene's hearing? According to Henry Smith, the London preacher Thomas Nashe dubbed "silver-tongu'd," hearers of a good sermon should "record" what they heard: mentally note what "speaketh to thine own sin" and send the lesson "to all the parts of thy soul and members of thy body."[25] Greene recorded a vivid experience, but named neither what spoke to his own sin nor how it affected his body and soul. Thus, the sensory cycle that should lead to a lively inward faith was incomplete.

The skeptical Greene had gadded to the parish of not just an admired preacher, but a famous advocate of preaching. What was known as "Mr Mores catechism" (which remained in print for sixty years after his death) is remembered for its bold claims for "The minister by whom the people do believe."[26] How, the catechism asks, is man saved? "The holy ghost hath appointed the preaching of the word to be the ordinary meanes, whereby he worketh in our hartes this true and lively faith, and without this preachinge of the worde, wee can never have faith" [A3]. More's syllogism of doom is a commonplace of the period's evangelical puritans, relying, of course, on Romans 10.[27] Contentiously, one Sunday when the Norfolk Justices of the Peace were gathered in his congregation, More thundered that "skarsly [one in twenty] parish hath a preacher, and can they be saved then? Shal we make God a lyer? He saith, whosoever doth not beleeve is damned; and none can beleeve

24 Perkins, cited in Crockett, *Play*, p. 12.

25 I:334, cited in Crockett, *Play*, p. 7.

26 Collinson, *Godly*, p. 299.

27 For other examples, see Carlson, "Boring," 270.

without a preacher. If then we will have the people of the Lord to be saved, let them have preachers"[28] His recommendation to this regional elite was that if the bishops wouldn't fund preachers, the gentry should endow their own. More is called seditious in one of the anti-marprelate tracts.[29] Greene might well have joined the anti-Martinists in mocking More. But instead of mocking More, Greene ventriloquizes that mockery in the teasing reaction of his "copesmates": When they heard

> that the Preachers wordes had taken a deepe impression in my conscience, they fell vpon me in jeasting manner, calling me Puritane and Presizian, and wished I might have a Pulpit, with such other scoffing tearmes, that by their foolish perswasion the good and wholesome lesson I had learned went quite out of my remembrance. (*Repentance*, C3)

The image of Greene in a pulpit positions More as a kind of alter ego to the much younger author: there is even a certain wistfulness in Greene's noting, amidst evidence of his own damnation, that this "learned man ... doubtles was the child of God," that is, elect.[30] A curious detail links the two men: More wore "the longest and largest beard of his time so that no act of his life should be unworthy the gravity of his appearance," and Greene in his London years affected a long, pointed beard, as Nashe would later record.[31] Greene lived, then, as a kind of anti-More, a celebrity preacher of failed faith. Both men maintained a theatrical appearance that made their authorial idiosyncrasies highly public.

Through Greene's doubts about both More's preaching and his own, *The Repentance* effectively questions whether it can be the minister "by whom we do believe," even if that minister is "sent" by "God's holy spirit." Greene insists that he received God's "call," that he did learn a "good and wholesome lesson," which took a "deepe impression" in his conscience; but once overwritten by the mockery of his copesmates, the original impression "went quite out of his remembrance" and he "regarded" it no more. The impression is as of wax, not as of print; these are senses under constant threat of erasure. More could have converted the greatest monster in the world, if any sermon could. Unless Greene is that monster, the inadequacy lies in the medium of the sermon: dependent on a human performer, removed from the sinner's experience, and inevitably fleeting in its impressions. A one-time event that only loosely matched his spiritual concerns, this sermon demanded and produced no action from Greene, no lasting engagement. It did, however, activate a vague worry that his earlier sins, more consequential than he had admitted to himself, had caused God to wipe Greene's name from the Book of Life. But then, Greene reports, the mockery of his friends drove out this impulse to repent, as if God's erasure of Greene's name was itself erased from Greene's memory.

---

28 Collinson, *Godly*, p. 299.

29 Collinson, *Elizabethan*, p. 403.

30 Perkins, "A Case of Conscience" (1592); cited in Green, *Print*, p. 314.

31 Collinson, *Religion*, p. 142.

Such concerns about the sensory impact of sermons are consistent with a new sermon topic that emerged around 1592, the sermon on hearing. The distinguished theologian William Perkins and the silver-tongued Henry Smith delivered (and, significantly, published) sermons urging believers to better habits of listening. These sermons repeatedly express or imply the worry that sermons will go in one ear and out the other, or, as Smith warned his listeners, that parishioners will "forget so fast as you hear."[32] Perhaps Greene had heard of these famous preachers' concerns (Perkins was Greene's exact contemporary at Cambridge: after a wild spell of his own, he had became "by far the most popular preacher in Cambridge," as Greene finished his degrees).[33] Or perhaps his uniquely public career as sinner with master's degree led him to a dirty secret of Elizabethan Protestantism: that even as the sermon became a successful popular practice, theologians raised doubts about its odds of producing salvation, particularly in resistant sinners and particularly given the stacked deck of election.

Certainly growing worries about the efficacy and ephemerality of sermon performances drove Henry Smith's advice that parishioners record sermons. Although Smith implied that these records should be held "in mind," he presumably also meant shorthand, invented in 1588. Shorthand made extemporaneous sermons reproducible for the first time, stimulating a steep rise in sermon publication that suggests widening doubts about a primarily aural Reformation.[34] The sermon boom also marks a convergence between commercial and devotional impulses in the print market. Sermons poured from the presses, taken down by dictation with or without the preacher's correction or permission. Indeed, both Smith and Perkins, like Robert Greene, would have titles falsely attributed to them after death.[35] Preachers still claimed that published sermons were mere stopgaps, but the demand for new titles suggests otherwise. In 1605 one self-defeating treatise claimed that "the word being urged and pressed by preaching" is "far more powerful, more piercing, ... more awaking to the conscience" than the "bare and naked reading" of scripture or sermons or treatises. Another preacher worried that spoken sermons offered the "gesture and countenance of a living man," and published sermons only the "dead letter of less effectual persuasion." But like Greene, this preacher published heavily, with the justification that in a "prodigal and intemperate age," "every man writeth more than need is."[36]

---

32 I335.

33 Norman Pettit, *The Heart Prepared: Grace and Conversion in Puritan Spiritual Life*, Yale Publications in American Studies (New Haven: Yale University Press, 1966), pp. 61–2.

34 Herr, *The Elizabethan Sermon*, p. 76.

35 Herr, *The Elizabethan Sermon*, pp. 28, 70.

36 Quoted in Crockett, *Play*, p. 14.

One of the most famous sectarian writers of the Restoration, Richard Baxter, would give lip-service to the efficacy of heard sermons while arguing that the "need" for published sermons was greater, especially among rural, self-taught believers such as himself:

> The Writings of Divines are nothing less but a preaching the Gospel to the eye, as the voice preacheth it to the ear. Vocal preaching hath the preheminence in moving the affections ... . But Books have the advantage in many other respects: you may read an able Preacher when you have but a mean one to hear. Every Congregation cannot hear the most judicious or powerful Preachers: but every single person may read the[ir] Books.[37]

At this later date in the spread of cheap print devotion, Baxter can assume that printed sermons will penetrate where good preaching may not, that "every single person" can read and presumably own some kind of devotional book. His pastoral philosophy is a long way from that of Elizabethan divines, when he asserts that "every single person" should read, and when he recommends "preaching the Gospel to the eye" without iconophobic apologies. Although Greene was no sectarian, his attention to audiences and their hunger for vivid sensory experiences made him a forerunner of the sectarians' populist and print-centered methods.

II. Looking in *A Looking Glasse*

Of course, even in the Elizabethan period "vocal preaching," in its "preheminence in moving the affections," drew some of its affect from the visual. For Elizabethan theorists, the visual appeal to audiences fell within the rhetorical art of delivery; in hindsight, we might call it performance. Critic Bryan Crockett emphasizes that the preacher was to be seen by congregants to embody, impersonate, or at least imitate a prophet.[38] More was not the only famous Elizabethan preacher to cultivate both a performative style of sermonizing and a prophet-like appearance to match. Certainly Greene and his fellow dramatists intuited the irony of such performative preaching as vehicle of an iconoclastic and antitheatrical theology. *The Repentance* continues a reflection on the English culture of preaching that Greene had taken up earlier in *A Looking Glasse for London and England*, the stage play he coauthored with Thomas Lodge around 1587–89. This belated morality play coordinates the stories of the prophets Oseas and Jonas, from the two Old Testament books now known as Hosea and Jonah. Not historically synchronous, both of these prophets warned the sinful Ninevites of the anger of the Hebraic God. Oseas appears first in the play: an angel has whisked him from Jewry, where he has been wasting his

37 Richard Baxter, *A Christian Directory: or, a Summe of Practical Theologies* (London, 1673), p. 60; quoted in Walsham, "Preaching," p. 232.

38 Crockett, *Play*, pp. 8, 11.

preaching, to the proud and corrupt city of Nineveh. He is to warn the Ninevites they face doom in forty days and then return to Jerusalem and tell them about the Ninevite object lesson. Meanwhile, Jonah is told by the angel that he, too, must take his preaching from Jericho to Nineveh, an assignment he flees until he is ejected from the whale. Repentant for his rebellion, Jonah starts warning the Ninevites. As Oseas and the angel observe Jonas's failure to reform the outrageous sins of King Rasni and his citizens, the angel impatiently remarks that "though the Lord forewarnes, yet they repent not," and recalls Oseas to Jerusalem before the forty days are up.[39] But Jonas is able to convince the Ninevites that a fasting penance is needed; only the clown, Adam, eats his way through the fast, and God spares the Ninevites. The play ends with Jonas turning his preaching to London.

Because one prophet begins the play and the other ends it in much the same apocalyptic mode, the two seem to be a tag-team, not unlike Lodge and Greene, whose shares of the authorship no one can separate. The prophets' interchangeability also suggests that of Greene and Chettle, the asynchronous coauthors of *The Repentance*. Whatever Greene's share of the cowriting of this early play, it demonstrates a topical awareness of the rise of urban preaching, as it mirrored Greene's own world of theatre and print. Both prophets speak to the Ninevites in biblical paraphrase so close that the play's source translation can be identified as the Bishops' Bible. However, both prophets also function outside the biblical frame, so that their warnings to various Ninevites alternate with direct addresses to the London audience, which is advised to regard Nineveh as its mirror. In the looking-glass world of this play, Ninevite's favorite sins are coincidentally those of Londoners. However, both Oseas and Jonas imply that Londoners will be harder to convert than most Ninevites, being rather like the resolutely contemporary character Adam. The prophets' heated apostrophes suggest the rhetoric of contemporary sermons; specifically, their addressing cities as corporate entities recalls the Paul's Cross Sermons that were a public sensation in Reformation London. The play's equation of London to Nineveh was itself a sermon trope, since Nineveh had been a favorite exemplum of Paul's Cross Sermons since the 1550s.[40] Bringing the Nineveh theme to the stage with plenty of spectacle—the worst sinners are struck by lightning—the play flaunts theatre's capacity to make visible the urban corruptions that sermons could handle only verbally.

A further challenge to the sermon culture, however, appears in the play's invented conversations between the prophets and God's angel, monitoring the missions to the Ninevites. In a play that generally follows Old Testament language closely, these interpolated lines are striking for their pervasive metaphors of

39 George Allen Clugston, ed., *A Looking-Glasse for London and England* by Thomas Lodge and Robert Greene (New York: Garland, 1980), G4v.

40 Susan Brigden, *London and the Reformation* (Oxford: Clarendon Press, Oxford University Press, 1989), pp. 461–2.

writing and publishing. First the angel tells Oseas to "Note" all the Ninevites' sins, so that "when thou hast written all," God can punish the offenders, and Oseas can "publish" God's judgment in the "open streetes" of Jerusalem (B1v). In another peculiar, non-Biblical line, Oseas concludes a warning to the Ninevites: "I speake although I write not" (G4v); it is unclear whether this line distinguishes the actor from the scriptural book, or fits into the play's characterization of Oseas as filing a report to HQ. Jonas, on the other hand, is worried about bad international press in the opposite direction: If he warns the Ninevites to obey the Jews' God when the Jews have failed to do so, then "I should publish to the world my countries blame" (E). Even if the verb "publish" is used primarily in its older sense of "make public knowledge," the printing of sermons as news must come to mind: for instance, Dering's notorious sermon, publishing to the nation the queen's blame in providing so few preachers.

How do these verbs connect to this play's performance and publication histories? Strikingly, Jonas concludes the play with this warning to London: "Thy Preachers crie, yet doest thou stop thine eares" [I4v]; instead, the play will "set a looking Glasse before thine eyes" (I4v). Indeed, throughout the play, London has been urged to "Look" upon the Ninevites, in their sin and in their repentance, and to learn from them. But the play has depicted the failures of looking at and learning from the most dramatic spectacles. Rasni, the king, fails to interpret the most literally striking scenes: he sees his queen "stroken with Thunder, blacke"; his young favorite Radagon "swallowed" by a "flame of fire"; his concubine threatened by "A hand from out a cloud [with] a burning sword." Still he believes his "sages" who assure him "these are but clammy exhalations (C2v; E4; G2).

We have no way of knowing whether any audience members were chastised by the play's images or words, as they were performed or published, but they had repeated opportunities. Apparently written before the Armada in late 1587 or early 1588, the play was revived in 1592, twice in March (near Easter), in April and June, Henslowe's accounts showing "respectable but not sensational" takings.[41] It may not be a coincidence that these revivals closely followed the publication of Greene's cony-catching pamphlets. The 1594 title page proudly states the play was "Made by *Thomas Lodge* Gentleman, and *Robert Greene, In Artibus Magister*," but Greene was dead by then. Lodge perhaps sold the play to raise money for a lawsuit; by 1596 he would swear off playwriting, as did Greene in his posthumous *Groatsworth*.[42] *Looking Glasse* has a surprisingly long publication history, with five extant quarto editions to 1617 (see Appendix C in this volume). The sole extant copy of the undated fourth quarto was used as a promptbook by Prince Charles' Company sometime after 1610.[43] The prompters' hand carefully emends the final lines, changing a reference to Elizabeth into one to James, and cutting out

---

41 Clugston, *Looking-Glasse*, pp. 1, 74–5.

42 Clugston, *Looking-Glasse*, pp. 15–18.

43 Clugston, *Looking-Glasse*, pp. 98–100.

the strongest attacks on whorish London. The "preachers" are now not just unheard but unmentioned, presumably by the company's self-censorship.[44] Lodge and Greene gave Lord Strange's Men a script that published their city's sins onstage, ironically claiming the efficacy of publication over the spoken word; a later acting company revised their words so as to pull that punch.

III. Reading

In *The Repentance*'s other report of a more successful engagement with a popular practice of devotion, Greene reports turning to a printed work of spiritual guidance, not a sermon but "the booke of *Resolution*" (B2). The circumstances of his reading are desperate: having mocked God and Church to a group of "welwillers" who staged an intervention, Greene comes home, falls sick, fears death, and "sodainely" takes up the book (its presence in his chamber is unexplained). In naming this printed work as in identifying a preacher, *The Repentance* makes another telling choice for a history of popular Protestantism. Once again, the representative of the practice is noted for its popular dissemination and its emotional affect; once again, its devotional authority is more contentious than it appears. Although we might expect a text chosen at random, recent work on devotional print culture identifies this particular book as virtually the only title then available to help a Protestant make a deathbed repentance. Moreover, the engagement with this book is specified down to the page, helping us surmise what sensory experience the medium of print offers him that the aural impact of a sermon did not. And finally, Greene misreads his intertext enough that we can see him intensifying its contribution to the Protestant textualization of devotion.

As the comprehensive work of Ian Green and Tessa Watt has shown, for all of its outpouring of religious commentary and disputation, sixteenth-century English print culture was surprisingly lacking in guides to lay belief, especially short, cheap titles. Sermons and catechisms were more common than guides to prayer or dying. The distinguished medieval genre of the art of dying handbook was thrown into remission, since deathbed repentance was itself suspect once extreme unction was desacralized. Sister Mary Catharine O'Connor comments that "the folly of postponing repentance till one's deathbed is condemned by many post-Reformation authors, and rarely do they offer hope of salvation for any sinner who procrastinates." She then refers specifically to *The Repentance of Robert Greene* as a rare post-Reformation expression of hope that Augustine would have endorsed his "tardy penitence."[45] The one early Protestant guide to dying, Thomas Becon's *Sycke Man's Salve*, was the exception and saw twenty-five editions from 1560 to

44 Clugston, *Looking-Glasse*, p. 269.

45 Mary Catherine O'Connor, *The Art of Dying Well* (New York, NY: Columbia University Press, 1942), pp. 39–40.

1632, but it was far too long, dull, and "daunting" to achieve real popularity.[46] The "booke of *Resolution*" filled that gap for Greene, and presumably for others, as Ian Green hypothesizes in accounting for its enormous publishing success.[47] However, its origins are peculiar. As Walsham explains, "Under Elizabeth, Protestantism itself was widely perceived to be lagging behind its pastoral adversaries in the publication of pastoral divinity." Since Reformed clergy were caught up in "the business of preaching, catechising, and casuistical instruction" while the "Catholic exiles [were] biding their time on the Continent," the former "sometimes resorted to appropriating and 'purging' classic works of popery like Robert Parsons' famous *First Booke of Christian Exercise*" [sic].[48] What Greene, and others, knew casually as "the book of Resolution" was originally *The First Book of Christian Exercise Appertaining to Resolution*, authored and published on the Continent by the prominent Jesuit Parsons, appropriated to English presses by the Puritan Edmund Bunny, and purged, although not to the satisfaction of the strictest readers. Parsons himself pointed out that Bunny's appropriation flagged the English clergy's failure to lead its flock. More temperately, Green proposes that "Bunny's choice of Parsons's work," virtually unrevised, evinces that even Puritans felt a "need for a greater emphasis on the affective elements in Christian doctrine than had existed in some earlier Calvinist works." Pointing to the importance of the Bunny/Parsons title to later sectarians including Richard Baxter, he hypothesizes that its attention to the needs of the dying specifically filled the need for an accessible "Protestant" *ars moriendi*. He notes that Bunny's commentary even refused to condemn deathbed repentance, as did most English Protestants, instead alluding to God's mysterious ways.[49]

The work's attention to the deathbed and hellfire, its generally affective or even lurid qualities, and even its doctrinal heterodoxy, all seem so right for Greene's sensibilities that they tend to confirm that Greene wrote the passage—or that Chettle knew how to extend Greene's persona. Its disputed origins, too, seem appropriate to the authorial tangles in which Greene and Chettle worked. Persons originally published the treatise at Rheims in 1582. It was republished in London in 1585 as an anonymous adaptation, with notes, minor emendations, and a "Treatise Tending to Pacification" of doctrinal differences. Parsons responded by expanding the work under the title of *A Christian Directorie*, with vigorous line-by-line rebuttals of Bunny's annotations, and a preface identifying Bunny as an appeaser with Catholicism, not to mention a thief. In 1589, Bunny wrote an

46 Green, *Print*, pp. 360–61; see also Nancy Lee Beaty, *The Craft of Dying: a Study in the Literary Tradition of the Ars Moriendi in England*, Yale Studies in English (New Haven: Yale University Press, 1970).

47 Green, *Print*, p. 361.

48 Walsham, "Preaching," p. 232. Robert Parsons, *The Christian Directory, 1607*, ed. D.M. Rogers, English Recusant Literature (Menston, Yorkshire: Scolar Press, 1970).

49 Green, *Print*, p. 361.

answer, hotly denying awareness that the text's original author was a Jesuit. The accretion of prefaces and marginal annotations created a paratext full of disputation, yet its language and its stake remained accessible to lay persons. Collectively, the Book of Resolution, under its various titles and the dual authorial hands of Bunny and Parsons, reached a remarkable thirty-four editions by 1600, including a bravura seventeen editions between 1584 and 1586, and it was still on the stationers' 1658 list of "vendible" books. Indeed, an earlier stationer characterized it as "the most vendible copy in our company these many years."[50] Its vendibility became as much a byword as Greene's ordinariness: Parsons wickedly noted that when Bunny discounted one patristic authority, it was as if saints "weighed not more in the affaires of our soule, then teen coople of Bunis, were they never so vendible."[51]

In his illness, Greene turns unerringly to the book's most lurid chapters on death, albeit by accident, and takes its affective descriptions as signals for his own physical reaction:

> at what time sodainly taking the booke of *Resolution* in my hand, I light upon a chapter therein, which discovered vnto mee the miserable state of the reprobate, what Hell was, what the worme of Conscience was, what tormentes there was appointed for the damned soules, ... nothing but feare, horrour, vexation of mind, deprivation from the sight and favour of God, **weeping and gnashing of teeth**, and that al those tortures were not termined or dated within any compasse of yeares, but everlasting world without end; concluding all in this of the Psalmes: *Ab inferis nulla est redemptio.*
>
> After that I had with deepe consideration pondered vpon these points, such a terrour stroke into my conscience, that for very anguish of minde **my teeth did beate in my head**, my lookes waxed pale and wan, and fetching a great sigh, I cried vnto God, ... If the rewarde of sinne be death and hell, how many deaths and hels do I deserue, that haue beene a most miserable sinner? (B2, emphasis added)

Greene's response to Bunny is remarkable in detailing both the specific phrases he read and the physical affect they produced. But his reading also is idiosyncratic, for Greene quickly seizes on the point that haunts *The Repentance*, the sense that he "cannot call to God for mercie" because his "faultes are beyond the compasse of [God's] favour": he is convinced that "there never lived a man of worser life" (B2–B2v) (although Greene certainly imagined worse sinners in his tragedies and crime pamphlets). The pamphlet seems obsessed with this point inasmuch as it queries which sins God is least likely to forgive, forget, or in the pamphlet's most striking phrase, "blot out." That fantasy itself seems to counter God's right to blot Greene

50 Brad Gregory, "The 'True and Zealouse Service of God': Robert Parsons, Edmund Bunny, and *The First Booke of the Christian Exercise*," *Journal of Ecclesiastical History* 45 (1994): 244–68.

51 Houliston, p. 170 quoting f12v of 1585 Parsons.

out of the book of life, an action on which he dwells, as though objecting to God's testy habit of revising his records. Greene "seemed as one of no religion, but rather as a meere Atheist, contemning the holy precepts uttered by any learned preacher: I would smile at such as would frequent the Church, or such place of godly exercise, ... so that herein I seemed a meere reprobate, ... one wipt out of the booke of life" (B1). Again, when he hears John More preach, he learns, "I should bee wipte out of the booke of life, if I did not speedily repent" (C2v). The book of life is Biblical, but Greene's repetition of the verbs "wiped" and, later, "blotted" suggests fascination with this authorial act, the fascination of an author who seldom blotted a line in his own manuscripts, but went on the record as regretting his previous publications. It also recalls the mockery of his friends wiping the efficacy of a sermon out of his conscience; it is as though Greene hopes God's memory is as poor as his own. This recalls that the letter to his wife asked her to "Forget and forgive my wronges done unto thee." Addressing God, he still is bold enough to imagine his soul as a book that can be rewritten, an extension of Calvinist thought into a textualized self that later writers, starting with Perkins and familiarly with Donne, would deploy often but with far more anxiety about the possibility of rewriting what has been predestined.

After a long description of Greene's horror at being beyond divine forgiveness, he skips to another chapter:

> In this despairing humor, searching further into the said Booke of *Resolution*, I found a place that greatly did comfort mee, & laid before me the promises of Gods mercie, shewing mee that although the Iustice of God was great to punish sinners, yet his mercie did exceede his works: and though my faults were as red as skarlet, yet washt with his bloud, they shoulde bee made as white as snow: therein was laid before mine eyes, that Dauid (Peter, and theefe all forgiven) ... I began to ... [take] great ioy and comfort in the pithie perswasions and promises of Gods mercie alleadged in that Booke.
>
> And yet I was not presently resolued in my conscience, that God would deale so fauorably with me, ... seeing all my life was lead in lewdnes, and I neuer but once felt any remorse of conscience ... . Yet calling vnto mind the words of *Esay*, that at what time soeuer a sinner doth repent him from the bottome of his heart, the Lord would **wipe away** all **his** wickednes out of **his** remembrance. (B3–B3v, emphasis added)

The final phrase confirms the ambiguity I have been tracing: What does it mean to "wipe away" wickedness"? Who is wiping whose wickedness out of whose remembrance? What is the relationship between Greene's (surely messy) book of conscience and God's infallible book of life? That Greene *is* rewriting Bunny very specifically is evident, for the exact page he summarizes can be found—and on it Bunny's shoulder note cites Ezekiel, not Isaiah. Bunny's main text paraphrases Ezekiel's promise that "At what time soever a sinner shall turn himself to me, I shall forgive his iniquities" (Bishop's, Ezekiel 33), as something more like Isaiah's chapter 55: "Let the ungodly man forsake his owne wayes, and the unrighteous his owne imaginations, and turne agayne vnto the Lorde, so shall he be mercifull unto hym: and to our God, for he is very redy to forgeve." Neither of these passages, of course, says "wipe away."

"Blot" occurs in the final prayer appended to the pamphlet, when Greene imagines God forgiving his sins: "Blot out my offences ... that they may not be a witnesse against me at the day of wrath" (D3v). According to the *OED*, "blot out" is more ambiguous than wipe, and can mean to blot pen ink away with water, or to blot out a written or printed word with more ink. The action might suggest, then, an author correcting printed proofs, God being the author of a printed book of life. Or the boldness of the request, and the notion of destroying a witness, might also suggest an angry reader defacing a written or printed calumny. Any reference to print is, of course, anachronistic in a Biblical paraphrase, but the pressure of Greene's context is strong.

That Greene's fascination with blotting reflects more than an authorial disposition, but an emerging textualization as English Protestantism takes in Calvinist ideas, can be suggested with another Biblical passage, from Acts, which Greene did not cite. In the Bishops' Bible this verse reads: "Repent ye therfore and convert, that your sinnes may be **done away**, when the tyme of refreshyng shall come, in the presence of the Lorde." But in 1611, the King James Bible uses "blot out": "Repent yee therefore, and bee conuerted, that your sins may be **blotted out**, when the times of refreshing shal come from the presence of the LORD" (Acts 3:19, emphasis added)

Greene's obsession with wiping or blotting away may arise from a writerly habitus, but it points to a deep concern with a sin that is truly unpardonable, one so unforgiveable in God's books that the only hope is that it will be deleted from the record. The structure of *The Repentance* suggests that the unpardonable sin on Greene's conscience is blasphemy. The event immediately precipitating Greene's illness and repentance was his boasting to his friends "that I feared the Judges of the bench no more than I dread the judgements of God or Hell itself" (Bv). This denial of God is, of course, blasphemy, to which Greene confesses in several of his autobiographical tracts, and to which Gabriel Harvey testifies. His blasphemy is reported later in this very pamphlet, in the "Life and Death," when he describes his youthful mockery of "the holy precepts uttered by any learned preacher"—and is implied when his friends scoff at him for being impressed by More's sermon. That mockery, too, was considered not just an offense to the Church but a blasphemous denial of the holy spirit. Hieron wrote, "he who thinks to be saved without preaching is damned"[52]; silver-tongued Smith said that "this refuse of preaching is but like swearing; for one takes the name of God in vain, and the other takes the word of God in vain" (I: 336), and Bishop Gardiner in 1599 alleged that "contempt for the ministry of the Word 'is the next dore to damnation it selfe.'"[53] The basis

52 Crockett, *Play*, p. 6.

53 Carlson, "Boring," p. 268.

for this claim was Mark, chapters 2 and 3; Jesus "forgives" a leper, and is charged by the scribes with blasphemy: "But there were certayne of the scribes syttyng there, and reasonyng in theyr heartes: Why doeth he thus speake blasphemies? Who can forgeve sinnes, but God only?" Jesus in turn charges the scribes themselves with blasphemy: "Veryly I say unto you, al sinnes shalbe forgeven unto the chyldren of men, & blasphemies wherewith so ever they have blasphemed: But he that speaketh blasphemie agaynst the holy ghoste, hath neuer forgeuenesse, but is in daunger of eternall dampnation" (Bishop's Bible, Mark 2–3). Greene may be conscious of this doctrinal position, for although the "Life and Death" reports the young scoffers' blasphemy, it carefully distances Greene from that act: "Thus although God sent his holy spirit to call mee, and though I heard him, yet I regarded it" only briefly. Greene admits that he *hears* the holy spirit, for to deny that is blasphemy; but then he must separate that hearing from his forsaken repentance, as he goes "forward obstinately in my misse" (C2v). As I have argued, however, the structure of the entire pamphlet, in questioning the efficacy of the best of preachers, counters the Elizabethan Church orthodoxy that preaching was an action of the Holy Spirit; in this particular doctrinal context, that questioning could seem to be the blasphemy against the Holy Spirit, which Jesus called unforgivable. Greene is entrapped by his own act of reporting his life, for if Greene's unpardonable sin is blasphemy, then publishing his prior blasphemies repeats, rather than blots out, the offense.

Why was reading so powerful in its effect on Greene that he not only was saved by a book but led to imagine his own life and God's mind as textual? If the "printing revolution" with its permanence and reproducibility rendered a change in him where the spoken word could not, did this anticipate the replacement of the Elizabethan puritans' emphasis on preaching with the later turn toward spiritual self-examination in devotional study and autobiography? Why was Greene in particular so unusually responsive to the change? As a playwright, why didn't he respond more powerfully to the performative as did most of his contemporaries? The answer could be that Greene was shaped by the particularity of his career, from his early scholarly training, through his authorial success, to his growing identification with cheap print as his "ordinary" means of expression, a biographical trajectory that itself charts the spread of the book. What we can be sure of is that this pamphlet's textual sense of devotion not only recapitulated his own move into vernacular culture, but also was offered influentially to his diverse readers, helping to popularize a recursively textualized life of faith.

IV. Writing

Of course, the literate practice of writing the self was familiar to the clergy through Augustine's *Confessions*, but this practice had been little imitated by English lay or popular authors in the sixteenth century. The seventeenth-century rise of spiritual autobiography is not the product of a continuous line of literate practice from Augustine, certainly not a continuous line of literate lay practice: the discontinuity makes Greene's pamphlet, even in its slightness and dubious sincerity, a significant landmark in the history of first-person writing. The primary early modern genres for writing the confessional self as narrative, other than the *ars moriendi*, were such second-person accounts as saints' lives, and their inverse, pamphlet accounts of murderers who repented at their executions. The Reformation disrupted these forms: saints' lives were outlawed (although Foxe certainly reinvented the genre to lasting effect), while gallows confessions had to inscribe eleventh-hour conversion as God's providence. The culture was not yet demanding orderly, continuous autobiographical accounts such as the conversion narratives (oral and written) or the spiritual autobiographies (private and published) that would come to characterize seventeenth-century sectarian experience. Crucially, however, that experience would stress life-long life writing, the continued struggle rather than the deathbed repentance, the Quaker conversion narrative rather than the criminal gallows conversion. One reason for distrusting autobiography written on the point of death was, of course, the problem of determining the authorial production was legitimate. Problematically, autobiographies written on deathbeds always require a ghostwriter for the final chapter. (Greene was unusual in also having ghostwriters who wrote sequels.) This is certainly the case with *The Repentance*, whose authorship has long been suspect. John Jowett has argued convincingly that Henry Chettle's editorial hand on this pamphlet was heavy, but that he was working with fragments generated by Greene.[54]

Crupi points out these questions of attribution and formal discontinuity echo the textual suspicions raised by the disorder of the pamphlets of 1590 (88–91). The fragmentary pieces that make up *The Repentance* certainly reinforce a sense that Greene's repentance is false, his faith insufficient.[55] As life narratives, Greene's pamphlets are disconcertingly discontinuous, but some of the textual problems require allowance for early modern generic expectations and publication conditions. The most immediate precedent in Greene's oeuvre for his repentance narratives demonstrates these fragmentary and collaborative qualities with a suspicious self-consciousness: his *Blacke Bookes Messenger* gives an account of "The Life and Death of Ned Browne" that is like a jestbook in its episodic form, but like a murder-pamphlet-gone-wrong in its rhetoric. Browne boasts that he is "resolutely, or rather reprobately given" but then scoffs, "But what should I stand heere preaching? I lived wantonly, and therefore let me end merrily" (C2). Why did Greene, then, stand there preaching? Modern editorial suspicions, and the probable skepticism of Greene's peers, discount all Greene's repentance writing. They certainly match Greene's worry about whether he has ever been effectually

---

54 John Jowett, "Johannes Factotum: Henry Chettle and Greene's Groatsworth of Wit." *Papers of the Bibliographic Society of America* 87: 453–86.

55 Clugston, *Looking-Glasse*, p. 41.

called to repentance. But in the later heyday of the spiritual autobiography, such self-doubts are not felt to render the entire work insincere. The uncertainty of Greene's sincerity may reflect his writing with uneven knowledge of an unevenly assimilated Calvinism in England: Predestination was kept under wraps by the theologians in this era—preachers were advised that "it were bad ... to dwell upon reprobation." The double decree would seize the popular imagination only when softened by the experimentalism that taught believers to read consoling signs of assurance in their lives.

Interestingly, an early work that modeled such experimentalism preceded Greene's *Repentance* (and Ned Browne's) by a year, and thus may furnish a kind of precedent for Greene's life writing. The collaged format of both *Blacke Bookes Messenger* and *The Repentance* corresponds to Philip Stubbes's equally brief and biographical *A christal Glasse for Christian women. Containing an excellent discourse, of the Godly life and Christian death of Mistresse Katherine Stubbes*: part spiritual biography, part dying prayer, part lay sermon. Stubbes's sentimental praise of his faultless nineteen-year-old dying wife went into a second edition within a year; its brevity allowed it to become a chapbook classic, exactly the kind of small book that Ian Green posits the market needed: at least twenty-four impressions by 1640, and chapbook adaptations afterward, are extant. Is it a coincidence that Stubbes's godly bestselling biography, Greene's sensational biography of Browne, and Greene's autobiographical last gasp, all constituted fragments into exactly one signature in quarto? In other words, were all these authentic biographies written to become bestsellers?

My questioning the motives for producing so popular a godly text might seem blasphemous, but, in fact, Walsham has already uncovered the chequered authorial history of the supposedly godly Philip Stubbes. In her article "A Glose of Godliness," she reconstructs Stubbes's career and finds that he was closer to a career writer like Greene than to the Puritan he has long been considered; his *Anatomie of Abuses*, infamous for its antitheatricality, may have been a written to sell or as a fairly conventional satire on pride. Walsham shows that his peers had their suspicions about his sincerity, too. She cites an anecdote about reverend P, "one learned Hypocrite, that could brooke no abuses in the Commonwealth," conspiring with his brother to represent his wealth falsely to a possible bride. But it is the detail about his first wife that connects P's identity to Stubbes's: P. is "so zelous that he bagan to put in English the she Saint in the Legend for the holinesse of her life: and forgot not so much as her dogge, as Tobies [dog] was remembred."[56] As it happens, Walsham found this anecdote in yet another one-signature popular pamphlet, the *Defence of Conny Catching* (1592), apocryphally

56 "'A Glose of Godlines': Philip Stubbes, Elizabethan Grub Street and the Invention of Puritanism," in Susan Wabuda and Caroline Litzenberger (eds), *Belief and Practice in Reformation England: A Tribute to Patrick Collinson From His Students* (Aldershot: Ashgate, 1998), p. 179.

attributed to the late Robert Greene. That this anecdote may be as apocryphal as Tobias or *Defence* is immaterial to Walsham's point that popular print culture freely depicted Stubbes as insincere, and as capable of rewriting the popular genre of the saint's life as a Protestant penny pamphlet. The same fragmentation, collaborative authorship, and questions of sincerity that haunt the textualized repentance penned about Ned Browne and Robert Greene (with some help from Chettle), could well have haunted that penned by Philip Stubbes about Katherine Stubbes. In light of the instability of the status of life writing in this era of emergent Calvinism and expanding cheap print, it may be wise to shift our interest in devotional texts from authenticity to affect, for then we can value Greene's contribution more fully.

Those insights might be carried back to Greene's other intertexts as well and help us see how print itself enables new kinds of affective experiences. There is no question that Greene's response to Bunny is intensely involved with its printed appearance. The detail from the chapter on presumption that Greene both quoted and physically imitated, the chattering teeth, is called out on Bunny's page by a shoulder note: "* Gnashing and chattering of the teeth are not alone, & proceede of diuerse causes" (Bunny, Part II chapter 4, p. 315). Of course, Greene has every reason to worry about presuming grace with his much-delayed resolution to repent; but that his teeth chatter at the thought seems to be a graphic cue, a fusing of verbal and visual information with bodily affect. For us to assume that such a material cue renders his spiritual experience more insincere than that of later spiritual autobiographers would itself be presumption. In the end, Greene's "literary" temper and his flair for spotting and using print commodities acquire greater devotional influence when he misperceives religion as printed record. In questioning the medium of the call to repentance, Greene asks questions that will become urgent in English Protestantism, even if they seem flippant in 1592. In the end, we cannot separate these writers' making of commercial texts from their writing to save their lives, and that makes Greene's repentance representative indeed.

Chapter 8

Robert Greene and the Uses of Time

Robert W. Maslen

I. Time-Wasting, Time-Serving, Trouble

By the time Greene died of a surfeit of pickled herrings and Rhenish wine in 1592, he had frittered away his talents as a writer in two spheres that he himself dismisses in his writings as a criminal waste of time: prose fiction and the theatre.[1] Yet the frequency with which he denounces his own productions as frivolous toys, evidence of a misspent youth and an addiction to physical and imaginative excess, betrays Greene's perverse pride in what he has done; a pride that manifests itself on every page of the so-called repentance pamphlets he published toward the end of his life.[2] In these he carefully retraces each twist and turn of his prolific career, showing off the creative energy of his work under the guise of rejecting it as useless—that is, as incapable of being accommodated among the narrow list of activities deemed morally profitable by the solemn elder statesmen of Elizabethan England. In doing so he calls into question the validity of these old men's definitions of productive labor, of time well spent, even of value or worth itself. With a strange mixture of tentativeness and arrogance he sets up his own writing as a wayward alternative to the literary canon they favor, offering a more realistic, if more disturbing, appraisal of how the world works than anything on offer in the official school curriculum.[3] And it is, above all, in their attitude toward the slippery concept of time that Greene's writings differentiate themselves from the

---

1 The circumstances of Greene's death-by-herring are given in Gabriel Harvey's pamphlet *Foure Letters and Certaine Sonnets: Especially Touching Robert Greene* (1592). See *The Works of Gabriel Harvey*, Alexander B. Grosart (ed.), 3 vols (London and Aylesbury: privately printed, 1884), vol. 1, p. 162 etc. It should be added that there is no hard evidence to support Harvey's account.

2 A fine account of these repentance pamphlets is given in Derek Alwes, *Sons and Authors in Elizabethan England* (Newark: University of Delaware Press, 2004), chapter 6.

3 I have discussed the idea of Elizabethan prose fiction as an alternative to the school curriculum in *Elizabethan Fictions: Espionage, Counter-espionage and the Duplicity of Fiction in Early Elizabethan Prose Narratives* (Oxford: Clarendon Press, 1997).

revered texts of the canon, and from the rigid system of values they supposedly represent.[4]

For Thomas Nashe, Greene was an exemplary user of his time as a professional writer. The sheer number of his publications, Nashe writes in his preface to Greene's *Menaphon* (1589), demonstrates his matchless capacity for improvisation, that is, for the spontaneous adaptation of his style to the needs of a given moment. "Let other men," he scoffs,

> praise the mountaine that in seaven yeares brings foorth a mouse… but give me the man, whose extemporall vaine in anie humor, will excell our greatest Art-masters deliberate thoughts; whose invention quicker than his eye, will challenge the proudest Rethoritian, to the contention of like perfection, with like expedition (sig. *b*1^{v}).[5]

Nashe's praise of the extraordinary *speed* of Greene's inventiveness pits him against the views of the famous pedagogue Roger Ascham, who held rapidity of thought and action to be signs of damaging rashness in his students, and who celebrated slow pensiveness as a prerequisite for good scholarship and a stable career.[6] For Ascham, the best of modern writers has his mind embedded in a few unchanging truths about religion and good government, laid down in the course of a lifetime's analysis of ancient authors. For Nashe, by contrast, the best of writers is the man who responds with greatest agility to sudden changes in fashion, shifts in political circumstances, reversals in the expected sequence of current events. Greene and his characters inhabit Nashe's world, not Ascham's: a world where Fortune rules instead of Providence, where the state authorities are invariably corrupt, and where the amorous women who were dismissed as fickle by contemporary moralists represent the sole stable feature in an ever-mutating landscape, stranded like incorruptible Patient Griseldas amidst a population of treacherous males while courageously laying about them with their unrivalled verbal artistry. In this world, virtue counts for nothing if you cannot respond with

---

4 My discussion here complements my discussion of Shakespeare's comic timing in *Shakespeare and Comedy*, Arden Critical Companions (London: Thomson Learning, 2005). My understanding of Greene owes a lot to two important recent discussions of his work, to which I was fortunate enough to have access before publication: Alwes, *Sons and Authors*, and Katherine Wilson, *Fictions of Authorship in Late Elizabethan Narratives: Euphues in Arcadia* (Oxford: Clarendon Press, 2006). Other major influences have been Arthur F. Kinney, *Humanist Poetics: Thought, Rhetoric, and Fiction in Sixteenth-century England* (Amherst: University of Massachusetts Press, 1986), David Margolies, *Novel and Society in Elizabethan England* (Totowa, NJ: Barnes and Noble, 1985), and Lori Humphrey Newcomb, *Reading Popular Romance in Early Modern England* (New York, NY: Columbia University Press, 2002).

5 *Menaphon: Camilla's Alarum to Slumbering Euphues*, 1589 edition. All quotations have been taken from the earliest editions available to me. Titles have been modernized.

6 See my *Elizabethan Fictions*, chapter 1, pp. 41–51, and introduction.

lightning reflexes to the shocking twists thrown up by time; and it's women and poets who possess these reflexes in most dazzling abundance.

Greene, then, is no acolyte of Ascham's, and he takes evident pleasure in confounding the expectations of readers who might share Ascham's understanding of the rights and wrongs of Elizabethan culture. His works proclaim their chronological displacement from the "official" calendar—the schedule set by schoolmasters, governors, and churchmen—in a number of ways. For one thing, they ostentatiously suspend official time in order to have their say. They take place in intervals of apparent inaction: truancy from study (*Ciceronis Amor*), truce in the midst of war (*Euphues his Censure to Philautus*), rest from labor (*Perimedes the Blacksmith*), periods of exile or displacement (*Pandosto*, *Menaphon*, *The Scottish History of James IV*), madness (*Orlando Furioso*), escape from affairs of state (*Friar Bacon and Friar Bungay*), crime sprees indulged in as a means of evading productive employment (the cony-catching pamphlets). For another thing, they write themselves into the gaps, so to speak, in the Elizabethan canon.[7] *Euphues his Censure to Philautus* (1587) makes a space for itself among the classical accounts of the Trojan War, as Greeks and Trojans take time off from slaughter to explore their differences in debate. *Penelope's Web* (1587) occupies one of the narrative lacunae in the *Odyssey*: What did Penelope and her women talk about as they unpicked her unending shroud during the long nights of Ulysses's absence? *Ciceronis Amor* (1589) takes the youth and leisure time of the most influential of Roman orators as its subject, absorbing Cicero's verbal skills into the despised mode of the love-story; while *The Mirror of Modesty* (1584) rewrites the story of Susanna and the Elders, a book of the Bible that had been ejected as apocryphal from the Protestant Scriptures. By interposing themselves *between* canonical texts, as it were—illuminating moments that have been left dark by the literary authorities—Greene's works imply that what is learned in school time does not adequately prepare young men for the bewildering range of experience they will encounter when they leave the safety of the schoolroom. The perceptions of his wily, worldly narrator/playwright are necessary if these pupils are not to be misled, as he was, when they emerge into the ever-shifting world of sexual and social interaction. But unlike canonical texts as taught by schoolmasters, Greene's works offer no promise of protection against such misleading. In them, passion is always overthrowing reason; vice always confounding virtue; and verbal and visual disguises are always impenetrable. They are filled with wily misleaders—tricksters, deceivers, traitors, politicians—whose actions can only be distinguished from those of honest folk by the inhuman operations of time, as seasons pass, new generations grow to maturity, and the lies of bygone ages are exposed at last to public scrutiny.

---

7 See Wilson, *Fictions of Authorship*, p. 86.

Ascham's pedagogic method was based on the art of imitation.[8] By mimicking the style of the ancients, he claimed, students could develop rhetorical skills that would prove invaluable in the cut-and-thrust of legal or parliamentary debate. Greene's reworkings of canonical texts, by contrast, ground themselves in the art of plagiarism, impudently hijacking other men's work for purposes of self-promotion. He admits as much in the dedication to *The Mirror of Modesty*, in a sentence that eerily foreshadows his famous attack on Shakespeare.[9] "Your honor may thinke I play like Ezops Crowe," Greene tells his dedicatee, "which deckt hir selfe with others feathers, or like the proud Poet Batyllus, which subscribed his name to Virgils verses, and yet presented them to Augustus" (sig. *a*3ʳ). At the same time, his impudent appropriation of a biblical story has been rewritten in Greene's inimitable style: it is "freshlie flourished with mine owne coulours." The word "coulours" carries implications of disguise and verbal trickery, qualities one might expect the notorious Roman plagiarist Bathyllus to cultivate.[10] Greene's preface to his fiction *Menaphon*, too, playfully links the author to Bathyllus, who figures here as the prolific generator of bad poetry, "that at everie winke of Caesar would deliver up an hundred verses, though never a one plausible" (sig. *a*2ᵛ). As he rewrites the canon, Greene implicitly revises Renaissance assumptions about the function of literature, discarding its claim to embody universal truths and good examples, and characterizing it instead as a shamelessly opportunistic medium that responds with chameleon promptness to the vagaries of the marketplace. Greene is the poet of time-serving rather than of timelessness, and many of the worlds he colors seem to challenge the notion that anything "timeless" exists at all.

It seems appropriate, in an essay on this time-bound writer, to confine oneself to a specific moment in his career: a moment when he seems to have been specially concerned with the question of the role of the author-playwright in the reign of Elizabeth I. From 1589 to 1590 Greene wrote a profusion of fictions and plays that paint a vivid picture of the writer's volatile relationship with the troubled times he

---

8 See especially his influential pedagogic tract *The Schoolmaster* (1570), in *English Works*, ed. William Aldis Wright (Cambridge: Cambridge University Press, 1904), pp.171–302. On the place of imitation in the Renaissance, see Thomas M. Greene, *The Light in Troy: Imitation and Discovery in Renaissance Poetry* (New Haven and London: Yale University Press, 1982).

9 The presumed attack on Shakespeare occurs in *Greene's Groatsworth of Wit, Bought with a Million of Repentance* (1592): "for there is an upstart Crow, beautified with our feathers, that with his *Tygers heart wrapt in a Players hide*, supposes he is as well able to bombast out a blanke verse as the best of you ..." (sig. F1ᵛ). For the question of Greene's authorship of this tract, see D. Allen Carroll (ed.), *Greene's Groatsworth of Wit*, Medieval and Renaissance Texts and Studies, vol. 114 (Binghamton, NY: Centre for Medieval and Early Renaissance Studies, 1994), introduction.

10 Bathyllus or Batillus was a mediocre poet who tried to claim some verses by Virgil as his own. The story is told in the *Life of Virgil* attributed to Aelius Donatus, which can be found at http://virgil.org/vitae/, translated by David Wilson-Okamura (1996; rev. 2005).

lives in.[11] In each case, a writer, poet, or scholar finds himself mixed up with tyrants, wicked old men, treacherous relatives, unscrupulous con-artists,or habitual abusers of the legal system. In each case, he finds himself on the wrong side of the law. And in each case he gets many chances to display his skills as an improviser as he seeks to disengage himself by cunning from the dangers that beset him.

Greene's impulse to plagiarize manifests itself frequently in these texts, as he plunders his own back catalogue in a bid to stave off starvation. Imagination clashes with pragmatism, the impulse to write literary and theatrical romance with a painful sense of the economic imperatives that fuel that impulse. And he is always aware that a similar conflict exists at the heart of Elizabethan culture, as idealized perceptions of the social hierarchy and its customs are repeatedly swept aside by the desires of the powerful or the demands of economic or political expediency. It is tempting, then, to read these pamphlets as a form of cumulative autobiography, a means by which Greene sought to write himself into the history of his time—and perhaps to change the way the people of that time saw themselves. I shall suggest here that this is a profoundly satisfying way of reading them.

II. "The Triumphes of inconstant Time": Greene's *Menaphon*

Nashe's comments on Greene's facility as a writer occur in his preface to the pastoral romance *Menaphon: Camilla's Alarum to the Slumbering Euphues* (1589). This is a book that presents itself as a summary and celebration of Greene's literary career so far. The book's subtitle sets it up in friendly rivalry with the two most popular fictions of the last decade, John Lyly's *Euphues* books (1578 and 1580), whose ornate prose style and scandalous domestic plot had a huge effect on the fictions that followed them—not least Greene's own. Nashe's preface implicitly develops this notion of *Menaphon* as the up-to-date successor to Lyly's bestsellers. In it Lyly figures as a plagiarist, whose "Italionate pen ... of a packet of pilfries [i.e. stolen goods] affoordeth the presse a pamphlet or two in an age, and then in disguised arraie, vaunts Ovids and Plutarchs plumes as their owne" (sig. *b*1^{v}), and whose sluggish work-rate compares unfavorably to Greene's hectic generation of narratives.[12] The preface is preceded by commendatory verses that continue to

11 These include the prose works *Ciceronis Amor*, *Menaphon*, *Greene's Never Too Late*, *Franscesco's Fortunes*, *Greene's Mourning Garment*, and *Greene's Vision*, and probably the plays *Friar Bacon and Friar Bungay*, *The Scottish History of James IV*, and (with Lodge) *A Looking Glass for London and England.* For the dates of *Greene's Vision* and *A Looking Glass*, see section 4 of this essay.

12 That Lyly is alluded to here seems probable since the first *Euphues* book was set in Naples (hence "Italionate pen") and contained extensive adaptations from Plutarch and Ovid ("Euphues and his Ephebus" and "A Cooling Card for Philautus"). See *Euphues:*

invoke the Lyly/Greene rivalry: "Of all the flowers a Lillie on[c]e I lov'd," they proclaim, "But now old age his glorie hath removd, / And Greener objectes are my eyes aboade" (sig. *a*3^r). *Menaphon*, then, is locked into its time and place, and Nashe proclaims its built-in redundancy even as he trumpets Greene's credentials as the darling of the moment, the young pretender to Lyly's laurel crown who will forfeit it by and by to someone younger still—perhaps Nashe himself, whose first literary fruits this preface is.

Greene's own allusion to Lyly in *Menaphon* is wittier and more affectionate than Nashe's crude dismissal. As two young people size each other up as potential lovers, each inwardly criticizes the other's prose style for its tasteless extravagance: Samela thinks Melicertus possessed by an "inkhorne desire to be eloquent" while Melicertus 'imagined she smoothed her talke to be thought like Sapho, Phaos paramour' (sig. F1^r). The style they are using at this point is euphuism, a system of balanced clauses and far-fetched comparisons which Lyly popularized in *Euphues* and refined in a series of court comedies, including *Sapho and Phao.*[13] Samela and Melicertus can only be united as lovers once they have discarded this style for something simpler and more modish. Greene's romance, then, like its preface, inhabits a world where literary tastes are always changing, writers and rhetorical techniques forever slipping out of fashion. And this is just one of the many ways in which time's inconstancy manifests itself in the narrative, rendering its version of Arcadia profoundly unstable and the inhabitants of that literary country both paranoid and aggressive, as the boundaries of their nation and their personal lives are repeatedly breached by calamities or ruthless outsiders.

What was it that made Nashe and Greene so fiercely competitive in 1589? And what made Greene so conscious of the fluctuations of stylistic fashion? One answer might be the meteoric rise of Marlowe, whose *Tamburlaine* took the stage by storm in 1587, and whose *Faustus* may have been the talk of the town when *Menaphon* was being written.[14] Nashe's preface alludes to Marlowe in the same disparaging terms he uses for Lyly,[15] and Greene's narrative invokes him twice:

The Anatomy of Wit and Euphues and his England, ed. Leah Scragg (Manchester and New York: Manchester University Press, 2003), p. 88 n. 2 and p. 99 n. 4. In addition, Lyly's dedication to the second *Euphues* book makes much of its belatedness (see *Euphues*, ed. Scragg, pp. 155–60); and Lyly had only published two "pamphlets" under his own name (the two *Euphues* books) by the time Nashe wrote these comments.

13 See Jonas A. Barish, "The Prose Style of John Lyly," *ELH* 23 (1956), pp. 14–35. On Greene's relationship to Lyly's style see Wilson, *Fictions of Authorship*, pp. 126–37.

14 On the arguments for an early date for *Faustus*, see *Doctor Faustus*, ed. David Bevington and Eric Rasmussen, The Revel's Plays (Manchester and New York: Manchester University Press, 1993), pp. 1–2. I adduce further evidence for the early dating of Marlowe's play in this essay, especially the echoes that seem to be present in *Greene's Vision* (see section 4).

15 That is, if the passage at sig. *b*1^r of the preface refers to Marlowe, who could be one of the "idiote art-masters, that intrude themselves to our eares as the alcumists of

once when the shepherd Menaphon woos Samela in a prose version of Marlowe's famous lyric "Come live with me and be my love" (sig. D1^r); and once when Samela mockingly compares Melicertus to Tamburlaine (sig. F2^r). Nashe also makes an abusive reference to Thomas Kyd, whose *Spanish Tragedy* was the biggest box-office hit of the late 1580s (sig. *b*3^r). With Nashe's help, Greene seems to be carving out a niche for himself in the steadily expanding mid-Elizabethan hall of literary fame. But it is a niche from which he might easily be toppled; part of what makes Greene's place in it so precarious is his class. He is a social parvenu with no hereditary right to the eminence he currently occupies. Time has not confirmed his position, and there is no guarantee that he will manage to retain it—hence, no doubt, his anxious insistence on repeating on every title page his principal claim to high social status, the fact that he has been awarded the degree of Master of Arts by both Oxford and Cambridge. Greene may, therefore, have read Nashe's scornful strictures on the class origins of his chief rivals with some discomfort, conscious that they could be as easily applied to him, should Nashe's loyalty prove as mercurial as his pen.

For Nashe, Kyd's work is to be dismissed because he is a scrivener's son who did not attend the university, and who depends for inspiration on English translations of the classics rather than Greek or Latin originals.[16] This allies him to the tasteless "mechanicall mates" or craftsmen who delight in ornate English, the language of the "inkhorne" (sig. *b*1^r); with "vainglorious tragoedians" or tragic actors who stake their claim to immortality on clichéd allusions to classical myth; and with the "idiote art-masters" (such as Marlowe, another Master of Arts from Cambridge) who supply these actors with "the swelling bumbast of a bragging blanke verse" in support of their aspirations. Springing up alongside these are the "ironicall censors of all" (sig. *b*1^v), uneducated satirists like the radical pamphleteer Martin Marprelate who take it on themselves to reprimand their "superiours" and to "correct Common weales" (sig. *b*2^v). In Nashe's world, in other words, there is a clear hierarchy of intellect, which operates hand in glove with the social hierarchy. Learning properly used upholds the status quo, and those who step out of line by harboring literary ambitions when they have no degree, or by feeding the egos of actors with the fruits of their university studies, or by interfering with affairs of state in popular print, become the targets of Nashe's own satire, which castigates them all as base-born hacks who steal their ideas and style

---

eloquence, who (mounted on the stage of arrogance) think to outbrave better pens with the swelling bumbast of a bragging blanke verse." The author of *Tamburlaine* fits the bill pretty neatly.

16 Nashe refers to writers who "leave the trade of Noverint [i.e. the scrivener's trade] whereto they were borne, and busie themselves with the indevors of Art," using "English Seneca read by candle light" as inspiration, and leaping into the playwright's profession as rashly as "the Kidde in Aesop" leapt into the fox's jaws (sig. *b*3^r).

from the "private devices" or unpublished work of the aristocracy and gentry, tricking themselves out with the feathers of well-born "Poets" (sig. A2^{v}).

Quite how far Greene would have concurred with this class-based critique of contemporary writers it is hard to tell. He certainly attacks the pretensions of common players elsewhere in his work, dismissing them as self-important practitioners of a merely "mechanical" art who are parasitically reliant on the skills of educated writers such as himself.[17] But by the time he wrote *Menaphon* he had probably been writing for the stage for several years, and had been guilty of some extravagant blank verse in his *Comical History of Alphonsus, King of Aragon* (c. 1587–88), a close imitation of Marlowe's *Tamburlaine*; so he could be said to have made a contribution to the swollen egos of the players which Nashe found so objectionable. In addition, Nashe's accusations of plagiarism against his contemporaries may have brought a faint blush to Greene's cheek. As we have seen, he had characterized his own work as plagiaristic in *The Mirror of Modesty*, and *Menaphon* is in several senses a parasitical text. For one thing, it draws heavily on Greene's own earlier romances, especially *Gwydonius* (1584) and *Pandosto* (1588). Like *Gwydonius* it culminates in a single combat between a father and son, and like *Pandosto* it features a tyrant who exiles his daughter to a pastoral setting and who conceives an incestuous lust for her in the book's last pages. It steals at least one of its episodes—the abduction of a beautiful boy by pirates—from Longus's erotic pastoral *Daphnis and Chloe*, published in English translation in 1587. And Greene's romance also draws on an unpublished text by a modern writer far superior to Greene in social status: Sir Philip Sidney. Sidney's *Arcadia* circulated widely in manuscript before its publication in 1590, and *Menaphon* looks as though it were written with a thorough knowledge of it.[18] Both books open with an ominous prophecy, later fulfilled; in both a king is humiliatingly subjected to the torments of "unnatural" desire. Both contain male members of the ruling class disguised as shepherds who court princesses, and in both the courtship culminates in abduction and civil war. Given these resemblances between his romance and the unpublished work of a dead aristocrat, Greene may have regarded Nashe's strictures on literary thievery as hitting a little too close to home.

But there are two major differences between Greene's *Menaphon* and Sidney's *Arcadia*: their relative length and the perspectives they adopt. Greene accelerates the pace of Sidney's text enormously, cramming sixteen years of his characters' lives into a narrative less than half as long as the shorter version of Sidney's epic. And Greene's work adopts at times the point of view of the shepherds, as Sidney's never does. *Menaphon*'s rapidity in getting through its plot marks it out as the

17 See Cicero's attack on the arrogance of the player Roscius in *Francesco's Fortunes: or the Second Part of Greene's Never too Late* (1592): "I grant your action, though it bee a kind of mechanicall labour, yet well done tis worthy of praise: but you worthlesse, if for so small a toy you waxe proud" (sig. I4^{v}). Cited from the 1600 edition.

18 See Wilson, *Fictions of Authorship*, pp. 4–8.

product of a working man with a living to earn, as does its preoccupation with the agricultural work done by the peasantry; so that in imitating Sidney's romance, Greene seems as much concerned to distance himself from its author as he does to emulate his achievements.

Paradoxically, one of the means Greene uses to distance himself from Sidney is to bring the social classes closer together. Greene's Arcadia, unlike Sidney's, is a place where the classes meet for a time on equal terms; where disguised lords, princesses, even kings rub shoulders with herdsmen; and where a person's worth is measured by verbal skill, not social standing. This temporary rapprochement between rich and poor is heralded at the beginning of the book by an outbreak of the plague, which affects all Arcadians equally, the ruling classes as well as the commons. The King of Arcadia reacts to the crisis with an acknowledgement of his responsibilities to his people, recognizing that "the strength of his subjects was the sinnewes of his dominions, and that every crowne, must conteyne a care, not onely to winne honour by forrayne conquests, but in mainteining dignitie with civill and domestical insights" (sig. B1^{r}). With parliamentary approval, he looks for such insights from the Delphic oracle, which responds with its wonted ambiguity, deferring the advent of "a happie time" until after a series of seemingly impossible conditions have been met (sig. B1^{v}). The romance takes place, then, during a period when normal rules have been suspended, so that the classes thrown together in the course of the narrative find it easier than usual to see what they have in common. Besides their disease-prone bodies, the shepherds and aristocrats learn that they share common passions (desire, irascibility, envy); common weaknesses (fickleness, pride); common skills (they are all accomplished versifiers); and common pursuits, as aristocrats learn to work with their hands and herdsmen learn to wage war. Under these circumstances, when a pair of banished aristocrats seeks shelter among the Arcadian shepherds they find themselves able to adapt with consummate ease to their humble environment. As soon as the princess Sephestia puts on pastoral clothes and assumes a pseudonym, Samela, even the shepherd Menaphon, who knows her royal status, is able to treat her as an equal. And Sephestia soon comes to love her new life, finding "such content in the cotage" that she begins "to despise the honors of the Court" (sig. D3^{r}). Her husband, Maximius, too, adapts with alacrity to his new context, blending in so well with the rural community that his identity as the shepherd Melicertus is not revealed until half way through the book. For a while, then, Greene's Arcadia looks almost Utopian, the egalitarian contentedness of its inhabitants marred only by the occasional outbreak of comic jealousy, the odd piratical raid on the coastline.

But the title page of *Menaphon* warns us not to expect this situation to last. The book here proclaims its preoccupation with "the variable effects of Fortune, the wonders of Love, the triumphes of inconstant Time"; all phrases that stress the waywardness of the book's events, their exceptional nature, their resistance to regulation or government. The phrase "inconstant Time", which echoes "the Triumph of Time" on the title-page of *Pandosto*, militates against the idea of stasis, or even of predictability. And as in all of Greene's romances, one chief reason for time's unpredictability in this book is the inconstancy of men; above all, royal men. Male monarchs and their offspring are rapacious egomaniacs, whose lusts are incestuous and whose wars are waged on a whim. Addicted to treachery, they get close to their inferiors only with the aim of betraying them; when all else fails, they set up kangaroo courts to dispose of those who resist their tyranny. The triumph of time in *Menaphon* is to expose the murderous inconstancy of these royal men to public scrutiny. And the process marks out *Menaphon*'s narrator as a political satirist of some courage, prepared to open up the fault-lines in monarchist culture for all to see, despite the modesty of his own class origins.[19]

The narrator-satirist's tool in this business of exposure is a literary mode that is often associated with the uncritical celebration of royalty: romance.[20] The plague precipitates Arcadia into what may be called "romance time," when the effects of Fortune and the wonders of love are everywhere in evidence. In romance, relatives lose and find one another by chains of outrageous coincidences, last-minute reprieves preserve the lives of men and women whose survival seemed past hope, and aristocrats find their natural nobleness rewarded with a happy ending. Greene's book contains all these ingredients and more. The aristocratic couple who have disguised themselves as Arcadian shepherds meet by chance and fall in love, before finding out years later that they were already husband and wife. Their son is kidnapped by pirates, raised by a king and queen, then falls in love with a picture of his own mother and hurries back to Arcadia to kidnap her for himself. Her husband, the kidnapper's father, still in his shepherd's disguise, leads a rustic army to her rescue and challenges his son to single combat. The combat is interrupted before any blood can be shed, and the book ends with a series of last-minute revelations that reunite all long-lost relatives and reconcile all enmities. So far so familiar; this might be the plot of any English or Hispanic tale of chivalry, of the kind whose popularity reached new heights in the 1580s.[21] But more even than most of these, the climax of Greene's romance is a family affair, and there is an element of pastiche in the extent to which all of the key players turn out to be interrelated. The final combat between father and son is fought over the former's wife and the latter's mother; it is interrupted by the young man's grandfather, the King

19 For the idea of the author as satirist, as developed by one of Greene's contemporaries and collaborators, Thomas Lodge, see my "Lodge's *Glaucus and Scilla* and the Conditions of Catholic Authorship in Elizabethan England," *EnterText* 3.1 (Spring 2003): 59–100.

20 For a full account of the romance tradition in Elizabethan England, see Helen Cooper, *The English Romance in Time: Transforming Motifs from Geoffrey of Monmouth to the Death of Shakespeare* (Oxford: Oxford University Press, 2004).

21 On the popularity of the English romance tradition in Elizabethan times, see Cooper, *The Romance in Time*, introduction. On the popularity of Hispanic—or more accurately Iberian—romance, see Helen Hackett, *Women and Romance Fiction in the English Renaissance* (Cambridge: Cambridge University Press, 2000), chapter 4.

of Arcadia, who throws the combatants in prison and proceeds to vent his spleen on the shepherd army by subjecting it to wholesale slaughter. The climactic battle, then, is a right royal rumpus, and most of the royals involved are unprincipled thugs. The effect of the wonders and coincidences that conclude the narrative is to underline the class antagonisms that have simmered beneath the surface of the text throughout its length. Like many of Greene's romances, *Menaphon* damages relations between the classes instead of shoring them up; it is hardly surprising when the withdrawal of the courtiers from the countryside at the end is greeted by the peasantry with resignation, even relief, instead of the universal acclamations that close (say) Sidney's *Old Arcadia* or Longus's *Daphnis and Chloe*.[22]

At the end of *Pandosto*, some shepherds acquire gentlemanly status as a reward for raising the Princess Fawnia. In *Menaphon*, by contrast, the humble benefactors of Sephestia are always harmed by close contact with royalty, and kings in pastoral garb prove as deadly to them as wolves in sheep's clothing. When King Democles falls in love with Sephestia, he dons shepherd's clothes to get at her; it is in these same shepherd's clothes that he persuades Prince Pleusidippus to carry her off, then stirs up the other shepherds to attack the prince in a bid to get her back—a bid that ends in a general massacre at the hands of King Democles's troops. The king, in fact, has nothing but contempt for what he calls "the basenesse of Shepheards" (sig. H4^{v}); which makes it all the more shocking that he can adopt their dress whenever it suits him, make an emotive appeal to class solidarity when he chooses to incite them to violence ("Shepheardes, you see my profession is your trade" [sig. I1^{r}]), and simulate grief over the abduction of Sephestia despite the fact that he masterminded the abduction himself. His hypocrisy is breathtaking, his sense of gratitude nonexistent, his morality unfathomable. Clearly by the end of the story, he has forgotten everything he said during the plague about a monarch's duty to his subjects. He has no consistent policies or values, and his ready self-adjustment to the whims of the moment prove deadly to those who try to trust him.

His grandson Pleusidippus is no better. Brought up by his banished mother, Sephestia, among shepherds, the child's royal blood manifests itself in his beauty, his blood-lust, and his tendency to treason. His favorite game with his friends the shepherd boys is to condemn them to death for resisting his "authoritie" (sig. F4^{r}). Abducted by pirates, Pleusidippus is raised by the King of Thessaly, but betrays his adopted father before he has come of age. On seeing a portrait of Sephestia he falls in love with her at once, abandons his fiancée—the king's daughter—and hurries off to woo his own mother instead. Like Democles he disguises himself as a shepherd to get at her, and like Democles he refuses to take no for an answer: on being rejected he carries her off to a nearby castle. When the shepherd army besieges the castle to win her back, he shows his contempt for them in a string of insults worthy of his grandfather, mocking them from the battlements as "sheepe

---

22 The most thorough account of Greene's relation to class is that of David Margolies, *Novel and Society*, chapter 7.

transformed into men, swaines into souldiers, and a wandring companie of poore shepheards, into a worthie troope of resolute champions" (sig. K1^{r}). Like Democles, then, he is a traitor both to his own class and to the laboring class who nurtured him in his hour of need. He is, in fact, a latter-day counterpart of the Trojan prince Paris, whose abandonment of the shepherdess Oenone for Helen brought about the destruction of Troy, and whose story is often invoked in Greene's romance. If time tries truth, as *Pandosto* and other Elizabethan fictions asserted,[23] then the outcome of this trial in *Menaphon* is to brand the men of the Arcadian royal family as vacillating tyrants, whose vacillations wreak havoc on their land and subjects.

Greene's own position in the romance seems closer to that of the peasantry than to that of the wayward royals. He is identified with the "scholler-like Shepheard" Menaphon both in Nashe's preface (sig. *b*1^{r}) and in the commendatory verses (sig. *a*3^{r}-*a*3^{v}), and at first it seems that the association is hardly a compliment.[24] Like Greene, Menaphon harbors high intellectual pretensions when we meet him. His lyrics are as fine as any Greene penned, and he considers his "sheep-walkes to yeeld as great Philosophie, as the Ancients discourse in their learned Academies" (sig. B2^{v}). But within a few pages, he falls for a woman above his station, and his change of emotional status plunges him at once into comic clownishness. He and his sister sit in their cottage bemoaning his condition: "she blubbered and he [sighed], and his men that came in and saw their master with a kercher on his head mournde; so that amongst these swaines there was such melodie, that Menaphon ... went to bedde" (sig. C3^{v}–C4^{r}). When he wakes next morning he goes "roundly to his breakfast" (sig. C4^{v}), then decides to subsist solely on "the contemplation of his Mistres beautie" (sig. D1^{r}), in a parody of the excesses of the Petrarchan lover. Later, Samela declares her preference for the disguised aristocrat Melicertus, and Menaphon flies into a jealous rage, which he expresses in crudely materialistic terms: "deceitfull woman ... either returne love for love, or I will turne thee forth of doores to scrape up thy crummes where thou canst ... then see which of our beardlesse yongsters will take ye in, when I have cast you foorth" (sig. G3^{v}). By this stage his philosophical pretensions have vanished, so that when he is finally defeated in a singing contest by Melicertus, one might suppose that he has been duly punished for his overweening aspirations—as Nashe would have expected him to be. One might suppose, too, that the superiority of the aristocracy has been confirmed, since the noble Melicertus has proved himself a better singer than the best of the Arcadian herdsmen, despite the ancient link between the Greek peasantry and song.

---

23 The title-page of *Pandosto* states "that although by the meanes of sinister fortune, Truth may be concealed yet by Time in spight of fortune it is most manifestly revealed."

24 For the identification of Greene with Menaphon see Wilson, *Fictions of Authorship*, pp. 6–7.

But Melicertus's defeat of Menaphon is a decidedly mixed blessing. As a result, he is made captain of the shepherd army, which he promptly leads to destruction at the hands of Democles. Menaphon stays behind, and ends the book with marriage to a woman as witty as Samela, whose name—Pesana—declares her affiliation to the peasantry. A similar trajectory is traced by another shepherd, Doron, who begins as a serious poetic rival to Menaphon—his verse description of Samela makes Melicertus fall in love with her—and ends as a figure of fun, the "homely blunt Shephearde" (sig. K2^{v}) who courts Menaphon's sister with verses that compare her lips to "Cowcumbers" and her teeth to "the tuskes of fattest swine" (sig. K3^{v}). But the verses with which he does this occur immediately after the massacre of the shepherd army; by taking time out to sing, he avoids a violent death. The shepherds, in other words, have the last laugh in the narrative; the book ends with them, not with the aristocracy, since the marriage of Doron and Carmela takes up the final sentence.

Indeed, the entire book could be said to adopt the herdsmen's point of view. Its running title is "The Reports of the Shepheards," and the poor light it casts on the world of the court seems calculated to recommend a modest life over an exalted one, and to put off artists like Greene from seeking to mix with their social superiors. The romance validates, too, the relaxed approach to love taken by Menaphon, who substitutes a willing partner (Pesana) for an unwilling one (Sephestia) without excessive agonizing, and by Doron, who makes a pig's ear of his love song but ends by "jumping" a marriage "with his old friend Carmela" (sig. L2^{v}). Courtly love, by contrast, comes across as a destructive waste of time for everyone but Sephestia. The anonymous narrator confirms this in the only song addressed to the reader, which analyses sexual attraction in terms that chime with Menaphon's and Doron's comically antiromantic stance. "Love's a desire," the song declares, "which for to waite a time, / Doth loose an age of yeeres, and so doth passe ... Leaving behinde nought but repentant thoughts / Of daies ill spent, for that which profits noughts" (sig. L1^{r}). Like Greene, Doron and Carmela are workers, who "after a little playing loath to depart" as lovers go "about their businesse." King Democles and his family, by contrast—with the exception of the pair who become honorary shepherds—are dangerous loafers, whose unwavering focus on desire instead of labor threatens to tear their kingdom to pieces.

All the same, the identification of Greene with Menaphon is too simplistic. In his preface, which precedes that of Nashe, Greene stresses the stylistic virtuosity of his text, telling his gentlemen readers that they will "finde my style either *magis humile* in some place, or more *sublime* in another ... as if Sphinx on the one side, and Roscius on the other were playing the wagges" (sig. *a*2^{v}). Roscius was the most celebrated of Roman comic actors, Sphinx the riddling female monster killed by the tragic hero Oedipus. Greene, in other words, claims in *Menaphon* to have aped the language of all classes and both sexes, drawing on both "high" tragic and "low" comic material to forge the "strange conceipts" of his story. He is not, then, solely to be identified with the comic poet-shepherd Menaphon—or with any other man in the text. Menaphon's eventual wife, Pesana, seems to have an equal claim to stand in for the writer. She is one of several witty female characters whose rapid-fire dialogue associates them with the brilliant improvisers admired by Nashe, whose critical faculties mark them out as expert readers, and whose unwavering loyalty under trying conditions confirms them as the sole guardians of faith in this version of ancient Greece. The subtitle of the romance, *Camilla's Alarum to the Slumbering Euphues*, seems to hint that women have as large a stake in its authorship as the male shepherds of whose "reports" it is supposed to consist (Camilla was the witty heroine of Lyly's second *Euphues* book). So, too, does its dedication, which is to the widowed Lady Hales. And these hints at the centrality of women to the text would have been borne out for its first readers by Greene's known association with fictional women.[25] At the start of his career Greene named his first romance after its heroine Mamillia and declared his desire "by wit or arte to be their defender"—to speak out on behalf of ladies—whenever he had the chance.[26] And Greene continued to ventriloquize the voices of clever women on page and stage till the end of his career, when one of his last pamphlets featured the first-person confessions of a witty English whore.[27] In between, Greene made women the titular protagonists of his romances more often than any other English author, earning him the epithet "Homer of women" in 1589.[28] Clearly there was something about adopting a woman's perspective that appealed to him as a writer, and prompted him to risk the charge of "feminizing" his readers by placing them at the centre of his fictions.[29]

---

25 Helen Hackett discusses Greene's association with women in *Women and Romance Fiction*, pp. 94–7. Alwes discusses it in *Sons and Authors*, chapter 5.

26 *Mamillia: A Mirror or Looking-Glass for the Ladies of England* (1583), fol. 30^{r}. See also the second part of *Mamillia* (c. 1583), subtitled *The Triumph of Pallas*, where Greene consolidates his credentials as women's champion: "I hope whatsoever the envious crue shall crow against me for defending the loyaltie of women, vertuous and wel disposed gentlemen wil neither appeach me of flattery, nor condemne me of folly" (sig. D2^{v}), and where he is heralded as such by the commendatory verses of Richard Stapleton ("champion like he challenge makes, with Ladie Pallas shield, / To stand in armes against your foes in open camped field") (sig. A4^{v}).

27 See "The Conversion of an English Courtizan," in *A Disputation between a He Cony-Catcher and a She Cony-Catcher*(1592), sig. D1^{r}–F4^{r}.

28 The phrase is used by Nashe in *The Anatomy of Absurdity* (1589), though it's not absolutely certain he was referring to Greene (see Nashe, *Works*, ed. Ronald B. McKerrow, 5 vols [London: A.H. Bullen, 1904], vol. 1, p. 12). Romances by Greene with women as their titular heroines include the two parts of *Mamillia*, *The Mirror of Modesty* (referring to Susanna), *Penelope's Web*, *Alcida* and *Philomela: The Lady Fitzwater's Nightingale.*

29 On the association between women and romance in the period, see Hackett, *Women and Romance Fiction*, chapter 1, especially pp.16–19. Derek Alwes gives a detailed assessment of Greene's attitude to his female readers in *Sons and Authors*; see especially the introduction, chapter 5 and the conclusion.

What this something is may be inferred from the effect on men of the conspicuous presence of intelligent, faithful women in *Menaphon*. Throughout the romance, as throughout Greene's work, the fidelity of women helps to expose and offer an alternative to the treachery of men. For every inconstant man in the text there is at least one constant woman: Pesana for Menaphon, Sephestia for Democles, Eriphila and Olympia for Pleusidippus; and these women are always defeating the men in contests of eloquence, wit, and resilience. As a reader one can only conclude that men's claim to deserve exclusive rights to social, intellectual, and moral authority in the kingdoms they inhabit does not stand up to scrutiny. Women are consistent and forgiving, men vindictive and unstable; and the marginalizing of the former may prove disastrous for a nation. This becomes obvious when one looks at the consequences of Sephestia's banishment from the court of her father, Democles. Cast out for marrying a man her father thinks beneath her, the disguised Sephestia becomes the catalyst for every complication in the narrative, from Democles's catastrophic infiltration of the pastoral community to the civil war that breaks out in the final "act." Sephestia possesses in abundance all the qualities associated with women in *Menaphon*: fidelity, endurance, wit, and a seemingly infinite capacity for forgiveness.[30] Only her restoration to her proper place at the center of power in Arcadia—where she can engage, presumably, in fierce but affectionate debates with her husband, as the Queen of Thessaly does with hers in the court where the kidnapped Pleusidippus grows up—can restore stability to the kingdom. Without women at the center, all kingdoms are condemned to suffer under the egocentrism of men, whose waywardness manifests itself in the violence with which Democles and Pleusidippus prosecute their incestuous obsessions with the disguised princess.

It is fitting, then, that Sephestia's return to her father's court should be brought about by the intervention of an "olde woman attired like a Prophetesse" (sig. L1^{v})—a Pythia, or priestess of Apollo—who explains how the prophecy delivered by Apollo's Delphic Oracle at the beginning of the story is to be fulfilled, then disappears as if to prove her own authenticity. Pythian pronouncements frame Greene's romance, so that the language of women dominates its rhetoric at every level—from the religious to the conversational. And many of the eloquent women in the narrative share with his male shepherd-poets a profound respect for labor and those who do it. Sephestia works alongside Menaphon and later Melicertus throughout her stay in Arcadia, using "countrey labours" to "avoide tedious conceipts" (sigf. D3^{r})—to forget her sorrows—and later to preserve her independence after she has freed herself from Menaphon's unwanted attentions. Pesana uses labour for the same purposes: she "thought to brave love with seeming not to love; and thus she daily drove out the time with labour" (sig. E4^{v}). The old prophetess who summarizes Sephestia's adventures at the end of the book describes her as having "livde in labours tempred with loves" (sig. L2^{r}), and in this

30 On women and forgiveness in Greene, see Alwes, *Sons and Authors*, chapter 5.

she echoes a sentence used by Democles to describe the rural subjects he dupes. "Arcadian Swaines," he calls them, "whose labours are tempered with sweete loves, whose mindes aspyre not, whose thoughts brooke no envie; onely as rivalls in affection, you are friendly emulators in honest fancie" (sig. $I4^v$). The association of love with labour flies in the face of the Elizabethan critics who saw all fictions as the fruits of idleness, while the egalitarianism of the shepherds and of the disguised princess puts to shame the snobbery both of the royal men in the book and of the arrogant young Cambridge graduate, Nashe, who introduced it. For Greene, love stories and labor not only *may* coexist but inevitably *must* do so—after all, he made a living from both. And the time put in to constructing the "honest fancie" of a romance is time well spent, like Sephestia's time among the shepherds. Both Nashe and the aristocracy he favours would do well to emulate her in escaping into the clear air of Arcadia when the opportunity presents itself, instead of heaping insults on its base-born inhabitants.

III. Time is, time was, time is past: *Friar Bacon and Friar Bungay*

As we have seen, *Menaphon* exists in romance time: hours purloined from the schedule set by schoolmasters, priests, and authoritarian parents, and given over instead to the words and actions of women and workers, people of no consequence in the eyes of the Elizabethan authorities. Although not located in Italy, Greene's book delivers just the sort of "bawdie" narrative condemned by the pedagogue Roger Ascham in *The Schoolmaster*, where he attacks the invidious effects on young readers of Elizabethan romances translated from the Italian.[31] In the love-language of Sephestia, in the lust-fuelled violence of Democles and Pleusidipppus, in the disguises and filial disobedience with which it is filled, Greene's book offers its readers a rich abundance of what Ascham describes as

> such subtle, cunnyng, new, and diverse shiftes, to cary yong willes to vanitie, and yong wittes to mischief, to teach old bawdes new schole poyntes, as the simple head of an English man is not hable to invent, nor never was heard of in England before, yea when Papistrie overflowed all.[32]

For Ascham, the reading of Italianate romances threatens to supplant the official canon altogether. "Suffer these bookes to be read," he warns, "and they shall soone displace all bookes of godly learnyng."[33] Greene's Greeks are as subtle as Ascham's Italians: as adept in the arts of seduction, as skilled in the donning of false identities, as devastating in their effects on the lands they infiltrate in pursuit of their

---

31 For a detailed account of Ascham's attack on Italianate prose fiction, see my *Elizabethan Fictions*, introduction and chapter 1.

32 Ascham, *English Works*, ed. Wright, p. 231.

33 Ascham, *English Works*, ed. Wright, p. 231.

illegal desires. Too long spent in their company might well prove infectious for Greene's naïve English readers, and the effect of such a Greek infection is hinted at in the many references to the disastrous adventures of Paris that punctuate the narrative.[34] As a reward for judging Venus to be the loveliest of goddesses, Paris was promised the hand of Helen; in snatching Helen from her husband, the young shepherd-prince kicked off the Trojan War. Romance, then, could destroy great civilizations. No wonder Ascham sought to ban it from his pupils' shelves.

But if romances could be seen as dangerously time-wasting trifles, which harbored the potential to lay England open to corrupting foreign influences, Greene's other sphere, the theater, seemed to some Elizabethan commentators to have already conquered a significant portion of territory in the heart of England and to be making daily inroads into the work-schedules of London's citizens. After the construction of the first purpose-built playhouse in the country, the Theatre (1576), a volley of antitheatrical tracts appeared, which accused the players of everything from the spread of crime and sexual diseases to the encouragement of insurrection.[35] The most prominent of the antitheatrical polemicists, Stephen Gosson, saw modern poetry in general as a Trojan horse designed to smuggle loose morals by stealth into English culture. "If you looke well too Epaeus horse," he wrote in *The School of Abuse* (1579),

> you shall finde in his bowels the destruction of Troy ... pull off the visard that Poets maske in, you shall disclose their reproach, bewray their vanitie, loth their wantonnesse, lament their follie, and perceive their sharpe sayings to be placed as Pearles in Dunghils, fresh pictures on rotten walles, chaste Matrons apparel on common Curtesans.[36]

As Gosson's metaphors of visards (masks), painted sets and borrowed clothing imply, dramatists are for him the worst of poets. "Playes," he claims in his most extended and aggressive assault on the theater, *Plays Confuted in Five Actions* (1582), "are the inventions of the devil, the offrings of Idolatrie, the pompe of worldlinges, the blossomes of vanitie, the roote of Apostacy, the foode of iniquitie, ryot, and adulterie" (197). In other words, they encourage their audiences to change religions, to indulge in thievery and sexual shenanigans, and to overthrow

---

34 See for instance sig. C4^v (judgement of Paris); sig. D3^r (Oenone and Paris); sig. D3^v (judgement of Paris mentioned in Doron's song; also "Priamus young boy" is Paris); sig. F1^r (where Paris is "Priamus Wanton," as well as being mentioned by name at the top of the page); sig. K1^r (where Pleusidippus is Priam defending Paris's Helen in Troy).

35 For accounts of Elizabethan attacks on the theatre, see Jonas Barish, *The Anti-Theatrical Prejudice* (Berkeley: University of California Press, 1981), chapter 1; Laura Levine, *Men in Women's Clothing: Anti-Theatricality, 1579–1642* (Cambridge and New York: Cambridge University Press, 1994); and my *Shakespeare and Comedy*, introduction.

36 *Markets of Bawdrie: The Dramatic Criticism of Stephen Gosson*, ed. Arthur F. Kinney (Salzburg: University of Salzburg, 1974), p. 77. All references to Gosson's work are taken from this edition.

the social order, and they are, therefore, "not to bee suffered in a Christian commonweale" (187). The players neglect their true "vocations" as craftsmen, tradesmen, or servants through an ambitious desire to "walke gentlemanlike in sattin and velvet," thus "dismembering" the body of the state (195–6) and putting its prince at risk through their gross disregard for the traditions of hierarchy. For Gosson, in fact, the playhouse represents a devilish alternative society, a kind of anticommonwealth designed to tear the nation apart from within by debilitating its inhabitants in body and mind.

From the 1580s onwards, the authorities of the City of London repeatedly echoed Gosson's strictures—especially with reference to the player's contempt for the city's official timetable. Year by year the Mayor complained about the players to the Queen's Privy Council, accusing them of staging plays at times when their audiences should be working, or attending church services, or avoiding public gatherings altogether for fear of plague.[37] Like other plays of the period, Greene's finest comedy, *Friar Bacon and Friar Bungay*, takes full advantage of both Gosson's and the Lord Mayor's antitheatrical polemics by embodying their worst anxieties about the theater in vigorous action on the London stage. In it, a low-born London magician-friar—the equivalent in the field of conjuring to the playwright in the field of imaginative writing—assumes a central position in a cast that includes the Kings of England and Castile and the Emperor of Germany. He summons up devils to do his will, as playwrights were always doing when they populated their plays with demonic vices. And he sends them hither and thither to do his bidding in an England that is stolen wholesale from the chronicles, those history books in which successive Tudor governments had taken such a close proprietorial interest. Moreover, the subplot of the play is a naturalized Greek romance: a love story with many features derived from *Menaphon*, but transplanted from the pastures of Arcadia to the English countryside. The subplot thus completes the surreptitious invasion of England by subtle foreign notions that Ascham predicted as the inevitable consequence of translating Italian fictions into English. *Friar Bacon*, then, is an act of brazen cheek, and all the more cheeky in that it takes as its climax an event involving a head made of brass, in which its own misuse of time is mockingly highlighted. One wonders if the London authorities noticed this when they attended its first performance.

Friar Bacon's plot resembles that of *Menaphon* in several ways. Both narratives involve a disguised aristocrat and a fickle prince competing for the affections of a countrywoman: a situation that invites comparison with Paris's courtship of the shepherdess Oenone, whom he abandoned for Helen, as well as provoking many hints at the tyrannical tendencies of royal men in love. And both narratives contain other competitions in addition to this amorous rivalry. In *Friar Bacon*, magicians engage each other in conjuring contests, just as the shepherds of Arcadia challenge each other to duels of song—or as English writers incited each other to gestures of

---

37 See my *Shakespeare and Comedy*, p. 66.

professional rivalry in the late 1580s. And like *Menaphon*, *Friar Bacon* stages a competition between the comic and tragic modes for dominance of its narrative. If *Menaphon* enacts a light-hearted struggle between the tragic Sphinx and the comic Roscius—a struggle that ends with the massacre of some shepherds and the marriage of others—*Friar Bacon* pits the tragic and comic consequences of love and magic against one another and turns the contest between alternative outcomes for the action into a meditation on the responsibilities of an imaginative writer in an age when the imagination was a source of deep suspicion.[38]

In fact, *Friar Bacon* injects a new sense of urgency into Greene's writing, an urgency that can be detected in nearly all his later works for page and stage. Its characters show a far greater fearfulness than Sephestia or the Arcadian shepherds did about the potentially lethal reaction of the ruling classes to any unauthorized deployment of their subjects' time. Where *Menaphon* allows itself to dwell on the details of a pastoral existence, eking out its romance plot over the leisurely span of sixteen years, the pastoral and romance elements in *Friar Bacon* are pitted against the timetable set by government, so that it seems only a matter of days or hours before the pleasant pastimes of its lovers turn tragic. The word "treason" is repeatedly linked with desire in the world of the play, and the possibility of personal betrayal and ruin is invoked even at its most light-hearted moments. This, then, is an anxious version of pastoral as well as a cheerful one, and there are two possible reasons for its anxiety. The first is its location in England, which brings the lovers Lacy and Margaret into direct conflict with the English royal family, fictionalized ancestors of the supreme authority over Greene himself. Second, the story unfolds within the purlieus of an English playhouse, with all the controversies and formal restrictions this carries with it. Its plot is circumscribed by the necessary limits of dramatic time: everything in it must happen within the two hours' traffic of the stage, so that each minute expended in the pleasures of courtship brings the action closer to a potentially drastic dénouement. And as we have seen, the Elizabethan theater had generated a far fiercer public debate than even the despised literary genres of the chivalric romance and the love story. For the theater-haters, time spent within the playhouse walls was time not merely wasted but gone to the devil; it seems likely that when *Friar Bacon* was written English theater audiences had just been given a particularly graphic demonstration of the implications of these antitheatrical prejudices.

Was Marlowe's *Doctor Faustus* first performed in 1589?[39] Plenty of scholars think so, and support for the date is provided by *Friar Bacon*, where a necromantic duel between an Englishman and a German seems to act out Greene's ambition to beat Marlowe at his own theatrical game, supplying a conjurer of their own for

---

38 For Elizabethan hostility to the imagination, see Sir Philip Sidney, *An Apology for Poetry*, ed. Geoffrey Shepherd, revised R.W. Maslen (Manchester and New York: Manchester University Press, 2002), introduction.

39 See note 14 above.

English spectators to cheer for (Bacon) in place of a morally dubious foreigner (Faustus).[40] If the date is right, then *Friar Bacon* is also a reply to Marlowe's use of stage time, which was the most ingenious in English theatrical history so far. In *Doctor Faustus*, the duration of a stage performance marks the limits of a scholar's life, and the protagonist transforms the last scene of the play into a countdown to his doom, as he tries to talk his way out of a contract with Lucifer in a speech whose every line represents a minute of the final hour before the deadline set for his damnation. Like *Friar Bacon*, then, the tragedy cheekily confirms the worst fears of the antitheatrical lobby, who had forged a direct polemical link between the imaginative territory of the theater and the circuit of hell to which it treacherously drew its English audiences.[41] Faustus's collaboration with Mephistophilis and Lucifer as he seeks more and more manic and offensive ways to delight his audience—culminating in sex with a demon in the shape of Helen of Troy—identifies the stage as an annex of hell: a notion that became entrenched in the imagination of Marlowe's contemporaries as rumors spread concerning the participation of actual devils in performances of his work.[42] The second English *Faust* book—a prose account of the adventures of Faustus's servant Wagner as he pursues his master's fearful trade after his death—includes an aerial stage constructed by devils for the entertainment of the people of Wittenburg, which collapses into the river Elbe at the end of a performance of "The Tragedy of Doctor Faustus."[43] Clearly Marlowe's calculated demonizing of time spent at the theater had struck a resonant chord with his literary as well as his theatrical inheritors.

But for all its resemblance to *Faustus*, Greene's *Friar Bacon* seems designed precisely to *rescue* the stage from the identification with harmful devilry with which Marlowe and Gosson had so gleefully smeared it. The play's magician-protagonist is a patriot, who uses his powers to strengthen the security of the nation rather than to undermine it, and who gives up these powers in ample time to supply the play with the wished-for happy ending. His ambition is to defeat his German rivals in a kind of conjurer's World Cup; to entertain his monarch, his fellow Englishmen, and his Elizabethan audience with a dazzling display of innovative special effects; and to wall his country round with brass as defense against foreign invasion. And although the last and silliest of these projects comes to nothing, the friar's success in two of his three ambitions means that his commitment to his country is never in doubt. It is for this reason, presumably, that Greene allows him

40 For the date of *Friar Bacon*, see Daniel Seltzer's edition, Regents Renaissance Drama Series (London: Edward Arnold, 1963), pp. ix–x (though Seltzer suggests that *Doctor Faustus* was written later). All references to *Friar Bacon* are taken from this edition.

41 See my *Shakespeare and Comedy*, introduction.

42 For one such rumor as reported much later by William Prynne, see *Doctor Faustus*, ed. Bevington and Rasmussen, p. 2.

43 See *The Second Report of Doctor John Faustus* (1594), reprinted in *Early English Prose Romances*, ed. William J. Thoms (London: Routledge and Sons, n.d.), pp. 914–21.

to see the error of his ways and renounce the black arts before the devil can carry him off to keep Faustus company. For this reason, too, there is no tension or fear involved in Bacon's final speech, where the magician makes one last use of his necromantic skills to predict a brilliant long-term future for England under the guidance of Elizabeth I. In this play, Greene gives short shrift to the enemies of the theater—or even of the black arts, whose resemblance to the theater here makes Bacon's decision to renounce them seem almost unnecessary.

Nevertheless, the play's second plot raises the spectre of treason, one of the crimes for which the theatre-haters vilified dramatists;[44] and treason runs alongside patriotism as an undercurrent of this comedy. Here as in *Menaphon* it is the vice of the ruling classes, who seek to divert attention from their own treachery by branding their innocent subjects as traitors. The king's son, Edward Prince of Wales, lusts after the milkmaid Margaret and plots to betray her by seduction or rape. He gives away his bad intentions when he tells one of his friends that any man would "with Tarquin, hazard Rome and all" to get her (i.85–86)—Tarquin being a prince, like himself, who brought down the Roman monarchy when he raped one of his subjects. His best friend Lacy is despatched to sound out Margaret's attitude toward Edward, but falls in love with the girl himself, and is subsequently tormented with fear of the royal reaction to his own "treachery" (vi.54–57). His fear is well founded: Edward observes the "comedy" of Lacy's courtship in a magic glass belonging to Bacon (vi.48), and his response is murderous. He flies into a jealous rage, accuses the earl of harboring "trait'rous thoughts" (viii.1), launches a volley of seductive verse at Margaret (viii.51–66), and prepares to "bathe" his dagger in Lacy's "bosom" (viii.79–80). Like Democles and Pleusidippus before him, Edward comes close to transforming Bacon's "comedy" into a tragedy, and he is only prevented from doing so at the last minute by reminding himself of his reputation as a soldier, which can only be sustained if he shows himself capable of "subduing fancy's passion" (viii.120). Throughout this part of the action, the genre of the play hangs in the balance, as in the central scenes of *Faustus*. Jests threaten to be converted into earnest, and the tone of events to be changed by violence, and it is the moment when Edward begins to echo Marlowe ("Like Thetis shalt thou wanton on the waves," he tells Margaret, "And draw the dolphins to thy lovely eyes, / To dance lavoltas in the purple streams" [viii.57–59]) that marks the point of gravest danger. The moment passes; but Greene has paid eloquent tribute to his fellow playwright, with his talent for rendering theatrical time problematic, the outcome of a dramatic plot uncertain.

By revealing Margaret and Lacy's courtship through his glass, Bacon associates himself both with the treachery of Prince Edward and with the doubts this casts on the play's eventual outcome. His use of his glass as a peepshow for erotic comedies associates him, too, with Greene the playwright: another university man from a humble background who specializes in purveying erotic illusions to

---

44 See my *Shakespeare and Comedy*, pp. 14–16.

voyeurs of all classes. And this last association is a troubling one, since the glass that almost causes a tragedy in the middle of the play really causes one before the end, once again validating the theatre-haters' anxieties about the impact of the imaginative arts on their consumers. After the prince has left him, Bacon invites two students to look into his glass, where they watch their fathers killing each other in a squabble over Margaret. The sight enrages its youthful spectators to the point of stabbing each other to death in horrific emulation of their elders. At this point, Bacon renounces his magic powers and smashes the glass, as if to absolve Greene of any complicity with the disastrous effects of conjuring—or the writing of plays and romances. And in the following scene, the chief clown of the play, Bacon's servant and fellow-conjurer Miles, completes the play's act of comic self-purgation by riding off to hell on the back of a devil. Penitence and purgation clear the air for the play's happy ending. Greene may flirt with the dark suggestions of Marlowe's masterpiece, but he is careful to disaffiliate himself from his dangerous colleague before his flirtations get too serious.

Yet the fact remains that Greene's alter ego Bacon presides over a decidedly ambiguous performance. For one thing, the play in which he stars mocks the English royal family on several occasions. At the beginning, Prince Edward changes clothes with a fool to seek Bacon's help in winning Margaret. Later, he bribes Bacon to impede the legitimate love of Margaret and Lacy. And although in the end he succeeds in bridling his desire for Margaret, he demonstrates in the meantime the ease with which royalty can turn tyrannous, terrorizing his subjects and pouring his financial resources into manipulating them for his own ends. Bacon is Edward's willing accomplice in all this; Bacon's own accomplices are devils. As a figure for the writer, then, the friar is more ambiguous than Menaphon was. He is a loyal servant of the crown, but the crown he serves is tainted with corruption. And the most famous scene in the play, which involves Bacon's celebrated brazen head, seems to embody (so to speak) the ambiguous status both of his loyalty and of his patriotism.

The brazen head represents the highest aspirations of the English conjurer. With it he aims to learn "strange and uncouth aphorisms" and raise brass ramparts round his island home (xi.19–20); plans more surreal and grandiose than anything Marlowe's Faustus imagined. And it is another of Greene's alteregos, the magician's comic servant-apprentice Miles, who exposes the folly of this project. Miles stakes his claim to the status of poet with the verse form he uses, a metrical jog-trot known as "Skeltonics," after its inventor, the satirist John Skelton. Indeed, the verse form identifies Miles as a specifically *satirical* poet, like Menaphon and Doron in the latter stages of Greene's romance. Armed with this verse and with his equally vigorous prose, Miles cheerfully cuts a range of authority figures down to size, from Master Burden, ruler of the "academic state" of Oxford (ii.6–7), to the disguised Prince of Wales (who tries to have him killed for his presumption [v.50]), the Emperor of Germany, even the English king himself. And Miles's satire culminates in a devastating critique of his master, Bacon. The apprentice is set to watch the brazen head at the crucial moment when its enchantment is to reach fruition, confirming Bacon's status as the preeminent magician in Europe; his failure to perform this simple task robs Bacon of his finest hour, the point at which he might have gained the status of a tragic figure. Miles's monologue in the brazen head scene is a comic parody of Faustus's final speech, with its countdown to perdition; by sabotaging this countdown—by ignoring his master's instructions to watch the clock—it is Miles rather than Bacon who rescues the play from a potential slide into ruin.

At the beginning of the scene, Bacon orders his servant to wake him as soon as the head begins to speak; having issued his orders, he promptly talks himself to sleep (xi.39). This is the first of the scene's comic echoes of *Faustus*, reminding us that Marlowe's garrulous conjurer effectively talked himself to death. The head *does* speak three times, of course, but Miles is less than impressed by its eloquence. All it utters at first is a single phrase, "Time is," which Miles thinks neither clever nor witty: "is this all my master's cunning, to spend seven years' study about 'Time is?'" (xi.53–57). And when the head goes on to declare "Time was," Miles's opinion of his master's work is confirmed: "Yea, marry, time was when my master was a wise man, but that was before he began to make the Brazen Head" (xi.65–70). The opportunity passes; the head declares "Time is past" and falls silent (xi.75); Bacon rushes in and bursts into a series of laments that again recall the final speech of Faustus: "Ah, villain, time is past; / My life, my fame, my glory, all are past" (xi.94–95). But these laments utterly fail to attain the tragic heights reached by Marlowe's doctor. Nothing much has been lost by the failure of Bacon's project—nothing, that is, but the fulfilment of his ambitions. None of his complaints hints at any loss for *England* as a result of Miles's negligence, and one can only conclude that Miles was perfectly justified in seeing the friar's experiments as worthless, the head as fundamentally hollow. And Bacon's reaction to his failure exposes something else: the extent to which his ambitions have corrupted him. He first sacks the unfortunate apprentice, then has him carried off to hell by one of his devils (xv.64); and the punishment is so disproportionate to the offence that it convicts the conjurer of a tendency to tyranny more terrible than Edward's. Clearly, Bacon has the potential to become a figure like Ateukin in Greene's other dramatic romance, *The Scottish History of James IV*: a Machiavellian scholar who will stop at nothing in his rise to power. In both plays, to meddle as he does with affairs of state is to enter an environment that is fundamentally rotten, and the clown Miles helps us to see the full extent of its rottenness.

The low verse of the clown, then, provides a necessary counterweight to the bombastic blank verse of the scholar. Without both figures the play's address to its audience would be fundamentally unbalanced. Between them they stand for two aspects of the dramatist: his humble origins and his high aspirations, which together enable him to address aristocrats and commoners with equal confidence. But there's a third figure in the play who helps to engineer its happy ending: Margaret of Fressingfield. Margaret recalls Sephestia in her beauty and her wit—though not in her class origins, since she is one of the few Elizabethan pastoral heroines with no claim to royal status. Like Sephestia, she is set up in direct opposition to the adulterous heroine of traditional chivalric romance.[45] And like Sephestia, she has a good claim to stand for the writer who invented her; as good a claim, at least, as either Bacon or his apprentice, whose humble birth she shares.[46] She brings to the play a third quality to match Bacon's art and Miles's humor: stability, a steadiness in the face of adversity that is inseparable from the fact that she is a woman and that she is in love. Bacon and Miles were seduced by devilry and the service of bad masters; Margaret remains constant both in affection and in moral integrity. As a result, she represents the most powerful response in the text to the hostility of Elizabethan critics of imaginative writing, the essential missing element in the formula for good authorship.

In fact, each aspect of Margaret's character responds to a specific contemporary criticism of poetic fiction and drama. Her work ethic, which displays itself in the country labors in which she is always engaged, absolves her of any suspicion of idleness, which romance was supposed to encourage. Her fidelity absolves her of sexual incontinence, which romance was supposed to arouse in its readers. And her resistance to the seductions and threats of her social superiors gives her a moral stature that romance was supposed to lack. She is independent in a way no other character in the play can claim to be; her independence manifests itself in the moral guidance she gives to her superiors by her own example. Twice she rejects Prince Edward's offer to make her his mistress, each time pointing him firmly in the direction of his duty as England's heir. She draws her suitor Lacy—a Paris figure who always harbors the potential to discard his Oenone—from his initial plan of seduction and abandonment to an honest proposal of marriage. She shames Prince Edward into an act of mercy by begging to be executed for treason in Lacy's place; when Lacy tests her love for him by pretending he has deserted her, she shames him into honoring their engagement by promptly dedicating the rest of her life to God. Her decision to "live in Framlingham a holy nun / Holy and pure in conscience and in deed" (xiv.23–24) confirms, of course, the purity of her love for Lacy, who she thinks she has lost; but it also makes her a female equivalent of Bacon, who rejects magic, the stuff of theater, for a life of prayer, just as Margaret

---

45 The most extended Elizabethan attack on chivalric romance and its encouragement of adultery was that of Roger Ascham in *The Schoolmaster* (1570): "bookes of Chevalrie ... were made in Monasteries, by idle Monkes, or wanton Chanons: as one for example, *Morte Arthur*: the whole pleasure of which booke standeth in two speciall poyntes, in open mans slaughter, and bold bawdrye: In which booke those be counted the noblest Knightes, that do kill most men without any quarell, and commit fowlest advoulteries by sutlest shiftes ... . What toyes, the dayly readyng of such a booke, may worke in the will of a young jentleman, or a yong mayde, that liveth welthelie and idlelie, wise men can judge, and honest men do pitie." *English Works*, ed. Wright, p. 231.

46 For women as surrogate authors in Greene's work, see Wilson, *Fictions of Authorship*, p. 83ff.

rejects love, the stuff of romance, for a life of sexual abstinence. However, Margaret is better than Bacon, since she never succumbs to arrogance or anger. No male character, in fact, comes close to matching her qualities; so that if she feminizes the men in the play, as poetry, fiction, and drama were supposed to feminize their male recipients, then to be feminized here is to be rescued from the savage self-centeredness of early modern masculinity.

For Ascham, Gosson and their fellow humanists, love of women was the principal means by which men were made effeminate. Love subjected their intellects to the irrational demands of the women who obsessed them, causing them to abandon their duties in the public sphere for the pleasures of the private boudoir. Chivalric romance was the literary equivalent of this erotic self-abasement, elevating women above men in the hierarchy of social values and celebrating male prowess on behalf of women in place of more legitimate male exertions on behalf of state and sovereign. Margaret rescues love as well as romance from these imputations. Her opposition to the chivalric ideal declares itself most openly in the episode of the two country gentlemen who kill each other for her sake. One gentleman tells the other that his willingness to fight for Margaret confirms his social status: "Th'art worthy of the title of a squire," he tells him, because he has "kept thine hour like a man" (xiii.37–38). But the useless deaths of the duelling lovers, and the consequent deaths of their sons who watch the duel in Bacon's glass, demonstrate the moral vacuousness of a literary tradition that identifies violence as the ultimate measure of male and female worth. Margaret is no Guinevere or Helen, her reputation built on the willingness of men to slaughter one another in her name. The love she bestows—as opposed to the love that is demanded of her—brings reconciliation rather than conflict between master and man, between king and subject.

But if Margaret is no Helen, she is also no nun. An English Protestant audience would hardly have applauded her decision to take the veil when Lacy deserts her. When she tells him she has been driven to penitence by the thought of the time she has wasted in his company ("How fond the prime of wanton years were spent / In love" [xiv.59–60]) it is difficult to imagine even a cynic responding with approval. And when she rescinds her repentance and flings herself into Lacy's arms ("The flesh is frail ... I cannot say him nay" [xiv.86–88]) it is still more difficult to imagine a spectator not applauding. Even theater-haters like Gosson could hardly have objected to the union, legitimized, as it is, by the promise of marriage and set in opposition to a religious vocation they rejected on principle. And if the theater-haters *did* withhold their imaginative assent from the wedding feast that ends the play, they would have shown themselves at odds not only with love but also with Greene's attractive fictional version of England, the nation in whose name Henry III declares the festivities open in the play's last lines: "the time / Craves that we taste of naught but jouissance. / Thus glories England over all the west" (xvi.74–6).

Margaret, then, is a kind of trick played on the theater-haters, the humble pearl of wisdom, as her name implies, embedded in Greene's comedy; the true champion of England in a play where all other champions fail; and a worthy precursor for the witty heroine/dramatists who dominate the comedies of Shakespeare. She is also, like Sephestia, either a figure for Greene himself or a necessary counterbalance for him: a fictional wife, as it were, flesh of his flesh, from whom he divorces himself at his peril. Throughout Greene's oeuvre, a loving and equal union between men and women offers the only escape route from the savage waywardness of unattached masculinity, and the only hope of security for a kingdom caught in the self-destructive trap of patriarchy. From this point of view—his acceptance of female as well as lower-class influences as a fundamental part of his make-up as an artist—it does not seem an exaggeration to describe him as a radical writer. He is an ambitious one, too, whose appropriation of the material of the English chronicles gave the romance plot of his play a direct bearing on the time and doings of his spectators.

IV. Time deferred: Greene's *Vision*

From the two cases we have examined so far, it is clear that Greene's understanding of the role of writer is highly complex. Counselor to kings and worker of wonders like Bacon; lyricist of love and beauty like Menaphon; clown and satirist like Miles and Doron; emblem of loyalty in adversity like Sephestia and Margaret; as godly as a heroine, as devilish as a Satanist; his complexity makes him slippery, impossible to pin down in a simple set of co-ordinates and definitions, or to confine in a single character. So when Greene seeks to do something straightforward, like repent of his sins and turn to God in his last years as a writer, one would expect this to be a difficult and extended process—perhaps an impossible one. It is for this reason, no doubt, that in about 1590 he introduced the important principle of deferral into his writing: the notion of putting off till tomorrow what he ought to do today, of extending the process of reconstructing himself as a plain model citizen until the moment when his economic circumstances and his own inclinations should find it convenient. In this year he wrote a quasi-autobiographical romance, *Greene's Never too Late*, which summarized the principle—as its title suggests. And in this year, too, he wrote a less readily categorized pamphlet, *Greene's Vision*, which helped to ensure that his process of deferred reformation continued until long after it was "too late"—until long after his death, in fact, which was brought about (we are told) by a thoroughly impenitent excess at his final banquet.

In his antitheatrical polemics, Stephen Gosson maintains that English playwrights are always claiming to have reformed themselves—that is, to have purged their work of the various forms of political and sexual corruption which are the targets of Gosson's polemics.[47] Such claims, he says, are spurious, and the

47 This view of Gosson's is most fully developed in his third antitheatrical pamphlet, *Plays Confuted in Five Actions* (1582). The pamphlet is reprinted in *Markets of Bawdrie:*

playwrights' reformation cosmetic. And from one point of view, Greene's *Friar Bacon* seems to ratify this assertion. As we have seen, Margaret and Bacon both claim to break their links with desire and devilry, the twin evils that for Gosson plagued theatrical history; yet both return like the proverbial dog to their vomit. On learning that Lacy still loves her, Margaret takes him back with barely a second thought, and Bacon's magic is still active as the play draws to a close, pursuing Miles with vindictive doggedness and inspiring the magician with the gift of patriotic prophecy in his final speech long after he has announced his retirement. It is as though Greene thinks that the mere *intention* to reform is enough to vindicate both characters from charges of self-interest. And Margaret goes a step further when she cries, as she sheds her religious vocation, "the flesh is weak." In this time-bound world all absolute commitments are impossible, perhaps pernicious. Even the greatest commitment of all, that of lifelong love—for God or man—needs always to be revised in the light of new demands and opportunities. As with Greene's other heroines, Margaret's revision of her position tends to reinforce, not negate, her constancy. But she lives in a world where *male* constancy seems almost nonexistent. One might ask of Lacy the question asked of the leading man in the sequel to Greene's first romance, *Mamillia*, whether he will prove "as inconstant a husband as a faithlesse woer" (sig. K4^{r}); and the answer would be as uncertain as it was in the case of Mamillia's suitor. Under these conditions, female fidelity needs to be as mobile as infidelity if it is to stand a chance of keeping level with the shifty male object of its desire.

Greene's own pose as a penitent has a good deal in common with the half-hearted reformations of Margaret and Bacon. At times, indeed, it has even more in common with the failed repentance of his model for Bacon, Faustus. His first experiment with the pose, *Greene's Vision*, was posthumously published in 1592 as part of a series of quasi-autobiographical texts that were printed throughout that year to mark the Faustian countdown of minutes until his death. The so-called "repentance pamphlets" made a drama out of Greene's last crisis, fusing hints in his own work with elements from Marlowe's masterpiece to build up a vivid picture of the dying man.

Like the doomed doctor, Greene figures in these pamphlets as a tormented and divided soul, desperately seeking to atone for past misdemeanours in life and print while at the same time frantically using up the last moments of his life in generating new printed texts which repeatedly rework the sins he claims to have abandoned. How far this picture is an accurate one we shall never know; but there is no doubt that it was collaboratively constructed by a number of writers including Greene himself. Henry Chettle contributed to it when he edited the most famous of the pamphlets, *Greene's Groatsworth of Wit Bought with a Million of Repentance* (1592), for posthumous publication; Gabriel Harvey capitalized on it in his

---

The Dramatic Criticism of Stephen Gosson, ed. Arthur F. Kinney (Salzburg: Institut für Englische Sprache, 1974), pp. 138–200.

scabrous account of Greene's demise in *Four Letters ... Especially Touching Robert Greene* (1592); and an unknown writer may have helped to flesh it out in the moralistic *Repentance of Robert Greene* (1592).[48] *Greene's Vision*, too, claims on its title page to have been "Written at the instant of his death"; but internal evidence shows it to have been written in 1590, soon after *Menaphon* and *Friar Bacon*. Its simultaneous status as one of his last productions and as a careful appraisal of his situation in mid-career makes it a fascinating tribute to his sense of timing. Clearly, Greene was intensely conscious of the fact that making a radical change to his authorial persona, as he proposes to do in this pamphlet, requires meticulous planning and split-second judgements concerning the current state of the book market. And clearly, too, his "repentance," like those of Margaret and Bacon, is by no means a simple affair.

Greene composed his *Vision* in response to the success of a book called *The Cobbler of Canterbury* (1590): a Chaucerian collection of stories purportedly told by a party of English travelers as they journey to Gravesend by barge.[49] Ostensibly stung to the quick by the widespread assumption that this mildly scurrilous collection is by him, Greene first disclaims his authorship of the text, then produces his own post-medieval document to rival it: an Elizabethan version of Chaucer's *House of Fame* in which the author falls asleep and dreams of an encounter with the spirits of Chaucer and Gower, who proceed to stage a debate over the merits and demerits of his career as a writer. The debate ends with the approach of a third spirit, that of the biblical King Solomon, who successfully persuades the dreamer to abandon love-literature for theology. Solomon's recommendation may explain why Greene did not publish his *Vision* in the year he wrote it: the pamphlet was to have been his Baconian recantation, modeled on Chaucer's famous retraction in *The Canterbury Tales*, and in 1590 he was not yet ready to recant.

When *Greene's Vision* was finally issued to the London public in 1592, its dramatic character must have been startlingly obvious to those many readers who were avid for further details of its author's scandalous death. The epistle to the Gentlemen readers is signed from the "dying" Robert Greene (sig. A4^{v}), and the opening of the narrative presents Greene as a scholar who has misused his talents and who articulates his consequent "trouble of minde" in the language of Faustus (sig. B3^{r}). "*Stipendium peccati mors*," he reminds himself as the Doctor does in the first act of the play (sig. B3^{v}),[50] and the quotation drives him into a series of echoes of the Doctor's frantic final oration:

48 For the authorship of *The Repentance of Robert Greene*, see Alwes, *Sons and Authors*, pp. 145–6.

49 For a detailed account of *The Cobbler of Canterbury*, see Margaret M. Schlauch, *Antecedents of the English Novel 1400–1600* (Warsaw: PWN and London: Oxford University Press, 1963), pp. 157–63.

50 See *Doctor Faustus*, ed. Bevington and Rasmussen, A-text, I.i.39 and B-text I.i.37.

> Oh then whether shall I flie from thy presence, shall I take the wings of the morning and absent my selfe? Can the hideous mountains hide me, can wealth redeeme sinne, can beautie countervaile my faults, or the whole world counterpoyse the ballance of mine offences? Oh no, and therefore am I at my wits end, wishing for death, and the end of my miserable dayes, and yet then the remembrance of hell, and the torments thereof drive me to wish the contrarie (sig. B3^{v}).[51]

These Faustian lines cast a gloom over the *Vision* that would have had readers in 1592 turning the pages rapidly, eager to find out whether Greene suffered the same calamitous fate—impenitence and damnation—as that other truant scholar, and relieved in the end to discover that, like Bacon, he did not.

As they read, however, they may also have found themselves uncertain of the true extent of Greene's repentance. For one thing, Chaucer's ghost undertakes a defense of Greene's books that is as spirited as anything Lodge or Sidney could have written. Laughing off Greene's reservations about the worth of his "amourous trifles," he reminds him that there are not one but nine Muses, "amongst whom as there is a Clio to write grave matters, so there is a Thalia to endite pleasant conceits, and that Apollo hath Baies for them both, aswell to crowne the one for hir wanton amours, as to honour the other for her worthy labours: the braine hath many strings, and the wit many stretches" (sig. C2^{v}). The cheery liberalism of this defense is wonderfully refreshing to readers familiar with the bullying assaults on poems and plays launched by Greene's more inquisitorial contemporaries. And when Chaucer begins to list the moral "sentences" he has found among Greene's works, in comic imitation of the collections of proverbs or improving *sententiae* that passed for moral philosophy among the Elizabethan booksellers, Greene's fans may well have concluded that the case has been well won.[52] Besides, the moralist John Gower, who puts the case against Greene's work "with a sowre countenance" that betrays his bias against literary pleasure (sig. C3^{r}), is as willing as Chaucer to rank Greene's "amourous trifles" alongside those of Ovid and Chaucer himself. And when the two ghosts launch into a storytelling competition to see which can paint a more instructive picture of the ill-effects of jealousy—Chaucer with a scurrilous *fabliau*,[53] Gower with a kind of saint's legend modelled on Chaucer's own tale of Patient Griselda[54]—the contest reads more like a virtuoso display of Greene's skill in different narrative modes than a serious effort to decide which style he should favor in his future publications.

---

51 A number of details in the passage repeat what Faustus says in the A-text at V.vii.65–123, in the B-text at V.ii.138–91 (Bevington and Rasmussen's edition).

52 On these sentences or *sententiae*, see my essay "William Baldwin and the Politics of Pseudo-philosophy in Tudor Prose Fiction," *Studies in Philology* 97.1, pp. 29–60.

53 For the *fabliau* tradition in medieval and early modern England, see John Hines, *The Fabliau in English*, Longman Medieval and Renaissance Library (London and New York: Longman, 1993).

54 See the Clerk's Tale in *The Canterbury Tales*.

Each tale plays on the title of *Greene's Vision* by including a kind of vision as an integral part of its plot. Gower's concerns a jealous Flemish husband, Vandermast (which is also the name of Friar Bacon's German rival), who visits an aged scholar and receives an effective cure for his jealousy. The scholar changes Vandermast's appearance by magic into that of a "beautifull young man" (sig. G1^{r}), in which form he visits his wife as a kind of erotic daydream to test her fidelity; her triumphant passing of the test ends his suspicions. Chaucer's narrative features a less reputable scholar, who uses a fake vision to instruct a country girl in the art of cheating on her own jealous husband. In contrast to Gower's moral academic, Chaucer's scholar favors the technique of seeming to *confirm* the jealous husband's worst fears before dismissing them. With all the wit of a comic dramatist, he arranges for the husband to catch his wife *in flagrante delicto*, sitting on a scholar's lap and "eating of a pound of Cherries" (sig. D4^{r}) with lascivious greediness. The scholar then puts the husband to sleep by magic and convinces him when he wakes that what he saw was an illusion, an "idle and a jealious fancie" conceived in a bout of sickness (sig. D4^{v}). The husband then gives up his jealous ways, and his wife is able to carry on her sexual pastimes unimpeded.

In both these stories, Baconian scholars occupy the position of artists who specialize in pulling the wool over people's eyes and conjuring up seductive fantasies, thus (once again) confirming the worst suspicions of Greene's critics regarding the bad effects of his scribblings. In the case of Chaucer's tale, the tableau of the cherry-eating wife has the added twist of being an accurate portrayal of her adultery: an imitation of fact that only *poses* as fantasy. And Gower's tale, too, has a twist. In the middle of it, the jealous husband goes mad and launches into a set of instructive "sentences" or *sententiae* that are little more than misogynistic rantings and that are confuted in every detail by the good behavior of his virtuous wife (sig. F2^{v}). Gower thus inadvertently calls into question the value of the glibly "sententious" form of philosophy favoured by Elizabethan educators. No wonder, then, that as Greene reluctantly agrees to follow Gower's example rather than Chaucer's, he quickly adds a proviso. I have one more romance to finish, he explains—the quasi-autobiographical narrative *Nunquam sera est* (*Greene's Never Too Late*, 1590)—before moving into fully fledged didactic mode (sig. H1^{v}). No wonder, too, if King Solomon, when he appears in *Greene's Vision*, dismisses the writings of both Chaucer *and* Gower as labor lost and time wasted. Only theology, he states, can claim to impart true wisdom; if you are not a theologian, it doesn't much matter *what* you write, since "the end of thy labours shall be vanitie" (sig. H3^{v}).[55]

---

55 Solomon was, of course, the ultimate author of *sententiae* or sentences; he supposedly wrote the biblical book of Proverbs, which provided a model for the many books of proverbial wisdom published in the sixteenth century. For an account of Medieval and early modern traditions relating to Solomon, see Donald Beecher (ed.), *The Dialogue of Solomon and Marcolphus*, Publications of the Barnabe Riche Society 4 (Ottawa: Dovehouse Editions, 1995), introduction.

The calculated nature of Greene's penitence is demonstrated both by the deferral of the *Vision*'s publication and by the ambiguity of the term "vision" in the book's title. The central vision of the book is supposedly heaven-sent, designed to call a sinner to repentance. But this vision gives rise to two stories containing apparitions of a very different kind, erotically charged and designedly misleading, which suggests that any abjuration of amorous fancies the book contains is being held in suspension for at least the length of the book. Quite simply, Greene does not seem to be taking it wholly seriously, despite the motto he chose for many of his publications after 1590, *sero sed serio*. Seriousness, Solomon implies, requires a monomaniacal commitment to a single course of action, a determined adherence to—or at least, seeking out of—a known set of values; a simplicity that is at odds with the art of producing literary or dramatic entertainment. Greene's pamphlets, by contrast, trace the destabilizing effect of time on values, commitments, even words themselves. Beginning a Greene romance, it is genuinely impossible to guess how it will end. The famous shock suicide of the title character in *Pandosto* is only one of a range of startling dénouements in his prose and drama: others include Mamillia's eventual choice of the philandering Pharicles over the virtuous Florion at the end of Greene's first romance; the execution of the clown Adam in *A Looking Glass for London and England*; the cheerful damnation of Miles in *Friar Bacon*. This refusal to honor the stability of genre conventions may have been one of the characteristics of Greene's writing that made it sell so well in a period when so many writers were content to peddle tamely to what was expected of them. And it is a principle he carried over into his life, deferring the repentance that was expected of him, and which he was always advertising, until after the moment of his death. Greene would seem in the end to have had more in common with Miles—who relishes the prospect of hell as a place full of "tippling houses" and "good drink" (xv.34–37), and for whom repentance is, therefore, finally unthinkable—than with Margaret or Bacon.

But it may also be that Greene's contemporaries saw in him someone much more like themselves than the exemplary figures offered up for their instruction in the more conventional productions of his colleagues. The lip-service he paid to repentance and the tension that arose from the question of whether he would ever manage to repent gave them a perfect reflection of their own collective dilemma, as Christians and as citizens of a thriving, commercial metropolis. This parallel between his situation and theirs is nowhere made more obvious than in the play Greene wrote with Thomas Lodge, *A Looking Glass for London and England*. The play was probably written and performed in 1590, and it extends the time-bound status of its authors to embrace the whole of the English capital.[56] In it, the

56 I take 1590 to be the date of the play's composition on the basis of two passages in books he wrote in 1590. The first is from *Greene's Vision*, in which Greene declares his intention "with the Ninivites [to] shew in sackcloth my harty repentaunce" (sig. H1^{v}). He takes up the theme at greater length in the dedication and conclusion of *Greene's Mourning*

decadent inhabitants of the mighty city of Nineveh are warned by successive prophets to abjure their wickedness before a deadline set by God. Should they fail to repent in time, their city faces annihilation, a *coup de foudre* as sudden and devastating as the lightning bolt that strikes dead their incestuous queen in the middle of the play (14.30–31). The play's plot puts the entire metropolis of Nineveh in the position of Marlowe's Faustus, of Greene's Bacon, of Greene himself; the parallel with Greene is pointed up in the final scene, when the prophet Jonah reassures the Ninivites, as Greene reassured himself, that "amends may never come too late" and that "A will to practise good is vertuous" (14.110).

Throughout the play, too, the parallel between Nineveh and London is stressed in a series of direct addresses from the prophets Hosea and Jonah to the audience. "Looke London, look," urges Hosea, "with inward eies behold / What lessons the events do here unfold" (14.86), and no doubt the citizens of London in Greene's time looked and listened with rapt attention. The *Looking Glass* takes up the mantle of *Dr Faustus* and spreads it over the population of England; its magic mirror informs its audience that their sins are equal to Bacon's, Greene's, or even the king of Nineveh's, who commits incest and innumerable acts of tyranny before humbling himself in sackcloth and ashes. As a dramatic device, one can think of nothing more impressive in an age of faith than a warning to the audience that it is in danger of damnation, that the very time taken up by the play they are watching is time that could be taken up with preparations for the day of judgement.

The *Looking Glass* informs Greene's public that they are no better than Greene himself; that they are a population of Greenes, just as Greene himself was an agglomeration of his own characters, the virtuous and the vicious, the constant and the unfaithful mingled promiscuously in a single mortal body. We could do worse, if we wish to understand the inhabitants of Elizabethan London, than look as closely as his public did into the dazzling hall of mirrors that is his work for page and stage.

Garment, where he speaks of the "wantonnesse" of the "Ninivites" (sig. A3^r) and urges his readers to "weare" the book "as the Ninivites did their sackcloth" (sig. K3^r). This dedication and conclusion appear only in the 1616 edition of the book, but since the sole surviving copy of the 1590 edition is imperfect, it seems reasonable to suppose that they were intended for the first edition, and that Greene wrote them. The supposition appears more reasonable when one considers that the dedicatee of the *Mourning Garment*, George Clifford Earl of Cumberland, died in 1605, long before the 1616 edition in which the dedication first saw print. Moreover, the conclusion speaks of the book as "the first of my reformed passions" and "the last of my trifling Pamphlets," which suggests that it was written before his other "repentance pamphlets" such as *Greene's Farewell to Folly* (1591). In both the *Vision* and the *Mourning Garment*, the various allusions to the Ninivites refer to the biblical stories of Hosea and Jonah that form the basis of the *Looking Glass*, and it seems likely that he made these references when the stories were fresh in his mind after adapting them for the theatre.

Chapter 9

Transplanting Lillies: Greene, Tyrants and Tragical Comedies

Katharine Wilson

> Of all the flowers a *Lillie* once I lou'd
> Whose labouring beautie brancht it selfe abroade;
> But now old age his glorie hath remoued,
> And Greener obiectes are my eyes aboade.[1]

Henry Upchear may be a marginal figure in literary history, but his own assessment of the contemporary, cultural landscape is uncompromising. The florid excesses of Lyly's style are dismissed as fodder for adolescent fantasies; Greene's writing is for grown-ups. Upchear is not an unbiased witness. His dismissal of Lyly's work occurs in a poem commending Greene's *Menaphon* (1589), a pastoral narrative that seems to have been inspired by Philip Sidney's manuscript fiction composed around the late 1570s, now known as *The Old Arcadia*.[2] Greene was in the process of rebranding himself. He had begun his career by imitating the plot and outlandish style of Lyly's bestselling stories about Euphues, a young Italian who finds himself forced to choose between friendship and love. But by the end of the 1580s, *Euphues* (1578) was looking a little tired.[3] Sidney's death in 1586 had generated a flurry of would be "arcadian" writing, and Greene was eager to present himself as a fashionable and upmarket pastoralist.

---

1 Robert Greene, *Menaphon Camillas alarum to slumbering Euphues, in his melancholie cell at Silexedra* (London, 1589), *3r.

2 The similarities between Greene and Sidney's plots suggest that Greene had some knowledge of one of the many manuscripts of *The Old Arcadia* then in circulation. The fullest argument for Greene's debt to Sidney is found in S.L. Wolff's *The Greek Romances in Elizabethan Prose Fiction* (New York: Columbia University Press, 1912), pp. 366–458, but his analysis is substantially updated by Lori Humphrey Newcomb's discussion of Greene and Sidney in *Reading Popular Romance in Early Modern England* (New York, NY: Columbia University Press, 2002), pp. 21–76, and H.R. Woudhuysen, *Sir Philip Sidney and the Circulation of Manuscripts 1558–1640* (Oxford: Clarendon Press, 1996), p. 264, pp. 300–303, pp. 328–31.

3 For changing attitudes to euphuism, see G.K. Hunter, *John Lyly: The Humanist as Courtier* (London: Routledge & Kegan Paul, 1962), pp. 257–97.

His method of doing so was characteristically economical. Greene wrote two pastoral fictions in quick succession, and they share many similarities. *Menaphon* is, in part, a revised version of Greene's own previous pamphlet *Pandosto. The Triumph of Time* (1588), itself a bestseller and the source of numerous imitations throughout succeeding centuries.[4] The change of direction in Greene's prose style in the late 1580s is paralleled by the development of his dramatic techniques. Greene's first play *Alphonsus King of Aragon* (c.1587) was a tragedy written in imitation of Marlowe's *Tamburlaine the Great* (c.1587), which appears to have failed disastrously. Greene turned to romantic comedy with far more successful results. *The Honorable Historie of Frier Bacon, and Frier Bungay* (c.1589) was probably his second and most successful theatrical work and demonstrates a characteristically astute combination of cultural topoi. Greene again invited his audience to associate his work with Marlowe by giving them a story about a magician forced to resign his conjuring—like Doctor Faustus.[5] But Greene hedged his bets by loosely adapting the popular chapbook history of the early exploits of the philosopher Roger Bacon, and interwove multiple plot lines, most notably the story of a prince courting a milkmaid. Some members of his audience might have remembered *Pandosto*, in which a prince courts a princess he believes to be a shepherdess. But readers and audiences might also have remembered another text by the author whom Henry Upchear was so keen to forget. Woven into both *Pandosto* and *Frier Bacon* are memories of Lyly's first play *Campaspe* (1584).[6]

This continued exploitation of Lyly's influence comes as no surprise in itself. Greene is as famous for plagiarism as he is for prodigality, and he built his literary career by ruthlessly mining and recycling every usable shard of literature that came his way, including his own earlier works. As both his friends and enemies were keen to point out, his attitude toward his sources was heavily influenced by commercial pressures. Yet to regard Greene's modes of imitation as wholly reductive is to ignore his ongoing assessment of his own place in the huge and amorphous canon of early modern fiction.[7] Greene freely borrowed words, phrases

---

4 The most famous of these is, of course, Shakespeare's *The Winter's Tale*, but see Newcomb's *Reading Popular Romance* for the phenomenal cultural history of *Pandosto*.

5 For the relationship between Marlowe and Greene's texts, see John H. Jones, *The English Faust Book* (Cambridge: Cambridge University Press, 1994), pp. 52–72.

6 The relationship between Lyly and Greene's texts is noted by G.C. Moore Smith in "Lyly, Greene and Shakespeare," *N&Q* 10th Series, 8 (1907): 461–2. See also Stanley Wells' introduction and commentrary on the text in *Perymedes the Blacksmith and Pandosto. A Critical Edition* (New York and London: Garland, 1988). All references to *Pandosto* are taken from this edition and are indicated parenthetically in the text by page number.

7 Of the extensive literature on early modern modes of imitation, see especially G.W. Pigman III, "Versions of Imitation in the Renaissance," *RQ* 33 (1980): 1–32. Pigman identifies three major types of imitation; "following," "emulative," and "transformative." However, it is difficult to read Greene's work solely in the light of these definitions, since Greene often performs a variety of imitative modes simultaneously.

and whole passages, but as his career progressed his works are increasingly marked by a tendency to find ways of drawing attention to his own combinations of different literary modes. Greene dominated popular prose and dramatic romance in the 1580s because of his ability to combine imitations of disparate generic and narrative traditions, and to see the parallels between them.

His use of *Campaspe* is a case in point. Although Lyly's first play was billed as a "tragical comedie," it looks like a love story that reflects the generosity of Alexander the Great. But Greene's use of the "tragic" elements of the text in *Pandosto* and *Frier Bacon* suggests he also saw how it could lend itself to more provocative readings, and as a way to develop a new genre after the failure of *Alphonsus*. Greene had plenty of other generically hybrid texts to consider. Both he and Sidney were reading the translations of sensational, ancient Greek fictions newly available in print. Heliodorus, Longus, and Achilles Tatius had opened up a treasury of stories and motifs about chaste heroines miraculously rescued from trials, shipwrecks and lascivious suitors, the "tragic" and "comic" elements of their adventures determined by random spins of the wheel of fortune.[8] Sidney's reading resulted in a story of the foolish duke Basilius who ends up embroiled in comically inappropriate pastoral courtship with members of his family. Both Lyly's Alexander and Sidney's Basilius lie behind Greene's eponymous Pandosto.[9]

Greene then had plenty of different literary experiences to respond to—like the heroines of his fictions. Nashe's celebrated nickname for Greene, the "*Homer* of women," aptly indicates the extent to which he was preoccupied with the question of female response to the ever present threat of male lust and oppression, a question that would doubtless have resonated with many of his readers.[10] And just as Greene constantly revised the parallels between different literary traditions, so the women in his narratives are constantly forced to reassess how to deal with the lustful suitors and tyrants with whom they are confronted. Greene had plenty of archetypes from which to choose, many of which had long been lodged in the folk memory of his readers: patient Griselda tyrannized by her husband, chaste Susanna ogled by the elders.[11]

---

8 See Wolff, *The Greek Romances*, pp. 366–458. The pastoral section of *Pandosto* is partly adapted from Longus's *Daphnis and Chloe*.

9 Compare also the hero of Lyly's *Midas*.

10 Thomas Nashe, *The Anatomie of Absurditie* (1589), in *The Works of Thomas Nashe*, ed. R.B. McKerrow (1904–1910; rev. F.P. Wilson, Oxford: Basil Blackwell, 1958), vol. I, 12. For the significance of women readers, real and implied, see Helen Hackett, *Women and Romance Fiction in the English Renaissance* (Cambridge: Cambridge University Press, 2000); Caroline Lukas, *Writing for Women: The Example of Woman as Reader in Elizabethan Romance* (Milton Keynes: Open University Press, 1989).

11 John Phillip's *The Comodye of pacient and meeke Grissill* (c.1556–61) is only one of the many contemporary examples of "patient Griselda" stories. Greene wrote a version of the biblical story of Susanna in *The myrrour of modestie* (1584).

But Greene was also interested in the women who managed to combine chastity and obedience with a more active and vocal solution to their problems. Again Greene had a vast range of perspectives to bring to the question. The heroines of ancient Greek fictions often give eloquent defenses of their chastity as well as having the ability to escape from their pursuers. In *Euphues* Lyly had highlighted the questions of exemplary behaviour, partly by crafting a style—euphuism—that is heavily dependent on excessive and unusual comparison. The text is constructed around eloquent monologues, many of them about young men confronted by impossibly beautiful women, and women wondering whether they can honestly consent to love.[12]

For Greene's protagonists, especially the women, the level of literary knowledge that can be brought to bear upon a situation often becomes a crucial factor in determining their fates. The self-reflexivity with which they approach their situations is part of Greene's legacy from his immersion in romances.[13] Ancient Greek fictions are full of narrators, storytellers, and inset tales; native romances are equally characterized by an awareness of the kinship between authors and readers inside and outside the text. George Peele's *The Old Wives Tale* (1595), probably written to satirize Greene, revolves around a garrulous old woman whose stories are repeatedly interrupted by romance protagonists. Chaotic and inconsistent as Greene's texts frequently are, they reveal an obsession with how to use and integrate literary allusions, a task that is often shared between the author and his self-conscious protagonists. Greene milked his sources for all they were worth, but he also evolved a variety of narrative modes to highlight his borrowings and assess their relevance to his own texts. When Greene read *Campaspe*, he found speeches he could imitate and a plot he could adapt. But he placed his responses within frameworks in which protagonists and readers are invited to respond actively to the process of imitation—to read, and talk back.

I

The theatrical conditions in which *Campaspe* was produced were as far removed from Greene's customary literary milieu as the subject matter of the text. First printed in 1584, Lyly's first play was designed to be presented by boy players at the court and at the Blackfriars, with Lyly contributing separate prologues for each venue. The plot is a dramatization of a popular anecdote from ancient history.

12 Affective monologues can be traced to multiple classical and native romance traditions. See Helen Moore, "Elizabethan Fiction and Ovid's *Heroides*," *Translation and Literature* 9 (2000), pp. 40–64; Helen Cooper, *The English Romance in Time* (Oxford: Oxford University Press, 2004), pp. 18–20.

13 See Simon Palfrey's discussion of romance in *Late Shakespeare: A New World of Words* (Oxford: Oxford University Press, 1997), pp. 36–56.

According to Pliny, Alexander the Great instructed one of his artists, Apelles, to paint a nude portrait of his favorite concubine Campaspe. During the course of the painting, Alexander realizes that Apelles has himself fallen in love with Campaspe, and gives her to him.[14] Pliny's portrait of Alexander is explicitly intended to showcase Alexander's magnanimity and emotional self-control.

Lyly's Alexander has traditionally been interpreted as an equally generous leader, whose virtues are probably a reflection of Elizabeth's own munificence.[15] However, as Michael Pincombe points out, Lyly seems at pains to contrast his version of Alexander with the more familiar image of him as a bloodthirsty tyrant, who is as likely to exhibit violent sexual tendencies as military ones.[16] The play starts with a discussion between two soldiers, Clitus and Parmenio, after Alexander's destruction of Thebes. In the play, this event is blandly described by Parmenio as "a conquest without conflict" (I. i. 5). Yet nobody seems very certain of Alexander's mercy. The soldiers soon encounter some of the captives from the siege, including two women, Campaspe and Timoclea. To quell their anxiety about their fate, Timoclea notes that even Alexander's power has its limits:

> *Timo*. *Alex*. hath ouercome, not conquered.
> *Par*. To bring al vnder his subiection is to conquer.
> *Timo*. He cannot subdue that which is diuine.
> *Par*. Thebes was not.
> *Timo*. Vertue is.
> *Clitus*. *Alexander* as he tendreth virtue, so he will you, he drinketh not bloud, but thirsteth after honor, he is greedy of victory, but neuer satisfied with mercy. In fight terrible, as becometh a captaine; in conqueste milde, as beseemeth a king. In al things, then which nothing can be greater, he is *Alexander*.
> *Camp*. Then if it be such a thing to be *Alexander*, I hope it shalbe no miserable things to be a virgin. For if he saue our honors, it is more then to restore our goods. And rather doe I wish hee preserue our fames, then our lyues; which if he do, wee will confesse there can be no greater thing then to be *Alexander*. (I. i. 43–57)

Campaspe's hopes appear to be fulfilled when Alexander himself comes on the scene, since he promises the women that they will be "honourably entreated." However, Alexander also turns out to be preoccupied with the degree of his own influence, and with the possibility of less honorable entreaties. When he is later alone with his general Hephaestion, Alexander taunts him with being in love with Campaspe. Hephaestion's denial leads Alexander to consider the benefits of emotional restraint:

---

14 Pliny, *Natural History* 35, cited in R. Warwick Bond's edition of *The Complete Works of John Lyly* (Oxford: Clarendon Press, 1902), vol. II, p. 306. All references to Lyly's works are taken from this edition.

15 See for example, Hunter, *John Lyly*, pp. 159–66.

16 See Michael Pincombe, *The Plays of John Lyly: Eros and Eliza* (Manchester: Manchester University Press, 1996), pp. 24–51.

> *Hep*. Could I aswell subdue kingdoms, as I can my thoughtes; or were I as farre from ambition, as I am from loue, al the world wold account mee as valiant in armes, as I know my self moderate in affection. (II. ii. 11–14)

But Alexander's teasing is a blind, as he then confesses: "I loue, *Hephestion*, I loue! I loue *Campaspe*, a thing farre vnfit for a Macedonian, for a king, for *Alexander*" (II. ii. 20–21). Hephaestion is also in no doubt as to the unsuitability of the match:

> *Hep*. But you loue, ah griefe! But whom? *Campaspe*, ah shame! A maide forsooth vnknowne, vnnoble, & who can tell whether immodest? Whose eies are framed by arte to inamour, & whose heart was made by nature to inchaunt. I, but she is bewtiful; yea, but not therefore chast: I, but she is comly in al parts of the body: yea, but she may be crooked in some part of the mind: I, but she is wise, yea, but she is a woman! (II. ii. 41–7)

And like Campaspe and Timoclea, Hephaestion knows that Alexander's agency cannot extend to the control of others' emotions:

> *Alex*. I am a king, and will command.
> *Hep*. You may, to yeelde to luste by force, but to consent to loue by feare, you cannot. (II. ii. 100–102)

Fortunately, nobody in the play is obliged to consent to lust by force. Alexander allows Apelles to court Campaspe, who is as sensitive as Hephaestion to social decorum in matters of love: "In kinges there can be no loue, but to Queenes, for as neere must they meete in maiestie, as they doe in affection" (IV. iv. 30–31). Even Alexander quickly reconciles himself to the situation and ends the play looking forward to future military campaigns.

Yet despite the harmonious ending, the play is littered with reminders of the historical Alexander's violent career and the fictional Alexander's desire to control everyone with whom he comes into contact. He and Hephaestion know the difference in rank between him and Campaspe means he could never court her. As Hephaestion points out, he could rape Campaspe, but not make her love him. Alexander's decision to bestow Campaspe on Apelles is a pragmatic recognition of his own limitations as much as an act of magnanimity. Nor is Campaspe the only potential victim of Alexander's desires. Apelles enjoys a questionable degree of freedom. He remains Alexander's court painter, forced to exercise his talent on subjects of his master's choice. In addition to having to paint Campaspe for Alexander, Apelles turns out to have a gallery full of mythological pictures of divine rapes, although whether these are indicative of Apelles' or Alexander's taste remains unknown.

As Pincombe argues, it is the hidden stories of rape and violence that make the play live up to the running title given in the earliest editions: "A tragical Comedie of Alexander and Campaspe." Lyly's experiments with dramatic genre were partly inspired by Richard Edwards' play about male friendship, *Damon and Pythias*

(1571). Tragicomedy was a hot topic, not least because it had also recently come under attack. In his *Apology for Poetry*, Sidney took the opportunity to fulminate against hybrid plays which "be neither right tragedies, nor right comedies, mingling kings and clowns."[17] His condemnation may have spurred Lyly into attempting to reform the genre. Rather than randomly stirring up comic and tragic elements, Lyly wrote a play that develops into a comedy despite featuring a protagonist who properly belongs in classical tragedy. Alexander plots rape, but has to give way to the comic love plot being enacted without his knowledge by Apelles and Campaspe. His boredom with his role is suggested by the haste with which he renounces all pretensions to Campaspe in favor of more fighting.

Alexander is increasingly sidelined as the comic plot takes over and unwittingly cedes his dominance of the play to Apelles when he commissions him to paint Campaspe. As is made abundantly clear in the play, Alexander cannot paint and has to use Apelles as a surrogate. But the surrogate ends up becoming the lead. Another layer of comic meaning is suggested by Apelles's situation at the end of the play. He attains the best possible outcome under the circumstances, by both remaining a favored court painter and winning Campaspe. The situation must have resonated for Lyly, who spent his career trying to attain royal favour. Yet if Lyly's Alexander was intended to provoke comparisons with Elizabeth, the compliment is at best double-edged; Alexander is as repressive and bored as he is magnanimous. Even his ambition could not entirely stop Lyly from depicting the consequences of dependence on royal favour.

II

Greene is unlikely to have got anywhere near royal favor, or probably any real patronage at all. By 1588, his career was defined by his ability to manufacture romance fiction for the popular press. And *Pandosto* looks like everything Sidney would claim to have hated.[18] Cashing in on the phenomenon generated by Sidney's own pastoral manuscript, *The Old Arcadia*, Greene created a narrative which oscillates wildly between comedy and tragedy until the very last sentence. But Greene also used the text as a way of responding to *Campaspe*. Like Sidney and Lyly, Greene wrote about an irrational ruler whose sexual desires are thwarted. In *The Old Arcadia*, Basilius ends up unwittingly courting his wife. Greene turns

---

17 Sir Philip Sidney, *An Apology for Poetry* ed. Geoffrey Shepherd, rev. R.W. Maslen (3rd edn, Manchester University Press: Manchester, 2002), p. 112. See Pincombe, *The Plays of John Lyly*, pp. 36–7. For the multifarious definitions of tragicomedy in this period, see Marvin T. Herrick, *Tragicomedy: Its Origin and Development in Italy, France and England* (University of Illinois Press: Urbana, 1955), pp. 215–60.

18 Despite his strictures, however, Sidney frequently breaks his own definitions of decorum in *The Old Arcadia*.

Sidney's comically confused families into tragically incestuous melodrama. Like Sidney, Greene concluded his depiction of pastoral courtship with the unfulfilled promise of a spectacularly tragic denouement—the execution of young lovers. But he reached his conclusion through his adaptation of the themes mingled in *Campaspe*: tyranny, sexual violence, surrogacy, and social rank.

Greene gives his readers a clue to the source of his inspiration before they reach the story. *Pandosto* is not written in a very euphuistic style (by Greene's standards, at least). The dedicatory epistle addressed to George Clifford, however, is larded with the elaborate modesty topoi employed by Lyly in the Blackfriars prologue to *Campaspe*. He compares Clifford to Alexander, and even adapts one of Lyly's compliments to Elizabeth's wisdom, in which Lyly claims "to sette before our owle *Pallas* shield, thinking by her vertue to couer the others deformitie" (lines 5–6).

The plot of *Pandosto* itself seems to be firmly anchored in the fortune driven world of ancient Greek romance. Yet despite the difference in literary environment, both Lyly and Greene unfold a plot in which a ruler creates a climate of fear, but is unable to control young love. Pandosto king of Bohemia is consumed by irrational jealousy and suspects his wife Bellaria of committing adultery with his friend Egistus, king of Sicily. Deprived of his friend, Pandosto has no equivalent of the counselor Hephaestion to whom he can confide his irrational passions. Instead, he tries to force his servant Franion to poison Egistus. Franion responds to the situation with a sentiment which would doubtless have been echoed by Lyly's Clitus and Parmenio: "Kings are knowen to commaunde, seruaunts are blamelesse to consent" (13). Franion, however, chooses to help Egistus escape, and Pandosto's suspicions are inflamed still further when Bellaria discovers that she is pregnant. Her daughter is born and cast adrift on the sea by Pandosto. Bellaria bears all her trials with patience. Her innocence is vindicated by the Delphic oracle, but her "extreame ioy" is overshadowed by her "heauie sorrowe" at the news of her eldest son's sudden death, and she dies of the tragicomic contrast of emotions (34).

Yet Greene's interpretation of tragicomedy encompassed more than seismic emotional shifts. It is in the pastoral section of the text, in which Greene might appear to be most dependent on an arcadian tradition, that he reassesses *Campaspe* most fully. Abandoning Pandosto to repentance, Greene relates how his daughter was saved and brought up by shepherds, unaware of her true identity. They name her Fawnia and raise her as a shepherdess. When she is sixteen, she happens to meet Egistus's son Dorastus out hunting. Both are instantly attracted to each other and later express their feelings alone in parallel monologues. Both believe that the difference in rank between them is an insurmountable obstacle to courtship, but resolve to submit to love anyway. As Fawnia puts it, "loue is a Lord, who will commaund by power, and constraine by force" (53).

Fawnia's formulation of the power of love sounds conventional enough. But its more sinister implications are touched on when Dorastus, like Lyly's Alexander, reveals that he knows there is no other way of achieving his ends. When he begins to court Fawnia, his language echoes the conversation of Lyly's Alexander and Hephaestion: "Why, *Fawnia*, perhaps I loue thee, and then thou must needes yeelde, for thou knowest I can commaunde and constraine" (57). Fawnia duly responds by also using *Campaspe* as her source text: "[C]onstrained loue is force, not loue: and know this, sir, mine honesty is such, as I hadde rather dye then be a *Concubine* euen to a King" (58).

Lyly confined the hints of sexual violence in his play to the realm of male fantasy. Greene, however, capitalized on them by giving Alexander's words to the romance hero, while his heroine resists his entreaties by quoting Campaspe's reflections on the possible consequences of her capture by Alexander. Dorastus' teasing threats are instantly deflected by Fawnia's ability to respond in kind, and she diverts the situation by moving away from Lyly's generic world to that of pastoral. Fawnia suggests that Dorastus become a shepherd in order to obliterate the difference in rank between them. But although Dorastus adopts a pastoral disguise, it convinces nobody, and he is later captured by Pandosto. With his reappearance in the narrative, the tragic potential of *Campaspe* is represented with even more sinister results. Pandosto is also bewitched by Fawnia's beauty, which he reflects on in the words of Lyly's Hephaestion: "Dooth *Pandosto* then loue? Yea: whome? A maide vnknowne, yea and perhapps, immodest, stragled out of her owne countrie: beautifull, but not therefore chast: comely in bodie, but perhappes crooked in minde" (80).

Fawnia finds herself confronting not only a lover who talks like Lyly's Alexander, but also her father. Once again, she combats the threat by returning quotations, with Greene dropping hints about his theatrical source by setting out her encounter with her father as dialogue. Pandosto tries to persuade Fawnia to love "vsing these familiar speaches" by stressing that "it is better to be fauoured of a King then a subiect" (84). Fawnia responds by echoing Lyly's Timoclea in her distinction between physical and mental states: "[T]he body is subiect to victories, but the mind not to be subdued by conquest." Pandosto's entreaties become more threatening: "[M]y power is such as I may compell by force." Fawnia quotes Campaspe: "[W]here lust ruleth it is a miserable thing to be a virgin, but know this, that I will alwaies preferre fame before life, and rather choose death then dishonour" (85).

Greene's creation and repetition of an unwritten scene from *Campaspe* create a disturbing link between the tragic element of the text, as embodied by the unwittingly incestuous father, and the comic romance of the hero and heroine. The language of *Campaspe* makes Dorastus into a surrogate of Pandosto, their shared emphasis on force yoking their parts of the plot together. Again Greene looks back to the male relationships in Lyly's play. By commissioning Apelles to paint Campaspe, Alexander tries to employ Apelles as a surrogate in his courtship—a plan which backfires when Apelles falls in love. This is not to suggest that *Pandosto* is based on an unremittingly bleak interpretation of *Campaspe*. Greene counterpoises his sensational cliffhangers with plenty of moments of sly comedy, not least those derived from Dorastus's limited interpretation of pastoral (very different from that of Sidney's Musidorus). But like so many of his later fictions, *Pandosto* is written with an awareness of the close kinship between scenes of courtship and scenes in which chaste women are forced to defend their honor. And in Greene's ongoing consideration of the female response to such challenges, his answers are increasingly literary. Fawnia is one of Greene's most eloquent heroines, and her ability to rewrite *Campaspe* to her own advantage helps her to repel both the hints of force from her lover and the promise of rape from her father.

But Greene characteristically saves plenty of surprises for the last page. Pandosto's passion turns to hatred when Fawnia rejects him, and instead of raping her, he plans to execute her and Dorastus. Only the unexpected revelation of Fawnia's origins by her foster father brings about recognition, depicted with deadpan understatement by Greene: "*Fawnia* was not more ioyfull that she had found such a Father, then *Dorastus* was glad he should get such a wife" (90). Despite the general reconciliation, however, Pandosto knows that he belongs in the tragic part of the story. After the marriage of Dorastus and Fawnia, he kills himself in despair, in order, as Greene helpfully points out, "to close vp the Comedie with a Tragicall stratageme" (92). Yet if the play ends with a tragedy, it is not of Pandosto's making. After Pandosto's funeral in Sicilia, "*Dorastus* taking his leaue of his father, went with his wife and the dead corps into *Bohemia*, where after they were sumptuouslie intombed, *Dorastus* ended his daies in contented quiet." Dorastus leaves Bohemia with a living wife and a dead father-in-law, but only achieves "contented quiet" after "they" were buried.[19] Greene's pronoun may be a mistake, but the intriguing possibility remains that Fawnia has fallen victim to her husband rather than her father. Even the eloquence borrowed from *Campaspe* is of limited utility in a world dominated by aggressive male relations.

III

Pandosto is full of protagonists and narrators eager to remind readers to note the contrasting generic elements of which the text is composed. But there is no equivalent of the most obvious author surrogate in *Campaspe*—the artist Apelles, who, like Lyly, was obliged to tailor his career to the artistic requirements of the ruler he needed to please. In *Frier Bacon* the eponymous magician himself

---

19 Greene may be suggesting a symmetry between the burial of Bellaria, which ends the first half of the narrative, and that of Pandosto and perhaps also Fawnia. Greene borrows heavily throughout *Pandosto* from his earlier fiction *Euphues his Censure to Philautus* (1587); see Wells's introduction, especially pp. lxxiii–lxxix. Dorastus's burial of his family echoes the end of Ulysses' tale in *Euphues his Censure*, a tragedy in which a wife's infidelity to her husband leads to her suicide.

becomes the mediator between the interlaced plots.[20] The play is set in more familiar locations than the exotic terrains of *Pandosto*: Bohemia and Sicilia are replaced by Oxford and Fressingfield. But the exploits that the play depicts are no less spectacular. Greene turns the medieval philosopher Roger Bacon into a magician who spends much of the play trying to conjure a homemade brazen head into speech. While the popular chapbook history that is Greene's major source depicts the rise of the philosopher to celebrity through scholarship, Greene's Bacon is obliged to win conjuring competitions in order to entertain his master, Henry III.[21] In *Campaspe*, Apelles's usefulness to Alexander was measured by his ability to produce lifelike portraiture. Bacon's main asset is his "glass perspective," a magic mirror with which characters can watch scenes happening in different locations.[22] Greene may be casting an ironic glance at the comparatively low technology of Apelles's painting.[23] But Bacon's glass also allows him to take on the status of author, and his interpretation of authorship again echoes *Campaspe*. In the prologue to the court, Lyly apparently invents an anecdote from ancient history:

> Whatsoeuer we present, we wish it may be thought the daunsing of *Agrippa* his shadowes, who in the moment they were seene, were of any shape one woulde conceiue ... . With vs it is like to fare, as with these torches, which giuing light to others, consume themselues: and wee shewing delight to others, shame our selues. (lines 13–18)

Greene's Bacon accompanies the revelations from his mirror with injunctions to his spectators to mark the "comedy" or "tragedy" that is about to unfold in front of them. Like Greene himself, he is engaged in an endless process of framing inset tales and combining genres. But his work itself ultimately helps to cause tragedy and makes Bacon renounce his magic. Like the actors of Lyly's play, Bacon learns that delight and shame are intertwined.

---

20 For a full analysis of Greene's complex combinations of plot lines, see Charles W. Hieatt, "Multiple Plotting in *Friar Bacon and Friar Bungay*," *Renaissance Drama*, NS, 16 (1985): 17–34.

21 The earliest surviving edition of the popular history of Bacon's life is *The Famous Historie of Fryer Bacon* (1627). See the extracts reproduced in J. Churton Collins's edition of *The Plays and Poems of Robert Greene* (Oxford: Clarendon Press, 1905), Vol. II., pp. 6–13. All references to Greene's plays are taken from this edition.

22 For a discussion of the issues involved in staging Bacon's perspective on the rest of the play, see J.A. Lavin's edition of *Friar Bacon and Friar Bungay* (London: Ernest Benn limited, 1969), pp. xvi–xxi.

23 See Charles W. Hieatt, "A New Source for *Friar Bacon and Friar Bungay*," *Review of English Studies*, NS, 32 (1981): 180–87, 185. The first recorded performances of *Frier Bacon* happened at the Rose in 1592, and Hieatt argues convincingly that Greene's response to *Campaspe* is partly defined by the greater theatrical opportunities afforded by the popular theater. Lyly, for example, includes a subplot involving the philosopher Diogenes' ability to fly; Greene's Friar Bacon flies across stage.

And like Apelles, Bacon is forced into the service of a lustful ruler. Within the framework provided by the exploits of his friar, Greene introduces a series of comic plots, the first of which involves the attempted seduction of Margaret, a keeper's daughter in Fressingfield, by the son of Henry III, the future Edward I. In this narrative, Greene leaves no room for ambiguity about his protagonist's intentions. The England in which *Frier Bacon* is set is a land of plenty in which the mentions of butter and cheese have an almost choric function. And, as is clear from the opening scene of the play, the most desirable object of consumption is Margaret the milkmaid, whose attractions are barely distinguishable from the dairy products she tends. Like Dorastus in *Pandosto*, Edward first encounters his would-be lover after a hunting expedition. As he explains to his courtiers, he accompanied her into the dairy and was immediately smitten:

> She turned her smocke ouer her Lilly armes,
> And diued them into milk to run her cheese:
> But, whiter than the milke, her christall skin,
> Checked with lines of Azur, made her blush,
> That art or nature durst bring her for compare. (I. i. 79–83)

Edward's intentions are strictly dishonorable. Margaret's appearance in the dairy immediately makes him think about the Roman legend of Lucrece, raped by the lecherous emperor Tarquin:

> *Ermsbie*, if thou hadst seene as I did note it well,
> How bewtie plaid the huswife, how this girle
> Like *Lucrece* laid her fingers to the worke,
> Thou wouldest with *Tarquine* hazard *Roome* and all
> To win the louely mayd of *Fressingfield*. (I. i. 84–88)

Yet Edward is a strangely reluctant Tarquin, and withdraws from his self-imposed role as rapist almost as soon as he proposes it.[24] Instead, he starts hatching a complicated ruse that again foregrounds the issues of surrogate courtship. On the pretext that Margaret is bound to impede his desires by demanding marriage, he seizes on his servant Rafe's idea of a substitute plot. While Rafe is to impersonate Edward at court, an earl called Lacy is to disguise himself as a farmer's son in order to assess Margaret's possible interest in Edward. Edward himself intends to watch Lacy in action by the agency of Bacon's magic mirror, or, as Bacon puts it, to "marke the commedie." (II. ii. 663)

Like Lyly's Alexander, Greene's Edward shows a limited commitment to the role of lecherous suitor. Greene, however, also complicates matters further by making Edward less interested in Margaret's intentions than he is in those of his

---

24 Compare the response of Iachimo in Shakespeare's *Cymbeline*, who also cites the example of Tarquin before deciding not to rape Imogen.

friend Lacy. By the time Lacy encounters Margaret in order to plead Edward's suit, Margaret is already attracted to Lacy. When she discovers his real identity, Lacy determines to marry her to save her from the prince. Edward is furious and later confronts Lacy in words which make it clear that he knows his sources:

> Iniurious *Lacie*, did I loue thee more
> Than *Alexander* his *Hephestion*?
> Did I vnfould the passions of my loue,
> And locke them in the closet of thy thoughts? (III. i. 947–50)

Edward has cast himself as Alexander in a revision of *Campaspe*. But instead of taking on the role of Alexander's intimate Hephaestion, Lacy has chosen to play Apelles. Like Lyly's Alexander, Edward soon gets over his disappointment. Within lines he moves from threatening to execute Margaret and Lacy to self-consciously practicing magnanimity, claiming that "So in subduing fancies passion,/ Conquering thy selfe, thou getst the richest spoile" (III. i. 1043–44). With the help of Lacy's promises of "butter, cheese and venison," reconciliation is confirmed. Edward later agrees to an arranged marriage to Eleanor of Castile. But he only shows any enthusiasm for it when Eleanor proposes that they share a double wedding with Margaret and Lacy, an idea he greets with "Gramercie, *Nell*, for I do loue the lord,/As he that's seconde to my selfe in loue" (IV. ii. 1726–27). Even Rafe the servant feels compelled to warn Eleanor. Edward's love, he tells her, is "like vnto a tapsters glasse that is broken with euery tutch; for he loued the faire maid of *Fresingfield* once out of all hoe" (IV. ii. 1731–33).

In *Pandosto* Greene had used *Campaspe* as a way of highlighting the network of potentially violent suitors. In *Frier Bacon* he returns to the male relationships in Lyly's play in order to suggest an equally contentious subtext. Edward identifies his most important relationship as that between himself and his "Hephaestion" Lacy, which is disrupted by Margaret playing "Campaspe." Greene does not pursue the relationship between Edward and Lacy, but he implicitly contrasts it to that between Lacy and Margaret. The question of love versus friendship was, of course, a standard topic, and one which Greene had been imitating since he first read *Euphues*. But the love triangle he creates is suggestive. Alexander and Hephaestion belonged in the canon of classical male relationships. In Marlowe's *Edward II* (1592), Mortimer the elder justifies Edward's love of Gaveston by placing it in this context: "The mightiest kings have had their minions;/ Great *Alexander* loved *Ephestion*."[25]

As in *Campaspe* the ruler's dominance of the plot line gives way to that of his surrogate. As in *Pandosto*, Greene depicts a world in which male cruelty is endemic. Greene does follow the relationship between Lacy and Margaret, which appears to be doomed before it starts. Before they are married, he pretends to cast

25 *Edward II* in *The Complete Works of Christopher Marlowe*, ed. Richard Rowland (Oxford: Clarendon Press, 1994), vol. III, scene 4, lines 391–2.

her off by writing a letter in which he professes his intention to marry one of Eleanor's maids. Margaret resolves to enter a nunnery ("Now farewell, world, the engine of all woe!" (V. i. 1880) only to be forced into a humiliating climb-down a few lines later when Lacy returns to confess that he was merely testing her constancy ("And all the shew of holy Nuns, farewell!" [V. i. 1942]). Even the on-stage audience seems nervous. In what is for Greene an unusually explicit pun, one of the attendant lords professes his amazement: "To see the nature of women, that be they neuer so neare God, yet they love to die in a man's arms" (V. i. 1954–5). Embarrassment is only dispelled by Lacy's promise of the universal panacea: butter and cheese for breakfast.

Greene was never averse to raising a cheap laugh at the expense of women, Catholicism, or anything else. Yet in comparison to Fawnia, actively repelling her suitors by exchanging quotations, Margaret appears unusually passive. The major difference between them lies in social rank. Fawnia is a princess disguised as a shepherdess; Margaret really is a milkmaid. Greene's transformation of her into the wife of an earl is more socially radical than Lyly's depiction of the match between Apelles the artist and the prisoner of war Campaspe. Campaspe is quite clear about the need to maintain appropriate social boundaries. But Greene also suggests that Margaret's humble background is related to her inability to decode the very literary machinations of Lacy. Fawnia's eloquence as a shepherdess betrays her noble origins—and by implication her level of literary knowledge. Like Pandosto and Dorastus, Fawnia appears to be familiar with the speeches in *Campaspe*. Margaret, however, turns out never to have read anything by Lyly. The letter in which Lacy pretends to renounce her is couched in the sort of heavily euphuistic style that Greene himself employed in his early works: "The bloomes of the Almond tree grow in a night, and vanish in a morne: the flies *Haemerae* (faire *Peggie*) take life with the Sun, and die with the dew ... ." (III. iii. 1481–3). But such explicit euphuism in Greene's later works is almost always a sign of self-consciously courtly artifice, which should be treated with suspicion or ridicule (as Henry Upchear would have agreed). Only Margaret, Greene implies, is simply too unfamiliar with contemporary literary style to understand how to interpret it.

As many of Greene's heroines discover, cultural knowledge is power, but most likely to be associated with those of a higher social rank. Unlike so many of the women in peril who feature in Greene's later works, Margaret is unable to find comfort in the positive exempla provided by mythology or history. The only female archetype she can summon up is the ultimate negative example, Helen of Troy. *Frier Bacon* is saturated in classical allusions, but almost all of them revolve around Ovidian narratives of rape and violence—like the paintings in Apelles's studio.[26] Margaret, of course, wins Lacy in the end; Greene liked rags-to-riches

---

26 See, for example, Lacy's allusion to Phoebus and Semele at i. ii. 363–4, or Edward's reference to Phoebus and Daphne at IV. ii. 1668–70.

stories.[27] But Margaret's lack of literary skills makes the transition from the world of butter, cheese, and venison to more seemingly courtly modes an unusually painful one.[28]

Fawnia and Margaret are only two of the many good women in Greene's fictions who are forced to reflect on their responses to the irrational men with whom they are surrounded. In Greene's works, the moral choice usually turns out to be a literary one, which reflects their author's own self presentation. Despite Upchear's determination to relegate Lyly to the bottom of the literary division, Greene never stopped assessing his predecessor's influence. *Campaspe* was such a provocative text for Greene precisely because it gave rise to so many generic possibilities. For Pandosto and Dorastus, it provided the language of tragedy—but for Fawnia an escape from male lust into the world of comic romance. For Edward and Margaret however, Lyly's text makes for uncomfortable reading. Edward thinks he has lined up his cast to reenact the play only to discover that one member of it has changed roles without telling him—the same dilemma encountered by Alexander when he found out that Apelles had turned into a lover rather than a servant. Margaret, meanwhile, is hampered by her ignorance of *Euphues*, which Greene presents as required reading at the court. But this is the court of Henry III; like Upchear, Greene puts Lyly in his place as hopelessly outdated. Reading too much Lyly can be just as dangerous. In *Menaphon*, which satirizes almost every current cultural debate, the hero and heroine waste time by exchanging meaningless hyperboles because each thinks the other can only talk in euphuism. Greene found ever more varied ways of making his debt to Lyly into a joke, but never escaped from his literary legacy.

---

27 Fawnia's foster father is knighted at the end of *Pandosto*.

28 Compare the response of Queen Dorothea in Greene's later tragicomedy *The Scottish Hystorie of Iames the Fovrth*. Faced with a similar dilemma to that of Margaret, she pragmatically concludes, "He does but tempt his wife, he tryes my love" (II.ii. 967), and sets out to reclaim her husband.

Chapter 10

Recent Studies in Robert Greene (1989–2006)

Kirk Melnikoff and Edward Gieskes

A.B. Grosart's *Life and Complete Works in Prose & Verse of Robert Greene*, 15 vols (1881–86) remains the only relatively complete edition of Greene's works. The only collected edition of Greene's plays is still J. Churton Collins's *The Plays and Poems*, 2 vols (1905). Useful earlier bibliographies of Greene criticism are James Seay Dean's *Robert Greene: A Reference Guide* (Boston: G.K. Hall & Co.,1984) and Kevin J. Donovan's "Recent Studies in Robert Greene (1968–88)," *English Literary Renaissance* 20.1 (1990): 163–75.

I. General

Biographical

Dan Brayton's "Robert Greene" in *British Writers Supplement VIII* offers a biographical sketch of Greene that follows the generally accepted account of his trajectory from Norwich to Cambridge to London and his early death. It also surveys his work, breaking it up into generic categories: Prose Fiction, Greene as Playwright, Greene as Poet, and Proto-Journalism. The essay looks briefly at Greene's afterlife in various late sixteenth-century narratives and in Woolf's *Orlando*. It offers a helpful overview of the works and is most useful in calling attention to Greene's poetry. Lori Humphrey Newcomb's entry for Greene in the recently revised *Oxford Dictionary of National Biography* offers a cogent retelling of the main biographical details of Greene's life along with an impressively detailed (especially in its discussion of the cony-catching pamphlets), genre-based overview of Greene's work. Like Brayton, Newcomb also considers Greene's surprisingly salient posthumous reputation. To these more standard elements, Newcomb adds a provocative section regarding Greene's invention of authorial celebrity.

General

In one of the few recent works that accounts for the entirety of Greene's output, Reid Barbour's *Deciphering Elizabethan Fiction* proposes that we read Greene's work according to its own stated and implied narrative design. It is Barbour's contention that Greene's productions should be understood as constituting two overlapping stages: an early stage where "deciphering" (defined by Greene and other prose pamphleteers as "a representational act of a narrator") is the dominant narrative mode, and a later stage where "discovering" (defined as a narrative mode of "uncovering") is the dominant mode. Notable is Barbour's chapter on "Greene's Discovering," which draws some provocative connections between Greene's prose designs of the late 1580s and 1590s, and the same period's theatrical interests. Specifically, Barbour sees a connection between the late Elizabethan theatre's thinking about the discovery space and Greene's construction of a narrative mode centered around moments of discovery. Barbour concludes that Greene's impulse in borrowing theatrical modes is politically conservative, and he makes this point most strongly when he shows how Greene's rogue pamphlets use moments of discovery to "map" potential moments of criminal disorder. Stanton J. Linden's *Darke Hieorogliphicks: Alchemy in English Literature from Chaucer to the Reformation* is designed to "examine literary reflections of alchemy in an attempt to discover their means, explore their contributions to literary art, and investigate the insights they provide into important but obscure habits of thought" (5) in English culture. Greene enters into this study as an example of the literary use of alchemy in both prose fiction and drama. Linden describes Greene's treatment of alchemy as moving from being more or less objective to being satirical. James P. Bednarz's "Marlowe and the English Literary Scene" is concerned with the intellectual exchanges between the London community of professional writers during the late 1580s and early 1590s, particularly with Marlowe's presence in these exchanges. In his relatively extensive consideration of Greene, he essentially relates what has become the conventional, critical narrative of an antitheatrical, increasingly desperate Greene being overawed first by Marlowe's and then by Shakespeare's literary experiments in the world of professional theatre.

As one of many recent works that focus on Greene's fiction, Steve Mentz's "Wearing Greene: Autolycus, Robert Greene, and the Structure of Romance in *The Winter's Tale*" explores the "unruly subtexts" of Shakespeare's late play: romance, cony-catching tracts, and repentance pamphlets (all genres used by Greene). It argues that Shakespeare's incorporation of such generic subtexts suggests his fashioning of romance as a genre of reconciliation. Mentz's monograph *Romance For Sale* explores the development of "Elizabethan-Heliodoran prose romance" in the 1580s and the turn away from it in the 1590s. Greene is the "common figure" in Mentz's discussion. For Mentz, Greene's legacy is a variety of images of prose authorship in early modern England. Derek B. Alwes's *Sons and Authors in Elizabethan England* focuses upon Greene's early romances and his cony-catching tracts. Heavily influenced by Richard Helgerson's *Elizabethan Prodigals*, the book explores the way in which writers like Greene, Sidney, and Lyly responded to the patriarchal Elizabethan imperitive of state service as each pursued a career in literature. According to Alwes, Greene, like Sidney and Lyly, "used his fictions to redefine his responsibilities [to self, family and commonwealth] in such a way that writing became, not rebelliousness, but a way of fulfilling those responsibilities" (20). Peter Mack's "Rhetoric in Use: Three Romances by Greene and Lodge" maps Greene's and Lodge's extensive and varied use of rhetoric and dialectic in their pamphlet material. Mack's overarching purpose is to show how important the conventions of formal oratory were to the production and presumably the reception of sixteenth-century fiction. Helen Moore's "Elizabethan Fiction and Ovid's *Heroides*" traces the lesser-known influence of Ovid's *Heroides* on Elizabethan fiction and upon the development of the modern novel. Focusing mostly upon Greene's fiction, the essay points out that *Heroides*' epistolary style, its store of exempla, and its construction of compelling female voices are important influences. Using the aesthetic theories of Bakhtin, W.W. Barker's "Rhetorical Romance: The 'Frivolous Toyes' of Robert Greene" argues that Greene's writing becomes dialogic in his repentance pamphlets. Barker concludes that Greene's thoroughly dialogic narrative voice in *Greene's Groatsworth of Wit* should be seen as a precursor of three-dimensional characters like Hamlet. Arul Kumuran is also interested in transformations in Greene's late-career writing. His "Robert Greene's Martinist Transformation in 1590" contends that Greene's turn from arcadian romances to cony-catching pamphlets and repentance pamphlets around 1590 can be best explained by the pamphlet phenomenon of Martin Marprelate, which "injected a new freedom into the language of the pamphlet and had energized Elizabethan prose satire" (245). Discussing several of Greene's prose works, Elaine Beilin in *The Uses of Mythology in Elizabethan Prose Romance* wants to establish "Renaissance moral or Neoplatonic meanings of various myths and mythological figures" (11). She argues that the "sixteenth century romancer wrote to satisfy other demands than those the twentieth century makes on its novels"; specifically, she shows how the period's prose fiction valued "the presentation of ideas in a sequence that is clever, witty, and conducive to thinking on the part of the reader" (12) over plot.

Greene's self-conscious response to a burgeoning print market is the focus of a number of recent studies. Katherine Wilson's monograph *Fictions of Authorship in Late Elizabethan Narratives* explores the modes and anxieties of popular prose authorship in the second half of the sixteenth century. Looking primarily at Greene's prose romances, Wilson's book considers "the way authors marked out ideas about writing within their novels, often through the creation of writers and readers within the text. The repetition of this theme suggests the authors' own uncertainty about the role of prose fiction" (4). Carmine DiBiase's "The Decline of Euphuism: Robert Greene's Struggle Against Popular Taste" is an effort to account for the rise and fall of euphuism between the 1570s and the 1590s. Turning to

Greene to discuss "one important reason for its decline" (88), DiBiase argues that *Greene's Vision* offers a "new approach to fiction" and expresses "frustrations with the demands of the popular reader who pretends to appreciate euphuism without really knowing what it is" (89). Greene's solution to this problem, suggests DiBiase, is to turn away from the aristocratic subjects of euphuistic narrative to the lives of his London contemporaries. Because literary decorum dictates that this material should not be expressed with an aristocratic style, Greene thus turned away from euphuism toward a plainer form of writing. Alexandra Halasz's *The Marketplace of Print* analyzes the early modern print market in order to develop a narrative of a changing discursive field; this narrative ultimately points toward the emergence of a public sphere. According to Halasz, Greene's work helps to articulate the problem of "how the discursive space of the pamphlet becomes the site of a contest for authority in relation to the marketplace" (38). In Halasz's account, "'Greene' emerges as an author in and of these texts in order to mark a claim of value apart from the marketplace, but that claim to discursive authority functions to establish the value and vendibility of commodity-texts associated with his name" (38). In other words, Greene comes to represent the convergence of market and nonmarket claims to authority in the author's name. Greene's writerly authority underwrites his saleability in the early-modern print marketplace. Halasz's book offers an important and influential characterization of the forces shaping the social space in which pamphlets were produced in early modern London.

As one of the recent works dedicated to gender issues in Greene's fiction, Derek Alwes's "Robert Greene's Duelling Dedications" contends that Greene's prose fictions appeal to women by simultaneously empowering them as figures of virtue and ascribing to them an interior life. Brenda Cantar's "'Silenced but for the Word': The Discourse of Incest in Greene's *Pandosto* and *Menaphon*" also considers the relationship between Greene's fiction and its female audience. Considering Greene's use of incest between fathers and daughters in his romances, particularly in *Pandosto* and *Menaphon*, Cantar's essay sees this recurring motif as the product of larger changes in familial relations at the beginning of the early modern period. It concludes that these fictions probably had an "ambivalent and polyvalent" message for their female audiences. Last, in *Writing for Women: The Example of Woman as Reader in Elizabethan Romance*, Caroline Lucas proposes that we read Elizabethan romance as an object in and of itself. Looking at the romantic fiction of Greene as well as of Pettie, Rich, and Sidney, Lucas argues of Greene that his romances consistently offer women powerful yet self-destructive self-images.

In one of the few recent studies to focus upon the whole of Greene's dramatic work, A.R. Braunmuller's "'Second Means': Agent and Accessory in Elizabethan Drama" turns to the early modern legal concept of agency as a way to approach the drama. The essay argues that "some Elizabethan playwrights use agency to create the illusion that the characters originate and prosecute the plays' action" (178).

Braunmuller offers a useful survey of the common law's understanding of agency (the legal fiction that makes two persons legally identical—a master and servant, for example, are one person under the law when the servant acts on behalf of the master) and uses the example of homicide to illustrate the legal idea. Braunmuller shows how plays like *The Spanish Tragedy* and *Friar Bacon and Friar Bungay* depict characters who depute agents to act for them in ways that are consistent with the law of agency. At the close of the essay, the discussion turns to Peele's *Old Wives Tale* and *James IV* to discuss ways that dramatists explore "the relation between a creative figure and the personages of a play" (199). Braunmuller suggests that these plays dramatize the "fictiveness of human identity and human action" (202) by merging frame and main action, by having characters occupy positions within and without the play proper in ways that echo the legal fiction that undergirds the law of agency. Peter Happé's *English Drama Before Shakespeare* sees Greene's dramatic output as part of the "vigorous life" of the professional stage in the late 1580s and early 1590s. Lamenting that Greene's dramatic skill has not been appreciated, Happé points to Greene's ability to combine theatrical effects and his significant contribution to the development of English comedy as a genre. Benjamin Griffin's *Playing the Past* concerns itself with the way that early modern history plays "were (and are) perceived" (xiii) and looks at *Friar Bacon and Friar Bungay* and *James IV* as examples of history plays that distance themselves from their putatively historical contents–turning the play in both cases into romance. Greene is one of many examples in the book of playwrights who write on historical subjects but do not feel compelled to retain much in the way of historical specificity. Instead, historical settings serve to protect plays from the charge of referring too closely to the present

II. Select Studies of Individual Plays

Friar Bacon and Friar Bungay

In the final chapter of his book *Theatre and Humanism: Elizabethan Drama in the Sixteenth Century*, Kent Cartwright contends that *Friar Bacon and Friar Bungay* embodies many humanist dramatic techniques as well as a developing epistemological uncertainty. Cartwright concludes that Greene's play ends by moving beyond radical uncertainty through a turn to dramatic spectacle as a redeeming source of communal experience. Kurt Tetzeli Von Rosador's "The Sacralizing Sign: Religion and Magic in Bale, Greene, and the Early Shakespeare" also sees a kind of uncertainty infecting the play. Reading *Friar Bacon and Friar Bungay* within the context of the Reformation tension between Word and sign, Rosador contends that the play undermines the authority of both. In the end, says Rosador, this instability is replaced by the relatively stable authorizing presence of Royal power. Richard Levin's speculative "Tarlton in *The Famous History of*

Friar Bacon and *Friar Bacon and Friar Bungay*" suggests, after analyzing the plays' identical title-page woodcuts and their similar constructions of Bacon's clownish servant, that Miles may have been originally written to be played by Richard Tarlton. In a wide-ranging essay, Kevin LaGrandeur in "The Talking Brass Head as a Symbol of Dangerous Knowledge in *Friar Bacon and Friar Bungay* and in *Alphonsus, King of Aragon*" draws a connection between Greene's use of the Brazen head in these two plays and a medieval tradition hostile to innovative, natural science. Alexander Leggatt's chapter on Greene in his *Introduction to English Renaissance Comedy* also underscores an interrogation of magic in the play. His focus, however, is on what he calls the play's construction of a debate between varying loci of power, a vestige from the debate-inflected tradition of the Tudor interlude. Ian McAdam's "Masculinity and Magic" asserts that *Friar Bacon and Friar Bungay* establishes a parallel between "the power of magic and the power of sexual desire" (37)—specifically desire for Margaret—and that "the responsibility for control falls almost wholly on the shoulders of the male characters, not because Margaret is weak, or uninteresting, or unimportant in the play, but because the play's social context radically limits her own effective control" (37). The essay concludes that the play's comic resolution and its vision of Elizabeth is "undercut by an assertion of masculine control that cannot, historically and psychologically, escape implications of its own potential sterility" (57–8). The essay offers an insightful reading of the play's representation of the links between magic, gender, and desire. Bryan Reynolds and Henry Turner's "Performative Transversations" examines the collaborative space of the university as imagined in Greene's play and suggests connections between that space and the contemporary university.

James IV

Following Braunmuller's important essay in 1973, the most compelling recent work on what was apparently Greene's last play has considered *James IV*'s frame as an important part of its meaning. In "Bohan and Oberon: The Internal Debate of Greene's *James IV*," Alexander Leggatt argues that the conflict between Bohan and Oberon is the central element of the play. He concludes that each character presents a different yet not altogether irreconcilable way of looking at the world. J. Clinton Crumley's "Anachronism and Historical Romance in Renaissance Drama: *James IV*" focuses specifically upon the "dramatic anachronism" created in the frame's relationship with the main plot. As character's shift effortlessly between the frame's and main plot's different historical moments, the play manifests a self-consciousness about history, showing itself to be aware of dramatic art's power to alter our understanding of history and the world.

III. Select Studies of Individual Prose Pamphlets

Ciceronis Amor

Both Constance Relihan and Kevin L. Gustafson offer provocative considerations of Greene's constructed female audience in *Ciceronis Amor*. Relihan's "Humanist Learning, Eloquent Women, and the Use of Latin in Robert Greene's *Ciceronis Amor: Tullies Love*" argues that the prose romance's representation of women reading and commenting upon Latin "reveals a deep distrust of the ways in which [the system of Latin education] reifies male speech and relationships and devalues women's intellectual and interpretive skills" (12). Gustafson's "Homosociality, Imitation, and Gendered Reading in Robert Greene's *Ciceronis Amor*" sees such a conclusion as "a bit too sanguine" (280), suggesting instead that the work's self-conscious engagement with its potential female readership ultimately still ends up idealizing homosocial bonds between men. Still, concludes Gustafson, Greene does so "in a way that embraces the diversity of the likely audience for vernacular fiction, at once amusing scholars and making classical oratory marketable to a non-scholarly reading public" (294).

Cony-Catching Pamphlets

Constance Relihan's "The Narrative Strategies of Robert Greene's Cony-Catching Pamphlets" (a portion of which is also published in her later book *Fashioning Authority*) considers the narrative strategies of Greene's cony-catching pamphlets and argues that they are all in one way or another conceived with a desire to draw attention to their author and his fictional art. In these works, "narrative control" and "artistic authority" are Greene's main concerns. Steve Mentz's "Magic Books: Cony-Catching and the Romance of Early-Modern London," one of a number of essays touching on Greene in the recent collection *Rogues and Early Modern Culture*, is also concerned with the formal strategies of Greene's cony-catching pamphlets, particularly those having to do with genre. According to Mentz, Greene's six cony-catching pamphlets work within the conventions of prose romance, ultimately serving to help "initiate [their citizen-readers] into the new languages of urban culture" (241). Michael Long's "Transgression and Cultural Taboo: Constructing the Criminal in English Renaissance Rogue Literature" concerns itself not with the narrative strategies of such literature but with the various ways in which a normative English nationalism is manufactured out the various "culturally forbidden practices" of the Renaissance rogue.

Greene's Groatsworth of Wit

The last two decades have seen a continuation of debates about the pamphlet's elusive referents. In "William Kemp as 'Upstart Crow,'" Winifred Frazer contends that Shakespeare's anonymity in the early 1590s made it highly unlikely that Greene would have subtly targeted him in a 1592 pamphlet. For her, William Kemp is a much more likely candidate. Both Robert F. Fleissner's "The 'Upstart Crow' Reclawed: Was it Kemp, Wilson, Alleyn. Or Shakespeare?" and D. Allen Carroll's "'For There is an Upstart Crow'" reconsider Frazer's arguments in favor of Kemp. Both conclude that the best evidence still points to Shakespeare as Greene's "upstart crow." W. Ron Hess's "Robert Greene's Wit Re-Evaluated" particularly calls into question the widespread "Stratfordian" assumptions that the pamphlet's "tygers heart wrapt in a players hyde" must be a reference to *3HenryVI* and that Greene was necessarily attacking Shakespeare as his "upstart crow." Carroll's "The Player-Patron in *Greene's Groatsworth of Wit*" considers the possible identity of the player-patron in *Greene's Groatsworth of Wit*. It contends that although there is evidence supporting either Burbage, Robert Wilson, or Munday, the "portrait teases with possibility, the specific disappearing into the generic" (312). In his "*Johannes Factotum* and Jack Cade," Carroll suggests that the pamphlet's "Johannes fac totem" is possibly a reference to Jack Cade in *2 Henry VI*. He points out that Cade was referred to as "John Mend-all" in both Holinshed and Stow. More recently, scholars like Arul Kumaran and Alexandra Halasz have read *Greene's Groatsworth of Wit* as a discursive and figurative recapitulation of Greene's experiences as a professional, university-educated writer with patronage, the pamphlet market, and the professional theatre.

Greene's Vision

In his "Gower, Chaucer and the Art of Repentance in Robert Greene's *Vision*," Jeremy Dimmick explores Greene's complicated engagement both with the pamphlet's disputants Chaucer and Gower and with the pamphlet's immediate precursors' *The Cobler of Canterbury* and *Tarlton's News out of Purgatory*. He argues that *Greene's Vision* deploys Greene's prodigal public persona in order "to perform a virtuoso mock-conversion in which claims to discursive authority made by the fictionalized Chaucer, Gower, and even King Solomon are called into question" (457).

Gwydonius

Robert B. Heilman's "Greene's Euphuism and Some Congeneric Styles" describes Greene's euphuistic style in *Gwydonius* and considers its tense relationship with the text's romance narrative. The essay also traces the development of euphistic style through the nineteenth century in works by Johnson, Burney, Edgeworth, Austen, and Charlotte Brontë. Anne Lake Prescott's "Through the Cultural Chunnel: The Robert Greeneing of Louise Labé" considers Greene's changes in translating Labé's *Débat de Folie et d'Amour* (1555) into *Gwydonius*'s appendix

The Debate between Folly & Love. Prescott is particularly interested in Greene's layering of gender and cultural differences onto Labé's original.

Pandosto

In a provocative revision of the traditional source study, Inga-Stina Ewbank's "From Narrative to Dramatic Language" considers the traces of Shakespeare's rich encounter with *Pandosto* in *The Winter's Tale* in the context of two modern RSC performances of the play: Trevor Nunn's in 1969 and John Barton's in 1976. Mapping the way in which *The Winter's Tale* self-consciously recasts what by 1610 would have been *Pandosto*'s familiar syntax, narrative mode, and assumptions about the relationship between language and truth, Ewbank then demonstrates the many ways that each production disrupts this recasting and as a consequence glosses over some of Shakespeare's more pressing thematic interests in writing the play. Lori Humphrey Newcomb's "'Social Things': The Production of Popular Culture in the Reception of Robert Greene's *Pandosto*" considers both *Pandosto*'s and its author's role as symbolic objects in the late-sixteenth- and early-seventeenth-century creation of a division between popular and elite culture. According to Newcomb, "Greene" and *Pandosto* functioned as discursive stakes in a social world more and more concerned with social mobility and the unstable social space of the print market in St. Paul's Churchyard. In their engagement with Greene's widespread dissemination, authors like Nashe, Harvey, and Shakespeare all contribute to what would become a culture of literary distinction. Newcomb continues her analysis of *Pandosto*'s place in English literary history in "The Triumph of Time: The Fortunate Readers of Robert Greene's *Pandosto*." In this essay she traces the fortunes of *Pandosto* through the eighteenth century and concludes that anecdotal evidence about the romance's primarily lower-order reception from the Jacobean period on is unreliable in the face of material evidence of upper-order readers. Her *Reading Popular Romance in Early Modern England*, which contains revised and expanded versions of both of these essays, "contends that two kinds of reading practices made early modern prose romances popular: fiction was read by increasingly diverse audiences, and their tastes were read as constituting a subordinate cultural category" (1). The book combines a study of *Pandosto*'s reception history with a consideration of early modern reading practices and their cultural meanings, arguing that readers of popular romance were engaged in making distinctions between "high" and "low" literary forms.

Penelope's Web

In an essay which consciously seeks to situate its understanding of Greene's work in the space between past and present conceptions of femininity, Georgianna Ziegler, in "Penelope and the Politics of Woman's Place in the Renaissance," compares the representation of Penelope in the Sala di Penelope of the Palazzo

Vecchio in Florence and in Greene's *Penelope's Web*. Ziegler argues that both works reinstate and subvert sixteenth-century assumptions about women.

Philomela

Katharine Wilson's "'Taking Choice of the Library': Greene's *Philomela* and the Unravished Nightingale" sees Greene's overt metamorphosis of Ovid's tale of Philomela in his pamphlet of the same name as a literary gambit, as a way of "establishing himself in the great tradition of English fiction" (42).

A Quip for an Upstart Courtier

In "Of Bonnets and Breeches: Sumptuary Codes in Elizabethan Popular Literature," Margaret Rose Jaster indentifies a subtle appeal to lower-order, sumptuary conservatism in Greene's popular pamphlet. Sarah Warneke's "A Taste for Newfangledness: The Destructive Potential of Novelty in Early Modern England" describes the English interest in novelty as growing in the period and uses Greene's *A Quip for an Upstart Courtier* as an example. She sees the fascination with novelty that she documents as a response to rapid social change, arguing that the only way period thinkers found to explain such change was to "discover" an overwhelming desire for novelty in the English character.

IV. Canon and Texts

Canon and Chronology

In a detailed reconsideration of the debate about the authorship of *Greene's Groatsworth of Wit*, John Jowett's "Johannes Factotum: Henry Chettle and *Greene's Groatsworth of Wit*" concludes that internal and external evidence supports the theory that the work was a Chettle forgery. Jowett continues by arguing that *The Repentance of Robert Greene*, despite critical arguments contending that it, too, is by Chettle, was, in fact, by Greene but edited by Chettle.

Apocrypha and Uncertain Ascriptions

In "George Buc, William Shakespeare, and the Folger *George a Greene*," Alan Nelson once again takes up the issue of the inscriptions on the title page of a copy of the 1599 edition of *George a Greene*. Part of these inscriptions identifies the play as being by Greene. Nelson concludes from examining previous arguments and the text itself that the inscriptions are not forgeries and that they are, as others have argued, by George Buc, Master of Revels between 1610 and 1622. He questions, however, the accuracy of Buc's ascription of the play to Greene.

Textual Studies

A part of the continuing challenge to New Bibliography by the likes of Laurie Maguire and A. Bradley, Michael Warren's "Greene's *Orlando*: W.W. Greg's Furioso" questions W.W. Greg's hypothesis in *Two Elizabethan Stage Abridgements* that Alleyn's Part from *Orlando Furioso* is a good text and that Q1 of the play is a "bad quarto," a memorial reconstruction. In a close reading of Greg's groundbreaking and essentially unchallenged work, Warren draws attention to many of its dubious assumptions and conclusions. Although he does not have his own explanation for the relationship between the Part and the first quarto of *Orlando*, he still has serious reservations about Greg's.

Other Editions

Of the plays attributed to Greene, only *Selimus* and *Friar Bacon and Friar Bungay* were republished during the last sixteen years. Interest in *Selimus* is clearly due to postcolonial explorations of the "Turk"'s early modern construction. Daniel Vitkus's *Three Turk Plays from Early Modern England* offers modernized editions of *Selimus* along with two other "Turk" plays: Robert Daborne's *A Christian Turned Turk* (1609–12) and Philip Massinger's *The Renegado* (1623–24). In his introduction, Vitkus combines an overview of English images of Islamic culture with individual sections discussing the background and themes of each play. The volume also includes a short section of early modern images of Islam and appendices containing three early modern ballads involving Turks and "A Proclamation against Pirates" issued by James I in 1609. *Friar Bacon and Friar Bungay* is collected with a number of other plays in both Gassner and Green's *Elizabethan Drama: Eight Plays* and in Bevington's *English Renaissance Drama: A Norton Anthology*.

Stanley Wells's critical edition *Perymedes the Blacksmith and Pandosto by Robert Greene: A Critical Edition* was initially intended for Parr and Shapiro's failed Oxford edition of Greene's complete works. It offers old-spelling editions of each work and includes helpful bibliographical and literary introductions along with extensive commentary notes and appendices on "Greene and Pliny," "Works Deriving from *Pandosto*," and "The Poem in *Pandosto*." Brenda Cantar's edition of *Menaphon: Camilla's Alarm to Slumbering Euphues in his Melancholy Cell at Silexedra* (1996) offers a modernized version of Greene's romance. It also provides a discussion of the text and a bibliography.

Bibliography

I. General Studies

Biographical

Brayton, Dan, "Robert Greene." *British Writers Supplement VIII* (New York: Charles Scribner's Sons, 2002).

Ide, Arata, "Robert Greene *Nordovicensis*, the Saddler's Son," *Notes & Queries* 53.4 (2006): 432–6.

Newcomb, Lori Humphrey, "Greene, Robert (*bap.* 1558, *d.* 1592), *writer and playwright*." *Oxford Dictionary of National Biography* (Oxford University Press, 2004). [http://www.oxforddnb.com/view/article/11418, accessed 27 July 2005]

General

Alwes, Derek, "Robert Greene's Duelling Dedications," *English Literary Renaissance* 30.3 (2000): 373–95.

———, *Sons and Fathers in Elizabethan England* (Newark, DE: University of Delaware Press, 2004).

Barbour, Reid, *Deciphering Elizabethan Fiction* (Newark, DE: University of Delaware Press, 1993).

Barker, W.W., "Rhetorical Romance: The 'Frivolous Toyes' of Robert Greene," in George M. Logan and Gordon Teskey (eds), *Unfolded Tales* (Ithaca: Cornell University Press, 1989).

Bednarz, James P., "Marlowe and the English Literary Scene," in *The Cambridge Companion to Christopher Marlowe* (Cambridge: Cambridge University Press, 2004).

Beilin, Elaine, *The Uses of Mythology in Elizabethan Prose Romance* (New York: Garland, 1988). Rpt. of Princeton dissertation, 1973.

Bevington, David, "Shakespeare's Predecessors: Lyly, Greene, Kyd, and Marlowe," in Stephen P. Thompson (ed.), *Renaissance Literature* (San Diego, CA: Greenhaven Press, 2001).

Braunmuller, A.R., "'Second Means': Agent and Accessory in Elizabethan Drama," in A.L. Magnusson and C.E. Mcgee (eds), *The Elizabethan Theatre XI* (Port Credit, ON: P.D. Meany, 1990).

Cantar, Brenda, "'Silenced but for the Word': The Discourse of Incest in Greene's *Pandosto* and *Menaphon*," *English Studies in Canada* 23.1 (1997): 21–36.

DiBiase, Carmine, "The Decline of Euphuism: Robert Greene's Struggle Against Popular Taste," in Donald Beecher (ed.), *Critical Approaches to English Prose Fiction 1520–1640* (Ottawa: Dovehouse, 1998).

Dionne, Craig, and Steve Mentz (eds), *Rogues and Early Modern English Culture* (Ann Arbor: University of Michigan Press, 2004).

Griffin, Benjamin, *Playing the Past* (Woodbridge: DS Brewer, 2001).

Hackel, Heidi Brayman, *Reading Material in Early Modern England: Print, Gender and Literacy* (Cambridge: Cambridge University Press, 2005).

Halasz, Alaexandra, *The Marketplace of Print: Pamphlets and the Public Sphere in Early Modern England* (Cambridge: Cambridge University Press, 1997).

Happé, Peter, *English Drama Before Shakespeare* (New York: Longman, 1999).

Holmes, Morgan, "Rogue Sirens: Urban Seduction and the Collapse of Amicitia," in Constance Relihan and Goran V. Stanivukovic (eds), *Prose Fiction and Early Modern Sexualities in England: 1570–1640* (New York: Palgrave MacMillan, 2004).

Kumaran, Arul, "Robert Greene's Martinist Transformation in 1590," *Studies in Philology* 103.3 (2006): 243–63.

Linden, Stanton J., *Darke Hieoroglyphics: Alchemy in English Literature from Chaucer to the Reformation* (Lexington, KY: University of Kentucky Press, 1996).

Lucas, Caroline, *Writing for Women: The Example of Woman as Reader in Elizabethan Romance* (Milton Keyes: Open University Press, 1989).

Mack, Peter, "Rhetoric in Use: Three Romances by Greene and Lodge," in Peter Mack (ed.), *Renaissance Rhetoric* (New York: St. Martin's Press, 1994).

Mentz, Steven R., "Wearing Greene: Autolycus, Robert Greene, and the Structure of Romance in *The Winter's Tale*," *Renaissance Drama* 30 (1999–2001): 73–92. Also appears in Jeffrey Masten and Wendy Wall (eds), *Institutions of the Text* (Evanston, IL: Northwestern University Press, 2001).

———, *Romance for Sale in Early Modern England: The Rise of Prose Fiction* (Burlington, VT: Ashgate, 2006).

Moore, Helen, "Elizabethan Fiction and Ovid's *Heroides*," *Translations and Literature* 9.1 (2000): 40–64.

Reynolds, Bryan, *Becoming Criminal: Tranversal Performance and Cultural Dissidence in Early Modern England* (Baltimore: Johns Hopkins University Press, 2002).

Sams, Eric, *The Real Shakespeare: Retrieving the Early Years* (New Haven: Yale University Press, 1995).

Spates, William Henry, "Proverbs, Pox, and the Early Modern *femme fatale*," *Notes and Queries* 53.1 (2006): 47–51.

Tobin, J.J.M., "A Touch of Greene, Much Nashe, and All Shakespeare" in Thomas A. Pendleton (ed.), *Henry VI: Critical Essays* (New York: Routledge, 2001).

Wilson, Katharine, *Fictions of Authorship in Late Elizabethan Narratives* (Oxford: Clarendon Press, 2006).

Woods, Paula M., "Greene's Conny-Catching Courtesans: The Moral Ambiguity of Prostitution," *Explorations in Renaissance Culture* 18 (1992): 111–24.

II. Studies of Individual Plays

Alphonsus, King of Aragon

Chandler, David, "An Incident from Greene's *Alphonsus* in *As You Like It*," *Notes & Queries* 42 (1995): 317–319.

Friar Bacon and Friar Bungay

Ardolino, Frank, "Greene's Use of the History of Oxford in *The Honourable History of Friar Bacon and Friar Bungay*," *American Notes & Queries* 18.2 (2005): 20–25.

Cartwright, Kent, *Theatre and Humanism: Elizabethan Drama in the Sixteenth Century* (Cambridge: Cambridge University Press, 1999).

Gibson, Marion, "Greene's *Friar Bacon and Friar Bungay* and *A Most Wicked Worke of a Wretched Witch*: A Link," *Notes & Queries* 44 (1997): 36–7.

LaGrandeur, Kevin, "Brasenose College's Brass Head and the Significance of Greene's *Friar Bacon*," *Notes & Queries* 47 (2000): 357–8.

———, "The Talking Brass Head as a Symbol of Dangerous Knowledge" in *Friar Bacon and Friar Bungay* and in *Alphonsus, King of Aragon*," *English Studies* 80.5 (1999): 408–22.

Leggatt, Alexander, *Introduction to English Renaissance Comedy* (Manchester: Manchester University Press, 1999).

Levin, Richard, "*Friar Bacon and Friar Bungay*, *John of Bourdeaux*, and the 1683 Edition of *The History of Friar Bacon*," *Research Opportunities in Renaissance Drama* 40 (2001): 55–66.

———, "Tarlton in *The Famous History of Friar Bacon* and *Friar Bacon and Friar Bungay*," *Medieval and Renaissance Drama in England* 12 (1999): 84–98.

McAdam, Ian, "Masculinity and Magic in *Friar Bacon and Friar Bungay*," *Research Opportunities in Renaissance Drama* 37 (1998): 33–61.

Melnikoff, Kirk, "The 'Extremities' of Sumptuary Law in Robert Greene's *Friar Bacon and Friar Bungay*," *Medieval and Renaissance Drama in England* 19 (2006): 227–34.

Reynolds, Bryan, and Henry Turner, "Performative Transversations: Collaborations Through and Beyond Greene's *Friar Bacon and Friar Bungay*" in Bryan Reynolds (ed.), *Transversal Enterprises in the Drama of Shakespeare and his Contemporaries* (Houndmills: Palgrave Macmillan, 2006).

Tetzeli Von Rosador, Kurt, "The Sacralizing Sign: Religion and Magic in Bale, Greene, and the Early Shakespeare," *The Yearbook of English Studies* 23 (1993): 30–45.

James IV

Abate, Corinne, "'Men Learn at Last to Know Their Good Estate': Dorothea's Triumph in *James IV*," *Explorations in Renaissance Culture* 29.2 (2003): 253–66.

Calvert, Hugh, and M.W.A. Smith, "Word-Links as a General Indicator of Chronology of Composition," *Notes & Queries* 234 (1989): 338–41.

Cavanagh, Dermot, *Language and Politics in the Sixteenth-Century History Play* (Houndmills: Palgrave Macmillan, 2003).

Crumley, J. Clinton, "Anachronism and Historical Romance in Renaissance Drama: *James IV*," *Explorations in Renaissance Culture* 24 (1998): 75–90.

Hopkins, Lisa, "Ford and Greene: Two Histories of James the Fourth," *Notes & Queries* 43 (1996): 193–4.

Leggatt, Alexander, "Bohan and Oberon: The Internal Debate of Greene's *James IV*," in A.L. Magnusson and C.E. Mcgee (eds), *The Elizabethan Theatre, XI* (Port Credit, ON: P.D. Meany, 1990).

Lekhal, Catherine, "The Historical Background of Robert Greene's *James IV*," *Cahiers Élisabéthains* 35 (1989): 27–45.

Orlando Furioso

Lawrence, Jason, "'The story is extant, and writ in very choice Italian': Shakespeare's dramatizations of Cinthio," in Michele Marrapodi (ed.), *Shakespeare, Italy, and Intertextuality* (Manchester: Manchester University Press, 2004).

Stern, Tiffany, "The 'Part' for Greene's *Orlando Furioso*: A Source for the 'Mock-Trial' in Shakespeare's *Lear*?" *Notes & Queries* 247 (2002): 229–31.

Selimus

Hutchings, Mark, "The End of *Tamburlaine* and the Beginnings of *King Lear*," *Notes & Queries* 245 (2000): 82–6.

III. Studies of Individual Prose Pamphlets

Arbasto

Luborsky, Ruth Samson, "Further Evidence for the 1593 Edition of Combe's Emblems: The Title Page of Robert Greene's *Arbasto*," *Emblematica* 8.1 (1994): 179–80.

Ciceronis Amor

Gustafson, Kevin L., "Homosociality, Imitation, and Gendered Reading in Robert Greene's *Ciceronis Amor*," *Philological Quarterly* 82.3 (2003): 277–300.

Relihan, Constance C., "Humanist Learning, Eloquent Women, and the Use of Latin in Robert Greene's *Ciceronis Amor: Tullies Love*," *Explorations in Renaissance Culture* 27.1 (2001): 1–19.

Relihan, Constance C. (ed.), *Framing Elizabethan Fictions: Contemporary Approaches to Early-Modern Prose* (Kent, OH: The Kent State University Press, 1996).

Cony-Catching Pamphlets

Bix, Karen Helfland, "'Masters of their Occupation': Labor and Fellowship in the Cony-Catching Pamphlets," in Craig Dionne and Steve Mentz (eds), *Rogues and Early Modern English Culture* (Ann Arbor: The University of Michigan Press, 2004).

Hansen, Adam, "Sin City and the 'Urban Condom,'" in Craig Dionne and Steve Mentz (eds), *Rogues and Early Modern English Culture* (Ann Arbor: The University of Michigan Press, 2004).

Long, Michael, "Transgression and Cultural Taboo: Constructing the Criminal in English Renaissance Rogue Literature," *Cahiers Élisabéthains* 54 (1998): 1–25.

Luborsky, Ruth Samson, "Telling a Book by Its Cover; Or, How Harmon Masquerades as Greene," *ANQ* 5.2–3 (1992): 100–102.

Mentz, Steve, "Magic Books: Cony-Catching and the Romance of Early-Modern London," in Craig Dionne and Steve Mentz (eds), *Rogues and Early Modern English Culture* (Ann Arbor: The University of Michigan Press, 2004).

Relihan, Constance C., *Fashioning Authority: The Development of Elizabethan Novelistic Discourse* (Kent, OH: The Kent State University Press, 1994).

———, "The Narrative Strategies of Robert Greene's Cony-Catching Pamphlets," *Cahiers Élisabéthains* 37 (1990): 9–15.

Greene's Groatsworth of Wit

Carroll, D. Allen, "For There is an Upstart Crow," *Upstart Crow* 15 (1995): 150–153.

———, "*Johannes Factotum* and Jack Cade," *Shakespeare Quarterly* 40.4 (1989): 491–2.

———, "The Player-Patron in *Greene's Groatsworth of Wit*," *Studies in Philology* 91.3 (1994): 301–12.

———, "Rich and Greene: Elizabethan Beast Fables and Ireland," *Eire-Ireland* 25.1 (1990): 106–13.

Chandler, David, "The 'Bed-Trick' in *Measure for Measure*: A Source Suggestion," *Notes & Queries* 42 (1995): 320–321.
———, "'Upstart Crow': Provenance and Meaning," *Notes & Queries* 42.3 (1995): 291–4.
Duncan-Jones, Katherine, "Who was Marlowe's 'brocher of Atheisme'?" *Notes & Queries*, 53.4 (2006): 449–52.
Farley-Hills, David, "Premature Foreclosure in the Henry VI Debate," *Notes & Queries* 44.4 (1997): 489–93.
Fleissner, Robert F., "The 'Upstart Crow' Reclawed: Was it Kemp, Wilson, Alleyn. Or Shakespeare?" *Upstart Crow* 15 (1995): 143–9.
Frazer, Winifred, "William Kemp, Shakespearean Clown," *Shakespeare Newsletter* 43 (1993): 10.
———, "William Kemp as 'Upstart Crow,'" *Upstart Crow* 15 (1995): 140–142.
Hess, W. Ron, "Robert Greene's Wit Re-Evaluated," *The Elizabethan Review* 4.2 (1996): 41–8.
Hoster, Jay, *"Tiger's Heart": What Really Happened in the "Groat's-worth of Wit" Controversy* (Columbus, OH: Ravine Books, 1993).
Kumaran, Arul, "'Hereafter suppose me the said Roberto': Greene's *Groatsworth of Wit* as an Allegorizing Pamphlet," *Yearly Review* 10 (2001): 29–45.
———, "Patronage, Print, and an Early Modern 'Pamphlet Moment,'" *Explorations in Renaissance Culture* 31.1 (2005): 59–88.
Lucking, David, "A Bird of Another Feather: Will Shake-Scene's Belated Revenge," *Upstart Crow* 25 (2005): 51–7.
Merriam, Thomas, "Groatsworth's Added Value," *Notes & Queries* 43.2 (1996): 145–9.
Wilkinson, Katherine, "A Source for *The City Wit*," *Notes & Queries* 52.2 (2005): 230–232.

Greene's Vision

Dimmick, Jeremy, "Gower, Chaucer, and the Art of Repentance," *The Review of English Studies* 57.231 (September 2006): 456–73.

Gwydonius

Heilman, Robert B., "Greene's Euphuism and Some Congeneric Styles," in George M. Logan and Gordon Teskey (eds), *Unfolded Tales* (Ithaca: Cornell University Press, 1989).
Prescott, Anne Lake, "Through the Cultural Chunnel: The (Robert) Greeneing of Louise Labé," in Peter C. Herman (ed.), *Opening the Border: Inclusivity in Early Modern Studies. Essays in Honor of James V. Mirollo* (Newark: University of Delaware Press, 1999).

Menaphon

McCluskey, Peter, "'Humors to Delight': *Menaphon* as Burlesque," *Publications of the Arkansas Philological Association* 21.1 (1995): 69–75.

Never Too Late

Austern, Linda Phyllis, "'Sing Againe Syren': The Female Musician and Sexual Enchantment in Elizabethan Life and Literature," *Renaissance Quarterly* 42.3 (1989): 420–28.

Pandosto

Baldwin, Anna, "From the *Clerk's Tale* to *The Winter's Tale*," in Ruth Morse and Barry Windeatt (eds), *Chaucer Traditions* (Cambridge: Cambridge University *Press*, 1990).

Davis, Joel, "Paulina's Paint and the Dialectic of Masculine Desire in the *Metamorphoses*, *Pandosto*, and *The Winter's Tale*," *Papers on Language and Literature* 39.2 (2002): 115–43.

Ewbank, Inga-Stina, "From Narrative to Dramatic Language," in Marvin Thompson and Ruth Thompson (eds), *Shakespeare and the Sense of Performance* (Newark: University of Delaware Press, 1989).

Mussio, Thomas E., "Bandello's 'Timbreo and Fenicia' and *The Winter's Tale*," *Comparative Drama* 34.2 (2000): 211–44.

Newcomb, Lori Humphrey, *Reading Popular Romance in Early Modern London* (New York: Columbia University Press, 2002).

———, "The Romance of Service: The Simple History of *Pandosto*'s Servant Readers," in Constance C. Relihan (ed.), *Framing Elizabethan Fictions* (Kent, OH: The Kent State University Press, 1996).

———, "'Social Things': The Production of Popular Culture in the Reception of Robert Greene's *Pandosto*," *English Literary History* 61.4 (1994): 753–81.

———, "The Triumph of Time: The Fortunate Readers of Robert Greene's *Pandosto*," in Cedric Brown and Arthur Marotti (eds), *Texts and Cultural Change in Early Modern England* (New York: St. Martin's, 1997).

Penelope's Web

Ziegler, Georgianna, "Penelope and the Politics of Woman's Place in the Renaissance," in Susan Cerasano and Marion Wynne-Davies (eds), *Gloriana's Face: Women, Public and Private, in the English Renaissance* (Detroit: Wayne State University Press, 1992).

Philomela

Wilson, Katharine, "'Taking Choice of the Library': Greene's *Philomela* and the Unravished Nightingale," *Imaginaires* 4 (1999): 41–51.

Planetomachia

Das, Nandini, "A New Source for Robert Greene's *Planetomachia*," *Notes & Queries* 53.4 (2006): 436–40.

A Quip for an Upstart Courtier

Jaster, Margaret, "Of Bonnets and Breeches: Sumptuary Codes in Elizabethan Popular Culture," *Proceedings of the PMR Conference: Annual Publication of the International Patristic, Medieval and Renaissance Conference* 16–17 (1992): 205–11.

Warneke, Sara, "A Taste for Newfangledness: The Destructive Potential of Novelty in Early Modern England," *Sixteenth Century Journal* 26 (1995): 881–96.

IV. Canon and Texts

Canon and Chronology

Erne, Lukas, "Biography and Mythography: Rereading Chettle's Alleged Apology to Shakespeare," *English Studies* 79.5 (1998): 430–440.

Jowett, John, "Johannes Factotum: Henry Chettle and *Greene's Groatsworth of Wit*," *Papers of the Bibliographic Society of America* 87.4 (1993): 453–86.

Apocrypha and Uncertain Ascriptions

Nelson, Alan H., "George Buc, William Shakespeare, and the Folger *George a Greene*," *Shakespeare Quarterly* 49.1 (1998): 74–83.

Textual Studies

Hanabusa, Chiaki, "The Printer of Sheet G in Robert Greene's *Orlando Furioso* Q1 (1594)," *The Library* 19.2 (1997): 145–50.

Maguire, Laurie E., "The Printer and Date of Q4 *A Looking Glass for London and England*," *Studies in Bibliography* 52 (1999): 155–60.

Ransom, Nicholas, "Indian/Judean Again," *Analytical and Enumerative Bibliography* 10 (1999): 29–35.

Warren, Michael, "Greene's *Orlando*: W.W. Greg Furioso," in Laurie E. Maguire and Thomas L. Berger (eds), *Textual Formations and Reformations* (Newark, DE: University of Delaware Press, 1998).

Other Editions

Bevington, David, et al (eds), *Friar Bacon and Friar Bungay. English Renaissance Drama: A Norton Anthology* (New York: W.W. Norton & Company, 2002).

Cantar, Brenda (ed.), *Menaphon: Camilla's Alarm to Slumbering Euphues in His Melancholy Cell at Silexedra* (Ottawa: Dovehouse Editions, 1996).

Carroll, D. Allen (ed.), *Greene's Groatsworth of Wit: Bought With a Million of Repentance* (Binghampton, NY: Center for Medieval and Renaissance Studies, State University of New York at Binghampton, 1994).

Das, Nandini (ed.), *Robert Greene's* Planetomachia *(1585)* (Burlington, VT: Ashgate, 2007).

DiBiase, Carmine (ed.), *Gwydonius, or, The Card of Fancy* (Ottawa: Dovehouse, 2001).

Gassner, John and William Green (eds), *Friar Bacon and Friar Bungay* (New York: Applause Theatre Books, 1990).

Raid, Nadia Mohamed (ed.), "A Critical Old-Spelling Edition of 'The Tragical Raigne of Selimus'" (Diss. Queen's University at Kingston, 1994. *DAI* 56 [1994]: 1372A).

Vitkus, Daniel J. (ed.), *Three Turk Plays from Early Modern England:* Selimus*;* A Christian Turned Turk*; and* The Renegado (New York: Columbia University Press, 1999).

Wells, Stanley (ed.), *Perymedes the Blacksmith and Pandosto by Robert Greene: A Critical Edition* (New York: Garland Publishing, 1988).

Appendix A

Apocrypha[1]

Composition Date	Work	Publishing Date	Company (if applicable)
1570–83	*Sir Clyomon and Sir Clamydes*	1599	Queen's
1585	*A Funeral Sermon*	1585	N/A
1586–93	*Job*	Lost	Unknown
1587–93	*George a Greene*	1599	Sussex's
1588–92	*Arden of Feversham*	1592	Unknown
1588–94	*True Tragedy of Richard III*	1594	Queen's
1588–94	*Chronicle History of King Leir*	1605	Queen's
1588–98	*Mucedorus*	1598	Unknown
1589–92	*Soliman and Perseda*	1592(?)	Unknown
1589–91	*Fair Em*	1593(?)	Strange's
1590	*The Cobler of Canterbury*	1590	N/A
1590	*Tarlton's News Out of Purgatory*	1590	N/A
1590–94	*John of Bordeaux*	MS	Strange's(?)
1590–95	*Edward III*	1596	Admiral's(?)
1590–1600	*Edmund Ironside*	MS	Unknown
1590–1601	*Sir Thomas More*	MS	Unknown
1591	*Troublesome Reign of King John*	1591	Queen's
1592	*A Knack to Know a Knave*	1594	Strange's
1592	*The Groundwork of Cony-Catching*	1592	N/A
1592	*The Defense of Cony-Catching*	1592	N/A
1594	*Locrine*	1595	Unknown

[1] The following list is not meant to be exhaustive. Plays listed are only those whose authorship is essentially still in doubt. See Alfred Harbage, *Annals of English Drama, 975–1700*, 3rd edn (New York: Routledge, 1989) for dates and company information. See James Seay Dean, *Robert Greene: A Reference Guide* (Boston: G.K.Hall & Co., 1984) and Kevin J. Donovan, "Recent Studies in Robert Greene" *ELR* 20.1 (1990): 163–75 for ascription information.

Appendix B

Edition Information (organized by presumed composition date)[1]

Year	Work	Format	Publisher	Printer	Edition	Patron	Stationers Register	STC
1580	*Mamillia. A mirrour or looking-glasse for the ladies of Englande* (pt. I)	4	Woodcocke	T. Dawson	1583	Darcy	"Manilia" (10.3.80)	12269
1583	[*Mamillia. The triumph of Pallas*]	4	Ponsonby	Middleton	1583	Lee & Portington	"Mamilia" (9.6.83)	12269.5
	Mamillia. The second part of the triumph of Pallas	4	Ponsonby	Creede	1593	—		12270
1584	*Gvvydonius. The carde of fancie*	4	Ponsonby	East	1584	DeVere	"the card of phantasie" (4.11.84)	12262
	[—]	4	Ponsonby	Charlewood	1587	—		12262.5
	Gwydonius The card of fancie	4	Ponsonby	Creede	1593	—		12263
	Greenes carde of fancie	4	M. Lownes	H.Lownes	1608		"the Card of phantasie" (11.5.04)	12264
	Arbasto, the anatomie of fortune	4	Jackson	Windet & T. Judson	1584	Mary Talbot	"Arbasto" (8.13.84)	12217
	Arbasto. The anatomie of fortune	4	Jackson	Charlewood	1589	—		12219
	Arbasto. The anatomie of fortune	4	Jackson	R. Field	1594	—		12220
	The history of Arbasto King of Denmarke	4	Jackson	Beale	1617	—		12221
	The historie of Arbasto King of Denmarke	4	Williams	Purfoote	1626	—	"The Anotomie of ffortune" (1.16.26)	12222
	The myrrour of modestie	4	R. Ward	R. Ward	1584	Margaret, Countess of Darby	No Entry	12278

	Morando the tritameron of loue (pt. I)	4	E. White	Charlewood & Kingston	1584	Philip, Earl of Arundel	(E. Allde)"The tritameron of love" (6.29.24)	12276
1585	*An oration or funerall sermon vttered at Roome*	8	G. Robinson	G. Robinson	1585	None	No Entry	12354.5
	Planetomachia	4	Cadman	T. Dawson & G. Robinson	1585	Dudley	No Entry	12299
1586	*Morando the tritameron of loue* (pts. I&II)	4	E. White	Wolfe	1587	Philip, Earl of Arundel	"Morando" (8.8.86)	12277
1587	*Greenes farewell to folly*	4	Gubbin & Newman	T. Scarlet	1591	Robert Carey	(E. Aggas) "Greene his farewell to follie" (6.11.87)	12241
	Greenes farevvell to follie	4	W. White	W.White	1617	—		12242
	Penelopes vveb	4	Cadman & E. Aggas	Orwin	1587	Margaret and Anne Russell	(E. Aggas) "Penelopes Webbe" (6.26.87)	12293
	—	4	Hodgets	E. Allde	1601	—		12294
	Euphues his censure to Philautus	4	E. White	Wolfe	1587	Robert, Earl of Essex	"Euphues his Censure to. Philautus" (9.18.87)	12239
	—	4	Eliz. Allde	Eliz. Allde	1634	—	(E. Allde)"Euphewes his censure to Philautus (6.29.24)	12240
	The comicall historie of Alphonsus, King of Aragon	4	Creede	Creede	1599	None	No Entry	12233
1588	*Perimedes the blacke-smith*	4	E. White	Wolfe	1588	Gervis Clifton	"Perymides the black smith" (3.29.88)/ (E. Allde) "Pyremedes the blacke smithe" (6.29.24)	12295
	Alcida Greenes metamorphosis	4	G. Purslowe	G. Purslowe	1617	Charles Blount	(Wolfe) "Alcida Grene's metamorphosis" (12.9.88)	12216
	Greenes Orpharion	4	E. White	Roberts	1599	Robert Carey	"Greens Orpharion" (2.9.90)/ (E.Allde) "Greenes Orpharion" (6.29.04)	12260

	A looking glasse for London and England (with Lodge)	4	Creede	Creede	1594	None	"the lookinge glasse for London by Thomas Lodg and Robert Greene gent" (3.5.94)	16679
	A looking glasse, for London and Englande	4	Creede	Creede	1598	—		16680
	—	4	Pavier	Creede	1602	—		16681
	A looking glasse for, london and England	4	Blower	Blower	1605	—		16681.5
	A looking glasse for…	4	B. Alsop	B. Alsop	1617	—		16682
	Pandosto the triumph of time	4	Cadman	Orwin	1588	George Clifford	(Orwin) "the complaint of tyme" (7.1.88)	12285
	—	4	J. Brome	Field	1592	—		12286
	—	4	J. Brome	Simmes	1595	—	"Pandosto" (4.12.97)	12287
	Pandosto. The triumph of time	4	J. Brome	Bradock	1600	Not seen		12287.5
	—	4	Potter	Purfoot	1607	—	"Pandosto" (8.23.01)	12288
	Pandosto, the triumph of time	4	Potter	Stansby	1609	—		12288.5
	Pandosto. The triumph of time	4	Potter	Creede	1614	—		12289
	—	4	Potter	E.Allde	1619	—		12289.5
	—	4	Faulkner	Purfoot	1629	None		12290
	—	4	Faulkner	Purfoot	1632	None		12291
	(New title) *The pleasant historie of Dorastus and Fawnia*	4	Faulkner	Purfoot	1635	None		12291.5
	—	4	Faulkner	E. Purslowe	1636	None		12292
	[—]	4			1640	None		12292.5
1589	*The Spanishe masquerado*	4	Cadman	R. Ward	1589	Hugh Ostley	"The Spanish Masquerado by Robert Grene collected" (2.1.89)	12309
	—	4	Cadman	R. Ward	1589	—		12310
	Menaphon	4	Clarke	Orwin	1589	Lady Hales	"Menophon" (8.23.89)	12272
	—	4	Ling	Simmes	1599	None		12273
	—	4	Ling	Roberts	1605	None		12273.5
	(New Title) *Greenes Arcadia. Or Menaphon*	4	Smethwicke	Stansby	1610	None	"master Greenes Arcadia" (11.19.07)	12274
	Greenes Arcadia, or Menaphon	4	Smethwicke	Stansby	1616	None		12275

	The honorable historie of frier Bacon, and frier Bongay	4	E. White	Islip	1594	None	"The Historye of ffryer Bacon and ffryer Boungaye" (5.14.94)	12267
	The honorable historie of Frier Bacon, and Frier Bongay	4	Eliz. Allde	Eliz. Allde	1630	None	(E. Allde) "Fryer Bacon and frier Bungay" (6.29.24)	12268
	Ciceronis amor Tullies loue	4	Newman & Winnington	R. Robinson	1589	Ferdinand Stanley	No Entry	12224
	Ciceronis amor = Tullies loue	4	Busbie	R. Robinson	1597	—	"Tullies love" (10.30.95)	12225
	—	4	Ling	Simmes	1601	—		12226
	—	4	Ling	Roberts	1605	—		12227
	—	4	Smethwicke	Windet	1609	—	"His [Greenes] Tullies love" (11.19.07)	12228
	Ciceronis amor. Tullies loue	4	Smethwicke	Stansby	1611	—		12229
	Ciceronis amor, = Tullies loue	4	Smethwicke	Stansby	1616	—		12230
	Ciceronis amor, Tullies loue	4	Smethwicke	Stansby	1628	—		12231
	Ciceronis amor. = Tullies loue	4	Smethwicke	R. Young	1639	—		12232
1590	*The Royall Exchange*	4	W. Wright	Charlewood	1590	John Hart	(T. Nelson) "Cornucopia, or the Royal Exchange" (4.15.90)	12307
	Greenes mourning garment	4	Newman	Wolfe	1590	[George Clifford]	(Wolfe) "Greenes mourninge garment" (11.2.90)	12251
	—	4	G. Purslowe	G. Purslowe	1616	George Clifford	(Pindley) "Greenes mourninge garment" (4.27.12)	12252
	The Scottish historie of Iames the fourth, slaine at Flodden	4	Creede	Creede	1598	None	"the Scottishe story of James the Ffourthe slayne at Fflodden intermixed with a plesant Comedie presented by Oboron kinge of ffayres" (5.14.94)	12308
	Greenes neuer too late (pts. I&II)	4	Ling & Busbie	Orwin	1590	Thomas Burnaby	No Entry	12253

	—	4	Ling	Roberts	1599	—		12253.7
	—	4	Ling	Roberts	1600	—		12254
	—	4	Ling	Simmes	1602	—		12254.5
	—	4	Ling	Simmes	1607	—		12255
	—	4	Smethwicke	Stansby	1611	—	“Greenes never to late” (11.19.07)	12255.5
	—	4	Smethwicke	Stansby	1616	—		12256
	—	4	Smethwicke	Stansby	1631	—		12258
	Greenes vision	4	Newman	E. Allde	1592	Nicholas Sanders	No Entry	12261
1591	*A maidens dreame*	4	T. Nelson	T. Scarlet	1591	Elizabeth Hatton	“A maydens Dreame” (12.6.91)	12271
	The historie of Orlando Furioso	4	Burbie	Danter & T. Scarlet	1594	None	(Danter) “The historye of Orlando ffurioso” (12.7.93)	12265
	—	4	Burbie	Stafford	1599			12266
	A notable discouery of coosenage	4	T. Nelson	Wolfe	1591	None	(White & T. Nelson) “The arte of Connye katchinge” (12.13.91)	12279
	—	4	T. Nelson	Wolfe	1591	None		12279.4
	—	4	T. Nelson	Wolfe	1591	None		12279.7
	—	4	T. Nelson	T. Scarlet	1592	None	(E. Allde)“The Art of Conycatchinge” (6.29.24)	12280
	The second part of conny-catching	4	W. Wright	Wolfe	1591	None	“The second parte of Connye katchinge” (12.13.91)	12281
	The second and last part…	4	W. Wright	Wolfe	1592	None		12282
	The first part of the tragicall raigne of Selimus		Creede	Creede	1594	None	No Entry	12310a
1592	*The thirde and last part of conny-catching*	4	Burbie	T. Scarlet	1592	None	(T. Scarlet) “the Thirde and laste parte of Connye Catchinge with the newe devysed knavyshe Arte of foole takinge” (2.7.92)	12283

	The third ...	4	Burbie	T. Scarlet	1592	None		12283.5
	Philomela. The Lady Fitzvvaters nightingale	4	E. White	R. Bourne & E. Allde	1592	Bridget Ratliffe	(Wolfe) "Philomela ... by Robert Greene" (7.1.92)	12296
	Philomela, the Lady Fitzvvaters nightingale	4	G. Purslowe	G. Purslowe	1615	—	(Pindley) "Philomela" (4.27.12)	12297
	Philomela, the Lady Fitz-vvaters nightingale	4	G. Purslowe	G. Purslowe	1631	—		12298
	A disputation, betweene a hee conny-catcher, and a shee conny-catcher	4	Gubbin	Jeffes	1592	None	No Entry	12234
	(New title) *Theeues falling out, true-men come by their goods*	4	Gubbin	W.White	1615	None		12235
	—	4	H. Bell	G. Purslowe	1617	None		12236
	Theeves ...	4	H. Bell	B. Alsop	1621	None		12237
	Theeues ...	4	H. & M. Bell	G. Purslowe	1637	None	(Haviland & W. Wright) "Theeves falling out true men come by their goods" (9.4.38)	12238
	A quip for an vpstart courtier	4	Wolfe	Wolfe	1592	Thomas Barnaby	"a Quip for an vpstart Courtier" (7.21.92)	12300
	—	4	Wolfe	Wolfe	1592	—		12300.7
	—	4	Wolfe	Wolfe	1592	—		12301a
	—	4	Wolfe	Wolfe	1592	—		12301a.3
	—	4	Wolfe	Wolfe	1592	—		12301a.5
	—	4	Wolfe	Wolfe	1592	—		12301a.7
	—	4	E. White	E. Allde	1606	—		12302
	—	4	G. Purslowe	G. Purslowe	1620	—	"A quippe for an vpstart Courtier" (1.7.20)	12303
	—	4	G. Purslowe	G. Purslowe	1622	—		12304
	—	4	G. Purslowe	G. Purslowe	1635	—		12305

	The blacke bookes messenger	4	T. Nelson	Danter	1592	None	(Danter) "The Repentance of a Conycatcher. with the life and death of ... Mourton and Ned Browne" (8.21.92)	12223
	Greenes, groats-vvorth of witte	4	W. Wright	Wolfe & Danter	1592	None	"vppon the perill of Henrye Chettle a booke intituled Greenes Groatsworth of wyt bought with a million of Repentance" (9.20.92)	12245
	Greens, groats-vvorth of vvit	4	R. Olive	Creede	1596	None		12246
	Greenes groatsvvorth of witte	4	H. Bell	B. Alsop	1617	None		12247
	Greenes groatsworth of vvitte	4	H. Bell	N. Okes	1621	None		12248
	Greens groatsworth of wit	4	H. Bell	J. Haviland	1629	None		12249
	Greenes groatsworth of wit	4	H. & M. Bell	R. Hodgkinson	1637	None		12250
	The repentance of Robert Greene Maister of Artes	4	Burbie	Danter	1592	None	"The repentance of Robert Greene master of Arte" (10.6.92)	12306

[1] "Year" of composition of print pamphlets has been derived from Charles W. Crupi's "Chronology" in his *Robert Greene* (Boston: Twayne Publishers, 1986). "Year" of composition for plays has been taken from Alfred Harbage, *Annals of English Drama 975–1700* (London: Routledge, 1989). "Work" titles are taken from extant editions. "Publisher" signifies the agent(s) who financed a work's publication. "Publisher," "Printer," and "STC" information has been derived from the ESTC. "Publisher" and "Printer" spellings come from R.B. McKerrow, general editor, *A Dictionary of Printers and Booksellers in England, Scotland and Ireland and of Foreign Printers of English Books 1557–1640* (London: The Bibliographical Society, 1968). "Patrons" are taken from A.F. Allison's *Robert Greene 1558–1592: A Bibliographical Catalogue of the Early Editions in English (to 1640)* (Old Working, Surrey: The Gresham Press, 1975). "Stationers Register" entries come from Edward Arber, *A Transcript of the Registers of the Company of Stationers of London 1554–1640*, 5 vols (New York: Peter Smith, 1950) and have been selectively shortened.

Appendix C

Editions Published by Year between 1583 and 1640[1]

Year	Work	Name on Title Page	Edition
1583	*Mamillia* (pt. I)	"By Robert Greene graduate in Cambridge"	1
	Mamillia (pt. II)	"By Robert Greene Maister of Arts in Cambridge"	1
1584	*Gwydonius*	"By Robert Greene Master of Arte, in Cambridge"	1
	Arbasto	"By Robert Greene Mayster of Arte"	1
	The Myrrour of Modestie	"By R.G. Maister of Artes"	1
	Morando (pt. I)	"By Robert Greene, Maister of Artes in Cambridge"	1
1585	*An Oration*	None	1
	Planetomachia	"By Robert Greene, Master of Arts and student in phisicke"	1
1587	*Morando* (pts. I&II)	"By Robert Greene, Maister of Artes in Cambridge"	1
	Gwydonius	"By Robert Greene Master of Arte in Cambridge"	2
	Penelopes Web	"By Robert Greene Maister of Artes in Cambridge"	1
	Euphues his Censure to Philautus	"Robertus Greene, in artibus magister"	1
	The Comicall Historie of Alphonsus, King of Aragon	—	P
1588	*Perimedes*	None	1
	A Looking Glasse for London and England	—	P
	Pandosto	"By Robert Greene Maister of Artes in Cambridge"	1
1589	*The Spanish Masquerado*	"By Robert Greene, in Artibus Magister"	1
	The Spanish Masquerado	"By Robert Greene, in Artibus Magister"	2
	Arbasto	"By Robert Greene Master of Arte"	2
	The Honorable Historie of Frier Bacon and Frier Bongay	—	P
	Menaphon	"Robertus Greene in Artibus Magister"	1
	Ciceronis Amor	"Robert Greene in Artibus magister"	1
1590	*The Royal Exchange*	"Rob. Greene, in Artibus Magister"	1
	The Scottish Historie of Iames the Fourth	—	P

	Greenes Never Too Late	"Rob. Greene in artibus Magister"	1
	Greenes Mourning Garment	"R. Greene Vtriusq Academia in artibus magister"	1
	The Tragicall Raigne of Selimus	—	P
1591	*A Maidens Dreame*	"By Robert Greene Master of Arts"	1
	Orlando Furioso	—	P
	A Notable Discouery of Coosenage	"By R. Greene, Maister of Arts"	1
	A Notable Discouery of Coosenage	"By R. Greene, Maister of Arts"	2
	A Notable Discouery of Coosenage	Not seen	3
	Second Part of Conny-catching	"R.G."	1
	Greenes Farewell to Folly	"Robert Greene vtriusque Academiae in Artibus magister"	1
1592	*Greenes Vision*	None	1
	The Second Part of Conny-catching	"R.G."	2
	The Third and Last Part of Conny-catching	"By R.G."	1
	The Third and Last Part of Conny-catching	"By R.G."	2
	Pandosto	"By Robert Greene Maister of Artes in Cambridge"	2
	Philomela	"By Robert Greene. Vtriusque Academiae in Artibus magister"	1
	A Disputation betweene a Hee Conny-Catcher and a Shee Conny-Catcher	"R.G."	1
	A Notable Discouery of Coosenage	"By R. Greene, Maister of Arts"	4
	A Quip for an Vpstart Courtier	None	1
	A Quip for an Vpstart Courtier	None	2
	A Quip for an Vpstart Courtier	None	3
	A Quip for an Vpstart Courtier	None	4
	A Quip for an Vpstart Courtier	None	5
	A Quip for an Vpstart Courtier	None	6
	The Blacke Bookes Messenger	"By R.G."	1
	Greenes Groats-worth of Witte	None	1
	The Repentance of Robert Greene	None	1
1593	*Mamillia* (pt. II)	"By Robert Greene Maister of Arts, in Cambridge"	2
	Gwydonius	"By Robert Greene Master of Arte, in Cambridge"	3
1594	*Arbasto*	"By Robert Greene Master of Arte"	3
	A Looking Glasse for London and England	"Made by Thomas Lodge Gentleman, and Robert Greene"	1
	The Honorable Historie of Frier Bacon and Frier Bongay	"By Robert Greene Maister of Arts"	1
	The Historie of Orlando Furioso	None	1
	The Tragicall Raigne of Selimus	None	1

1595	*Pandosto*	"By Robert Greene Maister of Artes in Cambridge"	3
1596	*Greenes Groats-worth of Witte*	None	2
1597	*Ciceronis Amor*	"Robert Greene in Artibus magister"	2
1598	*A Looking Glasse for London and England*	"Made by Thomas Lodge Gentleman, and Robert Greene"	2
	The Scottish Historie of Iames the Fourth	"Written by Robert Greene, Maister of Arts"	1
1599	*Menaphon*	"Robertus Greene, in Artibus Magister"	2
	The Historie of Orlando Furioso	None	2
	Greenes Orpharion	"Robertus Greene, in Artibus Magister"	1
	The Comicall Historie of Alphonsus, King of Aragon	"Made by R.G."	1
	Greenes Never Too Late (2 pts)	"Robt. Greene, in artibus Magister"	2
1600	*Greenes Never Too Late* (2 pts)	"Robt. Greene, in artibus Magister"	4
	Pandosto	Not seen	4
1601	*Penelopes Web*	"By Robert Greene Master of Artes in Cambridge"	2
	Ciceronis Amor	"Robert Greene in artibus magister"	3
1602	*A Looking Glasse for London and England*	"Made by Thomas Lodge Gentleman, and Robert Greene"	3
	Greenes Never Too Late (2 pts)	"Rob. Greene, in artibus Magister"	4
1605	*A Looking Glasse for London and England*	Not seen	4
	Ciceronis Amor	"Robert Greene. In artibus Magister"	4
	Menaphon	"Robertus Greene, in Artibus Magister"	3
1606	*A Quip for an Vpstart Courtier*	None	7
1607	*Pandosto*	"By Robert Greene Master of Arts in Cambridge"	5
	Greenes Never Too Late (2 pts)	"Rob. Greene, in artibus Magister"	5
1608	*Gwydonius*	"By Robert Greene, Master of Arte, in Cambridge"	4
1609	*Pandosto*	"By Robert Greene Master of Arts in Cambridge"	6
	Ciceronis Amor	"Robert Greene. In artibus Magister"	5
1610	*Menaphon*	"Robertus Greene, in Artibus Magister"	4
1611	*Ciceronis Amor*	"Robert Greene. In artibus Magister"	6
	Greenes Never Too Late (2 pts)	"Robert Greene, In artibus Magister"	6
1614	*Pandosto*	"By Robert Greene, Master of Arts in Cambridge"	7
1615	*Philomela*	"By Robert Greene, vtriusque Academiae in Artibus Magister"	2
	A Disputation betweene ...	None	2
1616	*Menaphon*	"Robertus Greene, in Artibus Magister"	5
	Greenes Mourning Garment	"R. Greene. Vtriusq Academiae in Artibus Magister"	2
	Greenes Never Too Late (2 pts)	"Robert Greene, in artibus Magister"	7

	Ciceronis Amor	“Robert Greene, in artibus Magister”	7
1617	*Arbasto* (rev.)	“By Robert Green, Master of Art”	4
	Greenes Groats-worth of Witte	None	3
	A Disputation betweene ...	“By Robert Greene”	3
	Alcida	“By R.G.”	1
	A Looking Glasse for London and England	“By Thomas Lodge Gentleman, and Robert Greene”	5
	Greenes Farewell to Folly	“Robert Greene. Vtriusq Academia in artibus magister”	2
1619	*Pandosto*	“By Robert Greene Maister of Artes in Cambridge”	8
1620	*A Quip for an Vpstart Courtier*	None	8
1621	*A Disputation betweene ...*	“By Robert Greene”	4
	Greenes Groats-worth of Witte	None	4
1622	*A Quip for an Vpstart Courtier*	None	9
1626	*Arbasto* (rev.)	“By Robert Greene, Master of Art”	5
1628	*Ciceronis Amor*	“Robert Greene. In artibus Magister”	8
1629	*Pandosto*	“By Robert Greene, Master of Arts in Cambridge”	9
	Greenes Groats-worth of Witte	None	5
1630	*The Honorable Historie of Frier Bacon and Frier Bongay*	“By Robert Greene, Master of Arte”	2
1631	*Greenes Never Too Late* (2 pts)	“Robert Greene, in artibus Magister”	8
	Philomela	“By Robert Greene, vtriusque Academiae in Artibus Magist.”	3
1632	*Pandosto*	“By Robert Greene, Master of Arts in Cambridge”	10
1634	*Euphues his Censure to Philautus*	“Robertus Greene, in Artibus Magister”	2
1635	*Pandosto*	“By Robert Greene, Master of Arts in Cambridge”	11
	A Quip for an Vpstart Courtier	“By Robert Greene”	10
1636	*Pandosto*	“By Robert Greene, Master of Arts in Cambridge”	12
1637	*A Disputation betweene ...*	“By Robert Greene”	5
	Greenes Groats-worth of Witte	None	6
1639	*Ciceronis Amor*	“Robert Greene, in artibus Magister”	9
1640	*Pandosto*	“By Robert Greene, Master of Arts in Cambridge”	13

[1] “Year” of publication is based on extant publications. “Work” titles are derived from earliest extant editions and modernized for capitalization. “Name on title page” is derived from a survey of available editions on *Early English Books Online* <http://80-eebo.chadwyck.com.researchport.umd.edu:2050/home> and from Allison. “P” in the edition column indicates a performance. “Edition” refers only to known editions.

Index

Note: for a list of recent critical work on Greene, see 216–24.

Abbott, Andrew 54–6, 64, 71
System of Professions, The 13n51, 16n60, 54n4
"affective presence" 77, 81, 81n18, 82, 86, 87, 91
Agrippa, Henry Cornelius 77, 80, 84, 85
alchemy 78, 80, 206
Alcida 3–4, 110n41, 124, 170n28, app. B, app. C
Alexander the Great 191, 193–7, 199, 200, 201, 202, 203
Alexander, Peter 121
allegory 25–6, 31–2, 36, 37, 68
Allen, Don Cameron 78n9, 85n29
Allison, A.F. 124n30
Allot, Robert *England's Parnassus* 112–13
Alphonsus King of Aragon 1n2, 7, 12, 17–18, 29–31, 40–45, 41n3, 46n20, 47, 105, 110n41, 164, 190, 191, 217, app. B, app. C
as foul papers 40–41n3
date 40–41n3
Alwes, Derek 127n37, 157n2, 158n4, 170n25, 170n29, 171n30, 184n48, 206, 208
antitheatricality 8, 83n24, 83, 155, 173–4, 184–6
Apelles 193, 194, 195, 197, 198, 199, 200, 201, 202, 203
apocrypha 213, 223, app. A
Arbasto 101, 124, 219, app. B, app. C
Arber, Edward 7n20, 95n2
architecture, theatre 65n28, 68
Arden of Feversham 26, 99, app. A
Ariosto, Lodovico *Orlando Furioso* 111–12
articulatory space 81, 81n19
Ascham, Roger 158, 160, 160n8, 181
The Schoolmaster 172, 180n45
Augustine, Saint *Confessions* 153
authorship 16, 19–20, 97–9, 99n11, 101–2, 102n18, 104, 107–8, 108n34, 111–13, 116–19, 122, 129–31, 130n41, 199, 206, 208
and authority 40, 51
and celebrity ("*poeta publicus*")19, 73, 75, 76–7, 82, 87, 88, 89, 92, 205
and narcissism 50
collaborative 2–3, 13–14, 89, 102n18, 115, 117–19, 117n10, 130, 156
surrogates 175n46
see also "bibliographic ego"; Foucault; playwriting; professional practice; symbolic power
autobiography 93, 115–16, 161
spiritual 134, 154, 155

Bacon, Roger 79–80, 80n14, 81, 86
Bakhtin, M.M. 207
Barbour, Reid 17, 206
Barish, Jonas A. 162n13, 173n35
Barker, W.W. 5, 119n16, 123, 127n36, 207
Barnes, Joseph 80
Barton, John 213
Bathyllus 160, 160n10
Baxter, Richard 145, 149
Beaty, Nancy Lee 149n46
Beaumont, Francis *The Knight of the Burning Pestle* 69n40, 71
Beckett, Samuel *Texts for Nothing* 115
Becon, Thomas *The Sick Man's Salve* 148–9
Bednarz, James P 8n25, 206
Beecher, Donald 186n55

Beilin, Elaine 207
Bennett, H.S. 9n31
Bentley, Gerald Eades 10n38, 11n41, 64n24, 98
Bergeron, David 64
"bibliographic ego" 6, 98, 130n41
biographical details 3, 6, 6n15, 6n16, 124–5, 129n40, 205, 216
Black Book's Messenger, The 125, 154–5, 211, 220, app. B, app. C
Boehrer, Bruce 98n8
bohemia 4, 12, 13, 24
Bourdieu, Pierre 15n58, 15n59, 16n61, 53, 53n1, 57–8, 73n2, 75, 75n6, 76, 86, 101, 102, 102n17
  "homo academicus" 73–4, 73n2, 76–7, 82, 86, 88, 92
  "homology" 15n58, 57, 76–7, 85, 88, 92
  "relative autonomy" 15n58
Boutcher, Warren 76n7
Brady, Jennifer 9n8
Braunmuller, A.R. 5, 70, 70n42, 72, 208–9
Brayton, Dan 205
Breton, Nicholas *Pasquil's Mad-Cap* 95n3
Brigden, Susan 146n40
Brown, Cedric 4n9
Brown, Sir Thomas 80
Bruno, Giordano 77, 80, 87n33
Bubb, William 2
Buc, Sir George 65, 66n32, 214
  Third University 65n31, 65
Bulwer, John *Chirologia* 64n27
Bunny, Edmund 149–51, 156
  Book of Christian Exercise 136
Burbage, Richard 212
Burbie, Cuthbert 1, 3, 5, 99, 108
Burnaby, Thomas 10n36, app. B

Cade, Jack 212
Cadman, Thomas 8n26
Campanella, Tommaso 77
canon and chronology 21, 40–1n3, 113, 157–60, 190, 214, 223
Cantar, Brenda 208, 215
capital 75, 92
  cultural 13, 16, 101–2
  social 68–9
  symbolic 69
Carey, Robert 10, app. B
Carlson, Eric Josef 135n5
Carroll, D. Allen 11n42, 102n18, 116n3, 117, 119, 121, 127–8, 128n39, 160n9, 212
Cartwright, Kent 209
Case, John 78, 79, 80
Cecil, William Lord Burghley 79n13
Chaucer, Geoffrey 184
Cheney, Patrick 8n25
Chettle, Henry 4, 11n42, 20, 102, 109, 114, 117, 118–19, 126, 135, 137, 154, 183, 214
Cicero 81, 92
Ciceronis Amor 42, 97n5, 106, 124, 159, 211, 220 app. B, app. C
Clark, Sandra 13
class 5, 163–9, 167n22, 175, 182
Clifford, George 10n36, 187–8n56, app. B
clowns and clowning 25n1, 32–5, 36n11, 48–9, 141, 146, 179, 182, 187
  see also Kemp; Tarlton
Clucas, Stephen 80n16
Clulee, Nicholas 79n12–13, 80n16
Cobler of Canterbury, The 184, app. A
Colet, John 77
Collins, John Churton 6n16, 205
Collinson, Patrick 76n7, 136, 137, 137n10, 139n12, 140n18, 141n23
comedy 22, 30, 70, 72, 89, 92, 111, 174, 177, 182, 190, 195, 196, 198, 199
Cooper, Helen 166n20–21, 192n12
Coryat, Thomas 95, 95n3
craftsmen, theatre 64–7, 71
Crockett, Bryan 145
Crumley, J. Clinton 70, 70n44, 72, 210
Crupi, Charles 3–4, 5n14, 6n16, 7n23, 8n25, 40n3, 104, 108, 115n2, 123n29, 124, 129n9, 131n45, 154
cultural field 15, 15n58, 16, 17, 53n1, 69, 75, 77, 88, 102n17
  and cultural production 61, 102

defined 15n59
dramatic 61n19, 70, 71
literary 24, 75
theatrical 18, 213
see also Bourdieu; manuscript culture; print; professional practice; social space; stage
culture industry, early modern 6
culture, official 19

Daborne, Robert 215
Danter, John 99
Dean, James Seay 205
dedications 9–10, 9n32, 114, 160, 187–8n56
Dee, John 77, 79, 79n12–13, 80
Defense of Cony-Catching, The 12, 12n47, 112n44, 125, 155, app. A
Dekker, Thomas 12, 13n50, 17, 67n37, 84
Knight's Conjuring, A 109
Dessen, Alan C. 16, 17–18, 41n4–6, 43, 43n10–11, 57, 58n12
Dessen, Alan and Leslie Thompson 43, 43n12–13, 46n22
De Vere, Edward, Earl of Oxford 9, app. B
devotion, popular 21, 134, 135, 136, 145, 148
devotional practices 135, 136
DiBiase, Carmine 207
Dickenson, John *Greene in Conceit* 22n63, 22–4
Dickinson, Thomas H. 104
Digby, Everard 78
Dimmick, Jeremy 212
Disputation between a He Cony-Catcher and a She Cony-Catcher, A 125, 170n27, 206, 211, 220, app. B, app. C
Donne, John 151
Donovan, Kevin J. 205
Du Plessis Mornay, Phillipe 84n27
Duffy, Eamon 136

Eamon, William 79n12
education 57–8, 64–5, 135, 137
Edward III 29, 34n9, app. A
Edwards, Richard *Damon and Pythias* 194
Elizabeth I 79, 86n31, 139, 140, 147, 177
Empson, William *Some Versions of Pastoral* 34
England 8, 16, 19, 55n6, 64, 116–17, 129–31, 133–5, 155, 158, 172–4
English literary canon 113, 157–60, 190
Erasmus 81
Erne, Lukas 109, 113, 118n12
Euphues His Censure to Philautus 21, 42, 159, 198n19, app. B, app. C
Ewbank, Inga-Stina 213

Farley-Hills, David 40n2
Fassler, Christopher 99n11
Feingold, Mordechai 78n10, 86n31
Ficino, Marsilio 77, 79, 80, 80n14, 84, 87n33
Field, Nathan *Actor's Remonstrance* 55n7
Fleissner, Robert F. 212
Fletcher, John 95n3, 95–7
Foucault, Michel 33, 98–9, 116, 118n12, 129, 130–31
"What is an Author?" 116n5, 130
Fowler, Alistair 125n31
Francesco's Fortunes 7–8, 11, 44, 44n16, 56–7, 56n10, 107–8, 111, 164n17, app. B, app. C
Frazer, Winifred 211–12
Friar Bacon and Friar Bungay 12, 18, 19, 21–2, 26, 32–5, 78, 86–93, 99n11, 106, 159, 172–82, 190, 198–9, 199n22, 203, 209–10, 215, 218–19 app. B, app. C

Garin, Eugenio 78–9n9
Gatti, Hilary 79n13, 80n16
generic form 5n14, 16, 17, 22, 26, 53n1, 57, 60n16, 69–71, 89–90, 111, 123, 125n31, 126, 128, 154, 191, 203, 206
and competition 16
see also professional practice; stage

George a Greene 214, app. A
Gieskes, Edward 13, 15, 15n57, 16, 18, 19, 54n2
Gohlke, Madelon 128n38
Gosson, Stephen 83, 174, 176, 181, 182, 183, 182n47
Plays Confuted in Five Acts 173–4
School of Abuse, The 55n7, 173
Grafton, Anthony 76n7, 77–8n9
Green, Ian 136, 137, 137n10, 148, 155
Greenblatt, Stephen 131n43,
Will in the World 4, 4n8, 12
Greene, John *A Refutation of the Apology for Actors* 83
Greene, Thomas M. 160n8
Greene's Farewell to Folly 7n23, 10, 10n37, 22, 101, 103n19, 188n56, 124–5, 187–8n56, app. B, app. C
Greene's Groatsworth of Wit 4, 7, 11, 11n42–4, 16, 20–21, 29, 44, 57, 95–7, 102–4, 102n18, 115–31, 160n9, 183–4, 211, 214, 220–21, app. B, app. C
Greene's Mourning Garment 10n36, 103n19, 124, 161n11, 187–8n56, app. B, app. C
Greene's Never Too Late 10n36, 124, 182, 186, 222, app. B, app. C
Greene's Vision 21–2, 103n19, 115, 115n2, 124–5, 161n11, 162n14, 182–7, 187–8n56, 208, 212, 221, app. B, app. C
Greg, W.W. 8–9n29, 11n40, 41, 41n4, 100n14, 215
Gregory, Brad 150n50
Grindal, Edmund 140–41
Grinkin, John 67n37
Grosart, A.B. 205
Grosseteste, Robert 79
Gustafson, Kevin L. 211
Gwinne, Matthew 78, 79
Gwydonius 9, 9n34, 101, 128n39, 164, 212–13, 221, app. B, app. C

Hackel, Heidi Brayman 136
Hackett, Helen 166n21, 170n25, 170n29, 191n10
Halasz, Alexandra 95–6, 120, 120n17, 208, 212
Happé, Peter 209
Harington, Sir John 112–13, 112n44
Harriot, Thomas 80
Harvey, Gabriel 12, 13n50, 24, 110n42, 73–6, 76n7, 82, 86–8, 86n31, 111–12, 117, 117n8, 129n40, 152
Four Letters 109–11, 110n40, 110–11n42, 157n1, 183–4
Pierce's Supererogation 84n27
Heilman, Robert B. 212
Helgerson, Richard 111, 114, 127n37, 207
Henslowe, Philip 11n40, 107, 107n30, 112n44, 147
Hephaestion 193–4, 196–7, 201
Herendeen, W.H. 98n8
Herrick, Marvin T 195n17
Hess, W. Ron 212
Heywood, Thomas 71n46
Apology for Actors, An 55n7, 83
Hieatt, Charles W 199n20, 23
Hines, John 185n53
history 21, 65–6, 70–71, 161, 202
Homer, *Odyssey* 159
Horace, *Third Epistle* 122
humanism 209, 211
Hunter, G.K. 189n3, 193n15

Ide, Arata 6n16
Ingram, William 64, 64n25

Jackson, Hugh 8n26
James IV 3, 12, 18, 19, 40, 45–51, 53, 57–63, 69–72, 159, 161n11, 179, 203n28, 210, 219, app. B, app. C
as foul papers 45n19
Jardine, Lisa 76n7
Jaster, Margaret Rose 214
Jones, Inigo 64n26, 65n29
Jones, John H. 190n5
Jonson, Ben 20, 35, 56, 65n29, 70n42, 96–9, 98n8, 101–2, 130
Catiline 95–6, 95–6n3, 114
Poetaster 55n9, 71n45

Jordan, John Clark 3, 3n6, 5n14, 40–41n3, 73n1, 123n29
Jowett, John 11n42, 98n8, 102n18, 117, 117n9, 118n11, 119n14, 125, 154, 154n54, 214

Kelley, Edward 79
Kemp, William 211–12
Kinney, Arthur 123n29, 158n4
Kumaran, Arul 10n36, 8n25, 207, 212
Kyd, Thomas 25–6, 28, 29, 31, 109, 163
Spanish Tragedy, The 26, 30, 99, 163, 209
Kyle, Barry 36–7

Labé, Louise 212–3
labor 21, 104, 157, 159, 168, 171–2, 186
LaGrandeur, Kevin 210
Lake, Peter 133n1
Larson, Magali *The Rise of Professionalism* 13n51
Lavin, J. A. 35, 35n10, 199n22
law 55–6, 208–9
Lee, Robert 9n33
Leggatt, Alexander 70, 70n43, 72, 210
Levin, Richard 106n27, 209
Levine, Laura 173n35
Linden, Stanton J. 206
Lodge, Thomas 4, 11n44, 127, 135, 145, 147, 166n19
Loewenstein, Joseph 6n19, 8n29, 98, 130n41
London 1, 10, 14, 22, 25, 40, 65–6, 65n31, 74, 96, 135, 146–8, 173–4, 188
culture of writing 22
Long, Michael 211
Long, William B. 41n5
Longus 191, 191n8
Daphnis and Chloe 164, 167
A Looking Glass for London and England (with Thomas Lodge) 12, 21, 28, 99n11, 106–7, 134, 135, 145–8, 161n11, 187–8, 187–8n56, app. B, app. C
"Lord Darcie of the North" 9n33, app. B
Lord Mayor's Show 63n23, 64, 66, 66n35, 67, 69
Love, Harold 117n10
Lucas, Caroline 191n10, 208
Lupton, Thomas 25
All for Money 27
Lyly, John 25n1, 125n32, 128n38, 161n12, 162, 162n13, 189–203
Campaspe 22, 191–203
Euphues 125, 128, 161–2, 170, 189, 192
Midas 191n9
Sapho and Phao 162

McAdam, Ian 5, 210
McCluskie, Kathleen 71, 71n46
McColloch, Samuel Clyde 79n13
McJannet, Linda 41n6–7, 42
McKerrow, R.B. 7n20
McMillin, Scott and Sally-Beth MacLean, 12n46
Mack, Peter 207
Mad Priest of the Sun, The 1, 40n2
magic 19, 77–80, 84, 85, 86n31, 87–93, 174, 175, 177, 178, 181, 183, 186, 199
as necromancy 19, 80n16
Magnus, Albertus 79
Magnusson, Lynne 64n24
Maguire, Laurie 100n14
Maiden's Dream, A 124, app. B, app. C
Malone, Edmund 120–21n19, 121
Mamillia (pts I & II) 7n20, 7n22, 9, 9n33, 124–5, 170, 170n26, 170n28, 183, 187, app. B, app. C
manuscript culture 2, 9, 11, 41, 42, 56, 80, 80n16, 86, 86n31, 100n14, 151, 164, 189, 189n2, 195
Margolies, David 14, 158n4, 167n22
Marlowe, Christopher 4, 11n44, 25–6, 25n1, 28, 29, 40–41, 40n2, 51, 51n24, 57–8, 69, 89–90, 103, 105, 116n4, 119, 162–3, 175–9,
Doctor Faustus 26, 28, 36–7, 162, 162n14, 175–7, 179, 190
Edward II 201
Jew of Malta, The 26
Tamburlaine 1, 7, 17–18, 25–6, 29–30, 40, 40–41n3, 44, 51,

51n24, 58, 68, 99, 100, 162, 163, 164, 190
Martin Marprelate 163, 207
Maslen, Robert W. 16, 21–2, 157n3, 158n4, 158n6, 166n19, 172n31, 173n35, 174n37, 176n41, 177n44, 185n52
Massinger, Philip 215
Masten, Jeffrey 14, 14n53, 98, 113, 117n10
mathematics 77, 79, 80, 91, 77, 79, 80, 83, 83n22, 87, 90, 91, 92
May, Steven 14n54
Mebane, John S 77–8n9, 80n15
Melnikoff, Kirk 16, 18, 51n24, 57, 58n12, 60n17, 61, 61n18, 107
Menaphon 21–2, 97n5, 105–8, 110, 110n41, 116n3, 124, 158–72, 174–5, 189–90, 203, 208, 215, 222, app. B, app. C
Mentz, Steven 16, 20–21, 125n33, 128n38, 206, 211
Meres, Francis *Palladis Tamia* vii, 109, 114
Middleton, Thomas 12, 67n37
Miller, Edwin Havilland 8n27, 12, 12n49, 14, 73n1, 74n3, 101n15
Mirandola, Giovanni Francesco Pico della 77, 80, 84
Mirror of Modesty, The 124, 159–60, 164, 170n28, app. B, app. C
Montagne, Renee (Morning Edition) 4n8
Moore, Helen 192n12, 207
Moore Smith, G.C. 190n6
Morando 9–10, 10n35, 101, 101n15, 124, app. B, app. C
More, John 136, 141–3, 151
More, Sir Thomas 77
Mucedorus 31, app. A
Muir, Kenneth 59n13
Munday, Anthony 66–7n35, 67n37, 83n24, 119
Munday, Richard 66–7n35

narrative 3, 17–18, 21, 26, 70, 104, 127, 131, 185, 191–2, 206, 211, 213
Nashe, Thomas 4, 11n44, 13n50, 17, 20, 73–6, 87–8, 89, 103, 105–6, 108–11, 110n41, 116–17, 122, 127, 158, 161–4, 163n16, 168
Anatomy of Absurdity, The 116n3, 191, 191n10
Nelson, Alan 214
Newcomb, Lori Humphrey 4, 5, 6n18, 16, 21, 22n63, 24, 74, 101n15, 104, 110n41, 158n4, 189n2, 190n4, 205, 213
Newton, Thomas *Seneca His Ten Tragedies* 91
Nicoll, Charles 79n13, 81n17
North, Marcy 117–18n10
Northbrooke, John 83
Norwich 6, 6n15, 16, 138, 141
Notable Discovery of Cozenage, A 101n15, 124, 206, 211, 220, app. B, app. C
Nunn, Trevor 213

occult 77, 77n9, 78, 79, 80, 83, 84, 85, 86, 85n29, 86, 87, 90, 92
O'Connor, Sister Mary Catherine 148
O'Day, Rosemary 14–15, 15n56
Office of Works 65n28, 66
Ogle, John 66–7n35
Orgel, Stephen 64n26
Orlando Furioso 12, 99, 100, 100n14, 106–7, 111–13, 112n44, 159, 215, 219, app. B, app. C
Orpharion 8, 8n28, 103n19, app. B, app. C
Orrell, John 64–5, 65n28, 66n34, 68, 68n39
Overbury, Sir Thomas *The Wife and Diverse More Characters* 4–5
Ovid 161n12, 185, 202, 214

Palfrey, Simon 192n13
Pandosto 5, 9, 10n36, 22, 97n5, 101n15, 110n41, 124, 159, 164, 165, 167–8, 168n23, 187, 190, 190n4, 191, 191n8, 195–8, 198n19, 201–3, 203n27, 208, 213, 222, app. B, app. C

Parsons, Robert "the book of Resolution" 148–50, 149n48
Pask, Kevin 101–2
pastoral 60, 70, 89, 175, 189–91, 196–8
patronage 9–10, 76, 106–9, 114, 123, 195
  see also manuscript culture; print; professional practice
Peele, George 11n44, 25n1, 66–7n35, 103, 109, 113n46
  Old Wives Tale, The 192, 209
Peele, James 66–7n35
Penelope's Web 7, 7n23, 21, 22, 110n41, 124, 125n32, 159, 170n28, 213–14, 222, app. B, app. C
Perimedes the Blacksmith 1–3, 7, 9, 39–40, 105–6, 108, 116n4, 122, 124, 159, 215, app. B, app. C
Perkins, William 137, 142, 143n30, 144, 151
Pettit, Norman 144n33
Phillip, Earl of Arundel 9, app. B
Phillip, John 191n11
Phillips, Edward *Theatrum Poetarum* 114n47
Philomela 4, 124, 170n28, 214, 223, app. B, app. C
Pigman, G.W. 190n7
Pinciss, G.M. 12n48
Pincombe, Michael 193
plagiarism 5, 160, 164, 190
Planetomachia 3, 4, 42, 85–6, 85n30, 124, 223, app. B, app. C
players 10–11, 12n45, 43, 44, 45, 47–9, 55n7, 66–7, 100, 103, 121, 163, 169–70, 173, 174
  Greene's relationship with 7–8, 11–12, 18, 40–41, 43–7, 57, 103–8, 121n22, 164
playing 39–41, 48, 51
  as "mechanical labor" 44, 46, 164n17
  and rescripting 37
  companies 10–11, 13, 64, 66, 71, 99n11, 106–7, 116, 147, 148
playwriting 10–11, 11n41, 12n45, 17–19, 20, 25, 28, 37, 40–44, 47–9, 59, 59n13, 63–4, 66, 89, 103, 104, 104n23, 106–8, 110, 114, 116, 163n16, 173, 177, 179, 182–3
  attitude towards 40, 44–7, 51, 69–70, 89, 97, 102n18, 103–9, 114, 121n22, 130, 160, 177, 210, 216–17
  see also authorship; professional practice
poetry 30, 55, 55n7, 84–5, 102
  and poets 55n9, 84n27, 85, 88, 122, 158–9, 178,
  and poetics 77, 83n22, 88
Pollard, A.W. 8n27, 8–9n29
Ponsonby, William 8n26, app. B
Portington, Roger 9n33, app. B
Prescott, Ann Lake 212
Prest, Wilfred 14, 14n55
print 100, 106, 120–21, 121n22, 123n27, 156
  culture 20, 21, 95, 98–9, 101, 115–16, 118–21, 133–9, 144–5, 148, 153
  devotional material 21, 133–4, 136–7, 144–5, 148, 153, 156
  market for 2–3, 5–9, 13, 20–22, 76, 93, 96, 98, 100–101, 104, 114, 116, 130, 144, 207–8, 213, 217
  printers 8, 13, 93, 98–9, 101
  publishers 2, 12, 12n48, 13, 80, 99, 108, 115–16, 126, 146–7
  Stationers' Guild, the 8, 100, 150
  "stigma of print" 14
  textual studies 214, 215, 223–4
professional practice 1–3, 6–17, 13n51, 16n60, 19, 24, 37, 53–5, 64, 67, 71, 74–7
  and definitions of "readers" 16, 96, 127, 134, 170, 191n10
  and education 66n32
  and playwrights 10–11, 11n41, 17–19, 39–46, 64, 67, 104
  and rivalry between writers 82, 87–9, 92, 161–2, 174–5

and theatre 1–2, 5–8, 10–13, 11n41, 17–19, 20–21, 37, 39–47, 56, 58, 64, 71, 83, 89, 104, 107, 121n22
and pamphlet writing 1–3, 8–10, 12–15, 12n49, 16, 17, 19, 24, 42, 50, 71, 73–7, 82, 93, 158, 206
see also Abbott; authorship; cultural field; Larson
prose 105–6, 190
fiction 3n5, 20–21, 116–18, 123–6, 131, 157
Protestantism 21, 134–7, 139, 148–9, 156, 209
Pruvost, Rene 73n1, 86, 123

Queen's Men 12, 12n45–6
Quip for an Upstart Courtier, A 10n36, 99n9, 214, 223, app. B, app. C

Rainolds, John 83
Raleigh, Sir Walter 80, 80n15
rape 194–5, 202
Rare Triumphs of Love and Fortune, The 26, 31
R.B. *Apius and Virginia* 17, 26, 27n2, 36, 37
realism 25, 25n1, 26, 36–7, 36n11, 71n46
recent studies 205–24
reception 1n2, 4–5, 7, 10, 108, 170, 191
Reiss, Timothy 70n41
Relihan, Constance 211
repentance 21, 93, 128–9, 133–4, 137–8, 148–9, 154–6, 157, 182–7
Repentance of Robert Greene, The 1, 5, 6n15, 21, 102, 102n18, 104, 108, 115, 133–8, 141–2, 145, 148, 150–52, 154–5, 184, 184n48, 214, app. B, app. C
Revels Office 18, 63–7, 65n28, 69, 71
Reynolds, Bryan 16, 19, 76n8, 82n20, 83n21, 83n24, 87n32, 87n33, 87n34, 210
Richardson, Brenda 6n16, 9n32
Riche, Barnabe 20
Roberts, Sasha 123n27
romance 22, 70, 90–91, 125n33, 126–9, 128n38, 162, 165–7, 166n20–21, 170, 170n29, 172, 175, 175n45, 187, 191, 192, 206, 207–8, 212–13, 216–17
chivalric 90, 166, 175, 180–81, 180n45
Greek 124, 127–8, 174, 191, 196
Iberian 166n21
Italian 172–4, 172n31
women as readers of 166n21, 170, 170n25, 170n29, 170n28
Royal Exchange, The app. B, app. C
Royal Shakespeare Company 36–7, 213

Saeger, James P. 99n11
Sanders, Norman 45n18–19, 48n23, 62n21, 63n22, 68n38
satire 72, 89, 124–6, 129, 155
Schmitt, Charles 78, 78n10, 79n13, 81n17
Second Part of Cony-Catching, The 101n15, 124, 211, 220, app. B, app. C
Selimus 5, 12, 215, 219, app. B, app. C
Seltzer, Daniel 35, 35n10
sermons
in print 133–48, 151–2, 155
sermonizing 137–46, 152–4
see also devotion; devotional practices; print
Shakespeare, William 4, 4n8, 20, 33n8, 34n9, 70, 89, 102n18, 115, 120–23, 120n8, 123n27, 181–2, 212–13
Cymbeline 90, 200n24
Hamlet 47
Henry V 69
1 Henry VI 26, 121–2n24
2 Henry VI 212
3 Henry VI 212
A Midsummer Night's Dream 39, 40, 47
Richard III 39, 47
Winter's Tale, The 189n4, 213
Shapiro, James 64n24

Sheavyn, Phoebe 104
Sherman, William 76n7
Shumaker, Wayne 77n9
Sidney, Sir Philip 77, 84–5, 85n29, 113, 189, 191, 195
  Apology for Poetry, An 55, 84–5, 92, 175n38, 195, 195n17,
  Arcadia 164–5
  Old Arcadia 167, 189, 189n2, 195–6, 195n18
Sir Thomas More, 118, app. A
Smith, Bruce R. 134n3
Smith, Henry 142, 144
social space 15, 16–17, 53–5, 64
"sociopolitical conductors" 19, 82n20, 83
Soliman and Perseda 31, app. A
Spanish Masquerado, The 125, app. B, app. C
Spenser, Edmund 112, 113
  The Faerie Queene 111
  The Shepherd's Calendar 111
stage 69, 116, 208–9
  and psychomachia 28
  "audition reading" 10–11
  culture 6, 120
  dumbshows 50, 60n17, 61–3, 62n20, 67, 68n39, 69
  history 64, 176, 183
  interludes 210
  jig 60, 60n16, 61, 62n20, 63, 68
  morality plays 26, 28, 72n47, 145
  "morall" 29, 29n4
  music 45–6, 75, 75n31
  performance 18, 39–40, 45, 47–8, 63, 92, 137, 144, 145
    unscripted 45–6
  spectacle 63
  stage directions 41, 42, 43, 46
  trades 18–19, 65, 67, 70–71
  tradition 36n11, 61, 69
  vocabulary 17–18, 28, 30, 36–7, 43–4, 64
  see also antitheatricality; clowns and clowning; players; playing; playwriting
Stanley, Ferdinando Lord Strange 106–7, app. B
Stern, Tiffany 11n39, 11n41, 12n45
Stern, Virginia F. 86n31
Storojenko, Nicholas 3n6, 5n14
Street, Peter 66
Streitberger, W.R. 64
Strong, Roy 64n26
Stubbes Philip 83
  Anatomy of Abuses 83n24, 155
  Chrystal Glass for Christian Women, A 136, 155–6
style of writing 22, 70, 158, 160, 161–2, 162n13, 189–90, 202
  euphuistic 196, 202, 207–8, 212, 216–17
symbolic power 74–5, 82, 87–8
  and recognition 19, 75–6, 87, 87–8

Tarlton, Richard 106, 209–10
Third and Last Part of Cony-Catching, The 211, 220, app. B, app. C
Thomas, Keith 77–8, 78n10
Thorp, Willard 25, 25n1
time 21, 157, 159, 160, 162, 163, 166, 168, 172, 174, 175, 176, 183, 186, 187
tradition, literary 18–19, 61, 70, 91–2, 181, 191
tragedy 2, 49–50, 105, 111, 177–8, 195, 199, 203
tragicomedy 22, 49, 191, 194–6
transversal theory 19, 77, 81, 81n18, 82, 83n21
treason 171, 175, 177
Tribble, Evelyn 98n8
Trithemius, *Steganographiae* 79n13
Troublesome Reign of John King of England 99, app. A
Tumelson, Ron 16, 19–20, 58n12
Turner, Henry S. 16, 19, 83n22, 85n29, 87n32–3, 88n34, 210
tyrants 161, 168, 191, 193

university 4, 6, 14, 75, 77–9, 82, 87, 89–90, 92–3, 103, 106, 210
University Wits 19, 25–6, 25n1, 37, 71, 73–5, 82, 117
Upchear, Henry 189–90, 202–3

Vickers, Brian 117–18n10, 131
Vitkus, Daniel 5, 215
Von Rosador, Kurt Tetzeli 209

Wacquandt, Loic 16n61
Wager, Lewis *The Life and Repentance of Mary Magdalene* 28
Wager, William 25, 28
  Enough is as Good as a Feast 28
Walker, D.P. 77, 77n9
Walker, Mike 60n17
Walsham, Alexandra 135, 136, 149, 155–6
Wapull, George 25, 28
  Tide Tarrieth No Man, The 28
Ward, Roger 8n26, app. B
Warneke, Sarah 214
Warning for Fair Women, A 17, 28, 32, 37
Warren, Michael 100, 215
Watt, Tessa 136, 148
Weimann, Robert 18, 39–40, 39n1, 44, 51
Weld, John 33, 33n8
Wells, Stanley 1n2, 190n6, 215
West, William N. 133n2
White, Edward 2, 8n26, app. B
Williams, Franklin B. 9n30
Williams, John 78, 80
Willing Suspension Productions 60–61n17, 61
Wilson, John Dover 121
Wilson, Katherine 16, 22, 158n4, 159n7, 162n13, 164n18, 168n24, 180n46, 207, 214
Wilson, Robert 25, 212
  Three Ladies of London, The 26
Wolff, Samuel L. 128n39
women 5, 112–13, 158–9, 166, 170–71, 170n25–6, 170n29, 171n30, 181–2, 191, 192–3, 202–3, 208, 216
  as author surrogates 180n46
  as readers 170, 191, 191n10, 208
  see also reception; romance
Woodcocke, Thomas 7, 7n20, 8n26, app. B
Wotton, Henry 76n7

Yarington, Robert *Two Lamentable Tragedies* 31
Yates, Frances 77, 77n9, 84n27
Yorkshire 6n16, 9n32

Zetterberg, J. Peter 79n12
Ziegler, Georgianna 213